Nietzsche and the Drama of Historiobiography

ROBERTO ALEJANDRO

University of Notre Dame Press

Notre Dame, Indiana

Manufactured in the United States of America

Library of Congress Cataloging-in-Publication Data

Alejandro, Roberto, 1955–
Nietzsche and the drama of historiobiography / Roberto Alejandro.
    p.   cm.
Includes bibliographical references and index.
isbn-13: 978-0-268-02037-8 (pbk. : alk. paper)
isbn-10: 0-268-02037-x (pbk. : alk. paper)
1. Nietzsche, Friedrich Wilhelm, 1844–1900.   I. Title.
b3317.a3975   2011
193—dc22

                                                2010049945

Contents

Acknowledgments

A book is a debt; this will not be the exception.

During my years of research and reflection on Nietzsche's philosophy, I had the privilege of finding scholars who shared my strong belief in the importance of rigorous exegesis of Nietzsche's texts. Daniel Conway read an initial version of chapter 1 and a story of Nietzsche's view of the soul. His comments and encouragement to pursue the project and to see it to completion gave an always appreciated impetus to my investigation. Keith Ansell-Pearson, John Seery, and Jeff Church read my analysis of Nietzsche's genealogy and made important suggestions. Kathleen Higgins, Michael Allen Gillespie, and Thomas W. Heilke read an essay on the metaphysics of meaning and alerted me about weaknesses and ways to improve my arguments. As always, George Kateb supported my project. All these scholars showed me deep generosity and acted as genuine teachers. If my arguments fail, it is not because they did not warn me. A sabbatical from my teaching responsibilities in the Department of Political Science at the University of Massachusetts, Amherst, gave me valuable time to deepen my research into the vast literature on Nietzsche. The institutional support that I have received from my department has been crucial.

The untiring support of Charles Van Hof and the attentive care and careful reading of the manuscript by Rebecca DeBoer at the University of Notre Dame Press allowed this journey to reach the stage of publication.

As a Nietzschean conception of indebtedness, my debt to all these people goes well beyond my abilities to repay them.

My greatest gratitude is owed to my wife and children who showed me, under trying circumstances, the loving environment that is needed to complete any intellectual endeavor.

Abbreviations and Editions of Nietzsche's Works

AC *The Anti-Christ*
AOM *Assorted Opinions and Maxims*
BGE *Beyond Good and Evil*
BT *The Birth of Tragedy*
CW *The Case of Wagner*
D *Daybreak*
EH *Ecce Homo*
GM *On the Genealogy of Morality*
GS *The Gay Science*
H *Human, All Too Human*
HC *Homer in Competition*
KSA *Kritische Studienausgabe*
PCP "The Philosopher as Cultural Physician"
PPP *The Pre-Platonic Philosophers*
PRS "The Philosopher: Reflections on the Struggle between Art and Knowledge (1872)"
PTA *Philosophy in the Tragic Age of the Greeks*
RWB *Richard Wagner in Bayreuth*
SE *Schopenhauer as Educator*
TGS "The Greek State"
TI *Twilight of the Idols*
TL "On Truth and Lies in a Nonmoral Sense"
ULH "On the Utility and Liability of History for Life"
UW *Unpublished Writings from the Period of Unfashionable Observations*

WLN   *Writings from the Late Notebooks*
WP   *The Will to Power*
WS   *The Wanderer and His Shadow*
Z   *Thus Spoke Zarathustra*

TRANSLATIONS

I have used the following translations with abbreviations listed above. References to Nietzsche's works are by section title, if applicable, and section number, unless otherwise specified. Titles of sections are usually shortened, for instance, "Expeditions" for "Expeditions of an Untimely Man" and "Good Books" for "Why I Write Such Good Books." Thus, "(EH; "Good Books"; 3)" refers to section 3 of "Why I Write Such Good Books" in the edition of *Ecce Homo* listed below.

Roman numerals following abbreviations identify a particular volume or major part, as in *Human, All Too Human*, volume 1, which is presented as "H; I;" followed by the relevant section number; or *On the Genealogy of Morality*, Second Essay, which is presented as "GM; II;" followed by the section number of the essay. Nietzsche's prefaces are identified with the letter "P". Due to length, citations to Letters, WPN, and UW are placed in notes rather than main text.

I use three translations of *On the Genealogy of Morality*. My preferred one is the translation by Carol Diethe, edited by Keith Ansell-Pearson. I have also consulted the translations of, respectively, Walter Kaufmann and J. Hollingdale, and Maudemarie Clark and Alan J. Swensen.

With the exception of "Letter to George Brandes, May 4, 1888" and "Letter to Jacob Burckhardt, January 6, 1889," listed separately below, all letters cited in the notes are from *Selected Letters of Friedrich Nietzsche*, edited by Christopher Middleton.

The Anti-Christ (1888). (AC) In *Twilight of the Idols and The Anti-Christ*. Translated by R. J. Hollingdale. New York: Viking Penguin, 1968.
Assorted Opinions and Maxims (1879). (AOM) Volume 2, part 1 of *Human, All Too Human*. Translated by R. J. Hollingdale. Cambridge: Cambridge University Press, 1986.

Beyond Good and Evil (1886). (BGE) Translated by R. J. Hollingdale. London: Penguin Books, 1990.

The Birth of Tragedy and The Case of Wagner. (BT, CW) Translated by Walter Kaufmann. New York: Vintage Books, 1967.

Daybreak: Thoughts on the Prejudices of Morality (1881). (D) Translated by R. J. Hollingdale. Cambridge: Cambridge University Press, 1982.

Ecce Homo. How One Becomes What One Is. (EH) Translated by R. J. Hollingdale. London: Penguin Books, 1979.

The Gay Science. (GS) Translated by Walter Kaufmann. New York: Vintage Books, 1974.

"The Greek State." (TGS) In *On the Genealogy of Morality*. Translated by Carol Diethe. Edited by Keith Ansell-Pearson. Cambridge: Cambridge University Press, 1994.

"Homer in Competition." (HC) In *On the Genealogy of Morality*. Translated by Carol Diethe. Edited by Keith Ansell-Pearson. Cambridge: Cambridge University Press, 1994.

Human, All Too Human (1878). (H) Translated by R. J. Hollingdale. Cambridge: Cambridge University Press, 1986.

"Letter to George Brandes, May 4, 1888." Quoted in George Brandes, *Friedrich Nietzsche*, p. 84. New York: Macmillan; London: W. Heinemann, 1909.

"Letter to Jacob Burckhardt, January 6, 1889." In *The Portable Nietzsche*. Edited by Walter Kaufmann. New York: Viking Press, 1954.

On the Genealogy of Morals. (GM) Translated by Walter Kaufmann and J. Hollingdale. New York: Vintage Books, 1967.

On the Genealogy of Morality. (GM) Translated by Carol Diethe. Edited by Keith Ansell-Pearson. Cambridge: Cambridge University Press, 1994.

On the Genealogy of Morality. (GM) Translated by Maudemarie Clark and Alan J. Swensen. Indianapolis: Hackett Publishing Company, 1998.

"On the Pathos of Truth (1872)." In *Philosophy and Truth: Selections from Nietzsche's Notebooks of the Early 1870s*. Translated by Daniel Breazeale. Atlantic Highlands, NJ: Humanities Press, 1979.

"On Truth and Lies in a Nonmoral Sense" (1873). (TL) In *Philosophy and Truth: Selections from Nietzsche's Notebooks of the Early 1870s*. Translated by Daniel Breazeale. Atlantic Highlands, NJ: Humanities Press, 1979.

"On the Utility and Liability of History for Life." (ULH) Translated by Richard T. Gray. In *The Complete Works of Friedrich Nietzsche*. Volume 2. *Unfashionable Observations*. Stanford: Stanford University Press, 1995.

"The Philosopher as Cultural Physician." (PCP) In *Philosophy and Truth: Selections from Nietzsche's Notebooks of the Early 1870s.* Translated by Daniel Breazeale. Atlantic Highlands, NJ: Humanities Press, 1979.

"The Philosopher: Reflections on the Struggle between Art and Knowledge (1872)." (PRS) In *Philosophy and Truth: Selections from Nietzsche's Notebooks of the Early 1870s.* Translated by Daniel Breazeale. Atlantic Highlands, NJ: Humanities Press, 1979.

Philosophy in the Tragic Age of the Greeks. (PTA) Translated by Marianne Cowan. Washington, DC: Regnery Gateway, 1962.

The Pre-Platonic Philosophers. (PPP) Translated by Greg Whitlock. Urbana: University of Illinois Press, 2001.

Richard Wagner in Bayreuth (1875). (RWB) Translated by Richard T. Gray. In *The Complete Works of Friedrich Nietzsche.* Volume 2. *Unfashionable Observations.* Stanford: Stanford University Press, 1995.

Schopenhauer as Educator (1874). (SE) In *Unfashionable Observations.* Stanford: Stanford University Press, 1995.

Selected Letters of Friedrich Nietzsche. Edited by Christopher Middleton. Chicago: University of Chicago Press, 1969.

"The Struggle between Science and Wisdom." In *Philosophy and Truth: Selections from Nietzsche's Notebooks of the Early 1870s.* Translated by Daniel Breazeale. Atlantic Highlands, NJ: Humanities Press, 1979.

Thus Spoke Zarathustra (1883). (Z) Translated by Walter Kaufmann. New York: Penguin Books, 1978.

Twilight of the Idols. (TI) In *Twilight of the Idols and The Anti-Christ.* Translated by R. J. Hollingdale. New York: Penguin Books, 1968.

Unfashionable Observations. Translated by Richard T. Gray. In *The Complete Works of Friedrich Nietzsche.* Volume 2. Stanford: Stanford University Press, 1995.

Unpublished Writings from the Period of Unfashionable Observations. (UW) Translated by Richard T. Gray. In *The Complete Works of Friedrich Nietzsche.* Volume 11. Stanford: Stanford University Press, 1995.

The Wanderer and His Shadow (1880). (WS) Volume 2, part 2 of *Human, All Too Human.* Translated by R. J. Hollingdale. Cambridge: Cambridge University Press, 1986.

The Will to Power. (WP) Edited by Walter Kaufmann. Translated by Walter Kaufmann and R. J. Hollingdale. New York: Vintage Books, 1967.

Writings from the Late Notebooks. Edited by Rüdiger Bittner. Translated by Kate Sturge. Cambridge: Cambridge University Press, 2003.

GERMAN EDITIONS

My own translations are based on the following German editions:

Ecce homo. In *Sämtliche Werke: Kritische Studienausgabe.* Volume 2. Edited by Giorgio Colli and Mazzino Montinari. Berlin and New York: Walter de Gruyter, 1967–1988.
Menschliches Allzumenschliches und andere Schriften. Cologne: Könemann, 1994.
Morgenrothe. In *Sämtliche Werke: Kritische Studienausgabe.* Volume 3. Edited by Giorgio Colli and Mazzino Montinari. Berlin and New York: Walter de Gruyter, 1967–1988.
Zur Genealogie der Moral. In *Sämtliche Werke: Kritische Studienausgabe.* Volume 5. Edited by Giorgio Colli and Mazzino Montinari. Berlin and New York: Walter de Gruyter, 1967–1988.

INTRODUCTION
"Wrecked against Infinity"

In 1888, Friedrich Nietzsche sensed that a calamity was closing in on him day by day. Nietzsche, the philosopher, was declining. Throughout the decade he had criticized the dominant morality of the West and chipped away at its most celebrated values and conclusions. Now, his inner strength and desire to fight were on the wane. His character Zarathustra, at least, had an eagle and serpent as his friends and companions, not to mention a monkey. Nietzsche was in solitude. He abandoned his projected book on the transvaluation of all values. One may well wonder whether, at this point in his life, he possessed the philosophical resources to embark on or to finish such an endeavor. "I have been thinking very clearly although not to my advantage over my general position," he wrote his friend Franz Overbeck. "Not only is health lacking, but also the predisposition to get healthy—the life force is no longer intact. The losses of at least ten years can no longer be made good; during that time I have lived entirely off 'capital' and added nothing to it, nothing at all."[1]

In the feeling that he was no longer alive, philosophically, he settled his final scores with Richard Wagner in *Nietzsche contra Wagner* and *The Case of Wagner;* summarized his philosophy in *Twilight of the Idols* and *The Antichrist;* and offered a self-portrait for posterity in *Ecce Homo.* It was as though he were preparing his own funeral—a mock funeral, to be sure. If his claim that he was born posthumously is open to question, the claim that he had died *pre*humously is more plausible.

I interpret Nietzsche's preparations as part of an "epic spirituality," defined by his quest for meaning through philosophical reflections, genealogical investigations, and the many stories he had been telling to himself and his readers for a long time. His stories were complex, and his philosophy burst out in many directions. But I will argue that, appearances to the contrary, the web he spun was very consistent; he was correct in declaring that all the threads of his thought fit together.[2] The idea of the whole, which he depicted in *Schopenhauer as Educator* and mentioned almost in passing in *Human, All Too Human*, returned with a sense of urgency in *Twilight of the Idols*. His philosophy was not a system, but it was certainly a whole. Moreover, I believe that it is incorrect to argue that his writings in 1888, by which I mean the ones he prepared for publication, bore the imprint of a man already descending into insanity. On the contrary, Nietzsche was as lucid as ever. Even if his philosophy presaged a gloomy future of nihilism, Nietzsche was also cheerfully reconciling himself with all the categories and events he had battled so fiercely.

Who was this Nietzsche who introduced his persona with "Ecce Homo"—the same phrase that Pontius Pilate used to present Christ to a hostile crowd? Apart from the obvious irony, is it symbolic that Nietzsche titled his self-portrait *Ecce Homo*, after writing a book titled *The Anti-Christ?* These are relevant questions, but any possible answers will probably fail to convey the depth of his philosophical travails. Can we trace the consistent patterns, as well as important shifts, in the evolution of his thought? The answer, I propose, lies in identifying the different layers of his philosophy, which is made up of a complex array of stories. In this book, I look at different stories of Nietzsche; place these stories within a tradition of genealogical theorizing, in which the philosopher discovers something that, according to him, lies underneath the surface and is the key to knowing what we are and how we ought to live; and interpret both the stories and the genealogy in terms of one of Nietzsche's unique features, namely, his use of historiobiography. Historiobiography blends the idea of an attunement with all history *and* one's awareness of this attunement. As a mode of philosophizing, historiobiography allows Nietzsche to view all human history as if it runs through his own life and thoughts. He thus can look at modernity from the eyes of a remote age (GS; 337), or so he claims. He prefers to live apart, "in past or future centuries" (GS; 377). He writes that Julius Caesar could have been his father. Of two master storytellers in Western philosophy—Plato and Nietzsche—Nietzsche has no parallel in his claim that he can examine unexplored depths of the past and ascertain the future as well. As in Plato's philosophy, Nietzsche's genealogies are myths that he creates to make sense of his world. But, in contrast to Plato, only Nietzsche is both the narrator and the actor; he is the scribe of his own drama. To him, his philosophy is much more than personal memoir or confession; it is historiobiography, a mode of awareness that seems to be a trademark of philosophical paradigms that flourished in the nineteenth century.

IN THE NINETEENTH CENTURY, WHEN MANY WERE ATTACKING the dominant class structures of European society, Nietzsche was harking back to a past in which the power and morality of an imagined nobility went unchallenged. While social and political revolts took place in the streets, and the boundaries of pleasure were being redefined, Nietzsche was arguing that an insufferable guilt choked the European soul. While science and new technologies were transforming urban spaces, Nietzsche delighted in writing about forests, mountains, and the splendid words of a solitary monk, Zarathustra. It was the age of newspapers, electricity, locomotives, and horrifying wars, but Nietzsche was thinking about Greek antiquity and the Roman Empire. He was, in an important sense, an antiquarian. Yet his foothold in the past gave him a perspicacity and a vantage point from which to interpret the momentous changes of the modern age. He was not only a modern thinker, but one ahead of his time. He initiated a concept of language and a critique of morality that tore apart received values and charted new territory. Like Socrates, who, Nietzsche claims, sensed that Athens was sick and coming to an end, Nietzsche sensed that the concept of universal reason of the

Kantian self was an illness, and the Kantian self was an undiag-
nosed patient. Nietzsche anticipated a moral climate that was bereft
of certainties, and he tried, against all odds, to warn his readers
about a culture that was both complacent and complicit with the
dangers of moral emptiness.

In Book 5 of *The Gay Science* (1886), he prophesied terrible wars
that would bring havoc to the world. In 1887 he saw a tired humanity, asphyxiated with guilt and ruining its health with pale visions of a supernatural world. Yet in the final year of his productive
life—1888—he proclaimed a philosophy of reconciliation, which
ameliorates the anguish that runs, either as a subterranean or open
current, through his texts. I refer here to the anguish of *apprehension,* in the varied meanings this word carries in the English
language—of grasping, arresting, understanding, and perceiving. It
also implies a foreboding, a barely discernible fear. In most cases,
philosophy is the apprehension of a lack. I seek to show that Nietzsche apprehends the problem of life, its lack of meaning, as anguish, and this anguish leads to an epic spirituality, in which his
philosophical reflections recount his explorations and discoveries in
the realm of human history, the inner world of people, and his own
soul. It is not for nothing that Nietzsche describes himself as a subterranean creature, and also as a circumnavigator of the inner world
(D; P; 1; H; P; 7).

In 1872, Nietzsche thought that there was no danger that human
beings would ever come to know themselves completely. But he believed that he knew humankind and himself all too well to treat the
question of the meaning of life as a disturbing problem that called
for an aesthetic justification of life.[3]

> I myself have attempted an aesthetic justification: how is the world's
> ugliness possible?—I took the will to beauty, to remaining fixed in
> *the same* forms, as being a temporary remedy and means of preser-
> vation. . . . Ugliness is the way of regarding things that comes from
> the will to insert a meaning, a *new* meaning, into what has become
> meaningless: the accumulated force which compels the creating
> man to feel that what has gone before is untenable, awry, deserving
> of negation—is ugly?[4]

His reflections do not aim exclusively at the acquisition of knowledge in order to create new meanings, but rather are part of a poem of self-creation.[5] Just as Homer invents his own divinities, Nietzsche strives to recreate his own life and the life of everything and everyone of importance who preceded him. His spirituality thrives on discipline and self-control, and takes the avoidance of self-deception as its moral compass.

This self-creation, however, is compromised—as I will argue here—when it is filtered through Nietzsche's natural determinism. What you are, according to him, has been decreed in advance. His fight against self-deception thus seems to be lost in advance, too. The dominant morality of the West, he argues, is an expression of sickness, yet a deterministic naturalism destroys whatever grounds he may have for his physiological analyses. He seems forced to accept that such "sickness" is a natural event, a necessity, and that nature bears no responsibility for it.

For reasons such as these, Nietzsche's spirituality is agonistic, not only in the Greek sense of trying, testing, and facing competing demands, but also in the sense of inner torture. The meaninglessness and goallessness of life, as well as its intrinsic sufferings, are recurring themes in his philosophy. So is Nietzsche's belief that individuals' souls are revealed in their creations. Artists are deceivers, because they throw a veil of beauty over the ugliness of life. Modern musicians do not realize that their music discloses "their own history, the history of the soul made ugly" (D; 239). Every philosophy is a biographical portrait, a personal confession (BGE; 6). A good biography must possess dramatic events, which Nietzsche finds clearly lacking in the philosophies of Kant and Schopenhauer: "their thoughts do not constitute a passionate history of a soul; there is nothing here that would make a novel, no crises, catastrophes or death-scenes" (D; 481).

Nietzsche's thought, in contrast, is full of crises and catastrophes, and, in writings of the late 1880s, images of death-scenes. He claimed to provide a detailed confession of the inner regions of the Greek, the Christian, the modern, the slave, and the noble soul, not to mention his own soul. But the project of taking every philosophy as a personal memoir, and of reading every person's soul through his creations, gestures, or language, is predicated on the reader's affinity with the "text." Just as Plato did his best to control the passions because he knew his kind—that is, he knew the nature of his fellow aristocrats—similarly, Nietzsche claims to know a person's secrets because he, too, has secrets (GS; 31). I "know you," he says to the practitioners of sacrificial morality, "better than you know yourselves" (D; 215). This affinity that he claims to possess ends up encompassing all the animal and human past. "Man is *not* just an individual but what lives on, all that is organic in one particular line."[6]

Nietzsche's spirituality is also epic in a figurative sense. He compares his philosophizing to a journey, to charting a road in a treacherous landscape, knowing the dangers but not their magnitude, and harboring doubts about where safety lies or even if there is any safe place. His texts abound in images of caves, tunnels, mountains, forests, and jungles, and he sees himself as an explorer. The open sea is, perhaps, the best trope of his epic journey. The sea possesses a powerful allure to Nietzsche, for its openness, vastness, and eternal becoming. The open sea is a portent of riches but also of the all too real possibility that, in attempting to cross it, one may be shipwrecked: "wrecked against infinity," or, in a literal rendering, "to fail because of infinity" (D; 575).[7]

A heroic spirit, according to Nietzsche, discovers that every type of knowledge amounts to self-knowledge. "Do you not fear to re-encounter in the cave of every kind of knowledge your own ghost—the ghost which is the veil behind which truth has hidden itself from you? Is it not a horrible comedy in which you so thoughtlessly want to play a role?" (D; 539). It may be a comedy, but the philosopher is fated to play it because knowledge is a drive in which the "sense for truth" is also the "sense for security." One "does not want to let oneself be deceived, does not want to mislead oneself"; like all animals, one wants to apprehend what is real in order to avoid dangers (D; 26). Still, the possibility of self-deception is always hovering over one. "Have you never been plagued by the fear that you might be completely incapable of knowing the truth?" (D; 539). This question, for Nietzsche, is anything but comical. Like Socrates, Nietzsche seeks to know the individual's soul, but his goal is not to tell whether it is a virtuous soul but to expand his knowledge of its depths.

I seek to show how the anguish that underpins Nietzsche's spirituality, an anguish which I will define as his "metaphysics of meaning," colored all of his reflections. I argue, moreover, that he deployed three strategies to find relief from his sense of the meaninglessness of life: his magnified concept of what he himself represented in human history; his doctrine of the eternal recurrence; and his philosophy of reconciliation. Although the doctrine of eternal recurrence seemed the solution to his quest for meaning, his idea of reconciliation provided the firmest ground for withstanding the anguish of life. He could withstand it because he understood that the futility, that is, the "in vain," which he abhorred in 1888, was a chimera. Nothing was in vain, nothing was dispensable, and the doctrines of eternal recurrence and reconciliation went together.

NIETZSCHE POSES QUESTIONS OF THE FOLLOWING SORT: What is the utility of history, art, myth, truth, and morality for life? How does one find the best possibilities for life?[8] In endeavoring to answer these questions, Nietzsche, since the early 1870s, equated the search for knowledge with the journeys of "the globe's greatest circumnavigators. In fact, the career of the thinker is of a somewhat similar sort: they too are circumnavigators of life's most remote and dangerous regions."[9] These "dangerous regions" evoke the idea of "life" as both an epistemological and moral problem. It is an epistemological problem in the sense that there are many gaps in our knowledge of human beings. It is a moral problem in the sense that the role of our individuality within the totality of life and history remains to be discovered. It is in the realm of morality that the individual can measure his or her inner strength to be responsible, that is (for Nietzsche), to be honest with oneself. To be sure, Nietzsche does not dissociate knowledge from morality. Knowledge involves describing and evaluating the way life is, and the morality that he defends will be attuned with "what is."

The attunement of knowledge and morality is not as straight-forward as it seems, however. Nietzsche also credits morality and religion for educating humankind and lifting it up from the animal realm. Humans, in his view, need to be lied to, and morality is a lie that they tell to themselves. Although this lie worked wonders through history and gave individuals their spirituality, he argues, history has now reached a point in which the restrictions imposed by morality are no longer lifting humanity up but dragging it down to an abyss of guilt. "The *power* man has achieved now allows a *re-duction* of those means of discipline of which the moral interpreta-tion was the strongest."[10] This situation makes it necessary to assess our past history anew and to invent new scales with which to weigh all current moral values and to determine, for the first time, the order or "rank" of greatness among humans.[11] In this dangerous journey, the attunement that he expects between knowledge and morality fails. Knowledge, he wrote in an early essay, "attains as its final goal only—annihilation."[12] Knowledge unveils life as meaning-less and goalless. And this leads to another sort of question: How do I live, once I know that life is meaningless? In coping with this question, Nietzsche must remind himself that he does not find any problem with his own life: "No, life has not disappointed me." He is doing fine since "the great liberator came to me: the idea that life could be an experiment of the seeker for knowledge," and knowl-edge a world of dangers, victories, and heroic exploits (GS; 324). *"How should I not be grateful to my whole life?"* he asks in *Ecce Homo.*

Nietzsche's philosophy is an attempt to endow life with the significance it lacks, through myths, art, and genealogical stories, and by posing questions that, for him, are turning points in human history. Unknowingly at times, and at other times utterly self-consciously, he constructs an epic story of his life, which achieves its highest meaning in his conclusion that he is both the awareness of all past missteps and the embodiment of the pregnant potentialities of all of human history. The past resurfaces in his own conscious-ness, and he will tell humanity what life really is and why it requires a philosophy of reconciliation. In achieving this, he becomes heroic, because he has faced his own highest suffering and hopes (GS; 268). Notwithstanding his claims to the contrary, this amounts to a philosophy of redemption.[13] He acts as a redeemer of life by presenting life as it really is and removing all the scoria that corrode human nature.

THE LITERATURE ON NIETZSCHE IS RICH IN VALUABLE interpretations of different strands of his philosophy or even of the entire corpus. However, my contention is that three themes—the metaphysics of meaning, the unconscious, and the philosophy of reconciliation—have not yet received the attention they deserve as defining Nietzsche's philosophical endeavors. This is a lacuna that my study seeks to fill. These three themes, moreover, are anchored on a superb storytelling, which he intimated very early in the connection he saw between philosophy and fiction: "*The natural history of the philosopher*. He knows in that he fictionalizes, and he fictionalizes in that he knows" (PRS; 53).[14]

Nietzsche's genealogical accounts, as well as his indictment of morality, are in my view both philosophical inquiries and also stories that he tells to himself and us in order to come to grips with his intellectual agenda. His writings contain a profusion of vignettes pointing to the origins of this or that phenomenon, yet one is at a loss to find instances in which he offers evidence, be it empirical or textual, to underpin his arguments. In *On the Genealogy of Morality*, the philological evidence he musters to derive "guilt" from "debt" is rather thin. In *The Birth of Tragedy*, his descriptions of Greek culture and his thoughts on the Greeks' attitude toward guilt are suspect. This thinness of evidence, however, does not matter, in the sense that it would be a major misunderstanding to judge Nietzsche's arguments by the standards of historiography. Nietzsche was even more dismissive: "All historians speak of things which have never existed except in imagination" (D; 307). He was not nor did he intend to be a historian. He was a philosopher, and, as such, he was working from within a tradition going back to Plato, in which archetypes condense or are a summation of an entire worldview. This is the case for Socrates' idea of virtue and for the Good in Plato's ideal polis. Nietzsche's conceptual archetypes are the Dionysian, the Apollonian, noble morality, slave morality, asceticism, decay, sickness, health, and so on. Usually, his genealogies are offered as tentative hypotheses and preliminary sketches, even where the tone of his writing is one of certitude. In many cases, his genealogical stories are modified or abandoned in favor of new ones.

Take, for example, Nietzsche's arguments about the origins of morality in *Human, All Too Human* (1878). In sections 39, 94, 96, and 99, respectively, Nietzsche offers four different accounts of the stages through which morality developed. These should be regarded as snapshots from different angles and, as such, not necessarily conflicting. In section 39 Nietzsche traces morality to the primeval times of an ancestral humanity;[15] in section 94 he discusses the stages of morality from the standpoint of the individual; in section 99 he does the same from the viewpoint of the state; and in section 96 he focuses on the relationship between morality, customs, and tradition. However, the version presented in section 96 establishes a succession that not only departs from the other versions, but will be reversed in *Beyond Good and Evil* (1886) and in *On the Genealogy of Morality* (1887). The "morality of piety," Nietzsche states in section 96, "is in any event a much older morality than that which demands unegoistic actions." That is, the morality of piety appears first and then is followed by the morality of egoistic actions. This view is completely absent from sections 39, 94, and 99. In 1886 and 1887, Nietzsche will reverse this order and claim that the first expression of morality was based on the egotism of the noble class, which was then followed by the morality of piety, namely, the morality of the slaves.

Nietzsche's genealogies, I suggest, should be understood by us as philosophical, anthropological, and literary devices, which neither prove chance or contingency, nor possess an epistemological superiority. Rather, they show how different or arbitrary a present-day meaning is, when compared to its origins. This reasoning presupposes, of course, that one accepts the validity of Nietzsche's accounts of the origins of a particular concept or institution. He frequently makes statements that expect our assent or rejection, without furnishing us with the grounds to assent or reject. Some of his genealogies appear as the lost thread of a larger picture, and the only one who has access to this picture is Nietzsche himself. Only he could understand the significance of the lost thread, by locating it in its proper place. In other cases, however, Nietzsche's genealogies are invitations to think differently and to see matters from a new vantage point.

As I mentioned above, the philosophical reflections and stories that comprise his genealogical inquiries do not attempt to demonstrate contingency. They also do not seek to avoid universal truths. Nietzsche believes in some truths that, in his view, are universal. Life is tragic for the universal truths and falsehoods it contains. And it is not the falsehoods that trouble Nietzsche; it is the truths of life, truths that in his assessment we fear and from which most of us recoil, but truths that he wants to face head-on. The standard of weakness, for him, is how much falsehood a person tamely accepts, and the standard of strength is how much truth the individual can bear.

Art, for Nietzsche, is a valuable help in bearing hard truths, but the aesthetic dimension is not enough to provide the spiritual solace he cherished. Art may weaken, strengthen, or mesmerize, but there is always a tinge of deception to it. Art must beautify and falsify life to make it bearable. Nietzsche eschews this dimension of art. In 1888 he writes about the importance of facing life as it is. As I will argue, the doctrine of the eternal recurrence is crucial to his philosophy to the extent that it provides a solution to, and reconciliation with, the metaphysics of meaning. The idea of eternal recurrence, not art, allows us to decipher and cheerfully bear the riddle of existence. "To the paralyzing sense of general disintegration and incompleteness I opposed the *eternal recurrence*" (WP; 417).

In the first chapter I spell out the relationship between meaning and storytelling in Nietzsche's philosophy. In chapter 2, I discuss Nietzsche's view of genealogy; examine its relation to physiology; and assess the epistemological superiority that is ascribed to genealogy in most interpretations of Nietzsche's philosophy. Building on the arguments advanced in chapter 2, I provide in chapter 3 a detailed revaluation of *On the Genealogy of Morality*. In chapter 4, I trace Nietzsche's conflicting examinations of art, and then turn to the role played by the unconscious in chapter 5. This chapter serves as a stepping-stone to a detailed examination of the metaphysics of meaning in chapter 6. Chapter 7 takes stock of important modifications in Nietzsche's arguments in 1888, and in chapter 8, I address his understanding of modernity. In chapter 9, I present Nietzsche's philosophy of reconciliation, review the epic character of his spirituality, and recapitulate my arguments on historiobiography and storytelling.

Chapter One

STORYTELLING
AND MEANING

Storytelling strikes us as an almost metaphysical need. It is the need to speak in complete sentences that reveal an order of beginning and end; the need for subjects and predicates that, when coupled together, provide explanations. Stories channel that need by offering plots, characters, causal links, and unexpected turns of event, and the whole brightens with life by feeding on the pleasure or ecstasy of expectation, which is one of the deepest qualities of human creatures. We prefer suspense, a temporary halt of knowledge, or, in some cases, even a permanent uncertainty. Complete stories build on suspense and end it. Unfinished stories build on suspense but never solve it, and thus inhabit the paradox of pleasure or cruelty: they can leave us in the realm of hope, which is pleasurable though unsatisfied, or in the vale of pain or resentment.

On another level, stories suggest an uncanny religiosity. Stories are told for the sake not of explanation but of *meaning*. Explanations are "surface creatures," acting as connectors of events; meaning is always subterranean. It is the answer to the interrogation that persists after all of the pieces are put together; it is the faith that responds to doubts that still linger after everything is explained and accounted for. Meaning is what we project on explanations, for we assume that explanations are the vehicles of meaning. All religions revolve around storytelling purporting to reveal the whys and hows of human existence. All cultures are organized around a web of stories, whose presence gives meaning.

Before there were novels, there were Platonic dialogues; before there were Platonic dialogues, there were the Homeric epics. But in their nature, the Homeric poems are separated from Plato's stories by an abyss. The *Iliad*, in particular, stands out as a story without beginnings. The wrath of Achilles is announced in the first sentence, like a bolt of lightning, as the cause of the misfortunes that have befallen the Achaeans. Soon, however, the story focuses not on Achilles but on the short-sighted and resentful Agamemnon. He is the cause of Achilles' wrath; but in Homeric storytelling, causal connections are kept to a bare minimum. The *Iliad*, in this sense, is a surface poem. Even when the gods intervene in human affairs, they show no inclination to explore the motives of the heart.

Agamemnon's refusal to return the captive Chryseis to her father brings a plague on the camp, and the soldiers are perishing. Why, then, does the poet pick on Achilles as personally responsible for the plague, apart from the fact that he is the main character of the story? The explanation probably involves the fact that the gods are arbitrary and unreliable, so much so that suppliants must design different strategies to gain the support of key divinities, who in turn may convince other deities to join the suppliant's cause. A pagan prayer is a convoluted display of manipulative tactics. In this environment, a character has broad leeway in his actions, even though those actions may amount to a permanent torture: one never knows whether one's relationship with one deity might displease another. Agamemnon is exempt from responsibility because he does not know the consequences of his actions. Achilles, however, knows the terrible consequences in store for the Achaeans if he does not join them in battle. Since reliable knowledge as to how the gods will respond to human actions is not at hand, it is especially important that people learn to discern the immediate and, in some cases, even remote consequences of their actions, even more so if the well-being of their community is at stake.

To take personal responsibility as the meaning that colors Achilles' wrath is, in all likelihood, a sublimated reading of the opening lines of the *Iliad*, but it is not an arbitrary one. The wrath is the main subject of the poem, followed by countless explanations of it. Similarly, the search for meaning is the defining motive that drives the Western philosophical canon in both its transcendental and secular metaphysics. In Plato's philosophy, both the sphere of meaning and the sphere of personal responsibility are enlarged. The immediacy of face-to-face enemies is replaced in his dialogues by refined conversations that are inquiries into the conceptual world. This activity presupposes a tradition informed by central agreements about vices and virtues in a person's life. But Platonic characters are not only historical or imagined human figures; transcendental concepts also figure prominently, as part of the plot. In some cases, they appear as unexpected guests, twisting the dramatic effect and pointing the conversation toward a world without language. Witness, for instance, Plato's reluctance or inability to provide a definition of the Good. And these concepts are, in an important sense, cut off from the traditional Greek view of the gods. Even they have to bend their knees to the *to agathon* (the Good), which is the highest Form of Plato's stories. Here we find an "archaeological" instinct that is absent in the Homeric epics: the quest for a cause behind a cause, which only arises when reflection has become an exclusive area of inner inquiry and self-inquiry. Whereas Homeric gods display neither inwardness nor any proclivity to see behind the actions of their subjects, Plato provides a detailed description of the structure of the soul and applies his view of rationality to all divine beings. And it is because both humans and divinities share the same faculty of reason that meaning can be found and expressed through language.

The metaphysics of meaning reaches a climax in Christianity, when the fullness of God's revelation displaces myths such as those of the Greeks. The past has been deciphered as a preparation for the First Coming, and the central traits of the future have been put in place. It does not follow, however, that God is now transparent. The Christian church, in both its Catholic and Protestant dimensions, has always stressed that God is beyond human understanding. Paul's epistles can be taken to deny this reading, in the sense that salvation is the revelation to Jews and Gentiles of a mystery hidden since the foundation of the world. But the whole prophetic sphere in the Testaments is shrouded in mystery, and the unfolding of God in history is still full of mysterious turns. Isaiah writes of a hidden God, but Amos confidently declares that God will not act without revealing his purposes to his prophets.

It is uncontroversial that both the Platonic and the Christian traditions treat human knowledge as a delimited sphere: for the former, we should seek the education and specialization required for a mystical encounter with the Good; for the latter, we should seek knowledge of God's grace and of the principles that ought to govern an individual's behavior. The function of knowledge is to provide a bridge to transcendence, through histories of origins deploying a meaningful plot. This paradigm governed the individual's attitude toward the external world and himself in the centuries of Christian dominance in western Europe.

This paradigm was to change. In what follows, I describe a trajectory toward what I call "the quest for transparency," which I treat as one of the most important and disturbing features of modernity. At times, admittedly, I will describe this trajectory in broad strokes. The reader should consider that my goal is to define this quest, to identify thinkers who took part in it, and to understand Nietzsche as a philosopher who extended that quest in all his theoretical endeavors. In Nietzsche's thought, transparency is the removal of layers, the quest for origins, and the interpretation of practices to see what is behind them and to uncover the "hidden" foundations that are the keys to explaining everything on the surface.

In the Renaissance, huge fissures developed in the Christian worldview. Ultimately, these destroyed the religious grip on the individual's subjectivity. They originally developed less from the impact of new scientific discoveries than from a return to classic literature and a new way of seeing reality as an aesthetic dimension. The return to the ancients was an eloquent example of how far the power of Christianity had eroded in the beliefs of certain circles of European culture. For although some aspects of classical Greek culture could be integrated with a Christian worldview (Plato, especially), the pagan soil of those expressions remained outside it. In the pagan perspective, truth is fluid and ultimately unknowable, given the great number of deities, each with special inclinations. The gods were unpredictable, which either made individuals timorous or expanded their sphere of action. But, more important than the rediscovery of ancient texts, the most subtle and fierce challenges to religious hegemony occurred in the aesthetic realm. Renaissance artists worked on religious themes but re-created them through the prism of the artist's perspective, thus carving out a niche in which the individual *qua* individual could express his judgment on the sacred and profane. The Renaissance artist, although immersed in a religious tradition, read the canon and interpreted it as a work of art in which the artist's judgment was paramount, outside the institutional boundaries of the church. The artistic creation was as much a personal interpretation of a religious tradition as it was a projection of the artist's individuality. In general, the Renaissance man inverted the dominant values of Christianity and put forward a new standard: man was the measure of man. The Reformation accelerated this inversion by returning to the idea of an apostolic church as interpreted through scripture and faith, which was, in turn, located in individual subjectivity.

The idea of the work of art as a showcase for individuality had a corresponding expression in the political realm, through Machiavelli's Prince. He, too, approaches the state as a work of art, on which he can leave the imprint of his *virtú*, along with a record of his success in attaining greatness. Machiavelli places the new ruler in an institutional vacuum, in which his qualities of judgment and character are the only measures for achieving his goal: legitimacy. The political sphere is conceived not only as independent of religious tradition, but as one in which the main tenets of that tradition are unworkable. *The Prince* thus shows, in a stark light, an epistemological crisis: traditional beliefs are found wanting. They cannot cope with the fluid reality of power. This is hardly a problem if public power is an insignificant aspect of a given political arrangement. But if public power is understood as the central sphere of social life, this calls for the eradication of religious beliefs from the strategies needed to obtain and to preserve power. Religion is still useful, but its world is upside down. The political realm is not a vehicle for religion. The opposite holds true: religion is a means to obtain power, and its efficacy ought to be measured by how successful it is as such a means. Man is the measure of man; power is the measure of power. An anti-Copernican revolution was in the offing: transcendence revolves around the axes of human creations and actions. In two words, this is a disguised paganism.

Nowhere is this pattern of thought more evident than in Hobbes's commonwealth, in which religion is not only explicitly relegated to an auxiliary role, but, more important, the central principle of Christianity—salvation—is redefined. Salvation is no longer achieved only through faith in Christ; it requires obedience to the sovereign.[1] This was Hobbes's hardly tactful way of affirming the irrelevance of religious beliefs in the constitution of society. The rationalistic approach of Descartes illustrates this pattern of thought on a new plane, that of the human mind. The Cartesian subject affirms his own existence, not because a religious text declares it to be true, but because he finds in himself the proof of what he is: a *thinking* being, which puts everything in doubt before arriving at itself as the source of validity. The Cartesian thinking "I" as the source of validity will soon become the Kantian agent, as the source of moral precepts.

These philosophical developments exemplify an assumption that both Greek culture and Christianity treated as hubris: reality, nature, and human life are transparent, that is, they can be understood through human reason. The Kantian view that the will, as an act of reason, can reduce moral rules to their bare essentials through statements that possess universal validity is rooted in this assumption. When the ethereal realm of Kantian reasoning is put aside in favor of anthropological stories about human nature, that assumption is still present. Rousseau in his *Second Discourse* claims to reveal what man "really" is: in a state of transparency and devoid of mystery, a state populated by compassionate beings.[2] The community based on the social contract, for Rousseau, is not a return to the state of nature but a conscious effort to re-create relations of transparency among individuals, whereby the vices and virtues of everyone are known to all.

This assumption about transparency and reason was in conflict with religious views about the constitution of society. In Kant's most hubristic moments, it legislates principles that even God, as a rational being, must respect. It also affects two other areas deserving of mention. For Descartes, the world and the human body in particular are organisms regulated by mechanical laws. Hobbes deepened this idea by a corporeal politics, in which the political body is a passive entity that receives stimuli from the external world and acts accordingly.[3] It is worth noting Descartes' description of the body in his *Treatise on Man* (1662):

> I suppose the body to be just a statue or a machine made of earth, which God forms with the explicit intention of making it as much as possible like us. Thus He not only gives its exterior the colours and shapes of all the parts of our body, but also places inside it all the parts needed to make it walk, eat, breathe, and imitate all those functions we have which can be imagined to proceed from matter and to depend solely on the disposition of our organs.[4]

The epitome of this mechanistic conception can be found in Julien Offray de La Mettrie's *Machine Man* (1747): "The body is nothing but a clock whose clockmaster is new chyle. Nature's first care, when the chyle comes into the blood, is to stimulate in it a sort of fever which the chemists, who are obsessed by furnaces, must have taken for a sort of fermentation."[5] By the nineteenth century, science had launched a full-scale assault on both body and mind, claiming them as its new territories for investigation. Physiology and psychology, respectively, sought transparency in these two frontiers of human existence, seeking to expel their mysteries.

Nietzsche enters the scene at a juncture when the body and mind were frequently explained as a transparent construction, composed of instincts that were always susceptible to physiological explanations. In 1878 he wrote about the prospect of identifying the chemistry of moral sensations, and in *The Anti-Christ* (1888) he paid homage to Descartes as follows:

> As regards the animals, Descartes was the first who, with a boldness worthy of reverence, ventured to think of the animal as a *machine:* our whole science of physiology is devoted to proving this proposition. Nor, logically, do we exclude man, *as even Descartes did:* our knowledge of man today is real knowledge precisely to the

extent that it is knowledge of him as a machine. (AC; 14, second emphasis mine)[6]

Nietzsche's genealogies are infused with the idea that life can be understood through a set of principles, which hold true even when they are consciously denied. Once those principles are identified, everything in human history and behavior will make sense and illusions will be dispelled. Every system of philosophy or morality is an "unconscious memoir" of the instincts of its founder (BGE; 6). One might apply this to three major nineteenth-century currents of thought: Marx's account of history and economics, Nietzsche's interpretation of life, and Freud's theory of psychoanalysis. Each is in the business of dispelling "illusions" that hold us hostage.[7] J. P. Stern has put this in an illuminating way:

> Their thinking is directed toward the uncovering of an immanent secret—a secret concealed in men's minds: . . . these minds they wished to change, and with them the world. Because they thought of their undertaking as the solving of a *secret*, they saw all opposition to it as a conspiracy: a conspiracy of men with vested social and material interests, thought Marx; of men with vested moral and religious interests, thought Freud; of men who choose to be only half alive and resent the few who live generously and dangerously, thought Nietzsche.[8]

Nietzsche, who possessed a keen genealogical instinct, is an emblematic figure of the "archaeological trade" in Western philosophy: the obsession to dig below the surface, or to see behind the mask, which acquires a troublesome dimension when one recognizes an inherent tendency to also plant the evidence for its findings. Moreover, although Nietzsche cultivates the genre of aphorisms and explicitly condemns consistency, his stories paint fairly coherent patterns underpinning events, individuals, and concepts. Commentators Arthur C. Danto, John Richardson, Richard Schacht, and Mark Warren, among others, have looked for and found coherent threads in Nietzsche's works.[9] The difference, not a minor one, between Nietzsche and other storytellers of Western philosophy is that Nietzsche is not only the narrator but also at times the actor, acting his own script. As Eugen Fink comments, Nietzsche "is a virtuoso of the artistic medium of suggestion, who can describe postures and fundamental stances toward the world and things, as well as existential attitudes and images of man with the sharpness of a silhouette while giving them the illumination of an icon."[10]

Nietzsche tells a variegated array of stories, ranging from the origins of nobles and slaves to the emergence of the political state. Most of his vignettes are deciphered when the philosopher sheds light on "hidden" motives, which puncture the halcyon facade of illustrious characters and venerable ideals that is widely accepted. These characters and ideals, according to Nietzsche, are powerfully colored by *ressentiment,* which serves as the *causa prima* of Christianity, democracy, Protestantism, the French Revolution, socialism, and anarchism. Any idea that challenges the "pathos of distance" and the value of rank—that is, of essential differences in merit and emotional strength between persons—must be anchored in resentment, according to Nietzsche: hitherto "mankind has been in the *worst* hands . . . it has been directed by the underprivileged, the cunningly revengeful, the so-called 'saints,' those world-calumniators and desecraters of man" (EH; "Daybreak"; 2).

Nietzsche is a master storyteller, and in his hands everything becomes a plot, a conspiracy, a sickness, a play, or even a secret and unknowable war. "I am going to tell the story—simplified—of certain philosophers"[11] (PTA; P); "This precisely is the long story of how *responsibility* originated" (GM; II; 2); "I shall now relate the *real* history of Christianity" (AC; 39); "I tell myself my life" (EH; Foreword). (His inclination to set the record straight is, in turn, a Protestant trait that confirms his views of scholars: they always inherit their parents' habits [GS; 348].) As he states, "It is a painful, a dreadful spectacle which has opened up before me: I have drawn back the curtain on the *depravity* of man. . . . A history of the 'higher feelings,' of the 'ideals of mankind'—and it is possible I shall have to narrate it—would almost also constitute an explanation of *why* man is so depraved" (AC; 6). But if Nietzsche's thought seems to enjoy a permanent attraction to us, this is due both to his credentials as a philosopher and to his ability to tell stories that are inscribed in the dominant movement of the last several centuries, namely, the quest for and the expansion of knowledge—of transparency.

Until the dawn of modernity in Europe, which for chronological purposes I identify as the development of mechanistic ideas in the seventeenth century, reality was perceived rather like the Earth was before 1492: a dense fog of ignorance or mystery covered huge expanses. What knowledge there was coexisted with mystery, signaling the limits of human reason and inquiry. But with the challenge initiated by the Renaissance and the advent of science as a new discourse possessing an encroaching nature—everything needs a scientific explanation, that is, an explanation according to the rules of science—the journey toward transparency gathered force. Nature had to be deciphered and harnessed through science, and even the most mysterious realm of all, human subjectivity, could be explored and deciphered through psychological interventions. It is not accidental that the three major traditions mentioned above—Marxism, Nietzschean stories, and psychoanalysis—insisted that almost everything humankind took to be knowledge so far was an illusion, which extended its shadow over religion, morality, human nature, and history. All three narrated other genealogies to account for the present, and through them the nineteenth century became the "hitherto" century.

"In direct contrast to German philosophy which descends from heaven to earth," Marx argued,

> here we ascend from earth to heaven. That is to say, we do not set out from what men say, imagine, conceive, nor from men as narrated, thought of, imagined, conceived, in order to arrive at men in the flesh. We set out from real, active men, and on the basis of their real life-process we demonstrate the development of the ideological reflexes and echoes of this life-process. The phantoms formed in the human brain are also, necessarily, sublimates of their material life-process, which is empirically verifiable and bound to material premises. Morality, religion, metaphysics, all the rest of ideology and their corresponding forms of consciousness, thus no longer retain the semblance of independence. . . .

In the whole conception of history up to the present this real basis of history has either been totally neglected or else considered as a minor matter quite irrelevant to the course of history.[12]

Similarly, Freud suggested that, up to now, the clear lines of the architecture of the mind had been buried under illusions, which thwarted a scientific explanation of sexuality, culture, religion, dreams, and even intoxication. The clear lines are there to be found: "in mental life nothing which has once been formed can perish . . . everything is somehow preserved and . . . in suitable circumstances (when, for instance, regression goes back far enough) it can once more be brought to light." And, in an archaeological metaphor, he compares the mind to an old city. "It is greatly to be regretted that [the] toxic side of mental processes has so far escaped scientific examination."[13] And hitherto, "no satisfactory solution of [dreams] has been advanced."[14]

Nietzsche was probably the most categorical of the three: "No philosopher hitherto has been in the right" (BGE; 25). One should take the world "together with space, time, form, motion, to be the result of a false *conclusion*" (BGE; 34). "All judgements as to the value of life have evolved illogically and are therefore unjust" (H; I; 32). "There is likewise a disinclination to admit that all that which men have defended in earlier centuries with sacrifice of happiness and life were nothing but errors: perhaps one says they were stages of truth" (H; I; 53). "[B]y inquiring after the criterion of certainty I tested the scales upon which men have weighed in general hitherto—and that the question of certainty itself is a dependent question, a question of the second rank" (WP; 587). This urge to test the scales by which values are assessed leads him to a reexamination of historical events and individuals.

Western thought is familiar with the search for "origins" and explanations; all theoretical paradigms deploy it. The Greeks told myths to explain their origins, Christians resorted to revelation to provide an account of our beginnings, and Renaissance philosophers turned to classical antiquity to explain the present. Myths, revelation, and antiquity *settle* a relationship with the past. The three frameworks of modern storytelling described above, in contrast, not only tell historical stories but continually turn to the past in order to measure the present. This is especially telling in Nietzsche's and Freud's interpretations, in which origins are the key to explaining both social pathologies and individual malaises.

Even a cursory reading of some of Nietzsche's texts will show numerous explanations of origins: the origins of knowledge, scholars, polytheism, the logical, the sound of German language, the age of fear; of poetry, prayers, faith in cause and effect, sin, morality, religion, religious wars, consciousness, guilt; of plastic arts, convictions, intoxication, intemperateness, ecstasy, the *vita contemplativa*, justice, intellectual consciousness, and asceticism; not to mention a "natural history of rights and duties" (D; 112); a "*history of the genesis of thought*" (H; I; 16); a "*history of the origins* of moral feelings" (GS; 345); and the need for a "*history* of the ethical and religious sensations" (WS; 16). In certain prominent cases, such as morality and religion, Nietzsche regales us with several accounts, each purporting to explain their origins. In *Daybreak* he criticizes the weight ascribed to origins (D; 44), and in *The Wanderer and His Shadow* he attacks the "poison of contempt for what is closest" (WS; 16), but he is clearly impervious to his own advice. There are no dams to stem the flood of Nietzschean stories about "origins."

This is historicity as frenzy. It is also historicity as transparency, as the quest for the "inner body" that is beyond the painter and the sculptor: "Plastic art wants to make characters visible on the outside; the art of speech employs the word to the same end, it delineates the character in sounds. Art begins from the natural *ignorance* of mankind as to his interior (both bodily and as regards character); it does not exist for physicists or philosophers" (H; I; 160). This ignorance, fortunately, will be superseded by the transparency that Nietzsche himself makes possible: "a word from me drives all bad instincts into the face" (EH; "Good Books"; 3). "Insight into the origin of a work concerns the physiologists and vivisectionists of the spirit; never the aesthetic man, the artist!" (GM; III; 4).

Our own century epitomizes the journey toward transparency and some of its fruits. We have the capacity to see, literally, beneath a person's skin; a chemical tune-up of the brain through chemical substances makes people functional; and by an accurate reading of the genome, society anticipates curing illnesses. Nietzsche was not entirely in the dark concerning these fruits, and he treats as hubristic the way experts of his time approached nature. "Our whole attitude toward nature, the way we violate her with the aid of machines and the heedless inventiveness of our technicians and engineers, is *hubris*" (GM; III; 9). But his own stories are implicated in this hubris. He is a member of the pack.

The century or so since Nietzsche has also been a time of storytelling *par excellence.*[15] A large part of our social life revolves around storytelling. From printed, televised, and Web news to soap operas, stories socialize our subjectivity. Science has erased the temporal distance between a story and its happening. In many cases, events need not be told; they can be *watched*. We have military actions on film (and other electronic media); beatings on film, executions on film, acts of political corruption on film, the results of state surveillance on film. This is, in another way, a transparency of origins and genealogy of transparency.

Although the quest for transparency plays an important role in accounting for Nietzsche's attraction to us today, it is not enough. Nietzsche's quest has a larger import in the context of developments that marked the twentieth century, especially its second half. First, what Nietzsche called the essence of life, namely, the will to power, achieved unheard-of proportions in the growth of national states and their military technology. This power was all too vivid in Nazism and the Soviet Union, and in the mega-state that is the United States. This has led to outcomes all too common throughout history, but which, in a time when mass media are ancillary to the exercise of power, have acquired new proportions. From Thrasymachus and Callicles, to Machiavelli, Hobbes, and Nietzsche, these outcomes have emphasized the ambiguous relationship between power and morality.

Second, Nietzsche argued that morality was always the expression of power. He was not saying something new; nor was he treading new ground in defending the importance of linguistic descriptions for the way people understand reality. Machiavelli has already noticed the importance of masks and deception in public life, and

Hobbes built a new reality on linguistic grounds, in his idea of a contract. But Nietzsche, more than any other philosopher in the Western tradition, hammered away at the two issues: the direct relationship between morality and power, on the one hand, and the way that language constructs reality, on the other. In the context of modern state apparatuses that literally create "reality," and in a world where a thug is an acceptable ally so long as he parrots the "right" concepts or joins with the gorgons of regional or global economic powers for his share of the spoils, it is clear that the bubble of belief in a universal rationality and universal morality has burst. Alas, instead of a deafening explosion, the evidence of its demise is a phlegmatic murmur. It is as if we knew all along that reason and morality were outsized costumes for dwarf-like concepts. And this is what Nietzsche is saying.

Third, Nietzsche's argument about a politics centered on the body has carried the day, though not necessarily according to his expectations. Physiology has been at the center of modern torture chambers and state goals of control, as well as in the general attempt to decipher what we are, with the explicit purpose of anticipating what we can be. True enough, the wars that Nietzsche anticipated came along, but the asphyxiating guilt and the nihilistic clouds that he abhorred and feared the most, on the whole, did not.

Together, such elements richly explain the contemporary relevance of Nietzsche's philosophical reflections and the pertinence of his stories. As in a Woody Allen film, Nietzsche offers carefully crafted stories and, at the slightest sign of inattention on the part of his readers/audience, walks to the screen and crosses over to the action. When the audience wakes up, a new character is in the plot. "Concerned but not disconsolate, we stand aside a little while, contemplative men to whom it has been granted to be witnesses of these tremendous struggles and transitions. Alas, it is the magic of these struggles that those who behold them must also take part and fight" (BT; 15). Narrator, actor, artist: Nietzsche himself wears multiple masks, for self-protection, both to conceal and reveal himself. As W. D. Williams claims,

[Nietzsche] is fond of isolating some aspect of his thinking . . . and then addressing it directly, or playing it off against himself, creating a tension whereby his thinking becomes a dramatic contest with the reader as spectator and, as it were, judge. Or, sometimes, it turns into a grandiose play within a play, with a carefully constructed mask being apparently ripped off for the reader's delight and satisfaction with further revelations and puzzles to follow, so that all is left shimmering and only half expressed.[16]

But this method is much more than a manifold display of masks. Nietzsche's stories about origins and future possibilities express a link between history and his personal story, between history and autobiography. That is, he is telling stories in which his self and the history of humanity meet, like two powerful currents, until they reach the point where all masks fall and a mysterious unity is revealed—when he sees all prehuman and human history enmeshed in his own life. This is what I call *historiobiography*: the belief that one life could contain the hieroglyphs to decipher human life as a whole; the idea that old voices are still resonating within the multiplicity of souls that are Nietzsche.

Nietzsche's script in his historiobiography follows a familiar and consistent pattern: the corrosion of life-affirming possibilities, the prospect of nihilism, and the daunting task of reversing the tide toward a philosophy of the future. This script suggests that he is still indebted to the most pervasive, and from his standpoint, presumably most corrosive form of metaphysics: the metaphysics of meaning, specifically, the meaning he has discovered through his storytelling. He readily admits that he does not want to be deceived, and that he might still be in the sphere of truth. But meaning and truth are two different categories, and meaning might well be at home with untruth.

The search for meaning is a two-dimensional quest, in which an agent tries to make sense of the world *and* to make sense of his place within it. This is, at bottom, an aesthetic project: the philosopher (it is invariably a philosopher) wishes to know the plot in which he finds himself, as well as his role in it. The assumption here is that there *is* a plot, with subjects and predicates, beginnings and ends; namely, that there are consistent patterns which can be told as stories. The plot can be purposeful or purposeless, but this is beside the point. And with a plot comes play-acting: "We should not forget that, without exception, our dear artists are, and have to be to some extent, actors; and without play-acting they would scarcely endure life for any length of time" (GS; 99).

The concepts of truth and untruth, appearances and deception, are relevant only as part of a quest for meaning. Nietzsche's philosophical critique of nihilism portends a mixture of despair and resignation. But his critique itself is strange, to the extent that it is deeply disturbed by a development that leads individuals and European culture in a *wrong* and *false* direction. But why should one be concerned about this? The answer is evident in his view that life is pregnant with life-affirming possibilities (the will to power, the noble morality) and life-denying ones (the herd instinct for self-preservation, the slave morality). On what grounds does one choose between these?

The idea of meaning is entwined with the idea of choice, but meaning seems to be at variance with the idea of change, or "becoming." For "becoming" might be read as a truncated meaning. When you are carried off by the flux, you do not have time to look backward, and you do not know where you are heading. There is no plot and, consequently, no role to play. Your meaning is a surface meaning, one of immediacy: you know you are in a permanent journey, in a permanent becoming that never ends. You do not reflect on your predicament, since reflection is the first stage toward "Egyptianism"—that is, an obsession with building conceptual walls.

As soon as you put your feet on what you perceive as solid ground, or throw out your anchor, and can *anticipate* possible shores; as soon as you can say, this is what life is, this is what I am; then you are no longer in the stage of becoming. You have stepped out of the flux. You are now a storyteller, a philosopher, or a pyramid builder. As Fink observes, "It is 'being,' according to Nietzsche, that is the delusion which conquers and enthralls the human imagination. It establishes a false network of concepts in which men com-

monly catch themselves and halts, binds, and lays to rest the supposedly actual." But this "being" is just the individual's own "net of
concepts that he throws time and again into the stream of becoming."[17]

Every time a philosopher throws his anchor to delimit his meaning, he needs to tell a story. In telling it, the narrator is forced to
have a beginning, which, from a temporal perspective, will be arbitrary, like the wrath of Achilles. The beginning could be in the past,
the present, or the future. The arbitrary character of the point of
departure is somewhat lessened by the causal links that the narrator
puts forward. When those causal links follow the pattern of deduc-
tions from specified assumptions, the story is in the realm of truth,
meaning, and even logic. Nietzsche, the avowedly self-proclaimed
immoralist, operates in this realm as well.

My approach differs from others, for instance, that taken by
Alexander Nehamas, who argues that Nietzsche "looks at the world
in general as if it were a sort of artwork; in particular, he looks at it
as if it were a literary text."[18] He assumes that Nietzsche arrives at
many of his positions by taking the "literary situation" as his point
of departure.[19] One problem is the lack of a clear definition of "literary situation," but even if this were defined, the idea of treating the
world as a literary construction is so broad that it requires a good
measure of filling in the details to make it a distinctive one. Assuming that a "literary situation" involves plots, characters, suspense,
dilemmas, mysteries, dangers, and dramatic effects, it is difficult
to say what would be unique about Nietzsche's perspective. Most
philosophers narrate a story or a plurality of stories, regardless of
whether the characters are actual or imaginary people, political re-
gimes, or even concepts. For instance, Machiavelli's *Prince* can be
read as a literary text that teaches the treacherous nature of power
and the way to survive and to keep it. Rousseau's *Second Discourse,*
not to mention his *Émile,* is a drama that includes both good and
bad characters; it has a climax—the rich, inventing, civil society—
and it has an end, which is the corrupt civilization in which his readers live. Even in Kant's system, one finds the denouement of a play
of concepts and the struggle to provide a persuasive ending. The
best example of the literary paradigm in philosophy is, of course,

Plato. The *Apology* can be read as a tragedy with comic moments; the *Euthyphro* as a comedy with tragic elements. The *Republic* might provide a script for the movie industry.

Thus, to argue that Nietzsche treats the world as a literary device or as artwork runs the risk of emptiness. The assumptions that I intend to test against the textual evidence are quite different. Nietzsche's philosophy, I argue, is the creation of stories that seek to find a meaning both for Nietzsche himself, who emerges as one of the main characters of his stories, and for all of humanity, which, he believes, has come to full consciousness in himself. What is new here? After all, Nietzsche insists that he, the author, is one thing, and his writings are another. But he also volunteers in his letters that *The Gay Science* and *Zarathustra* contain an "image" of him.[20] This contention can be applied to all his texts. I seek to show the centrality of what I call the metaphysics of meaning in the development of Nietzsche's philosophy. And this metaphysics of meaning can be constructed only by weaving the philosopher Nietzsche into the totality constituted by history. Hence, this is an exercise in *historiobiography*, a genre in which one individual—Nietzsche—is subsumed into all history, and all history coalesces in him.

I also avoid a perspectival stance in my interpretation of Nietzsche. Nietzsche admittedly claims that there are no facts, only interpretations, in *The Will to Power*. If there are no independent facts that will serve as a measure in judging an interpretation, then, as Nehamas argues, "every interpretation creates its own facts [and] it may seem impossible to decide whether any interpretation is or is not correct. . . . the very idea of interpretation, which seems to require at least that there be something there to be interpreted, begins to appear itself suspect."[21] Yet, as I demonstrate, Nietzsche does have a fairly long list of facts that he takes seriously and that explain why he, at times, sinks into despair. The will to power is a fact, even if he offers it as "my theory," and so also is the slave morality. Above all, the body, the instincts, suffering, discipline, and democracy are facts. Like Nehamas, I think that some interpretations are better than others. Unlike him, I think that perspectivism offers no ground to distinguish itself from relativism. If there are no facts behind the interpretation, and each interpretation creates its own facts, then we do not have independent standards to determine the validity of our positions.

The question that should be posed is: In terms of what is an interpretation better than another? I find "better interpretations" in Nietzsche when they are located within a script of missed opportunities and within the fact of storytelling as a way to find meaning for one's own life. It is from within the metaphysics of meaning that some interpretations are better than others. In this book I explore some of Nietzsche's stories to see how he dealt with meaning and constructed his philosophy. My arguments are also intended to show, in part, that the metaphysics of meaning inverts some of Nietzsche's most cherished values: he ends not as a triumphant Dionysus, but as a trapped Dionysus. On another level, I assess the avenues that may be closed by interpreting Nietzsche in terms of a style revolving around storytelling. As Robert C. Solomon argues, "style in philosophy . . . is first of all a style of thinking, an approach to life and not just a way of writing. A style is not superficial but deep, not word play but itself a worldview, a profound expression of *who one is.*"[22] My approach to Nietzsche from the perspective of storytelling is not meant to imply that he is primarily a literary figure, with secondary or even little philosophical significance. He is, primarily, a philosopher, but the most fruitful way of engaging his philosophy is through the stories he tells in his own quest for meaning.

Chapter Two

GENEALOGY, PHYSIOLOGY, AND NATURALISM

Genealogy, as I understand it, is an account of how events, values, and concepts arising from different sources and at different times were integrated into an interpretive framework to mold the culture that we now inhabit. These events, values, and concepts, once fluid and malleable in their interpretation, coalesced and were transformed into a yardstick to judge the past, or a measuring rod to select, reject, celebrate, and condemn other events, values, and concepts. The original historical soil was thus shaped and forced in one direction. Here, I express my own view; several authors' positions are addressed in the next section of this chapter.

To put it another way, a genealogy is the construction of a conceptual space that is deemed indispensable to explain another conceptual space. How and why did this construction, or this shaping and forcing, take place, and what does a genealogy mean for our culture, morality, and, ultimately, our present and future life? These are central questions that animate the genealogical method, and they reflect a search for transparency. For a genealogy is an unveiling: a removal of layers that, in the form of concepts and interpretations, erased certain historical marks and presented themselves as signposts of new beginnings. Genealogy is thus a task of disentangling the constituent elements of the past and reassembling them to explain why they now form a new whole. It is both a descent and an

ascent, both a retracing backward of the path that explains our existing moral views and a look forward to the genealogist's own predicament. It is also a history centered in nature: in how certain bodies,
certain instincts, and even certain illnesses evince ways of life, along
with a conceptual framework to justify them. Hence, in Nietzsche's
philosophy, genealogy and physiology are entwined.

In this chapter, I examine these two modes of interpretation in
Nietzsche's thought—the genealogical and the physiological. In so
doing, I hope to map out the salient traits of his view of the philosopher, to address the value of genealogy and its relationship to physiology, and to suggest the possible limits of Nietzsche's naturalism:
that is, the possible limits of Nietzsche's answers to the question of
why a certain shaping and forcing occurred in that landscape where
nature and culture mold one another. I will examine Nietzsche's genealogical method by discussing some of his accounts of the origin
of morality. At the same time, this chapter lays the foundation for
a detailed revaluation of Nietzsche's *On the Genealogy of Morality,*
which is the topic of the next chapter.

Here, I introduce a distinction between "archaeology" and "genealogy." I use the term "archaeology," the account of beginnings
(arkē), to refer to a search for that which lies buried but exercises a
powerful influence on, or determines, a person's character. In this
usage, archaeology is confined to investigations into the soul. I follow the traditional understanding of "genealogy" as the identification of origins and of the evolution of concepts, events, and people.

Why is physiology so important in Nietzsche's philosophy, and
how and why is Nietzsche's genealogy connected to his physiological claims? My hypothesis is that genealogy, for Nietzsche, turns out
to be a dead end when it is understood against the backdrop of his
"ontology of becoming" and the will to power. If this hypothesis is
sound, Nietzsche's naturalism, with physiology as the cardinal element, emerges as a strategy to rescue Nietzsche's arguments. But
the same naturalism that is supposed to salvage his genealogy, via
physiological diagnoses, destroys the epistemic claims of both genealogy and physiology. Yet genealogy and physiology are intrinsic
components of Nietzsche's epic spirituality of redemption; namely,

Nietzsche wants to cure people of errors that once lifted up human nature, but that are no longer necessary or, even worse, produce the lethal sickness of guilt and nourish a universal mediocrity.

GENEALOGY: AN OVERVIEW

In carrying out my task, I am well aware of the theoretical status that genealogy now enjoys. Commentators treat Nietzsche's genealogical approach as the right method to unveil origins, to trace their development, and to show that initial and unsavory traits are indelible. In some cases, this approach is treated as orthodoxy, which goes unchallenged even within its own assumptions. My goal is not to deny the validity of genealogy wholesale but to ascertain its nature and to ask whether genealogy supports the epistemological edifice—the critique of morality—that Nietzsche builds on it.

Gilles Deleuze defines genealogy as "both the value of origin and the origin of values." "Genealogy means nobility and baseness, nobility and vulgarity, nobility and decadence in the origin. The noble and the vulgar, the high and the low—this is the truly genealogical and critical element."[1] Michel Foucault understands genealogy as "gray, meticulous, and patiently documentary. It operates . . . on documents that have been scratched over and recopied many times." Genealogy is not a mere concern for the identification of origins. It is a cultivation of the "details and accidents that accompany every beginning." "The genealogist needs history to dispel the chimeras of the origin," and "he must be able to diagnose the illnesses of the body, its conditions of weakness and strength . . . to be in a position to judge philosophical discourse."[2] Genealogy, contrary to a traditional history that contemplates "distances and heights," stands for an "effective history" that "shortens its vision to those things nearest to it—the body, the nervous system, nutrition, digestion, and energies."[3] Raymond Geuss, focusing on Nietzsche's examination of Christianity, describes his genealogy as a "historical account" that considers how new meanings are imposed on events, how the defeated meanings are not totally obliterated, and how a new synthesis comes into being: "Instead of a 'definition' one must try to give an 'analysis' of the contingent synthesis of 'meaning' Christianity (for instance) represents. This process of disentangling the separate strands will take the form of a historical account. . . . The appropriate historical account is a genealogy."[4]

Along similar lines, Daniel W. Conway regards genealogy as a "case history" but introduces an important distinction between genealogy and symptomatology. Genealogy "supplies the empirical 'case history' that enables the 'immoral' philosopher to detect and interpret physiological symptoms, and to do so more accurately than priests and moralists. Genealogy thus informs Nietzsche's later writings with the validity that he is entitled to claim for them." Further, "Nietzsche's turn to symptomatology as a critical method makes sense only as presupposing the validity of genealogy."[5]

David Couzens Hoy defines genealogy in terms of the coherence or incoherence of people's self-understanding:

> Genealogy tends to find an incoherence in our own self-understanding (for instance, between our various self-descriptions, or between the way we think and the way we act) and then to show how that incoherence is produced from within us. Rather than confirm the adequacy of our present self-descriptions and the coherence of our practices, genealogy makes us more intelligible to ourselves by showing us the *inadequacy* of our present self-understandings and practices, and then giving an interpretation of how such an inadequacy could have come about.[6]

Eric Blondel argues, in contrast, that genealogy draws on natural history to explain the evolution of an event; on psychology to denude and unmask the affects; and on philology to interpret the "hidden meaning . . . of the *Semiotik* which morality is. This *philology* is at once a physiology, a medicine (semiotics means: the science of the interpretation of signs and of diagnosing maladies), a natural history of *evolution* and at the same time a *psychology* (the unveiling of affects)."[7] According to Blondel, genealogy is not the specification of "a temporal or essential origin" but the identification of a "development and a derivation." Genealogy transforms history into a "metaphor for *interpretation*," which is not concerned with historical facts. Interpretation is reading without being able to fix the origin [or] proper place . . . of the text." The interpretation of the text is thus "plural."[8] Conflict and a plurality of interpretation are imprinted in the nature of genealogy, which "is properly the language of the *life* of the body."[9]

These six views are representative of the importance of genealogy in studies of Nietzsche's philosophy. Let us take a look at what Nietzsche had to say about genealogy. In his view, "the democratic prejudice in the modern world toward all questions of origin" had hindered the project of a "moral genealogy" (GM; I; 4). He, by contrast, is undeterred by that prejudice and willing to heed a "new demand," which calls for a critique of moral values and an examination of the conditions under which *"the value of these values"* has developed and changed (GM; P; 6). The values to which Nietzsche refers are pity, self-denial, and self-sacrifice, that is, the values of Christian morality. He will pose questions that no one has posed before; and, contrary to the genealogies of English psychologists, which come "out of the blue" (*ins Blaue*)—namely, contrary to their random descriptions—Nietzsche will provide a "gray" account, though not "gray" in the sense of ambiguity. "Gray," for Nietzsche, meant "that which can be documented, which can actually be confirmed and has actually existed, in short, the whole, long, hard-to-decipher hieroglyphic script of man's moral past!" (GM; P; 7). More important, his critique of morality, via a genealogical inquiry into how morality emerged, is driven by his belief that the morality of pity—a morality that is "against life"—was "the *great* danger to mankind" and to European culture (GM; P; 5). Genealogy not only unmasks the past but also reveals the hidden nature of present-day culture. Genealogy thus bridges the past and the present and identifies dangers by deciphering the meaning of factual events and providing an account that goes in "the direction of a real *history of morality*" (GM; P; 7). In *Schopenhauer as Educator*, Nietzsche referred to a life that could contain the hieroglyphs to understand all other lives. In his *On the Genealogy of Morality*, his endeavor is equally encompassing: to read properly the entire past of humankind.

Both genealogy and archaeology occupy a prominent place in the annals of Western philosophy. Democracy, for example, is a contemporary conceptual space that can be understood as drawing its meaning from a chain of historical events, regarded as the foundations or origins of democratic institutions. Or, democracy can be understood, not in the light of historical developments, but as the expression of certain dispositions, such as free will and the capacity for voluntary consent, which are inscribed in human nature. The first scenario is built by the genealogist of the past; the second, by the archaeologist of the soul. In the Western philosophical tradition, some philosophers excel in one of these two spheres. Plato is primarily an archaeologist of the soul. Machiavelli is primarily a genealogist of the past. For most philosophers, however, the meanings read into history and into a person's soul are intertwined. History and the soul become a single interpretative unit. Kant is both; and Nietzsche is both.

The genealogist goes to past events or texts; demarcates a moment or event that will be considered the "origin"; and arranges an account purporting to explain the origin and its subsequent development. Since every morality, according to Nietzsche, is a biography of its founder and of his dominant drives and their conflicts (BGE; 6), every genealogical account also reveals the interpreter's subjectivity. The archaeologist of the soul, in contrast, resorts to history only incidentally, as a dispensable background of a struggle that takes place, as it were, behind closed doors. He descends into himself, but he is not content with his own inner travels and invariably begins to analyze other people's souls. In other words, this archaeology reveals not only the need of origins but also the need to decipher, to medicalize, and to cure: the need to be a physician, which is a dominant theme in Nietzsche's philosophy.

The assumption of this deciphering is that there is a hidden meaning that ought to be found or constructed, thereby linking genealogy and philology. This *ought* suggests an obligation, which is the foundation of knowledge. For Nietzsche, knowledge is a drive, which in its most rudimentary expressions is a search for security. We do not want to be deceived. Nietzsche mixes philology and physiology in such a way that wrong interpretations in the former are treated as having a degenerating root in the latter.[10] "I was moved by compassion when I saw myself quite thin, quite wasted away: *realities* were altogether lacking in my knowledge . . . thenceforth I pursued in fact nothing other than physiology, medicine, and natural science" (EH; "Human"; 3).

Nietzsche's Medical Diagnoses: The Body

In his essay "Nietzsche's Use of Medical Terms," Malcolm Pasley argues that, up to 1875, Nietzsche's medical language was "essentially figurative." But, beginning with *Human, All Too Human* (1878), his

> use of health/sickness terminology becomes a problem, as he begins to couch his general theory of man's cultural development— from which his moral, aesthetic and political theories are derived—ever more exclusively in physiological and medical terms. . . . he begins to suggest, further, that his own physio-psychological explanations of individual cultural behaviour can also be applied, literally, to the 'organisms' of advanced human societies and cultural groups.[11]

For his part, Gregory Moore provides evidence that the centrality of physiology in Nietzsche's thinking is explained by the influence of several authors in the early 1880s. As Moore shows, Nietzsche took elements from Carl Nägeli, Wilhelm Roux, and William Rolph, all of whom were exploring aspects of the natural sciences, to develop his own notion of the will to power.[12]

I refrain from Pasley's assertion that matters of health and sickness became so prevalent in Nietzsche's thought that, "by 1888, one can almost say that there *are* no other topics, that the question of health has swallowed up everything else."[13] It is abundantly clear, however, that Nietzsche's role as a philosophical physician and psychologist increases, and that his philosophy emphasizes the idea of historical epochs and conditions in which his notion of health and life-affirming possibilities prevailed.[14] A wide variety of events and characters afforded him the opportunity to philosophize, not with a hammer, but, so to speak, with the knives and forceps of the surgeon.

Beginning with *Human, All Too Human* (1878), Nietzsche grew increasingly certain of the importance of good physicians for humankind. In 1881, in a section of *Daybreak* beginning "Where are the new physicians of the soul?" he wrote: "The worst sickness of mankind originated in the way in which they have combated their sicknesses, and what seemed to cure has in the long run produced something worse than that which it was supposed to overcome" (D; 52). It was thus necessary to find the right diagnosis and the right prescription. In his role as philosopher and physician, the illness of the epoch—bad conscience—is presented as an emotional reflection of a physiological condition: it is the inability to discharge the individual's instincts (GM; II; 16). The ascetic priests are a "degenerating" form of life; the saint's visions and terrors are "familiar pathological conditions" which he is unable to interpret as illness (H, I; 126). The standard to measure the "highest humanity" in the Middle Ages was the capacity to see visions, which was "a profound mental disturbance!" (D; 66). The religious nature is a form of neurosis (BGE; 47); and similarly, physiological facts underlie Buddhism (AC; 20).

Socrates, the dialectician, was a sick person who infected the Athenian aristocracy; his daemon, according to Nietzsche, "was perhaps an ear-infection" (H; I; 126).[15] Plato, "the great slanderer of life," was corrupt, that is, sick (GM; III; 25). Jesus had a "morbid" condition, probably "susceptibility of the *sense of touch*" (AC; 29). Saint Paul, Alexander, Caesar, Napoleon, Mohammed, and Byron were epileptics (D; 68, 548), Rousseau was "mentally disturbed," Voltaire enjoyed "an uncommon health," Lord Byron induced in himself a "vindictive rancor" (WP; 100), and Spinoza was "consumptive" (GS; 349).

When savage or tame people experience an outburst of voluptuousness that suddenly turns into denial of the world and penance, this might be "interpretable as masked epilepsy" (BGE; 47). The "origin" of the German spirit is found in the "disturbed intestines" of the Germans (EH; "So Clever"; 1). "The German discontent with life" is produced by a "winter sickness" that is aggravated by "the effects of stuffy cellar air and the poison of stove fumes in German living rooms" (GS; 134). Skepticism "is the most spiritual expression of . . . nervous debility and sickliness; it arises whenever races or classes long separated from one another are decisively and suddenly crossed" (BGE; 208). "Three-quarters of all evil done in the world happens out of timidity: and this is above all a physiological phenomenon!" (D; 538).[16] The educated classes of Europe are "neurotic, and almost every one of its great families has come close to lunacy." "The sum of sensations" in the European culture poses the universal danger of "an over-excitation of the nervous and thinking powers" (H; I; 244). Everywhere in the civilized world of modernity, "*language* is diseased" (RWB; 5). A philosophy could be "at bottom the instinct for a personal diet" (D; 553), and a dietary mistake would give way to a gloomy view of life (GS; 134). As for Wagner's choice of heroes and heroines, "consider them as physiological types (a pathological gallery)!—all of this taken together represents a profile of sickness that permits no further doubt" (CW; 5).[17] The physician is even capable of identifying the age at which the thinker brings forth his philosophy (AOM; 271). As Blondel rightly comments, in Nietzsche, "[g]enealogical 'medicine' and physiology are *readings* oriented toward a semiotic (or symptomatology) as a science of the *signs* of sickness."[18]

Nietzsche's unceasing medical diagnoses rest, for him, on the simplest foundation: "life is sick and needs to be cured" (ULH; 10). They climax in his history of asceticism, which stems *"from the protective instinct of a degenerating life"* and "indicates a partial physiological obstruction and exhaustion" (GM; III; 13). The ascetic priest induces hypnosis to deaden pain and, as a bad philologist, shows a consistent will to misunderstand a physiological condition. In its simplest form, this is a "feeling of physiological inhibition," probably due to incorrect diet (GS; 134; D; 203; GM; III; 17).[19]

VIVISECTIONS OF THE SOUL

Nietzsche applies his diagnoses not only to the physical constitution of people but to their character, or souls, as well. In 1876 he referred to "the magical eye of the dramatist, who can read souls as easily as the most familiar text" (RWB; 8), and he scrutinized Wagner's development as a dithyrambic dramatist, as a human being, and as a writer (RWB; 8–10). The "new philosophers" of whom Nietzsche dreams are those who laid "the knife vivisectionally to the bosom of the very *virtues of the age* [and] betrayed what was their own secret: to know a greatness of man, a new untrodden path to his enlargement" (BGE; 212; see also 210).

The German soul, according to Nietzsche has "corridors," "interconnecting corridors," and "hiding-places and dungeons." The German "is acquainted with the hidden paths to chaos" (BGE; 244).[20] Nietzsche credits himself with the capacity to read Thucydides' "hidden thoughts" (TI; "What I Owe"; 2), and qua archaeologist/genealogist he is even able to reconstruct a scene that took place in the secrecy of Socrates' soul (BGE; 191). "One cannot begin to figure out Wagner until one figures out his dominant instinct," which, unsurprisingly, Nietzsche claims to have done: "he *became* a musician, he *became* a poet because the tyrant within him, his actor's genius, compelled him" (CW; 8). Schopenhauer, in turn, suffered from a secret guilt (SE; 3). Before "vivisecting" Wagner and Schopenhauer, Nietzsche had put his talent to work on the souls of saints and ascetics. "Let us therefore venture first to isolate individual drives in the soul of the saint and ascetic and then conclude by thinking of them entwined together" (H; I; 136). In discussing the ascetic individual's lust for power, Nietzsche muses about whether the souls of Saint Paul, John Calvin, and Dante may have consorted with "the gruesome secrets of such voluptuousness of power" (D; 113). For the followers of the "morality of sacrificial beasts," Nietzsche had a warning: "I know you better than you know yourselves" (D; 215). He identified the dominant instinct in the artist, an instinct "directed toward the meaning of art, which is *life*" (TI; "Expeditions"; 24). As he made clear in one of his letters, he counted himself among "the most experienced and tested of people," and immediately posed a question whose affirmative answer he knew in advance: "[I]s it my lot that I should be equally so experienced and tested in the torments of the soul?"[21]

The same thinker who was able to identify the dominant instinct in Wagner was even more versatile in his art: he could read the "'entrails' of every soul." His most encompassing declaration of the unity of the physician and the psychologist is expressed in *Ecce Homo,* perhaps self-mockingly:

> I possess a perfectly uncanny sensitivity of the instinct for cleanliness, so that I perceive physiologically—*smell*—the proximity or . . . the innermost parts, the 'entrails' of every soul. . . . I have in this sensitivity psychological antennae with which I touch and take hold of every secret: all the *concealed* dirt at the bottom of many a nature, . . . is known to me almost on first contact. (EH; "So Wise"; 8)

And here he reveals the area in which he was a "master." He could read "the secret labour of the instinct of *décadence*—that is what I have practised most, it has been my own particular field of experience, in this if in anything I am a master" (EH; "So Wise"; 1). What is buried is brought to the surface and what wishes to remain silent is forced, in Nietzsche's presence, to become audible (TI; Foreword). He can hear sounds from the instrument "man," sounds that the instrument itself did not notice (EH; "So Wise"; 4). He can smell the odor of words (WS; 119). A fragment from 1887 sums up this vocation as a reader of souls: "To explore the whole sphere of the modern soul, to have sat in its every nook—my ambition, my torture, and my happiness" (WP; 1031).

Not by accident, Nietzsche presents himself as a subterranean creature and as the "last disciple" of Dionysus, "that great hidden one, . . . whose voice knows how to descend into the underworld of every soul" (BGE; 289, 295). The allure of secret scripts, secret paths, and even secret labors becomes the lode star of his genealogical quests (BGE; 32).[22] A good physician acts like a good police agent (H; I; 243).

As a physician, Nietzsche intends to lay bare the underlying and transparent difference between those who are strong and those who are weak. Thus, his claim in *The Gay Science* that an unveiled truth is not his goal is unpersuasive (GS; P; 4). Even in this text, he embarks on his genealogical quests for a transparent and underlying dimension. In *Beyond Good and Evil*, he argues that even "the spell of definite grammatical functions is in the last resort the spell of *physiological* value judgements and racial conditions" (BGE; 20). In the *Genealogy*, he promises a *"physiology of aesthetics"* (GM; III; 8); claims that science has a physiological foundation (GM; III; 25); and stipulates a new task for medical science: "Indeed, every table of values . . . known to history or ethnology requires first a *physiological* investigation and interpretation, rather than a psychological one; and every one of them needs a critique on the part of medical science" (GM; I; 17). In claiming that the value of moral evaluations should attract the interests of physiologists and physicians, and that philosophers should act as mediators, he credited academic philosophers for having transformed "the originally so reserved and mistrustful relations between philosophy, physiology, and medicine into the most amicable and fruitful exchange" (GM; I; 17). It is hardly surprising that Nietzsche cites the phrase that Goethe used to express his delight in his "anatomical discovery" of the *Zwischenkiefer* (a bone that would separate human beings from the animal kingdom): all his "innards" were "set astir."[23]

In a word—as mentioned above—every philosophy is an "involuntary and unconscious memoir" of its founder (BGE; 3, 6). This view was put forward, from a different standpoint, by Goethe:

> The philosophers, for their part, can offer us nothing but patterns of life. The strict moderation of Kant, for example, required a philosophy in accordance with his innate inclinations. Read his biography and you will soon discover how neatly he blunted the edge of his stoicism, which in fact constituted a striking obstacle to social relationships, adjusted it and brought it into balance with the world. Each individual, by virtue of his inclinations, has a right to principles which do not destroy his individuality. Probably the origin of all philosophy is to be sought for here or nowhere. Every system

succeeds in coming to terms with the world in that moment when its true champion appears. Only the acquired part of human nature ordinarily founders on a contradiction; what is inborn in it finds its way anywhere and not infrequently even overcomes its contrary with the greatest success. We must first be in harmony with our-selves, and then we are in a position, if not to eliminate, at least in some way to counterbalance the discords pressing in on us from outside.[24]

Nietzsche goes further than Goethe, however, and builds a physio-logical type to explain a person's inclinations. In an early formula-tion of his physiological program, in 1878, he referred to the need to know "a *chemistry* of the moral, religious and aesthetic conceptions and sensations, likewise of all the agitations we experience within ourselves in cultural and social intercourse, and indeed when we are alone" (H; I; 1). Eight years later, in 1886, the physician was more confident in his diagnosis:

Behind the highest value judgments that have hitherto guided the history of thought, there are concealed misunderstanding of the physical constitution—of individuals or classes or even whole races. All those bold insanities of metaphysics, especially answers to the question about the *value* of existence, may always be considered first of all as the symptoms of certain bodies. (GS; P; 2)

The metaphors of dissection and diagnoses, of vivisection and knives, turn up prominently in Nietzsche's lab, and his program en-tails a triple dissection. History is opened by the genealogist; the body, by the physiologist's knives; the soul, by the archaeologist, the reveler of the inner world, the Odysseus of his Hades and other people's Hades. The philosopher reads the signs (the "effects") and then writes the genealogical account.

The sheer frequency of Nietzsche's medical diagnoses estab-lishes that physiology was a central component in his evaluations of individuals and cultural phenomena. But what exactly is the link between genealogy and physiology?

GENEALOGY AND NIETZSCHE'S ACCOUNTS OF MORALITY

Genealogy, in Nietzsche's philosophy, is a methodology that looks for (1) an identification of facts, in which facts are understood as the *truth* of reality in its historical, physiological, and psychological dimensions;[25] (2) a distinction between the origin of value and the usefulness and meaning of these values; (3) a process of disentangling the various strands that are woven into a morality that is understood as a whole; (4) an examination of the consequences of past events for (a) modern culture, (b) people's health, and (c) Nietzsche's own health; and (5) a specification of measures that ought to be taken to prevent further damage from the one already inflicted. Moreover, (6) genealogy is also characterized by a conception of time in which the past "continues living on," in both individuals and cultures. Prehistory, for example, "exists at all times or could possibly re-occur" (GM; II; 9). These six methodological strategies shed light on the central concern of genealogy, which is a critique of the value of certain values. This critique will be achieved by examining the origin of certain values and the consequences of these values for bodies (causing sickness), for culture (causing decadence), and for the human species as a whole (causing the diminution of human beings).

Genealogy thus begins as an inquiry into the origins of events, moral ideals, and institutions.[26] Once the historical origins have been identified, it examines the physiology of the creators of those events, moral ideals, and institutions; and their physiological traits are then expected to reveal the grounds of their psychology.[27] In these three areas (history, physiology, and psychology) of inquiry, it is possible to see the genealogist, the archaeologist, the physician, and the philologist at work. Nietzsche's analysis of Christianity, for example, furnishes ample evidence of these three areas. After journeying through history to find the origins of this religion in the cultural milieu of the Jewish people, Nietzsche analyzes the physiology and psychology of Jesus and Paul. The same methodology is at work in his reflections on the ascetic ideal. Nietzsche identifies the

origins of the ascetic priest in a past split within the noble caste between warriors and priests. As a physician and psychologist, Nietzsche then diagnoses the physiological illness—depression—as well
as the psychological trait of the ascetic, which includes a strong (yet
sick) will to power, accompanied by a strategy of looking for pleasure in pain and in tending the sick. As a philologist, Nietzsche then
interprets the value and meaning of the ascetic ideal. These three
dimensions are woven into his philosophy.

Genealogy, however, has another dimension that is often overlooked in discussions of Nietzsche's philosophy.[28] At the beginning
of his preface to the *Genealogy of Morality*, Nietzsche declares that
"we are unknown to ourselves" and indicates that his thoughts on
the origins of morality go back to the period when he wrote *Human,
All Too Human*. Genealogy is inextricably linked to the search for
self-knowledge, a program that he had announced in *Human* when
insisting on the need to know the chemical origins of moral sensations. Genealogy understood as both a quest for origins and a quest
for self-knowledge will allow Nietzsche to understand his own spirituality and to find traces of himself in the wide gamut of human
history.

Yet when we introduce Nietzsche's views of becoming and
knowledge into this mix, we find that genealogy does not seem to
measure up to the demands of his ontology of becoming. On the
one hand, in the process of going to the past for an "origin," the interpreter has already experienced so many metamorphoses himself,
as a cultural creation, that the particular perspective he uses when
he reaches the original site—be it a cultural event (e.g., the ancient
Greeks) or a type of person (e.g., the ascetic priest) or a way of life
(e.g., that of the slaves)—is likely to be deceptive or irremediably
damaged. It will be damaged if the genealogist does not recognize
his own historical standpoint. It will be deceptive if he is unaware
that he is not the fixed entity that is necessary to be the measuring
rod of an event.[29] Evaluation, in its natural roots, is unjust. It springs
from necessity (the way we are) and not necessarily from a drive toward knowledge. In order to evaluate, Nietzsche argues, we must be
fixed entities, which we are not (H; I; 32).

On the other hand, the original site will never be an untouched object, waiting in its pristine purity to disclose itself to the dissecting and discerning eye of the genealogist. The original site is a web of layers. These layers constitute multiple interpretations that cover up the origins under investigation, and when the genealogist unwraps those layers, he finds himself in a dead end. There is no "thing in itself" behind the layers. There is no "origin in itself," either. And if there were one, this "in itself" would be beyond our cognitive capabilities. It follows that the origin is a construction, an arrangement that interprets an encrypted reality and reflects an external world as refracted by the interpreter's propensities. Genealogical accounts are contrived with the express purpose of giving meaning to the genealogist's life, by placing it within a cultural context whose moral values, namely, the authoritative criteria to make and settle moral evaluations, are based on reasons other than the ones stipulated by those moral values.

Genealogy traces a boomerang route, in which the genealogist stands at both the beginning and end of the quest. The "knowledge" thus produced is a protective device for the genealogist to escape from the "goallessness" of human existence. Every interpretation has to do with the world that is of concern to us (WP; 521). As Christopher Janaway observes,

> Genealogy is a vertical study, rooted in ourselves as the eventual outcome, and so lacking the horizontal spread of interest characteristic of much historical work. So too with Nietzsche's genealogy: it is extremely selective of its past and always guided by the question, "How did I come to feel and think in *these* ways of mine?"[30]

But genealogy is also meant to be much more than a statement about the genealogist's predicament. As both Aaron Ridley and Keith Ansell-Pearson argue, it concerns our future or, better still, the futures available to humankind. In Ridley's account, it asks "what future ways of relating to ourselves are possible, ways of forging and testing values are possible, given our current self-relations and how we have come to stand in them."[31] For Ansell-Pearson, "Nietzsche's exercise in historical genealogy is informed by some basic but none-theless crucial questions: How and why does one engage with the past? What are one's hopes for the future?"[32]

The two sides of my critique—namely, that both the genealogist and the "origin" possess a fluidity that makes knowledge claims about them impossible—are, I think, reasonable, but Nietzsche appears to deny them. Although he stresses the impermanence of nature and the chance occurrence of events, he also describes individuals who, under the aegis of moral constraints, are uniform, stable, and capable of establishing fixed values. Furthermore, in the *Genealogy* he believes that he can find something factual and essential (sickness, for example) behind the dominant moral values. But these positions are not enough to abandon my critique.

It is perhaps more fruitful to pose, point-blank, the following question: What is the epistemic value of Nietzsche's genealogies? They are stories he tells as a philosopher, historian, anthropologist, physiologist, and psychologist, and these stories are guided by three assumptions. First, the most remote as well as the most recent past of the organic world continues in the human body.[33] "Man is *not* just an individual but what lives on, all that is organic in one particular line."[34] Second, this past can be recaptured. Third, he wants his life to be the foundation to decipher "the hieroglyphs of life in general," a goal he delineated as early as 1875 (SE; 3). The first and second assumptions allow him to make knowledge claims. The third assumption becomes the central goal of his epic spirituality. It is the burden he must bear and the duty he must fulfill.

In my introduction I referred to several stories that Nietzsche told about morality and the fact that some of these stories modify or contradict one another. Here I discuss a genealogical account of morality that he developed in 1881 and radically changed in the *Genealogy*. My goal is to show how his genealogical explorations in the realm of morality are stories that he crafts and alters as he deepens his reflections. To conceive of genealogy as storytelling is not to deny the validity of the genealogical method. But it is a reconceptualization of its epistemological status.

In *Daybreak*, as in all his texts, Nietzsche offers a variety of genealogical accounts. As a sample, I refer the reader to sections 26,

35, 38, 42, 62, 68, 95, and 188. In section 42, "Origin of the *vita contemplativa*," Nietzsche describes individuals who, in the fullness of their power, rob, attack, and murder. When their powers decline, these individuals become "less harmful" and put forth pessimistic ideas, which reflect their declining powers. People who live in melancholy and are poor in deeds become "poets or thinkers or priests or medicine-men." Their lack of power should warrant contempt, but they manage to frighten the community by deceiving it into thinking that they possess divine powers. In section 68, "The first Christian," Nietzsche narrates the story of Paul's conversion to Christianity; namely, Paul tried to abide by the commandments of the Jewish law, failed, and this failure led to a hatred of the law, until this hatred found in Christ the idea of "the *destroyer of the law*" and this destruction erased his sense of guilt (D; 68).

These stories are not, in my understanding, genealogical analyses but archaeological ones: an unearthing of the unseen developments and the inner logic operating in persons' souls. Similarly, Nietzsche depicts a "primeval delusion" concerning the relationship between knowledge and action, and describes how people thought in earlier times and how they still think of this relationship (D; 116). In *The Wanderer and His Shadow*, Nietzsche tells a parable to show the origin of nonegoistic actions. It goes like this: Two chieftains used to quarrel on a regular basis. Another chieftain, whose kingdom was somehow distant but still exposed to the violent inclinations of his two neighbors, summoned them to a peace conference, having previously told each of them, individually, that if their quarrels continue, he would ally with one of them to put an end to the ambitions and existence of the other. The quarrelsome chieftains agree to live in peace and begin to improve their economic condition and quality of life. Since the third chieftain does not receive these benefits directly, they think that he acted out of a lack of egoism (WS; 190).

In section 18 of *Daybreak* (1881), Nietzsche describes eras, preceding recorded history, in which a morality based on custom prevailed. On his account, these are "*the actual and decisive eras of history which determined the character of mankind.*" Suffering, cruelty, dissembling, revenge, and denial of reason all counted as virtues, while the desire for knowledge and peace were treated as dangers. With the entrance of the ascetic priest on Nietzsche's horizon, however, this story goes through a process of redefinitions and reallocations.

In the first story of 1881, cruelty, both in its external and internal dimensions, is the "greatest pleasure" for *one community* of souls "full of strength, revengefulness, hostility, deceit and suspicion, ready for the most fearful things and made hard by deprivation and morality." External cruelty refers to acts directed at other persons, while internal cruelty takes the form of self-chosen laceration. In the second story, the one deployed in the *Genealogy*, the community is divided into two opposing classes and moralities—those of the nobles and the slaves—in order to make room for the pathos of distance between them, which is absent from *Daybreak*. External cruelty is the exclusive domain of the nobles. Internal cruelty, in turn, is divided into two kinds: voluntary suffering as a form of self-control and discipline, which is now a sign of nobility; and suffering as the expression of bad conscience, which is the trademark of all people enclosed within social boundaries and especially those who are oppressed. Along similar lines, revenge is redefined and presented in two guises: noble revenge, an ephemeral act in which the nobles regard their enemies as good; and slave revenge, a permanent condition in which the slaves regard their enemies as evil. In the second story, dissembling is removed from the nobles; confident of their power, they do not need dishonesty. Dissembling, deceit, and suspicion are represented as the exclusive attributes of the slaves.

In the first story, inner cruelty occurred as an act of propitiation, to curry favor with the gods on behalf of the community. This understanding of cruelty reappears in the *Genealogy* when Nietzsche discusses the Greeks and describes their cruelty as a festive spectacle for the gods' enjoyment (GM; II; 7). This view is then superseded by the inner cruelty practiced by the ascetic priest on behalf of himself (to show his power) and the inner cruelty suffered by the herd, which is produced by their senseless suffering. In other words, in the case of the ascetic priest and the slaves, inner cruelty is a self-laceration in front of God to seek his favor, not for the community's sake but for the sake of the individual. It is the individual, not the community, who needs redemption.

In a nutshell, all the distinguishing marks—thirteen in total—of the eras of the morality of custom are redefined and reallocated.[35] All the signs that were considered virtues in the story told in *Daybreak* become signs of sickness in the version narrated in the *Genealogy*. Dissembling, cruelty, suffering, and denial of reason are no longer the virtues formed in the furnace of the eras of the morality of custom, the eras that "determined the character of mankind." They are redescribed as inventions of the ascetic ideal. Likewise, the ascetic ideal, not the nobles, treats well-being as hazardous. The nobles, not the ascetic ideal, envision peace and pity as dangers and treat work and being pitied as affronts. Both the nobles and slaves view the desire for knowledge and change as dangers. The outstanding feature of the second story is that "the character of mankind" is no longer the end result of the morality of custom. Rather, this character becomes the direct outcome of the victory of the ascetic priest and the morality of the slaves. The ascetic priest and the sick herd rule, and the earth is now a madhouse. The community ruled by the morality of custom was one hardened by "deprivation and morality," but the one in which the ascetic ideal is dominant—modernity—is one in which weakness reigns.

We can summarize these results as follows:

GENEALOGICAL ACCOUNTS OF MORALITY

Daybreak	*On the Genealogy of Morality*
One community	Two communities: nobles and slaves
Virtues (for all)	*Virtues for the nobles*
Suffering	Suffering as a means to self-discipline
Cruelty	Cruelty as an external discharge of their will to power
Dissembling	Honesty

GENEALOGICAL ACCOUNTS OF MORALITY (*cont.*)

Revenge	Revenge as an ephemeral act
Denial of reason	Denial of reason
Madness (counted as godliness)	Well-being
Dangers (for all)	*Virtues for the slaves*
Well-being	Suffering as self-denial
Desire for knowledge	Cruelty as inner guilt
Peace	Dissembling
Pity	Revenge as a permanent
	condition that is spiritualized
	as love
Change	Denial of reason
	Peace
Affronts (for all)	Pity
Being pitied	Being pitied
Work	Work
	Dangers for the nobles
	Desire for knowledge
	Change
	Dangers for the slaves
	Well-being
	Desire for knowledge
	Change

Even before *Daybreak,* in *Human, All Too Human* (1878), Nietzsche presented a genealogical story in which the nobles, "the good," belong together and are defined by their capacity for requital; but "the bad" do not form a community. "As a bad man one belongs to the 'bad', to a swarm of subject, powerless people who have no sense of belonging together. The good are a caste, the bad a mass like grains of sand" (H; I; 45). In the *Genealogy,* the nobles still form a community, but the bad are replaced by the slaves, who possess the instinct to congregate. The isolated "grains of sand" are now the herd.

Two more eloquent examples of different versions of stories are the evolution of the concept of "evil" and the idea of redemption in Nietzsche's genealogies. In *Human, All Too Human*, the concept of evil is born in individuals on a low social stratum, *not* in suffering people. The people of low social status are "the bad," that is, people who lack the capacity for requital (H; I; 45). In *Daybreak*, evil is a judgment made by the community about individuals whose originality challenges the morality of custom (D; 9, 15). In the *Genealogy*, however, evil arises from the resentment of the slaves.

In *Human, All Too Human*, the story of redemption follows this pattern: humans conceive of nature as bad; by encouraging suspicion toward nature, all religions and metaphysical systems that think of man as evil and sinful "*make* him himself bad"; and the idea of sinfulness becomes such a heavy burden that people rely on supernatural powers to free themselves from the idea that they are bad; that is, they need supernatural powers to obtain redemption. Hence this strategem: the Christian religion devises moral demands that are impossible to obey, because the intention of these demands is to make us "feel *as sinful as possible*." However, in *Human, All Too Human*, people derive pleasure from the feeling of sin. "If man had failed to find this feeling *pleasant*—why should he have engendered such an idea and adhered to it for so long?" (H; I; 141). In the *Genealogy*, in contrast, the feeling of sin is anything but pleasant. The ascetic priest is the only type of person who derives pleasure from his inner cruelty. The herd will obtain pleasure only after the ascetic priest serves up his prescriptions for dealing with suffering. Sin is bad conscience, as reinterpreted by the ascetic priest. Sin is *guilt*, and guilt bestows meaning on suffering. And, contrary to Nietzsche's argument in the *Genealogy*, guilt creates a powerful sense of individuality among the members of the herd, since each person is responsible for his sins.

Even in the *Genealogy* we find shifting assessments. These are striking in view of Nietzsche's insistence on precision. In the first essay, for instance, the conflicts between good and bad, and good and evil, are portrayed as ones that are present in "higher natures." In some passages this battle is also described as "undecided" (GM; I; 16). In the second essay, Nietzsche concludes that in the struggle between Rome (good versus bad) and Judea (good versus evil), Rome's defeat is complete. In the third essay, the weak have won decisively, and it is never clear whether there are any places where the conflict is still "undecided." As for the reference to "higher natures," Nietzsche conceives of the ascetic priest as more spiritual and, in this sense, as "higher" than other types of persons, but this "height" involves sickness. Only the strong possess the credentials for a genuine higher nature.

In describing the "advantages" of the Christian moral viewpoint in an 1887 notebook entry, Nietzsche asserted that this viewpoint "shielded man from despising himself as man, from taking sides against life, from despairing of knowledge: it was a *means of preservation*—in sum, morality was the great *antidote* to practical and theoretical *nihilism*."[36] This passage did not make it into the published text of the *Genealogy*, and the reason for its omission is clear. In the *Genealogy*, Christianity is described as a religion that leads to a nausea toward humanity and that incites individuals to contemn themselves.

Nietzsche's genealogy is also baffling at another juncture. In Book 5 of *The Gay Science* (1886), he praised the Jews in the following terms:

> Europe owes the Jews no small thanks for making people think more logically and for establishing *cleanlier* intellectual habits— . . . Wherever Jews have won influence they have taught men to make finer distinctions, more rigorous inferences, and to write in a more luminous and cleanly fashion; their task was ever to bring a people 'to listen to *raison*.' (GS; 348)[37]

But in the *same* year, in *Beyond Good and Evil*, his genealogical exploration takes a darker turn. Jewish culture is described as the soil that nurtured the cravings and principles of the slave morality (BGE; 195). How could the genealogist credit the same group, in the same year, with both improving the European cultural milieu and impoverishing it? How could the same group come to possess both a rigorous logic (GS) and a faulty one (BGE)? These divergences call the genealogist to task, but Nietzsche appears unaware of his inconsistency. The possible reply on his behalf—that I am applying to Nietzsche the constraint of a logical discourse that he rejects—is not helpful. Nietzsche makes logical connections, and he believes in the epistemic superiority of his genealogy. In the *Genealogy*, when Nietzsche refers to his earlier assessments of morality in *Human, All Too Human* and characterizes them as "the same thoughts" that he will expound upon here, he resorts to a familiar theme: he claims that he had an instinct that led him, inevitably, to a better knowledge (GM; P; 2). But, as my arguments on the evolution of his thought show, this is not an answer. Nietzsche reconfigures and refurbishes his earlier accounts of morality, but he never discloses his reasons for doing so.

GENEALOGY, PHYSIOLOGY, AND NATURALISM: A CRITICAL ASSESSMENT

To assess the epistemic value of Nietzsche's genealogies, we should address the goals his method seeks to achieve. A genealogy is expected to demonstrate:

(1) contingency: for example, moral values arose from a historical situation of oppression.
(2) a physiological state of nature: people were oppressed because they were weak.
(3) a psychological state: The oppressed grew resentful: "for powerlessness against men, *not* powerlessness against nature, is what engenders the most desperate bitterness against existence."[38]
(4) a physiological state of the body: the resentful people were sick.
(5) and a physiological state of the body that becomes a cultural problem: slave morality engenders a sick culture.

The uncovering of contingency, in this genealogy, destroys any supernatural basis for the origin of Christianity. The uncovering of resentment should lead Christianity to reassess its origins and to accept the fact that these origins (resentment, hatred) deny its highest values: love, compassion, and so forth. As a result, Christianity should effect an internal reconfiguration of its values (a "revaluation of values"). It does not follow, however, that genealogy makes a convincing case in inviting Christians to abandon the virtues of love, compassion, and the like. In fact, Christians can construct a Nietzschean argument and turn it against Nietzsche's genealogy. It could take the following form: "It is true that the origin of our morality was historical and represented the negation of the virtues we now uphold. However, though we ought to reject the supernatural basis, we can still defend the validity of our virtues and advocate love on the following grounds: through the sheer force of constraints (a 'new' morality of custom), these virtues have been severed from their origin and are now a second nature. In this second nature, love arises from love. The first nature, in which love was tethered to hatred, is no longer active." This argument satisfies Hoy's criterion for a genealogy, namely, of finding coherence in the knowledge claims people make about themselves.

This is a Nietzschean argument, but, as I will show in chapter 8, Nietzsche would not accept it, for he denies the authenticity of all altruistic virtues. Egotism, for him, is inscribed in nature. His retort is predictable: your virtues are still founded on your egotism and on your ignorance of what life is (the will to power) and of what nature is (becoming and necessity).

It is worth noting, however, that contingency, referring to the historical basis that genealogy uncovers, has been assigned a disproportionately large role in Nietzsche's philosophy. For Nietzsche goes a step further and reaches a paradox that, to my knowledge, is still barely explained by other commentators. The paradox is that the contingent character of the historical situation of oppression is, in fact, a *necessity*. The necessity stems from Nietzsche's naturalism and, as such, significantly weakens the role of contingency. There are accidents in nature, but the relationship between the strong and the weak, between nobles and slaves, is one of natural necessity. The weak are weak by nature, and so are the strong. It is the nature of the strong to subdue and prey upon others. It is the nature of the weak to resist and capitulate. In any case, they are the prey. Nietzsche explicitly says as much. The conquest of the weak by the strong was "a fate which *nothing* could ward off" (GM; II; 17, emphasis mine). "Everything is necessity." No one is accountable for what he is (H; I; 107). Genealogy leads back to nature, and nature leads to physiology. Science should be understood *"as the imitation of nature in concepts"* (H; I; 38). But if this is the case, Nietzsche's naturalism drives him into an epistemological quicksand. Morality and sickness, too, must be by necessity. Life-enhancing possibilities and life-denying ones are all necessary. Judging them is unavoidable—but also unjust (H; I; 32, 39).

The genealogical accounts presented earlier clearly suggest that a genealogical analysis, in Nietzsche's rendition of it, is not the "historical account" or the meticulous and documentary cultivation of details that Raymond Geuss and Michel Foucault, respectively, ascribe to Nietzsche's genealogy.[39] In Nietzsche's texts, a genealogical account mixes events that happened in history (the triumph of Christianity, for example) with events that take place within the genealogist's moral and intellectual horizon. Geuss's claim that the imposition of meanings by a genealogical analysis does not completely vanquish the original, existing meanings is valid, in light of Nietzsche's view of the organic world, but is not supported by Nietzsche's arguments in the *Genealogy* (the text Geuss analyzes). In the *Genealogy*, defeated meanings are obscured or completely obliterated (GM; II; 12). Blondel argues that Nietzsche's genealogy does not deal with historical facts, but rather transforms history into "a metaphor for *interpretation*." "For instance," Blondel states, "when Nietzsche attributes the 'beginning' of the 'slave revolt in morality' to the Jews (GM; I; 7), he does not situate his genealogy as a necessary historical fact, but as an interpretation."[40] This, too, does not survive serious scrutiny. Similarly, Blondel's claim that Nietzsche's genealogy is meant to reflect conflict, plurality, and ambiguity to the extent that it is a reflection of life, is plausible but only in part.[41] There is conflict and plurality, if by plurality we mean that Nietzsche's stories give different versions of the same event, but there is no ambiguity. Nietzsche criticizes other genealogists for their lack of intellectual rigor and makes definite claims about the truth (GM; II; 4, 12). The strictures of Nietzsche's genealogical examinations leave no doubt about his strong belief that he had found an unambiguous foundation to explain existing values and to revaluate them.

In the preface to the *Genealogy,* Nietzsche declares that his thoughts on the origins of morality are part of a will to knowledge that demands "greater precision" (GM; P; 1). In *The Anti-Christ,* he is so confident of the validity of his method that he defines the boundary separating the "correct" relationship of Israel with God from the wrong turn that it took when the priests became power holders.

Hoy's argument, described above, that a genealogy intends to show the inadequacy of people's current self-understanding is contingent on the validity of Nietzsche's claims about history, health, and sickness, which must be subject to verification. Hoy believes that Nietzsche's genealogy is verifiable, and this is in part the case. Nietzsche's account of the slave origins of Christianity can be verified; that is, one can examine the historical record to see if his views are accurate. But his arguments about health and sickness are not. They are circular: the healthy are the strong, and the strong are the healthy. Life-enhancing possibilities come from the strong, and the strong stand for life-enhancing possibilities. This circularity depends on the validity of the direct link that Nietzsche makes between morality and physiology; and, as I have argued above, his arguments here capsize on the banks of his naturalism. If sickness is a natural occurrence, then a morality arising from a physiologically defective body must also be natural. If instincts are the basis of everything, this excludes the possibility of the anti-natural sphere that Nietzsche abhors. Hoy explicitly poses but does not answer the question of whether Nietzsche has grounds to distinguish health from sickness.[42] My argument acknowledges this as a problem and adds that, given Nietzsche's naturalism, the opposition of health and sickness that he decries is already *justified* by virtue of their natural character.

I am now on better grounds to reformulate my critique of Nietzsche's conception of genealogy and to present it in Nietzschean terms. First, the "origin" identified by the genealogist will be an unstable site, given an ontology of becoming. Second, even if the genealogist found a stable origin, it is bound to vanish in light of Nietzsche's epistemology: we are never able to reach "the thing in itself," which is inaccessible. We only have access to effects, *not* origins (D; 307). It follows, third, that the origin will be an interpretation imposed by the will to power. The placement of the origin within a sequence of events, which is a faithful rendition of what Nietzsche does in the *Genealogy*, is the labor of the will to power. Genealogy is thus knowledge as an expression of power, a view that fits neatly with Nietzsche's idea of the organic world as a permanent struggle for domination. Everything in existence, he asserts,

> is continually interpreted anew, . . . transformed and redirected to a new purpose by a power superior to it; . . . everything that occurs in the organic world consists of *overpowering, dominating,* and in their turn, overpowering and dominating consist of re-interpretation, adjustment, in the process of which their former 'meaning' and 'purpose' must necessarily be obscured or completely obliterated. (GM; II; 12)

For the sake of argument, we could put aside the inaccessibility of an origin as a "thing in itself," and grant that Nietzsche has accurately identified a stable origin in a genealogical account. These concessions present genealogy as Nietzsche understood it. But, at the same time, the contrast deepens between his ontology and his knowledge claims. To put it starkly: his ontology of becoming is at odds with his view of the origin. The origin is bound to "become," but Nietzsche assumes an unchangeable chain of events. As I discuss in the next chapter, for instance, the weak are *fated* to be oppressed. And the oppressed will tunnel a way out of their torture chamber through cunning. They become *rational,* and their rationality will crush the strong. As Tracy B. Strong points out, "what happens is that the *Unbewusstheit* of the noble is unable to resist the dialectics of the slave: *the victor is always the weak.* Nietzsche is quite clear on this: the ability to induce the knowledge that one could have done otherwise is a decisive weapon."[43] And, we might add, this weapon is fated to be manufactured in the bitter soul of the slave.

My argument, which I thoroughly discuss in the next chapter, is that the origin, in Nietzsche's arguments, is never overcome. This is why he believes that his critique of the debilitating effects of the ascetic ideal is still valid for modernity. The origin of the ascetic ideal (resentment, i.e., a physiological illness) is still present in modern

European culture, and this accounts for Nietzsche's characterization of this culture as sick. This kind of reasoning is an instance of the genetic fallacy, and I do not see how Nietzsche escapes it. The logic is flawed. Baseness in the origin does not imply baseness in its offspring. But, for Nietzsche, the origin and its subsequent offspring constitute a single entity, which cannot be disentangled or taken apart. "In the community of the good goodness is inherited; it is impossible that a bad man could grow up out of such good soil" (H; I; 45). The origin and its offspring do not "become." As I argued above, in discussing Hoy's characterization of genealogy, if we sever current moral values and their origin, genealogy provides, at best, reasons to revaluate the *origin* of values. Genealogy does not provide any reasons to revaluate the values themselves.

Which of the genealogical and valuating accounts of morality in *Daybreak* and the *Genealogy* is closer to reality, or the "true" one? If we take seriously Nietzsche's argument that valuations are expressions of self-glorification,[44] which in turn express the will to power, we are in an epistemological quagmire. Which forms of moral valuation, that is, of self-glorification, are the best ones? After the genealogist of the past and the archaeologist of the soul identify the "origin" of an event and trace the evolution and transformation of that event, physiology has the task of sorting out different wills to power: that is, the task of establishing a new system of valuation, which is *only possible* through the proper identification of the signs of weakness and strength, sickness and health. A psychologist will define criteria to distinguish a weak will from a strong one. A physician will detect the nature and symptoms of sickness and health. These two processes—the distinction between weakness and strength and the right detection of sickness and health—will determine the validity of knowledge, thus showing the proper role of physiology. The validity of knowledge is established by resorting to physiology and diagnosing the health of the will to power that begot this knowledge in the first place. If it enhances life, in Nietzsche's notion of enhancement, it is a better or "truer" knowledge. If it diminishes life, it is a lower form of knowledge or even false. The priest is false because he is sick (AC; 52). The nature of the will to power, namely, whether it is healthy or sick, will settle the status of knowledge claims. As physician, psychologist, and philosopher, Nietzsche will measure the past in order to prepare new grounds for both his present and the future of humankind. "The order of rank of greatness for all past mankind has not yet been determined" (D; 548).

The link between genealogy and physiology is thus explained. Life evaluates through us, and "even that *anti-nature of a morality* which conceives God as the contrary concept to and condemnation of life is only a value judgement on the part of life—of *what* life? of *what* kind of life?" Nietzsche's answer is: "of declining, debilitated, weary, condemned life" (TI; "Morality"; 5). Is, then, an attack on a sick morality an attack on *life?* Is an attack on life an attack on *nature?* After all, sickness is a *natural* event. And though nature is chance and innocence, where innocence is understood as absence of responsibility, certain predictable patterns do not belong in the sphere of contingency, but are necessary, or fated. The strong are fated to act out their strength; and the weak and sick are fated to act out their nature; no other option is available to them.

The proper identification of the kind of life, that is, the type of will to power that is at work, becomes extremely complex when we consider that Nietzsche emphasizes the preeminence of sickness in the constitution of humanity, as well as the existence of different types of sickness. A sick type, the slave, channeled his energies in what later became the soul. Sickness brought forth the most delicate specimen of humankind, the ascetic priest. And it is also clear that sickness can be the route toward reason. At least, this was the case for Nietzsche: "sickness . . . compelled me to reason, to reflect on reason in reality" (EH; "So Clever"; 2).

This complexity deepens when Nietzsche joins instincts and happiness in all forms of ascending life (TI; "Socrates"; 11), and then invokes "the *instinct of décadence* itself" as that which is responsible for any will to deny life (TI; "Morality"; 5). And *décadence* turns out to be inescapable:

> It is self-deception on the part of philosophers and moralists to imagine that by making war on *décadence* they themselves elude

décadence themselves. This is beyond their powers: what they select as an expedient, as a deliverance, is itself only another expression of *décadence*—they *alter* its expression, they do not abolish the thing itself. (TI; "Socrates"; 11)

Is this also Nietzsche's predicament? Or is his self-characterization as an anti-moralist sufficient to elude the trap of decadence? In *Ecce Homo*, he asserts that his instincts always found the way out of decadence.

Nietzsche's medical diagnoses are necessary to his role as surveyor of the past and to the duty he takes on himself of being a *"new Columbus."*[45] They make possible his scrutiny of the origin and history of moral sensations in order to "solve the sociological problems entangled with them" (H; I; 37). This is, I think, a reasonable answer to the hypothesis I posed at the beginning of this chapter, namely, that genealogy would become a dead end when confronted by an ontology of becoming and by a diversity of wills to power. The idea of becoming means that the interpreter and his object, or the genealogist and the origin, are unstable, and it brings out the fact that the origin is itself an interpretation. A diversity of wills to power opens only one door: some wills are sick. It is no wonder that, in his autobiography and in a discussion of nutrition, place, and climate as medical remedies, Nietzsche confesses to "the real fatality of my life," which was "[i]gnorance *in physiologis*" (EH; "So Clever"; 2).

Here it should be noted that physiology is effective only in discerning a hierarchy of wills to power, but is unable to demonstrate that something sick is also anti-natural. Further, in Nietzsche's naturalism, to attack sickness is to attack nature. For this sickness is bound to be an expression of the will to power in its permanent effort to interpret, to dominate, and to arrange the world in its own image: "everything that occurs in the organic world consists of *overpowering, dominating*. . . . [E]very purpose and use is just a sign that the will to power has achieved mastery over something less powerful, and has impressed upon it its own idea [*Sinn*] of a use function" (GM; II; 12). In Nietzsche's view, the tragedy for humanity is that a sick, but more powerful, will to power triumphed.

His naturalism leads to *amor fati*. In their very nature, humans are the only animals that *need* to justify life (GS; 1), and this need demands forms of morality that will find justification, that is, meaning, in something "outside" life. For life, alone, cannot furnish its own justification. Life is meaningless and has no goal (H; I; 33, 34). Whatever the justification of life might be, it must come from something that, according to Nietzsche, is not life. It must come from something "higher," or "transcendental," that therefore negates what life is. The epistemological trap of genealogy thus remains. The transcendental domain, which is an eloquent manifestation of sickness, is fated to become. It is inscribed in a human need. Genealogy explains this process; could it alter it? This is a critical problem for Nietzsche.

Given the fated character of sickness, a passage from *Daybreak* strikes an ominous note in view of the precise and factual knowledge that Nietzsche seeks for his genealogical accounts. We only have access to "effects," that is, to "symptoms." "A historian has to do, not with what actually happened, but only with events *supposed to have happened:* for only the latter have *produced an effect.*" World history

> is opinions about supposed actions and their supposed motives, which in turn give rise to further opinions and actions, the reality of which is however at once vaporised again and produces an *effect* only as vapour—a continual generation and pregnancy of phantoms over the impenetrable mist of unfathomable reality. All historians speak of things which have never existed except in imagination. (D; 307, first emphasis mine)

Genealogy can do nothing about this epistemological problem. We can only grasp "effects." This is one of the "truths" of a "true" assessment of the human condition. If we had access to the truth of what life is, we would not be able to bear its meaninglessness. But even the "effects" are ugly enough as to demand the veil that art throws over them.

The preceding discussion allows me to put forward these conclusions:

(1)   To show the origin of some values *is not* to show that these values must be revaluated.[46]

(2)   To show that the will to power behind some values is sick *is not* to show that this sickness erodes the epistemic and moral validity of those values.

(3)   To find a sick will to power is not to find an anti-natural will to power.

(4)   In a naturalism ruled by necessity and the innocence of becoming, there is no place for blaming someone or regretting something. No one is responsible for what he is. "No one is accountable for his deeds, no one for his nature; to judge is the same thing as to be unjust" (H; I; 39).[47]

Nietzsche's interest in physiology explains the lengths he went to dissect and to diagnose Socrates and the ascetic priest. They were, after all, the competition. And in both of them he finds the same faults. Socrates "seemed to be a physician, a saviour," but he "was a misunderstanding: *the entire morality of improvement, the Christian included, has been a misunderstanding*" (TI; "Socrates"; 11). The old Athens "was coming to an end," and Socrates appeared "as the apparent *cure* for this case" (9). Philosophy turns into ventriloquism when Nietzsche, so to speak, enters into Socrates' soul: "'Socrates is no physician,' he said softly to himself: 'death alone is a physician here. . . . Socrates himself has only been a long time sick'" (12). The same verdict awaits the ascetic priest: "He combats only the suffering itself, the discomfiture of the sufferer, *not* its cause, *not* the real sickness: this must be our most fundamental objection to priestly medication" (GM; III; 17). The ascetic priest alters the direction of resentment (GM; III; 15), just as philosophers of the Socratic brand alter the expression of *décadence* (TI; "Socrates"; 11). Nietzsche's critique of counterfeit physicians even reaches the poets who wish to alleviate life. They "soothe and heal only provisionally." As in the case of Socrates and the ascetic priest, such poets "even hinder men from working for a real improvement in their condition" (H; I; 148). In all three cases—Socrates, the ascetic priest, and poets—we have physicians as tricksters and medications as palliatives or comedies of self-deception.

The prevalence of counterfeit physicians helps explain why Nietzsche seeks to identify the true causes behind the symptoms. It invites the question of whether he succeeded in offering genuine remedies rather than hypnotics to ameliorate pain temporarily. But this question seems to be intractable. In his late works, Nietzsche's remedy is straightforward: everyone should accept the fact that everything is an expression of the will to power and that nature stands for unequal and fixed body types. The order of rank is the supreme law of nature (AC; 57). Those endowed with the traits of the lowest type should accept their status at the base of a pyramidal society. For this type, presumably, the palliatives of art and religion will still be needed, just as, in Plato's republic, the workers need myths to accept their place in the ideal city. For the highest type of individual, no remedy, seemingly, is required to curb any possible sense of despair. They recognize what they are by nature and are sufficiently strong to affirm life as it is. This lack of a remedy is deceptive, though. Even the most spiritual type needs a palliative—which emerges in Nietzsche's idea of eternal recurrence. This palliative, as I argue later in this volume, does not cure, but it furnishes life with its highest meaning, and thus acts as the cornerstone of Nietzsche's epic spirituality and its self-therapy.

Philosophy, understood as physiology and divination, expresses not only the genealogical condition but also the centrality of nature in the constitution of a person. Nietzsche wields physiology as a philosophical weapon and philosophy as a physiological reaction because he regards the body as the only genuine battlefield. It is, at least, the original one, since the soul emerged from the body as a more dangerous and, for this very reason, more promising arena for higher battles. The awareness of suffering and beauty is born in the soul (GM; II; 18), and the soul emerges as a conscience of difference from the body.

The philosopher/genealogist/archaeologist/physician forms a powerful alliance. The genealogist and the archaeologist "find" evidence in history and in the soul, respectively; the physician diagnoses the philosopher; and the philosopher writes the prescriptions in the form of stories that offer redemption and self-therapy.[48] This alliance was eloquently spelled out early in Nietzsche's writings, in a section of *Human, All Too Human* with the apt title *"The future of the physician."* In a specific list of criteria for the modern physician, he had to possess "the subtlety of an agent of police or an advocate in comprehending the secrets of a soul without betraying them." Once the physician reaches the stage of proficiency in his trade, "he is then in a position to become a benefactor to the whole of society" through a wide spectrum of tasks that range from "the prevention of evil thoughts" to "the production of a spiritual-physical aristocracy (as promoter and preventer of marriages)." He will "cease to be a 'medicine-man' and become a saviour" (H; I; 243). In *Daybreak*, Nietzsche specifies his project as a physician, a project that is, on the surface, eerily similar to that of the ascetic priest: Nietzsche's future task is "to calm the imagination of the invalid so that at least he should not, as hitherto, have to suffer *more* from thinking about his illness than from the illness itself" (D; 54).

The irony here is that the philosopher turns out to be a sick physician in a state of permanent convalescence. But he claims to be healthy enough to take advantage of his sickness. Nietzsche probably took this insight from Plato's view of physicians:

> Doctors, it is true, would become cleverest if, in addition to learning the craft of medicine, they associated with the greatest possible number of the most diseased bodies right from childhood, had themselves experienced every illness, and were not, by nature, very healthy. After all, they do not treat a body with a body. If they did, we would not allow their bodies to be or become bad. But it is with a soul that a body is treated, and it is not possible for a soul to treat anything well if it is or has become bad itself.[49]

My contention that Nietzsche emerges as a sick physician— which he admits, to the extent that illness was his path to reason— refers us back to the quest for transparency that guides him as genealogist, archaeologist, physician, and psychologist. This quest is reflected in the causal links of his stories and in the intentions he discovers in the "secrets" of the souls of his patients/characters. The philosopher is trained in inner journeys, cherishes inner recesses, and possesses a soul that makes him aware of both beauty and suffering, malice and masks, cruelty and a cliff of thorns. Like the slave, he, too, is malicious: "I am too malicious to believe in myself" (EH; "Destiny"; 1). Like the ascetic priest, he is acquainted with religious sensibilities. "[W]e also know religious feelings better!" (GS; 122). His soul thus combines the delicate nature of the ascetic priest and the cunning and malice of the slave. He himself has attained the marks of a "higher nature": "[T]here is today, perhaps no more distinguishing feature of the *'higher nature'*, the intellectual nature, than to be divided in this sense and really and truly a battle ground for these opposites," namely, the slave values and the noble values (GM; I; 16).

Alas, Nietzsche's training in inner journeys and unknown regions will be sorely tested when we take a closer look at the central text in which he explains his genealogical method and seeks to demonstrate its epistemological power in elucidating the value of the morality of self-denial.

Chapter Three

ON THE GENEALOGY OF MORALITY
A Revaluation

Nietzsche, one might say, is concerned to give himself a new genealogy.

—Tracy B. Strong, "Genealogy, the Will to Power,
and the Problem of a Past"

Nietzsche wrote two lengthy genealogical analyses—*On the Genealogy of Morality* and *The Anti-Christ*—though all his texts include stories, parables, and investigations into the origins of a variety of events and concepts. His analysis in the *Genealogy* is presented as a "polemic" that will continue the themes of *Beyond Good and Evil,* and, as he makes clear in the preface, his concern with morality has also been addressed in previous works, particularly *Human, All Too Human* and *Daybreak.* The continuity of *Genealogy* with ideas advanced in *Beyond Good and Evil* should not obscure, however, the obvious departure that the *Genealogy* represents. It is about facts, truth, and reality, and apart from a few passages, Nietzsche eschews his inclination, so evident in *Beyond Good and Evil,* to question the validity of his thinking process and of his truth claims, where truth is something verifiable against the yardstick of an objective reality.

The preface to the *Genealogy* also makes clear that Nietzsche does not intend to examine all types of morality, but rather, one in particular, which he calls the morality of self-denial and self-sacrifice. He wants to know the *value* of these values, and this requires an investigation into the conditions in which these values arose. Contrary to Nietzsche's expressed goals and interpretation of his view of morality, however, the *Genealogy* is not, primarily, a text about the origin of morality. It is, in its structure and content, *an examination of the origin and transformation of guilt and their consequences*. The morality of self-denial and self-sacrifice follows as *one* of the reactions to these events. But Nietzsche's stated program is to investigate the conditions under which human beings invented the value judgments of good and evil, and to answer a central question: *"what value do they themselves have?"* "For me," he stresses, "it was a question of the *value* of morality" (GM; P; 3, 5).

Barely a year later, after writing *On the Genealogy of Morality*, Nietzsche had a disheartening answer: *"the value of life cannot be estimated."* "In themselves" values concerning life are "stupidities" (TI; "Socrates"; 2). The problem of life is "inaccessible" (TI; "Morality"; 5). It is only as symptoms that moral judgments about life have an "incalculable value." These judgments reveal "the most precious realities of cultures and inner worlds which did not *know* enough to 'understand' themselves" (TI; "Improvers"; 1). As argued in chapter 2, genealogy and the quest for transparency go together. "What defines me, what sets me apart from all the rest of mankind, is that I have *unmasked* Christian morality" (EH; "Destiny"; 7).

In the *Genealogy*, Keith Ansell-Pearson asserts, Nietzsche "provides us with a stunning story about humanity's monstrous moral past . . . [and] he also wants us, his readers, to read the text of our past in such a way that it becomes possible to discover 'a new twist and possible outcome for the Dionysian drama of the "fate of the soul"' (*GM* P:7)."[1] In this chapter, I intend to scrutinize this drama and assess Nietzsche's arguments about the origin and development of guilt. I will rely on several Nietzschean principles, some already suggested in chapter 2, as guidelines for my interpretation:

(1) the ontological principle: life is will to power, which means that will to power is the "essence" of life; life is, by its nature, violent and injurious; and the will to power, as an aggregate of instincts, always emerges victorious (GM; II; 11, 12). The ontological principle expresses itself in the individual organism and in the whole history of things and events; namely, in the whole history of culture.[2]

In the individual organism, the "highest biological point of view" signifies that the meaning and purpose of individual organs shift, and that even their destruction works toward the "true *progressus*" of life, "*always appearing,* as it does, in the form of the will and way to *greater power* and *always emerging victorious* at the cost of countless smaller forces" (GM; II; 12, second and fourth emphases mine). In the cultural domain, everything is the end result of an interpretation, a meaning, imposed by the will to power (GM; II; 12).

(2) the pleasure principle: guilt, as inner cruelty, is produced because the individual derives pleasure from this cruelty.

(3) the cruelty principle: cruelty is a constitutive element of higher cultures. Cruelty runs through and constitutes the "whole history of higher culture" (GM; II; 6; BGE; 229).

(4) the physiological principle: man is "the *sick* animal."

To these four principles I add what I call the Danto proviso:

(5) One should not say things that possess a clear meaning and then attempt to soothe their sting by invoking an imaginary fine print. "A man cannot write this way and then stand back in mock innocence and point to the fine print, to the footnote, to the subtle conciliatory phrase written in all but invisible ink, or say that we were expected to be subtle enough to read between the lines."[3]

In a detailed discussion of Nietzsche's genealogy, Brian Leiter argues that it "presupposes that its object has a stable or essential character—its *Brauch*—that permits us to individuate it intelligibly over time. What the genealogist denies is that this stable element is to be located in the object's purpose or value or meaning (its *Sinn*): it is precisely *that feature* which is discontinuous from point of origin to present-day embodiment."[4] Nietzsche is "concerned precisely to break the chain of value transmission by showing that the value or meaning of the genealogical object is discontinuous over time for two reasons: first, because there is no unitary value or meaning transferred from point of origin to contemporary object; and, second, because there is more than one point of origin."[5]

Leiter, relying on Nietzsche's "mini-genealogy" of punishment, in which Nietzsche differentiates between the stable element of punishment and its relative meaning, asks whether morality has a "permanent" element that could be individuated in an intelligible way over time. According to him, Nietzsche is unclear about this "permanent" element, and so Leiter makes "a proposal on [Nietzsche's] behalf: Let us say that the 'permanent' element in morality is *the practice of evaluating oneself and others*—call it the Anthropocentric Evaluative Practice."[6] But it is doubtful that Nietzsche needed help in this area; he provides not only a "permanent" component of morality but also the reasons that explain it. In Nietzsche's text, morality is always a means for the preservation of a way of life, even when this preservation may lead, as in the case of the warrior, to a short-lived existence. The preservation of a way of life takes the form of a code of conduct by which human beings give meaning to their lives and determine their worth. These three elements—preservation, meaning, and worth—are the "permanent" component in Nietzsche's view of morality. Nietzsche does not spell out his reasons for this systematically, but they lie in his characterization of man as, first, a reverent animal, that is, the only animal that needs to find meaning for its life (GS; 1); second, a valuating and sick animal, whose sickness is a demand for reasons to explain suffering (man yearns for reasons) (GM; II; 22; III; 20); and third, a vain creature who needs lies (morality is the lie the human beings tell to themselves), and whose vanity is his belief that he possesses a higher nature (BGE; 230).

Leiter concludes that Nietzsche's genealogy is inconsistent with his internal critique, that is, his view that his genealogies encourage people to revaluate the values they esteem; and that Nietzsche does not fall into the genetic fallacy, namely, the idea that the value of something is determined by its origin. Leiter also accepts the argument that the morality of self-denial, what Leiter calls "morality in the pejorative sense," is an obstacle to the flourishing of higher human beings. I will use Leiter's interpretation as a springboard to present my understanding of Nietzsche's genealogical stories as they are given in the *Genealogy*.

BAD CONSCIENCE AND AFFIRMATION

In the *Genealogy*, the first essay traces the emergence of two kinds of valuations and pinpoints one of the origins of the morality of self-denial; the second essay traces the genealogy of guilt; and the third essay identifies a second origin for the morality of self-denial. At the same time, the third essay is not so much concerned with the origin as with the meaning of the ascetic ideal and the protective measures that ought to be taken to shield those few individuals—the "unusual cases," *"man's strokes of luck"*—who are strong enough to act in a manner different from the one dictated by the sickness from which they suffer (GM; III; 14). Hence, the goal Nietzsche expressed in the preface, that of examining the conditions under which the value of the values of selflessness and self-denial arose, is reached in the first essay through one story, which is significantly different from the stories told in the second and third essays. As Leiter points out, there is more than one origin given for the morality of self-denial. It is also necessary to emphasize that Nietzsche sees genealogy as a "descent," which will reveal different expressions of guilt as well as different origins for this morality.

The story about the origin of this morality told in the first essay is fairly straightforward. The slaves—a group that develops cunning as a form of compensation for its weakness in front of the masters— transform their impotent hatred into love in order to gain a sense of superiority over their oppressors. The second story is narrated in the third essay through an examination of the meaning of the as-cetic ideal and is more complex. The slaves of the first essay dis-charge their hatred outwardly on the nobles by inverting the nobles' values. In the third essay story, however, the ascetic priest convinces the herd to discharge their suffering inwardly by accepting the idea of sin. Between these two stories, there are important gaps that

Nietzsche attempts to bridge by offering a detailed discussion of the prehistory of humankind in the second essay. I propose to reconstruct his argument by tracing the different stages that he describes in his quest for the conditions under which the morality of self-denial arose and developed. The descent toward this morality has five stages, which Nietzsche treats as strands that can be disentangled from a whole and analyzed as events that stand on their own.

Nietzsche locates the creation of society in the prehistory of mankind as his first case study. In the realm of history, Nietzsche presents four additional case studies that narrate the origin of guilt and purport to achieve the goal stated in the preface of the *Genealogy*, namely, an identification of the conditions that account for the value of the morality of self-denial. These stages and the five case studies can be listed as follows:

(1) the creation of society in prehistory
(2) the debtor-creditor relationship at the individual level
(3) the debtor-creditor relationship at the communal level
(4) the slaves' revolt
(5) the rise of the ascetic priest

Before discussing these case studies, however, we should consider some of the ramifications of Nietzsche's characterization of the prehistory of humanity. Here, I concentrate on the creation of society and of the sovereign individual.

The beginnings of Nietzsche's genealogy are found in the prehistory of humanity, when some populations were conquered and shaped by stronger groups or races. Such conquests were an act of fate and ushered in the internalization of man, that is, the bad conscience. Those who were subjected to the power and oppression of a stronger race were forced to abide by the social norms imposed by the artists of cruelty and violence, called "the blond beasts of deed," the creators of the state. The oppressed individuals who found themselves within the boundaries of society could not vent their instincts outwardly, and these instincts, always seeking satisfaction in actions, turned inward. Though Nietzsche is not entirely clear on this issue, he seems to suggest that the conquered population was already living under the aegis of some form of social organization, which was superseded by the new order imposed by their conquerors. People who were used to displaying their power in the open were now caged animals. Once the natural outlets for the expression of instincts were blocked, these instincts found a new outlet, with far-reaching consequences. This new outlet is the soul, the inner world that attempts to replace the natural wilderness as an arena of new adventures. But this inner world is a torture chamber, and the adventures in cruelty that are played out in it are expressions of a sick organism. And yet, in this story, this first manifestation of inner cruelty is not produced by guilt. Nietzsche later describes this cruelty as a "piece of animal psychology" and a stratagem that the will to power uses to express itself and to find *pleasure*. As Christopher Janaway puts it, "Nietzsche relies on the proposition that human beings find pleasure in *inflicting* suffering on themselves."[7]

In Nietzsche's analysis, the creation of society is an act of fate. The weak are destined to be forced by the strong to dwell within social norms. Society is also an abrupt change that sundered man from his natural wilderness and forced him to live within the confines of new rules. In this new and unknown environment, human beings no longer have "their familiar guide," the instincts that "unconsciously led them to safety" in their former habitat. Still, these instincts continue pressing for the gratifications to which they were accustomed. But human beings are not in a position to oblige. They must now learn, on the spot, by making inferences and establishing causal and logical connections; that is, they have to depend on their consciousness, "that most impoverished and error-prone organ!" This obstruction of the discharge of the instincts expands the inner world that will later be called the soul (GM; II; 16). Driven by "homesickness for the desert," man has "to create from within himself an adventure, a torture-chamber, an unsafe and hazardous wilderness" (GM; II; 16). That is, man substitutes a sick wilderness, a "torture chamber," for the healthy wilderness in which he once lived and enjoyed. "Lacking external enemies and obstacles, and forced into the oppressive narrowness and conformity of custom, man impatiently ripped himself apart . . . *that* is the origin of 'bad conscience'" (GM; II; 16). The *"instinct of freedom . . . incarcerated within itself* and finally able to discharge and unleash itself only against itself: that, and that alone, is *bad conscience* in its beginning" (GM; II; 17). This is why Nietzsche places so much importance on clarifying the proper relationship between punishment and guilt. Punishment socializes individuals into the habit of remembering and serves different purposes, but it is not the foundation of guilt. If anything, punishment makes its victims more cunning and more intelligent, but it fails completely to engender a sense of guilt.

This gives rise to the paradox that an incarcerated freedom and "the instinct of freedom" fight against each other. How can we envision an "instinct of freedom" incarcerated within itself? I offer a tentative answer, which seems to be in line with Nietzsche's reasoning. Freedom seeks more freedom, that is, power, and this additional freedom is only found within the existing boundaries where freedom is already located. For freedom is always located somewhere—in an organism, a culture, or a group. That is, freedom fights to expand itself, to widen the borders of its confines. It is precisely this expansion of the existing boundaries of freedom (the instinct of freedom "incarcerated within itself") that opens the way for a new world of optimum conditions: the inner world. But the struggle that creates an inner world is also the beginning of bad consciousness—an uneasiness in the face of an unknown environment where external enemies are lacking—and so the instinct of freedom battles against itself.

This tentative answer should not obscure one certainty: the "facts" promised in the preface to the *Genealogy* vanish from Nietzsche's radar screen as soon as he embarks on the journey to explain the origin of society. The signposts of this journey are assumptions and inferences, not facts.[8] In his view, the establishment of society is anchored on two assumptions. First, society comes into existence, not gradually, but as a result of a radical change brought about by compulsion. Second, this compulsion was the deed of creatures from the wilderness, creatures who discharged their instincts on other populations and shaped, through repression, a new type of person. The creatures from the wilderness, a "pack of blond beasts of prey," a "master race," are "the most involuntary, unconscious artists there are." They are the first embodiment of the state; they possess no notion of guilt and responsibility; and they are so different, so foreign to the ones oppressed, that their victims are not even able to hate them (GM; II; 17). "*They* are not the ones in whom 'bad conscience' grew"; but they created the conditions for the appearance of this phenomenon.[9] Reasonably, however, they, as representatives of the state, also begin to live in society, and slowly, begin to decay themselves.

Section 18 of the *Genealogy* deserves special mention in Nietzsche's account. First, Nietzsche's argument clearly indicates that bad conscience is not guilt. Bad conscience should be understood in the terms Nietzsche cites approvingly from Spinoza: as something that did not turn out as expected, as a "piece of animal-psychology, no more" (GM; II; 15; III; 20). But although bad conscience as the internalization of instincts is not guilt, it is, as Janaway puts it, "one crucial component in the genesis of guilt-consciousness."[10] Second, bad conscience is an "active force," an act of affirmation. Third, we find a bifurcation in Nietzsche's argument. Instead of one process of kneading and shaping the old animal self, an act performed by the "blond beasts" on the conquered, we find *two* processes of shaping.

The "master race" shapes the vanquished into a new form. *But the conquered, too, begin a process of self-creation.* If the conquerors are "artists of violence and organizers," the oppressed become only "artists of violence," and this violence has a different direction. It is not violence against other men, violence discharged externally. It is violence against themselves, violence discharged internally. This sick violence is, precisely, what engenders an inner world in which man becomes a conscious creator, an artist who gives form to himself and seeks pleasure in inner cruelty. Thus the instinct of freedom both expands its horizon, in creating an inner world, and constrains itself by shaping itself into a particular form.

"This secret self-violation, this artist's cruelty, this desire *to give form to oneself* as a piece of difficult, resisting, suffering matter, to brand it with a will, . . . this uncanny, terrible but joyous labour of a soul *voluntarily split within itself,* which makes itself suffer out of the pleasure of making suffer, this whole *active* 'bad conscience,'" spawns a "disconcerting beauty and affirmation" (GM; II; 18, first two emphases mine). The same "active force," the will to power that drives the "artists of violence and organizers" on the grand scale of the state, operates "on a smaller, pettier scale" and creates "negative ideals." This "smaller scale" is the inner world, the "soul" of the vanquished.[11]

To put it differently, bad conscience, a *sickness*, will allow human beings to obtain consciousness of their individuality and to engage, for the first time, in a process of self-creation in which they give form to themselves and derive pleasure from a self-inflicted cruelty. As Robert Guay observes, "With the bad conscience the story truly starts to be about us: self-determining, even self-inventing persons, rather than just animals who talk. More than self-inflicted suffering for the sake of socialization, the bad conscience was what created the self-distance needed to take oneself as an object."[12] This self-distance, however, naturally leads to a question, as expressed by Janaway: Why does this self-inflicting punishment lead to a guilty feeling, and not, as alternative candidates, to fear, jealousy, shame, or anger at the self's "own impotence?"[13] Nietzsche allows that internalized cruelty leads eventually to anger in the "herd." But my answer to the question is that none of Janaway's alternative candidates are self-empowering. In contrast, a guilty feeling enhances the feeling of power. In the case of fear, jealousy, and shame, the more powerful subject is always external, that is, the one who produces the fear, or provokes the jealousy, or incites shame from his position as an external witness. Only in guilt is the self able to affirm and give shape to itself.

It is worth emphasizing that the inner cruelty engendered by bad conscience is not described by Nietzsche as anti-natural. Rather, bad conscience is the "will to torment oneself, that suppressed cruelty of animal man who has been frightened back into himself and given an inner life, incarcerated in the 'state' to be tamed, and has discovered bad conscience so that he can hurt himself, after the *more natural* outlet of this wish to hurt had been blocked" (GM; II; 22). The "wish to hurt" is a natural element of the individual's constitution, and the unleashing of this wish on external objects is merely a "more natural" outlet.

In bringing forth a "disconcerting beauty," bad conscience creates an awareness of its opposite, of ugliness. In Nietzsche's view, the concept of the ugly appears first as an awareness of ugliness, and the concept of beauty follows as awareness of being different from the ugly. His reasoning is that something beautiful could be found in self-contradictory concepts such as selflessness, self-denial, and self-sacrifice. The preliminary theory of the origin of the value of the unegoistic, as expressed in these concepts, is located in the fact that they produce pleasure, and "this pleasure belongs to cruelty" (GM; II; 18). In joining cruelty and pleasure, the *Genealogy* is a return to Nietzsche's position in *Human, All Too Human* on the centrality of pleasure in determining fundamental dispositions of human nature (H; I; 34). On this view, pleasure possesses explanatory power to account for guilt, cruelty, and suffering.

In Nietzsche's reasoning, "only the will to self-violation provides the precondition for the *value* of the unegoistic" (GM; II; 18). In other words, if a person is willing to inflict pain and suffering on himself and derives pleasure from this, he will regard his action as "unegoistic." But this does not follow. The individual is deriving pleasure, that is, his ego is gratified. It is not clear, then, why Nietzsche talks about self-denial and self-sacrifice as being produced by "the will to self-violation," when it is precisely this will that *affirms* a person's individuality by allowing him to give form to his character.

Nietzsche's story faces other entanglements in his investigation of the origin and nature of bad conscience. Bad conscience is described as both a sickness "to which man was forced to succumb" and as something that man *invented:* "this fool, this prisoner consumed with longing and despair, became the inventor of 'bad conscience,'" the inventor of that "torture-chamber" that was the soul (GM; II; 16). These two descriptions are not consistent. The first makes bad conscience the end result of circumstances that were beyond the individual's control. The second emphasizes the individual's need to invent a sick adventure as a surrogate for the real thing. The soul is the product of an act of cruelty forced on individuals, yet Nietzsche also claims that the soul is "voluntarily split within itself." I fail to see any convincing way to reconcile these two versions.

At this point, I pause to identify some questions relevant to Nietzsche's genealogy. How did the state, a social institution that suddenly began at a particular place and time, become the *norm* for all humans? This is not explained. Why did the creatures enjoying the freedom of the wilderness not take precautionary measures, on seeing the suffering of those confined within social structures? How and why do the master organizers, the "unconscious artists" who, in light of Nietzsche's philosophy, must have been a *minority* produced by *fate,* continue to appear on earth, founding new societies and shaping animals into humans? How did the ancient Greeks and Romans manage to escape the scourge of bad conscience (as Nietzsche argues they did), despite the fact that both cultures have a division between a noble class and a lower social stratum? These questions challenge the precision and historical basis that Nietzsche claims for his account. His reflections, however, provide a sufficient explanation of why the masters themselves succumbed to bad conscience and guilt.

Yet how can we explain his argument about the people who are forced into the confines of society, given his argument that punishment is not the original cause of the bad conscience? Do these people experience punishment? These questions, which are brought to the fore in Matthias Risse's discussion of Nietzsche's genealogy of guilt,[14] require distinguishing several senses of "punishment." At first, the oppressed are punished if they deviate from the norms imposed on them by their conquerors. The punishment to which Nietzsche refers in discussing the debtor-creditor relationship between individuals is an ephemeral blow that leaves an imprint on the flesh of the victim (GM; II; 14). Punishment in the context of the creation of society is quite different. It is the protracted socialization of the oppressed into a completely new way of behaving, a socialization that entails two elements: the oppressed are left without enemies and obstacles, and they are forced into "the conformity of custom" (GM; II; 16). How could the oppressed be "without enemies" when their masters surround them? The explanation is found in Nietzsche's peculiar way of characterizing the masters. The deed of conquest is so abrupt and pulverizing that they provoke shock and awe in the oppressed, but not the *ressentiment* and hatred that are defining marks of the slaves. The masters appear "too terrible, sudden, convincing and 'other' even to be hated" (GM; II; 17).

Thus, punishment as ephemeral torture and punishment as protracted impositions are distinct. In the latter sense, the masters cage the oppressed in society. The oppressed also cage themselves in an inner chamber of torture. Yet they suffer the "hammer blows and artists' violence" of the masters (GM; II; 17), which means that they are punished.

POWERFUL COMMUNITIES AND GUILT

In the second essay of *On the Genealogy of Morality*, Nietzsche spells out the beginning of guilt in terms of the origins of responsibility. The animal, man, began to make evaluations and calculations and to fix prices, and this capacity produced a sense of superiority, perhaps the origin of human pride, when the individual compared himself to other animals. Evaluation and the fixing of values are tools to establish uniformity and predictability in a universe that is ruled by randomness. Once society and its morality of custom had socialized human beings to become predictable, and once they began to see reality as equally predictable, the "sovereign individual" came into full view. The individual who evaluates reality, thus escaping the arbitrariness of the real, concludes that he can evaluate and make himself predictable. He possesses "responsibility" and, accordingly, "has *the right to make a promise*." He is so confident of his control of himself and of reality that he feels able to make a pledge and to fulfill it, regardless of what fate might have in store for him.

Responsibility, Nietzsche clearly suggests, is not a universal attribute. The person who possesses responsibility is, rather, a special specimen, one who is *aware* of "this rare freedom and power over himself and his destiny" (GM; II; 2); he possesses free will and self-mastery and deserves trust, fear, and respect. He has the right to exercise mastery over nature and over all those creatures who have not reached the level of responsibility. Responsibility as the possession of an unbreakable will, that is, as the reliability to deliver on promises, is the defining trait of the strong, and this will is their "own *standard of value*" (GM; II; 2). Responsibility is man's "conscience." And this "conscience," as Ansell-Pearson points out, "is to be understood not simply as the superior moral faculty which makes each one of us uniquely human but as an interiorized form of social control, the disciplined product of the civilizing process of ancient morality."[15] Further, in Nietzsche's account, only the sovereign individual will be able to feel guilt by virtue of his free will.[16] It should be noted immediately that in the first essay, free will is invented by the slaves, but in the second essay, free will, along with self-mastery, is one of the defining features of the sovereign individual.[17]

And yet, after exalting the emergence of responsibility in such a way, Nietzsche excludes it when discussing the relationship of creditor and debtor. When the debtor, that is, the responsible man who has the right to make promises, fails in his promise, Nietzsche's arguments take an unexpected twist. Those who punish the debtors who fail to fulfill their promises do not consider them "guilty." Their inability to fulfill the promise was "an irresponsible piece of fate." And for the one who is at the receiving end of the punishment, who was formerly a "sovereign" individual, his chastisement is regarded "like a piece of fate." He feels no "'inner pain' beyond what he would feel if something unforeseen suddenly happened, a terrible natural disaster . . . where resistance is futile" (GM; II; 14).

As in Nietzsche's discussion of bad conscience, pleasure and suffering are entwined; pleasure is the basis of cruelty. Suffering is a compensation for unpaid debts because "*to make* someone suffer is pleasure in *its highest form*" (GM; II; 6, second emphasis mine). The punishment of the powerless is a privilege that belongs to the "*rights of the masters,*" and this privilege is given to the creditor as compensation for unpaid debts. This privilege and its concomitant pleasure increase, "the lower and baser the position of the creditor in the social scale" (GM; II; 5).

If the debtor, due to a trick of fate, falls into the hands of a creditor occupying a lower social stratum, a creditor who, according to Nietzsche, will most enjoy his power to inflict pain on someone in a higher social stratum (GM; II; 5–6), it is not unreasonable to think that the "sovereign man" will feel an inner pain, in the face of such a humiliation. This inner pain would not be due to guilt, however, but rather to a shattering loss of confidence in himself, as a proud person who had the power to make promises without regard for fate. But given the fixed boundaries of Nietzsche's social universe, this scenario is implausible. In his universe, it is inconceivable that individuals occupying a higher position in society would ever be debtors to those below them.

Having spelled out the origin of bad conscience and its evolution toward a process of cruelty as pleasure, Nietzsche proceeds to identify the conditions, or rather one condition, in which this sickness developed and reached its peak. This condition is indebtedness, which furnishes two case studies of guilt in the realm of history. The first takes place at the individual level in the sphere of debtors and creditors, a sphere in which, as we already know, the debtor feels no special inner pain when punishment is visited on him (GM; II; 4). But eventually, a feeling of indebtedness arises in the debtor; bad conscience darkens his inner world, and duty and guilt appear as an irredeemable debt. The soul has expanded, and guilt becomes permanent. Bad conscience *"now so firmly establishes itself,* eating into him, broadening out and growing, like a polyp, so wide and deep that in the end, with the impossibility of expiating the guilt, is conceived the impossibility of discharging the penance, the idea that it cannot be paid off ('eternal punishment')" (GM; II; 21, emphasis mine).[18]

This prepares the ground for the second case study, which occurs at the communal level and involves the community's feeling of indebtedness toward its ancestors. Here, Nietzsche establishes a correlation between the growth of the community's power (emergence of "universal empires"), the progress toward "universal deities," and an increase in the feeling of guilt, but the exact picture is elusive. He refers to a "conviction" and a "suspicion" (GM; II; 20), and, following the pattern established in the first essay, describes a crucial development that was *reversed,* just as the slaves inverted the noble scale of values (GM; II; 21).

This crucial development is vaguely portrayed as something "transformed through interpretation, in a historically strange and curious manner" (GM; II; 19). This description is odd, in light of Nietzsche's insistence on rigor and his critique of the sleight-of-hand of English psychologists who reach their conclusions out of the blue. In any case, in the second case study the community grows stronger and becomes aware of its strength. Although its awareness of power ameliorates the punishment visited on transgressors, the same awareness *increases* the sense of indebtedness toward the community's ancestors. That is, the community becomes more lenient toward lawbreakers but more harsh toward itself: "Following this line of thought, the *dread* of the ancestor and his power, the consciousness of debts towards him, increases inevitably, in direct proportion to the increase in power of the tribe itself, that is, in proportion as the tribe itself becomes ever more victorious, independent, honoured and feared" (GM; II; 19). The ancestors are transformed into powerful gods, and the community feels unworthy of them. The cruelty principle, man's wish to hurt himself, seeks greater cruelty by establishing a causal connection between guilt, duty, and religious precepts, whereby conscience "is woven together with the concept of God." This step completes the moralization of guilt and duty (GM; II; 21).

What is the "moralization" of guilt and duty? It is the weaving into a single strand of the feeling of bad conscience and the concept of God. Nietzsche explains this key element of his genealogy in terms of a sense of indebtedness that pervades powerful communities and leads to feelings of unworthiness in the face of their ancestors, turned gods. This unworthiness produces a guilt that increases when all the ancestors are unified into the idea of one, all-powerful god, who expresses both the community's power and its deep sense of indebtedness and unworthiness.

Once again, the cruelty principle is essential to Nietzsche's story. Because of the will to hurt himself, which was born when the animal man was caged in society and bad conscience came into the world, the man of bad conscience "*re-interprets* [his] self-same animal instincts as guilt before God." This "reinterpretation," presumably, grows slowly throughout the prehistory of humanity until it is ingrained in our inner world. This man of bad conscience resorts to "religious precepts" to provide his self-torture with the "most horrific hardness and sharpness," the "most terrible sickness," its "absolutely unparalleled" mental cruelty. It is a "madness of the will": "man's *will* to find himself guilty and condemned without hope of reprieve" (GM; II; 22, first emphasis mine).

In other words, before the emergence of the ascetic priest, man had already invented the most powerful means of self-torture: the feeling of guilt toward God. In the *Genealogy*, Nietzsche does not explain why man invented a God in whose presence he could feel irredeemably guilty. And, as Leiter points out, Nietzsche does not provide an explanation of why the moralization of guilt and duty occurs at all (GM; II; 21).[19] But Nietzsche's arguments clearly indicate that this inclination is a part of the human will, a part of our nature. It is also a *sick* will. Moreover, the explanation for the moralization of guilt that is lacking in the *Genealogy* can be found in *Human, All Too Human*. The "exaggerated" moral demands of Christianity, Nietzsche claims, had the explicit intention of inciting people to "feel *as sinful as possible*." "If man," Nietzsche asks, "had failed to find this feeling *pleasant*—why should he have engendered such an idea and adhered to it for so long?" (H; I; 141). The highest possible feeling of sinfulness is discussed in a section in which cruelty (the saint, for example, who ruins his health) and pleasure (the saint who elicits admiration) are entwined. That is, the joint operation of cruelty and pleasure, both natural occurrences, explains why people are driven to a deep feeling of indebtedness to God.

How does the powerful community ameliorate its guilt? It does so by killing its god. It supposes that this god sacrifices himself on behalf of the community, to wipe the slate clean and to free the community from its debt. But the idea of such a redemption makes matters worse for the community. Redemption magnifies the sense of guilt and makes it permanent. For the debt is unpayable, which means that the community's guilt will be unredeemable. In *Daybreak*, Saint Paul is freed from guilt when he finds in Christ the destroyer of the law. This freedom is not available to the members of powerful communities whose all-powerful god sacrificed himself voluntarily on behalf of his debtors.

The two case studies discussed above show, first, that when the feeling of indebtedness grows and tightens its grip on individuals, it leads to the notion of "eternal punishment." And second, when the feeling of indebtedness increases in powerful communities, it leads to the "most terrible sickness" of guilt before God, and this sickness explodes into the concept of divine redemption. The strong (not the weak), following a sick but natural instinct for cruelty, first invent a powerful god in whose presence they feel unworthy, and then kill him to find redemption. It may come as a surprise, however, that the "most terrible sickness" arises among the strong.

So far, we can identify six stages in the evolution of bad con-science. In the first stage, bad conscience is not guilt. It is an inner cruelty that produces pleasure. In the second stage, bad conscience is mired in a paradox: it is supposed to create guilt in the sphere of debtors and creditors, but the one who administers punishment does not treat the debtor as guilty, and the one who receives punish-ment does not see himself as guilty, either. His punishment is an act of fate. The debtor regards himself as *unfortunate*, not guilty. In this stage, punishment never goes below the culprit's skin. and his "guilt" is treated as "a boulder falling on him and crushing him, where resistance is futile." "'Bad conscience' did *not* grow in this soil," according to Nietzsche, the soil of hangmen and victims (GM; II; 14). In the third stage, bad conscience is associated with indebtedness toward ancestors, deepening a sense of guilt. In the fourth stage, people inherit the divinities of their tribes and clans, along with "the burden of unpaid debts and the longing for them to be settled."

Here Nietzsche introduces an important parenthesis. He refers to a "transitional stage": "Those large populations of slaves and serfs who adapted themselves to the divinity cults of their masters . . . form a transitional stage: *from them*, the inheritance overflows in every direction" (GM; II; 20, emphasis mine). The phrase "from them," which changes the location of guilt from masters to slaves, is problematic for two reasons. First, in the "transitional stage" man inherits the burden of debts toward divinities of tribes and clans. This burden is heaviest in the most powerful communities (vice versa, "the weakening of the tribe . . . always *lessen(s)* . . . the dread of the spirit of the founder" and, consequently, reduces the feeling of indebtedness toward this founder) (GM; II; 19). It follows that the burden of unpaid debts falls on the nobles, who rule in power-ful communities and who *impose* their divinities on their slaves. Second, man inherits the burden of indebtedness within a struc-tured social order, in which the slaves are still subject to their mas-ters. The indebtedness, then, must flow both from masters and slaves, and not only, as Nietzsche argues, from the latter. In the "transitional stage," the feeling of guilt as indebtedness continues growing through millennia in "the same proportion as the concept and feeling for God" increases in strength (GM; II; 20).

In the fifth stage, the moralization of guilt occurs; bad con-science and the concept of God are woven together. Bad conscience is now "firmly" established; as quoted above, it is growing "like a polyp" and "eating into" man (GM; II; 21). In the sixth and final stage, God sacrifices himself to redeem people of powerful commu-nities, who are already well on their way to creating empires. Nietz-sche finds in this stage the conditions in which bad conscience "reached its most terrible and sublime peak" (GM; II; 19, 20). But none of these stages makes mention of sin. None of these stages is the morality of self-denial and self-sacrifice.[20]

In Nietzsche's story, the powerful people who lived in strong communities that aspired to the formation of "universal empires," and who had ample opportunities to display their power, invented a universal and all-powerful deity that reflected the community's sense of growing strength. Since these people were powerful, unlike the caged animals that succumbed to the "blond beasts," how could they also be the suffering and sick animals that yearn for reasons to explain their inner pain?

Risse reverses a part of Nietzsche's sequence. He holds that "it is *only* through the impact of Christianity that the bad conscious-ness as a feeling of guilt arises."[21] Ridley has responded, compel-lingly, "that the plausibility of Nietzsche's account is entirely inde-pendent of any presuppositions concerning Christianity or God; and this is because he regards the concept of guilt as one of the condi-tions that makes the invention and success of Christianity so much as intelligible."[22] My discussion departs from Ridley's important contributions, but it shares his interpretive framework. At the same time, my arguments differ substantially from Risse's conclusions.

In Nietzsche's sequence, described above, guilt is already present in the transitional stage, between bad conscience as animal cruelty and the stage of indebtedness toward the Christian conception of God (GM; II; 20). It is worth emphasizing that at this stage, human beings have already inherited from their tribes and clans not only their divinities, but also "the *burden* of unpaid debts and the longing for them to be settled" (emphasis mine). This "burden" is best explained as tied to several assumptions that lead, necessarily, to that inauspicious event, that psychical conflagration that became the source of the greatest guilt. Although neither Ridley nor Risse specifies these assumptions, they are especially damaging for Risse's view that guilt "only" comes "through the impact of Christianity."

What are these assumptions, found in section 19 of the Second Essay of the *Genealogy?* First, the feeling of indebtedness between individuals was expanded and came to encompass the relationship between individuals and their ancestors. The notion of a duty toward one's ancestors was born. Second, just as the conquest of weaker populations by stronger ones is inscribed in nature, so also with this feeling of indebtedness toward the ancestors of the tribe. It is conceived as continually increasing. For the ancestors are transfigured into spirits, who keep making demands on the living from the realm they now inhabit. The "continuous" increase of indebtedness, which is presented by Nietzsche as a "given" in the intricate web of obligations between tribes and their predecessors, then takes a dark turn in the form of the third assumption, or suspicion. The tribe members are afflicted by a nagging thought: do they give enough to their ancestors? From here we reach the fourth assumption: this suspicion "remains and grows," and is powerful enough to demand human sacrifices as the highest price to pay to assuage this lingering shadow, this feeling of human insufficiency before the ever-demanding gods.

In the second, third, and fourth assumptions we have explosive materials: the continuous growth of the feeling of indebtedness, the suspicion that the tribe members' offerings always fall short of the ancestors' expectations, and the introduction of human sacrifices, conceived as the highest payment. These materials are enough to suggest that any resolution will be nasty. And so it is, but a fifth assumption is also needed. That is that the dread of the ancestors grows in direct proportion to the power of the tribe, until the ancestors become gods, not merely spirits. Nietzsche qualifies this assumption by stating that during the middle periods of humankind, the tribe honors its ancestors by ascribing to them the attributes of its ruling nobility.

What can we expect from the second assumption (continuous growth in the feeling of indebtedness) and the fifth assumption (the power of the tribe grows in direct correlation with the dread of the ancestors)? Exactly what Nietzsche offers: the emergence of the concept of an all-powerful God, who expresses the power of a strong community and in whose presence people will always be debtors. And what can be expected from the third and fourth assumptions, namely, the permanent suspicion that remains and *grows*? We can expect the idea that human sacrifices will never be enough. And if this is so, another type of payment, one which, by necessity, must be *higher* than the one humans offer and, accordingly, one that must come from *outside* our humanity, will settle the debt and put an end to the tormenting sense of inadequacy. The stage is set for the entrance of the Christian solution: God erases the debt by sacrificing Himself.

The suspicion inscribed in the third and fourth assumptions leads to the self-flagellation induced by a simple belief that is part of the psychological profile of people who feel indebted to spirits. Our offerings are always fated to fall short. We are always tortured by the same question: do we give enough? And what is this self-flagellation that is provoked by the idea that we never give enough? It is guilt. Ridley summarizes what I take to be the dominant interpretation of Nietzsche here: that is, it "is the slavish version of the bad conscience that is responsible for the transformation of the concept of debt into the concept of guilt."[23] But this is not the case. In light of the sequence that Nietzsche describes, guilt first appears in powerful communities and is *not* an exclusive trait of the slaves. Nietzsche's arguments allow for the possibility that other conceptions of

God arose in the world, until this tendency reached its zenith in the Christian concept of God, who in turn produces not merely guilt but the "greatest" feeling of guilt.

Thus, Nietzsche posits bad conscience as an anguished and firmly established guilt, which is antecedent to Christianity. The feeling of indebtedness and the suspicion of never being able to pay off the debt until the suspicion is "firmly established" in the debtor's bad conscience are the hallmarks of the pre-Christian world, the conditions that prepare the way for Christianity's "stroke of genius" (GM; II; 21).

A permanent suspicion easily slides into the domain of certainty. It is reasonable to infer that the outcome is liberating, since the problem no longer lies in suspecting one's inability to pay back. That inability is settled in the debtor's conscience. When the suspicion turns into certainty, the human race (via Adam), nature, and existence all become culprits and thus worthless. It is then, according to Nietzsche, that Christianity shows its genius by providing a temporary relief. The all-powerful God sacrifices Himself, and the debt is settled. How temporary is this settlement? Nietzsche does not say. To Saint Paul, this sacrifice is an eternal act of reconciliation. "All this is from God, who reconciled us to himself through Christ and gave us the ministry of reconciliation: that God was reconciling the world to himself in Christ, not counting men's sins against them" (2 Cor 5:18–19). But Nietzsche thinks differently: the debt is now bound to be eternal.

In terms of the sequence I described above, we can say that in Nietzsche's first case study, sin comes from the feeling of indebtedness toward God, and this feeling is born within powerful communities, *not within the herd.* Curiously, Nietzsche does not call this indebtedness "sin," but he furnishes reasons that undercut the distinction he will later impose between the moralization of bad conscience by powerful communities and the manufacture of the notion of sin. The moralization of guilt leads to the need for punishment, a view that, according to his arguments in *Daybreak,* "robbed of its innocence the whole purely chance character of events" (D; 13).

This moralization entailed the "most terrible and supreme peak" of the sickness represented by bad conscience; the "impossibility of expiating the guilt"; "the impossibility of discharging the penance"; and the fabrication of a curse over the human race (original sin), over nature (which is seen as "evil"), and over existence (which is considered "worthless") (GM; II; 19, 21). And yet, the powerful communities he describes may have needed a universal God but not the tricks and medications of the ascetic priest. And if they needed the ascetic priest and thus became the herd of suffering and sick animals, Nietzsche fails to explain why and how this transformation came about. In his second story, sin is the "reinterpretation" of guilt by the ascetic priest.

Here we arrive at two sources for the eventual development of the morality of self-denial. The feeling of *resentment* is born among the slaves, and the feeling of *indebtedness,* which evolves into the greatest feeling of guilt on earth, is born among the powerful. We also arrive at a position that has been glossed over by most interpretations of Nietzsche's genealogy. The feeling of indebtedness toward God, *not resentment,* is the cause of the greatest dangers that humanity faces: nausea at ourselves and pity for our fellow man. This means that the role of resentment in Nietzsche's thought has been blown out of proportion, though Nietzsche himself is responsible for this misunderstanding of his own arguments.

Nietzsche's own summary of the evolution of guilt in the second essay clearly leaves much to be desired. In his summary there are only two stages: first, guilt as "a piece of animal-psychology," "guilt in its raw state," and second, guilt reinterpreted by the ascetic priest as sin (GM; III; 20). But his genealogical accounts are far more complex than these two stages would imply. They include the deepening of guilt in the individual, as well as the most crucial stage, guilt as torture in the face of a divine being. This takes root in powerful communities well *before* the emergence of Christianity. Indeed, Christianity brought a "temporary relief" to the self-imposed torture arising from an irredeemable debt to God. "Christianity's stroke of genius" lies within the confines of this self-inflicted and magnified cruelty. God, the creditor, paid the debt (GM; II; 21).

TWO ORIGINS OF THE MORALITY OF SELF-DENIAL AND
WEARINESS OF LIFE: A DETOUR

We can now turn to the fourth and fifth case studies (the slave revolt
in morality and the ascetic priest), which Nietzsche's genealogy
identifies as the two origins for the morality of self-denial. The first
is located in the historical experience of the Jewish people, discussed
earlier. The second and more detailed origin is found in the medications invented by the ascetic priest. These two origins are marked by
important differences.[24] The slaves of the first essay of the *Genealogy*
do not suffer from guilt; their main weapon is resentment, and they
embody "the vindictive cunning of powerlessness" (GM; I; 13). The
priest's main weapon is guilt. Both depend on cleverness and self-
deception. In the first essay, the slaves' morality, namely, the transformation of their hatred into love, is an act that comes *from within*.
It is a morality of self-affirmation, a carving out of an identity for
themselves, against the nobles. The slave, as the person who believes in the free will of the strong to act differently, "*needs* to believe
in an unbiased 'subject' with freedom of choice, because he has an
instinct of self-preservation and *self-affirmation* in which every lie is
sanctified" (GM; I; 13, second emphasis mine). But in the third essay,
the morality of self-denial comes *from without*. It is invented by the
ascetic priest as a prescription for the sick herd. Moreover, this prescription is explicitly designed to cope with the feeling of weariness
of life. It is not devised to assuage the guilt brought about by sin.
The morality of self-denial is thus not responsible for "the two worst
epidemics" that Nietzsche ascribes to Christian morality, namely,
nausea at and pity for mankind (GM; III; 14).

    In the preface to the *Genealogy*, Nietzsche presents these
"epidemics" as the end result of the morality of self-denial: "Precisely here [in 'the instincts of pity, self-denial, self-sacrifice'] I saw
the great *danger* to mankind, its most sublime temptation and
seduction—temptation to what? To nothingness?—precisely here
I saw the beginning of the end, standstill, mankind looking back
wearily, turning its will *against* life" (GM; P; 5). But it is far from

clear whether he succeeds in establishing the connection between the morality of self-denial and the nausea and pity for man that supposedly arises from it. The third essay of the *Genealogy* paints a different picture, which requires an examination of Nietzsche's account of the feeling of weariness of life.

In certain historical epochs, Nietzsche claims, tiredness and heaviness of life [*Müdigkeit und Schwere*] are epidemic and are produced by a feeling of obstruction that arises "almost from necessity." The causes of this feeling are strictly physiological, but, due to a lack of knowledge of physiology, the feeling is misunderstood and treated as a psychological and moral problem. Actually, "with all great religions, the main concern is the fight against a certain weariness and heaviness which has become epidemic" (GM; III; 17). Though the ideas of weariness of life and of sin seem to be entangled, Nietzsche treats them as two separate entities. Sin is the ascetic priest's reinterpretation of guilt, the trademark that displays his quackery. Weariness of life, by contrast, is the end result of different physiological factors. The priestly medications are intended not *to assuage the feeling of sin,* but to deal with feelings of obstruction and lethargy, that is, weariness of life.

Two errors result. First, the physiological fact of depression is misinterpreted as a moral problem, as sin. The ascetic priest's "main contrivance" is "his utilization of the *feeling of guilt.* . . . Only in the hands of the priest, this real artist in feelings of guilt, did [sin] take shape—and what a shape!" (GM; III; 20). Second, the physiological fact of a feeling of obstruction is treated with the morality of selflessness, self-denial, and self-sacrifice. In a word, it is treated with the *wrong* cure, which is in effect a morality of hibernation, the anaesthetization of life.[25] It is worth repeating: this morality does not cope with sin. It copes with the feeling of weariness of life that Nietzsche refers to as "lethargy" and "obstruction."

The ascetic priest combats the weariness of life in two ways, which are contradictory. He uses "innocent means" and strives to achieve the maximum reduction of the awareness of life (a psychological hibernation). He also resorts to "guilty" means and provokes an "excess of feeling," an excess that, according to Nietzsche, only leads to exhaustion (GM; III; 20).

Nietzsche explicitly states that the attack that religions launch against the sensation of weariness of life is temporarily successful (GM; III; 17, 19), although he is inconsistent on this point. Presumably, the guilt caused by the idea of sin lies at the root of this weariness. However, *none* of the causes that Nietzsche lists to explain this weariness is related to sin. All are physiological conditions produced by circumstances *unrelated* to sin. They include the mixing of races and social classes; immigration with unhealthy results (a race moves to a climate that is inhospitable to "its power of adaptation"); the consequences of "age and fatigue" of a race; faulty diet; and physical illness ("corruption of the blood, malaria, syphilis and such like") (GM; III; 17). It is important to mention that Nietzsche introduces the morality of self-denial as the first remedy the ascetic priest uses against this weariness. "*Firstly,* we fight against that dominant lethargy with methods" that induce hibernation and define the morality of self-denial: "no loving, no hating; . . . no taking revenge; no getting rich; no working; begging; if possible, no consorting with women or as little as possible of this." The direct consequence of these remedies, which aim to reduce the awareness of life, is "*loss of self*" (GM; III; 17). The remedies are thus both behavioral (selflessness, self-denial, and self-sacrifice) and organizational (the creation of the herd). As remedies against weariness, *not against resentment* and *not against suffering,* they are the origin of the morality of self-denial. The value of this morality lies in the fact that its values of selflessness, self-denial, and self-sacrifice are effective means of combating the two great dangers of nausea and pity (GM; III; 14, 17). These values do work.

Despite Nietzsche's objections to the priest (he is not a real doctor) and his medications (they fail to address the real physiological cause) (GM; III; 17, 20), he concedes that the priest's medications work, though this concession is mixed with statements to the contrary: "As a matter of fact, there can be no doubt that such sportsmen of 'holiness' have found a real redemption from that which they fought against with such rigorous training" [Dass solche sportsmen der 'Heiligkeit' . . . in der That *eine wirkliche Erlösung* von dem gefunden haben, was sie mit einem so rigorösen training bekämpften, daran darf man *durchaus nicht zweifeln*] (GM; III; 17, translation mine). Nietzsche states further: "[T]hey finally *rid* themselves of that deep, physiological depression with the help of a system of hyp-notizing methods in countless cases: for which reason their meth-ods belong amongst the most general ethnological facts" (GM; III; 17, emphasis mine). "In fact, the old depression, heaviness and fa-tigue were thoroughly *overcome* [*gründlich überwunden*] by this sys-tem of procedures, life became *very* interesting again: . . . eternally awake, . . . exhausted and yet not tired. . . . Man was thirsting for more pain" (GM; III; 20). The *"formation of a herd* is an essential step and victory in the fight against depression." The growth of the community will kindle "a new interest . . . for individuals as well, which often enough will lift him out of the most personal element in his discontent, his aversion to *himself*" (GM; III; 18).

To sum up: the ascetic priest triumphs over the physiological problem of depression by deploying both his "innocent means" and his guilty ones. The morality of self-denial is part of the ascetic priest's arsenal of "innocent means." The excess of feelings, the "guilty" means, is equally effective. Against the suffering among the herd, the ascetic priest shapes the idea of sin to make this suffer-ing meaningful. Against the weariness of life, the ascetic priest pre-scribes the morality of self-denial. The unintended but clear out-come of sin is to redirect resentment, whereby the ascetic priest preserves the herd by protecting it from the strong, the envy of the strong, and from itself (GM; III; 15); however, this does not alleviate the suffering. The intended purpose of the morality of self-denial is to alleviate weariness of life; it does soothe the suffering.

By finding that "absence of suffering" is "the highest good, the value of values," which good the ascetic priest strives to achieve, Nietzsche accomplishes the goal he stated in the preface: to explain why self-denial, self-sacrifice, and pity had value. They pursued the absence of suffering (GM; III; 17), and did so effectively.

GUILT IS NOT THE ORIGIN OF THE MORALITY OF SELF-DENIAL

Contrary to Nietzsche's stated position in the preface, then, the mo-rality of self-denial is not "the *great* danger to mankind" and is not responsible for opening the gate to "the onset of the final sickness" (GM; P; 5). His arguments demonstrate instead that this morality is a device of nature to preserve itself against the weariness of life. The orgy of feeling, which is quite *different* from the morality of self-denial, is another device of nature to preserve itself through sickness, pain, and cruelty. Nietzsche's aversion to the cruelty of the ascetic priest, however, finds an obstacle in what I called above the Danto proviso.

The two great dangers that Nietzsche identifies—nausea at mankind and pity for mankind—come from the feeling of indebtedness toward God, *not* from the values of selflessness, self-denial, and self-sacrifice. These values merely act as tranquilizers that provide pleasure and a sense of superiority, and that help people overcome their disgust with themselves (GM; III; 19). But then, Nietzsche posits these values as also being responsible for the nausea and pity. The irony of this position is evident: it is a case of confusing cause and effect, a type of confusion that Nietzsche identifies as one of the major flaws of Western philosophy. It does not help him to say that this form of indebtedness arose from a "bestiality of thought" that developed when man was prevented from being a beast in deed. This "bestiality" is inconsistent with his claim that the feeling of indebtedness to God arose within powerful communities, communities in which individuals were still "beasts in deed." If he cannot find a link between nausea and pity, on the one hand, and the morality of self-denial, on the other hand, Nietzsche would still be able to identify the conditions under which the value of certain values emerged, but he would not be able to prove that the morality of self-denial is responsible for the two great dangers. There is another option at his disposal: he might argue that the morality of self-denial is not originally responsible for the two great dangers, but once it is in place, this morality increases the nausea and pity. Yet the textual evidence proves the opposite. The morality of self-denial alleviates and even cures depression. More specifically, it is an antidote, and an effective one, to the feeling of weariness of life.

The ascetic priest shapes sin in order to deal with suffering by giving it meaning. Sin individualizes and empowers its bearers. But sin and its corrosive sense of guilt are not the origin of the morality of self-denial. The ascetic priest invents that morality as a remedy against the feeling of weariness of life, not against sin. Weariness of life does not come from guilt. *Indeed, guilt is severed from the morality of self-denial.* Nietzsche never connects that morality with the guilt that is epitomized in sin. It should be remembered that Nietzsche includes the morality of self-denial as part of the ascetic priest's "innocent means." It is in the "guilty" means, the "excess of feelings," that Nietzsche introduces, *for the first time,* the concept of sin and portrays the ascetic priest as shepherding the sinners to a frenzy of terrors that make them thirst for more pain as compensation for their guilt (GM; III; 20). In short, the morality of self-denial *deals with weariness, and the excess of feelings deals with guilt.*

We thus have two stories and two origins for the emergence of the morality of self-denial, as well as two origins for the notion of sin. In the first story, the slaves find in love a way to circumvent their hatred and to achieve a feeling of superiority. In the second story, love is a remedy introduced by the ascetic priest, in the same way that he introduced sin into the conceptual world of the herd. In the first story, the morality of self-denial is the direct outcome of the slaves' resentment; in the second, it comes from a cunning and strong-willed individual who strengthens the will to power of the herd. The organization of the sufferers into a herd leads, "if only in miniature, to a new and much fuller outbreak of the will to power: the *formation of a herd* is an essential step and victory in the fight against depression" (GM; III; 18).

Equally important, the first origin of sin is indebtedness toward God, though Nietzsche does not call it sin; and, as already indicated, it develops among powerful communities. The second origin of sin is the ascetic priest's invectiveness, in his effort to rule over the suffering and to protect the herd from the strong and from itself (GM; III; 15). After discussing the idea of indebtedness to God in the second essay, Nietzsche goes on to examine the ascetic ideal. It is not until section 20 of the third essay that he returns to the notion of indebtedness toward God and makes an explicit connection between it and the "excess of feelings" and sin. But before discussing the second origin of sin, Nietzsche asks his readers "to remember the last essay," that is, the second essay that concluded with indebtedness to God, "the most terrible sickness ever to rage in man" (GM; II; 22). In the third essay, sin is called "the greatest event in the history of the sick soul up till now: with sin, we have the most dangerous and disastrous trick of religious interpretation" (GM; III; 20). Thus, sin and indebtedness to God are *textually connected*, but the two origins of sin are *disjointed*. In the second essay, the concept of sin was the offspring of man's will to hurt himself through the moralization of guilt, but in the third essay it becomes something shaped by the ascetic priest. In the third essay there is no longer any trace of the powerful communities who hit on the idea of the highest level of indebtedness. Sin is not a fact but a faulty interpretation of the physiological fact of depression. The will to misunderstand suffering and a lack of physiological knowledge are the two reasons that help explain the misinterpretation of the ascetic priest.

GREEKS AND CHRISTIANS: OTHER DETOURS

Nietzsche credits the ascetic priest with providing, for the first time, a meaning to suffering. However, other discussions of his are at variance with this. He also argues that the ancient Greeks and Christianity (before the ascetic priest) had already dealt with the issue of senseless suffering. For the Greeks, the meaning of suffering lay in the delight it afforded to the gods, who feasted on a good spectacle. For Christianity, suffering was part of a machinery of salvation: "neither for the Christian, who saw in suffering a whole, hidden machinery of salvation, nor for naïve man in ancient times, who saw all suffering in relation to spectators or to instigators of suffering, was there any such *senseless* suffering" (GM; II; 7).

In *Schopenhauer as Educator*, Nietzsche writes about the human experience of senseless suffering, but in the *Genealogy* he introduces an important clarification. Man needs to justify life, and the senselessness of suffering appears to be an overwhelming obstacle to reaching this goal. For senseless suffering is equated with a meaningless life. But ruses are always available; and in order to ascribe meaning to his suffering—that is, to justify life by justifying his suffering—man invented gods who became the spectators of a festive play of torments. These gods would not let a joyous play of pain go unnoticed.

The invention of gods was thus the *first* justification of suffering; it was a spectacle of cruelty meant to give pleasure to divine agents. Man's inventiveness did not stop here, however. Rather, he contrived the idea of free will to make the spectacle even more enjoyable to those hidden and divine creatures. Without free will, the gods would have been bored by knowing, in advance, how the spectacle would play out. Life itself is enclosed within a need for meaning, and "[w]ith the aid of such inventions [gods and free will], life then played the trick which it has always known how to play, of justifying itself, of justifying its 'evil'" (GM; II; 7). Well before the entrance of the ascetic priest, man had already found a way to explain and give meaning to his suffering. Nietzsche's own account of the ascetic ideal as *the first* interpretation that provided meaning to suffering is then inaccurate (GM; III; 28).

The ascetic priest comes with a different account. First, he provides meaning to suffering, not to justify life but to justify punishment.[26] Second, instead of justifying suffering by finding an *external* cause (such as the frivolous gods' enjoyment of suffering), a cause outside the sufferers' physical and emotional horizon, the ascetic priest looks for an internal cause that is located within them: the sufferers, not the gods, are responsible for their suffering. They are sinners, and sin stands for a responsibility that moves away from pleasure and is converted into guilt. Third, the ascetic priest concocts a different notion of the divine realm; in his view, God does not feel pleasure at the sight of pain. Rather, God himself is suffering, so much so that He decides to redeem the sufferers and, presumably, free himself from the disquieting vision of torture. Here the story is interrupted, and, in Nietzsche's account, God's plan is thwarted by both the ascetic priest and the herd's ingrained proclivity toward guilt. Redemption only deepened the human sense of guilt. Nietzsche claims that the "primeval" idea of the gods as "the friends of cruel spectacles" is still felt in modern culture; his proofs, he claims, are Luther and Calvin (GM; II; 7).

The Ascetic Priest and Nature

The ascetic priest reinterprets "the greatest feeling of guilt" (guilt before God) (GM; II; 20) as sin, and thus guilt is severed from the pleasure that human beings once found in inner lacerations. Here, Nietzsche seems to pose a distinction between the pleasure principle operating in the herd and the pleasure principle that is active in the ascetic ideal. His distinction suggests that the sickly type congregated in the herd separates cruelty from pleasure. The sickly type, the sinner, has an inner cruelty and an external pleasure: he suffers internally, but he enjoys the pleasure of giving pleasure through the morality of self-denial. The ascetic ideal, by contrast, keeps intact the connection of inner cruelty and pleasure. It seeks "pleasure in hurting," which is probably its "only pleasure." Its "satisfaction is *looked for* and found in . . . pain, voluntary deprivation [and] self-sacrifice" (GM; III; 11).

The ascetic priest organizes the sufferers into a herd; reconceptualizes the sufferers as sinners; identifies the feeling of weariness and its dangers; and prescribes "medications" to alleviate this weariness, that is, to anaesthetize depression.[27] These medications constitute the morality of self-denial, and in this morality, the herd finds the "pleasure of *giving pleasure*" (GM; III; 18). Thus, if we follow Nietzsche's genealogical account, the meaning of the ascetic priest rests in his role as doctor of the sick. His "historic mission" is to rule over suffering, and his purpose is making "the sick *harmless* to a certain degree" (GM; III; 15, 16). His value encompasses, as well, protecting past and present philosophers (GM; III; 6, 10, 13, 15, 16, 28). Moreover, by organizing the herd into a church, the ascetic ideal served a higher and more important purpose, in creating a barrier between the sick and the healthy. Though it was a "provisional safeguarding of those in better health, . . . for a long time that was all! And it was a great deal! It was a *very great deal!*" (GM; III; 16). The "provisional" barrier eventually crumbled, though Nietzsche never states how or why this took place. He also admires the safeguarding that the ascetic priest provided for the healthy, and the depth of the knowledge this priest attained from his perspective. If "we just put ourselves into the only perspective known to the priests for a moment, it is hard to stop admiring how much he has seen, sought and found within this perspective. The *alleviation* of suffering, 'consolation' of every kind—are where his genius lies" (GM; III; 17).

In his genius for contriving consolations, the ascetic priest behaves in a way that is similar to the master organizers of society: he "direct[s] the less ill strictly towards themselves" and "give[s] their *ressentiment* a backward direction" (GM; III; 16). This is a process of internalization of the instincts, but it is completely different from the internalization that resulted from the conquering deeds of the "blond beasts," for two reasons. First, those who were conquered and oppressed by the "beasts" built their inner chamber by themselves, while the herd lacks agency altogether. Second, the "blond beasts" pay scarce attention to the oppressed and instinctively possess a "pathos of distance" from them. The ascetic priest, in contrast, seeks out the vanquished, the sufferers, to be their doctor and to establish his kingdom among them.

Nietzsche's "most fundamental objection" is not to the priest but to his medications, and he never underestimates the cunning of the slaves or the ascetic ideal. He describes Christianity as bold in its search of narcotics to soothe suffering, and as "refined in guessing which emotion to stimulate in order to conquer the deep depression, the leaden fatigue and the black melancholy of the physiologically obstructed, at least temporarily" (GM; III; 17).

Just as the priest is a magician in narcotizing life and unleashing the emotions, he is also relentless in imposing his will to power. The nobles seek to overpower the weak. The ascetic priest seeks to overpower the weak *and* the strong. The ascetic ideal thus shows an overbearing and hubristic attitude: it seeks power, not over one form of life, but over life itself. The strong will settle their disagreements by establishing rules of justice that reflect an equilibrium of equal forces. The ascetic priest will settle nothing. His goal is total victory, which means that his will to power is stronger than any other will and that he will not refrain from using anything that will enhance his power. Here, it is important to realize that Nietzsche is not concerned so much with the ascetic priest's *ressentiment* as he is with this priest's strong will and cunning. The ascetic priest of the first essay belongs to the aristocratic caste and is depicted as impotent, resentful, and moved by a consuming hatred of particular individuals, that is, of the strong (GM; I; 7). The ascetic priest of the third essay reflects an "unparalleled *ressentiment*," but also embodies a sick and strong will that applies medication with good intentions: "However, we have to insist all the more firmly, as fairness demands, that this remedy ['excess of emotion'] was applied with a *good conscience,* that the ascetic priest prescribed it with the utmost faith in its efficacy, indeed its indispensability—often enough nearly collapsing himself at the distress he caused" (GM; III; 20). More important, the ascetic priest is not defined by hatred of particular individuals but by his cunning and his nature as a delicate animal. He is "a new kind of predator," who excels as a "magician and tamer of predators" (GM; III; 15).

Intriguingly, the ascetic priest's cunning seems to represent a problem for Nietzsche: since honesty is a key element of his morality, he does not include cunning among the features of the will to power. In fact, the nobles display "a certain lack of cleverness" anchored on their forgetfulness, while the slaves, by not forgetting and exploring secret corners, grow cleverer (GM; I; 10). But the ascetic priest's dissembling is hardly a reproach. Dissembling, for Nietzsche, is a legitimate form of self-protection. Again, Nietzsche's way out, his only way out, is to make a distinction between a healthy dissembling (that of the first and the new philosophers) and a sick one (that of the ascetic priest).

Contrary to Nietzsche's conclusion, the ascetic ideal is not "counter-nature" (GM; III; 12). Nor is it something alien to us. On Nietzsche's own description, the ascetic ideal is one of the expressions of the deepest instincts of life. It is one of the expressions of nature. To Nietzsche's chagrin, and in light of his own positions, there are contradictions in nature. The contradiction between the will to power and the will to self-preservation is one of them. The contradiction between the delight in cruelty as an affirmation of life (a heroic feast) and delight in cruelty as a suicidal inclination (the herd's sickness) is another. Within Nietzsche's philosophy, the only solution seems to be one couched in medical terms. There is a sick cruelty or, better still, a *sicker* cruelty, since the beginning of cruelty is rooted in sickness, namely, in the internalization of man.

My argument is that Nietzsche significantly alters his genealogy and balks at following the consequences of his historical explorations. In *Ecce Homo* he will put an end to his reluctance and will accept, joyfully, the consequences of *amor fati*. In the *Genealogy*, however, his stories go in one direction, and then he forces them to return to a plot in which the herd plays the role that he, Nietzsche, assigns to it: the role of sufferers looking for a guilty party and for explanations of their suffering. Nietzsche writes a genealogy of sin, a "descent" of bad conscience toward sin, and then changes his story. Sin is presented on the one hand as a feeling of indebtedness toward God, a feeling that arises in the heart of the blond beasts, the master organizers of powerful communities. But he does not follow through this line of thought. Rather, he posits another origin for sin, in terms of the ascetic priest's exceptional weapon to wound the sick herd. Thus, Nietzsche's summary (GM; III; 20) of how bad conscience became sin does not correspond to his own stories.

I do not place too much weight on the fact that Nietzsche does not live up to the rigorous standards of truth he requests from other genealogists, although this is certainly a valid objection. He is not a historian. My argument is that even if we accept the truth claims of his genealogies, we find conclusions that Nietzsche hinted at, but moved away from or glossed over altogether. His failure to face the logical consequences of his own arguments indicates a stunted naturalism, one that recoils from the fact that otherworldliness and the ascetic ideal are natural phenomena, part of the innocence of becoming.

By nature, man wills suffering (GM; III; 28).[28] By nature, all suffering people need to find someone to blame, and, as Nietzsche suggests in *Twilight of the Idols*, this need for revenge is also "a need for *pleasure*" (TI; "Expeditions"; 34). The ascetic priest does nothing but to follow his instinct. His instinct leads him "towards [ruling over suffering] and his own special skill, mastery and brand of happiness are to be had in it" (GM; III; 15). And despite all appearances to the contrary, the ascetic ideal is not a contradiction of life against life but the opposite: a tight defense of life. "Allow me to present the real state of affairs . . . : *"the ascetic ideal springs from the protective and healing instincts of a degenerating life* which uses every means to maintain itself and struggles for its existence" (GM; III; 13). In this well-known formulation, commentators tend to place the emphasis on the form of life, which is degenerating, and pay less attention to the source of this form, which is "the protective and healing instincts." The remainder of Nietzsche's formulation tends to receive even less attention: the ascetic ideal "indicates a partial physiological inhibition and exhaustion against which the deepest instincts of life, *which have remained intact,* continually struggle with new methods and inventions. The ascetic ideal is one such method" (GM; III; 13, emphasis mine). It is a method in which "life struggles with death *against* death" (GM; III; 13). But Nietzsche's conclusion does not follow. The "deepest instincts of life" cannot be equated with death, even less when these instincts are still impervious to the degenerating effects of the ascetic will. They "have remained intact."

The ascetic ideal is thus anchored on *healing instincts* and is one of the inventions the deepest instincts of life, *still intact,* use to preserve life [*die tiefsten, intakt gebliebenen Instinkte des Lebens*]. Seemingly, the ascetic priest never reconciles himself with his nature and this world, which explains his "wish for being otherwise, being elsewhere" (GM; III; 13). But in this very fighting against nature, nature is at work.

According to Nietzsche, "the intertwining of bad conscience with perverse inclinations, all those other-worldly aspirations, alien to the senses, the instincts, to nature" is present in all the ideals that are hostile to life (GM; II; 24). But "other-worldly aspirations" are *not* alien to the instincts. These aspirations are part of human nature and its instincts. Otherwise, these inclinations would be caused by something *outside* life, and there is nothing outside life. When one person soldiers on the battlefield and risks his life, he displays a strong and healthy instinct. When another person starves his body as a means to get access to "another" world, he displays a strong but sick instinct. Both are expressions of nature.

The ontological principle necessarily leads to the conclusion that the triumph of Christian morality is the triumph of a will to power. And so it is; but physiology offers a way out, for Nietzsche, in claiming that it is a sick will to power, a will to power that defines a degenerating way of life. Yet the facts that Nietzsche invokes are stubborn, and the direction of Nietzsche's arguments is clear, though he stops following the consequences of his genealogy. Although the ascetic priest's main contrivance is the utilization of guilt to protect life and to preserve his dominion over suffering, one should not lose sight of the fact that, according to Nietzsche, the introduction of God into the concepts of guilt and duty (the "moralization" of guilt) is also the direct outcome of man's will to hurt himself, a will that Nietzsche associates with pleasure. The ascetic ideal is thus the highest expression of this quest for pleasure through self-flagellation. The ascetic ideal is a *natural phenomenon*. It is instinct. It is a will to misunderstand. And above all, it is the supreme paradox: life protects life by using the fight of nature against nature. Nietzsche's protestations to the contrary, this fight is not anti-natural and does not stunt human flourishing. Sickness is the precondition for this flourishing; and sickness and cruelty are inscribed in nature. They come with life and its territory.

Nature and Necessity

Nietzsche's genealogy, according to Tracy Strong,

> does not seek out and describe the "things" that phenomenology holds to be the world, but rather delineates the *manner* in which the "things" are "made" into "facts." Nietzsche tries to bring out precisely how a particular world is put together and made a world; he shows thereby that that world *has no natural necessity*. Indeed, for Nietzsche, no world has any justification—nor can it, since it must repose on human action.[29]

On my argument, this requires some qualifications. It is true that for Nietzsche, no particular religion was fated to triumph over others. The Greek religion, to him, is the best evidence for this assertion. The Christian ascetic priest, moreover, is very different from the Hindu ascetic monk. But there is an overarching theme, like the plot in a Greek drama, in Nietzsche's analyses. Society is fated to develop, and oppressed individuals are fated to turn inward. The slaves might have developed another moral code, one in which they accepted their condition. But this condition, though plausible, would be a rare occurrence in Nietzsche's universe. Slavery is a form of life, which means that it is a form of the will to power. And, as will to power, the slaves will continue to reflect until they reach a point where they are confident of their superiority. This point is reached through the inversion of values, not through a passive acceptance of their predicament. The will to power assesses, sifts, and interprets the world in order to dominate it, and not merely to find ways of adaptation. Seen in this light, the reflective creatures, the oppressed and downtrodden, against which the nobles are no match, will prevail again and again.

There is a necessity inscribed in life.[30] Before humans are allowed to indulge in the pleasant activities of their inner cruelty, their conquest and taming is presented as an act of fate. The internalization of man, brought about by powerful creatures preying upon weaker ones, was also an act of nature and of fate. Sooner or later, the weak were fated to succumb to the power of the strong. The subjugation of masses of people by the "unconscious artists" of violence was "a compulsion, a fate which *nothing* could ward off" (GM; II; 17, emphasis mine). This means that bad conscience, too, was inscribed in the order of nature. Likewise, the feeling of obstruction is "almost" a necessity (GM; III; 17), and responsibility was a *necessary* development. Responsibility, "*the right to say 'yes' to oneself*," was a "fruit," but everything in the "tree," that is, in the circumstances of the animal man, "was ready and growing towards it!" (GM; II; 3). As Guay notes, "For all Nietzsche's attention to lacunae and contingency within historical processes, the focus of his argument was the discernment of an underlying directionality that has determined the present situation."[31]

Nietzsche traces the different stages of development once humans are fettered by social boundaries, but he never explicitly acknowledges that man's will to hurt himself by inventing the greatest feeling of guilt was a *natural* outcome. The "greatest feeling of guilt" is the advent of the Christian God, and the ascetic ideal is the greatest manifestation of power on earth. Nietzsche tries to find a way out of his dilemma through the physiological principle that human beings are sick animals. But this principle only shows that there are sick forms of pleasure, sick forms of flourishing, and sick forms of the will to power. Since nature does not disown sickness, and sickness cannot renege on its own genealogy, it follows that nature is the origin of sickness. To think otherwise, in Nietzsche's own terms, would be a "violation of reality." Sickness is a natural event. Not until *Ecce Homo* does Nietzsche realize this and provide, not a revaluation of all values, but a philosophy of reconciliation.

THE PATTERN OF GROWTH AND DESTRUCTION

In *The Birth of Tragedy*, Nietzsche describes a pattern, which seems to be inscribed in cultural events, of growth and destruction. Certain cultural events carry the seeds of their own demise. This happened to the Alexandrian culture and is happening in modernity.

Modern society, which is steeped in the Alexandrian and Socratic culture, is struck by a frightening realization: the belief in a universal happiness on earth, a happiness that only knowledge can make possible, turns into "the threatening demand for such an Alexandrian happiness on earth," and this demand can only be met by a "Euripidean *deus ex machina*." The optimism of knowledge leads to an ideal culture that extols the "dignity of man" (via the ideas of democracy and enlightenment) and the "dignity of labor" (via socialism). But this principle—the dignity of man—is predicated on another principle: social and moral equality. Alas, the Alexandrian culture was built on the institution of slavery. The Socratic optimism in knowledge thus brings about expectations that it is unable to satisfy (BT; 18).

Nietzsche invokes this pattern in the *Genealogy*, but he only does so in the case of Christianity and of a will to truth that announces the demise of Christian morality. Christian morality, translated into scientific conscience and intellectual purity, is unable to sustain the Christian dogmas, and the consequence is that truth turns against

Christianity. "In this way," Nietzsche asserts, "Christianity *as a dogma* was destroyed by its own morality, in the same way Christianity *as a morality* must also be destroyed—we stand on the threshold of this occurrence" (GM; III; 27). Nietzsche's words make it clear that the pattern of growth and destruction is "the law of life," and, in this sense, it must be equally applicable to the noble morality, Greek culture, the Roman Empire, and all the events whose downfall he saw as proofs of a degenerating humanity. He states categorically: "All great things bring about their own demise through an act of self-sublimation: that is the law of life, the law of *necessary* 'self-overcoming' in the essence of life" (GM; III; 27).

This pattern, inscribed in an "act of self-sublimation" that is the "law of *necessary* 'self-overcoming,'" is also tunneling its way through the society ever since its creation by the master organizers. The nobles/masters are pregnant with their own annihilation. Their need to master others brings about the oppression and confinement that will spawn the cunning of the slaves. While the nobles are dancing and hunting, the slaves are plotting. The life-denying world of the weak will obliterate the life-affirming world of the nobles. Yet if the nobles/masters succeed—as in the form of a Hindu caste system or the ideal society described in *The Anti-Christ*—then Nietzsche's encompassing notion, the will to power, is placed on a precarious footing. If the weak/slaves are domesticated, where is their will to power?

Is the pattern of growth and destruction depicted above relevant to the will to power? I argue that it is. I suggest taking another direction in examining this concept, in light of Nietzsche's analysis in the *Genealogy*. The will to power demarcates, sifts, chooses, interprets, and stamps a particular seal. It aims at domination and everywhere encounters resistance. But while life-affirming individuals are valuating and reverent animals by *nature*, their will to power is not inclined to the type of meditation that could guard them from the sophisticated barbs and deep valuations of the weak. Because of their physiology and the material conditions in which they live, life-affirming individuals are inured against reflection. Their lives are celebratory, cheerful, and marked by short spurts of energy. They do not ask questions. *That* is their problem. They rejoice in the deeds of the Homeric gods and goddesses, for instance, but compared to Socrates' questions and to the impressive accomplishments of Plato's dialogues or Sophocles' and Euripides' dramas, the Homeric descriptions are games for children. The life-affirming individuals could not and did not last long against the systematic assault launched by Greek rationality and the tragedians' insistence on posing uncomfortable questions. Their will to power fails to create its own spiritual scaffolding; it fails because it is fated to fail. This is "the law of life, the law of *necessary* 'self-overcoming' in the essence of life." This is also one of the reasons why Nietzsche came to use one formula—*amor fati*—to define his philosophy. *Amor fati*, the love of fate, entails a recognition and celebration of one's limits. The world of the nobles sublimates itself through its most forceful creation, which is a mass of enslaved creatures. And that world is bound to perish.

The previous arguments respond to a reasonable reply: even if sickness is a natural event, it does not follow that one ought to prefer it; there are still better possibilities in nature. Applied to a point in time, this argument is correct. As a description of historical processes in Nietzsche's genealogy, however, it is not. Sickness for Nietzsche, as a deepening of the first forms of internalization, is the precondition for cultural achievements. These accomplishments, as Nietzsche's genealogy and cultural analyses intend to show, carry the seeds of an eventual self-overcoming that will take the form of a partial or total obliteration. Apollo is reflecting, while Dionysus is reveling. Socrates is asking questions, while the Athenian aristocracy is memorizing the *Iliad*. Christians are discovering the comforts of life as members of the church, while the Empire is conquering.

These trajectories, still present in *The Anti-Christ*, take a different detour in *Twilight of the Idols*. In 1888, Nietzsche regrets, in rather poignant terms, the triumph of life-denying moralities, bodies, and cultures; defends the innocence of becoming, first mentioned in *Human, All Too Human* in 1878; and writes of the fatality and indispensability of everything. He summarizes his philosophy in *Twilight of the Idols* as follows:

What is the only teaching *we* can have?—That no one *gives* people their qualities, not God or society, parents or ancestors, not even *people themselves*. . . . The fatality of human existence cannot be extricated from the fatality of everything that was and will be. . . . The fact that nobody is held responsible any more, that being is not the sort of thing that can be traced back to a *causa prima*, . . . *only this can constitute the great liberation,*—only this begins to restore the *innocence* of becoming. (TI; "Errors"; 8)

No one is responsible for the way she or he is. As I have already mentioned, this and similar passages point toward Nietzsche's final philosophy of reconciliation.

Chapter Four

ARTISTS, ACTORS, AND
THE AESTHETIC PROJECT

In the last chapters I discussed Nietzsche's genealogy of guilt and his account of the way in which the internalization of instincts led to the morality of self-denial and a gnawing nausea toward life and mankind. But his accounts are hardly complete without taking into consideration the role of art and the artist. Art is necessary to drive away the nausea. And the artist appears as the only one who can act as a bridge to primeval times.

Nietzsche, in his own view, is a philosopher, a poet, a physician, an actor, and an artist. All these dimensions mingle in a rich mosaic that is a sign of an exuberant nineteenth-century individuality. The aesthetic dimension, combining art and acting, is one of the dominant spheres of Nietzsche's theorizing. Ultimately, however, Nietzsche's aestheticism is a refuge, from which he witnesses to and prophesies about the catastrophe that he thinks surrounds him. He confesses that "the problem of the actor" has attracted his attention for a long time (GS; 361), but that the actor is important for the artistic possibilities he makes possible for humankind. Actors, like religious leaders, have disciplined men, allowing them to contemplate themselves at a distance (GS; 78). But perhaps more significant is the actor's constant use of deception, namely, the representation of something different from what he is (even if this something is not so alien as might first appear). Deception, like nearly every idea in Nietzsche, can be understood, originally, as a physiological trait that developed in the right environment and was passed on to future generations. The art of deception originated in the lower classes; they refined the arts of dissembling for the sake of their utility (GS; 361).

LIFE AND AESTHETICS

In *Human, All Too Human,* Nietzsche argues that a true assessment of life will lead us to despise our predicament. Even in the present period of unabashed optimism about science, he states, both philosophy and art want "to bestow on life and action the greatest possible profundity and significance" (H; I; 6).[1] But how can this propensity to ascribe something deeper or higher to life be explained? The answer lies in the lack of any ultimate goal or meaning to life. If an individual, through the use of his imagination, managed to participate in the fortunes and suffering of other people, he would "despair of the value of life; if he succeeded in encompassing and feeling within himself the total consciousness of mankind he would collapse with a curse on existence—for mankind has as a whole *no* goal" (H; I; 33). In "On the Utility and Liability of History for Life," he claims that we have taken a path that leads to disgust with life. For life and injustice go together, and this truth is painful (ULH; 2; 9). Even worse, nature seems to have turned her back on us, by leaving us with a lethal combination of instincts, suffering, and the disposition to console ourselves through metaphysics. "Usually we do not transcend animality, we ourselves are those creatures who seem to suffer senselessly" (SE; 5).

Nature does not provide any help. She "does not take aim, and . . . misses the mark countless times. Artists and philosophers perish because their arrows do not hit their mark."[2] In *Thus Spoke Zarathustra,* Nietzsche introduces the "murderer of God," who was the "ugliest man," a person who could not bear to be seen "through and through," and who decided to kill the witness of his inner secrets (Z; IV; "Ugliest Man"). He represents the individual, who suffers, knows the depths of his own soul, and does not find any reason to justify his existence. In addition, he is consumed by the thought of an ever present spectator. With a God in place, the burden of knowing one's secrets was at least a shared experience. But once this eternal spectator is "murdered," the ugliest man realizes that now he, alone, will be his own witness; and it is far from evident that he possesses the strength to withstand this realization. It was no small consolation that God, as witness, provided him with a "purpose" for his life, a "purpose" that the murder seems to extinguish forever. This context explains a sentence in a fragment of Nietzsche's dated "Summer 1872–Early 1873," on the meaning of life and history: "The *purposes* are what *perplex* us."[3]

Against the backdrop of this perplexity, the idea of life as an aesthetic phenomenon became for Nietzsche an important philosophical project.[4] Presumably, it is the only strategy to make our existence bearable. In 1882, in *The Gay Science*, he extols the arts because of their power to save people from nausea and suicide: "If we had not welcomed the arts and invented this kind of cult of the untrue, then the realization of general untruth and mendaciousness that now comes to us through science—the realization that delusion and error are conditions of human knowledge and sensation— would be utterly unbearable. *Honesty* would lead to nausea and suicide" (GS; 107). Fortunately, art stands in the way of self-immolation, "art as the *good* will to appearance." "As an aesthetic phenomenon existence is still *bearable* for us" (GS; 107). Artists make things bearable to us, but how? They succeed in presenting things as "beautiful . . . and desirable for us," although these things in themselves are not. Art teaches us to look at all the manifestations of life "with pleasure and interest" and educates "our sensibilities so far that we at last cry: 'life, however it may be, is good'" (H; I; 222). Artists act as physicians who "dilute what is bitter" (GS; 299). "Art is above and before all supposed to *beautify* life, thus make *us* ourselves endurable, if possible pleasing to others" (AOM; 174). The artists "of all ages" "are the glorifiers of the religious and philosophical errors of mankind," and their greatest works would have not been possible without metaphysical beliefs (H; I; 220).[5] They are thus deceivers (AOM; 32, 188). Morality itself is an artistic "forgery" that was necessary in order for us to experience pleasure at the sight of the soul.[6] A similar view is presented, almost in passing, in the *Genealogy*[7] and expanded in *Twilight of the Idols*. The dominant instinct in the artist is "directed toward the meaning of art, which is *life*." "Art is the great stimulus to life" (TI; "Expeditions"; 24). As early as 1872, in *The Birth of Tragedy*, Nietzsche identified the Socratic, the artistic, and the tragic culture as three stages of illusions "designed only for the more nobly formed natures, who actually feel profoundly the weight and burden of existence, and must be deluded by exquisite stimulants into forgetfulness of their displeasure" (BT; 18; see also H; I; 148). And in the preface he wrote for this text in 1886, he categorically declared that "the existence of the world is *justified* only as an aesthetic phenomenon" (BT; P; 5).

Nietzsche's most eloquent conceptualizations of art, however, are presented in *Richard Wagner in Bayreuth.*

> The battles art shows are simplifications of the real battles of life; its problems are abbreviations of the infinitely complicated equation of human acting and willing. But the greatness and indispensability of art lies precisely in the fact that it arouses the *semblance* of a more simple world, of an easier solution to the riddles of life. No one who suffers from life can do without this semblance, just as no one can do without sleep. (RWB; 4)

In the tension between the desire for universal knowledge and the individual's capacity to know, art comes to the rescue: "Art exists *so that the bow does not break*" (RWB; 4). Here, in a nutshell, are anticipations of crucial ideas that define Nietzsche's philosophy: the need for appearances, the need to simplify, the riddles of life, and the problem of suffering.

The artists of the theater, that is, the actors, add a new dimension to the stimulants that life requires: "they have taught us the art of viewing ourselves as heroes," of seeing ourselves from a distance that hides the ugliness and meaningless of life (GS; 78). Theater arises when the imagination of people wanes and requires "its legends presented to it on the stage" (D; 265). In the case of the musician, aesthetics comes at a high price. The musician "discovers the tones out of the realm of suffering"; "he finds sounds for those secret and uncanny midnights of the soul"; he knows how to conceal

pain. Unfortunately, despite his mastery in understanding the suffering soul, he is unable to understand what his own spirit wants.
The musician's vanity, according to Nietzsche, spoils and ruins him,
and prevents him from knowing his "real masterpieces" (GS; 87).
Despite his role in deceiving human beings, the artist, Nietzsche
claims, is himself always in danger. He can easily return to the
moods pertaining to the childhood of human history (H; I; 159).

Nietzsche, in fact, came to think that "nothing is more easily
corrupted than an artist" (GM; III; 25). He thus opted for admiring
the work of art and forgetting about the artist (GM; III; 4). His disappointment in the artist led him to revert to the view he had once
expounded, and criticized, in Human, All Too Human. As I will
show, in the latter, Nietzsche describes the artist's work as a trick, in
presenting the work of art as it if were free from the process of becoming. That is, the work appears as the sudden deed of a genius—
or so the artist wants us to believe. In the Genealogy, however, Nietzsche prefers to go along with the trick and regard the work of art as
completed. But his goal here is to send the artist into oblivion. In
most cases, Nietzsche argues, the creator is "something one must
forget if one is to enjoy the work itself" (GM; III; 4). After all, the
artist was only the soil from which the work sprang, suggesting that
the artistic creation was fated to come to be.

Even more disturbing than the corrupting bent of the artist, according to Nietzsche, is that the artist's life is mired in falsity. He is
cursed to represent what he is not. If he were Achilles, he would not
be Homer; if he were Faust, he would not be Goethe; and, we might
add, if he were the philosopher/legislator, he would not be Nietzsche.[8] The artist's destiny is to be eternally separated from the "real,"
and his great temptation is to attempt "to lay hold of actuality." That
is, "one can understand how [the artist] may sometimes weary to the
point of desperation of the eternal 'unreality' and falsity of his innermost existence—and that then he may well attempt what is most
forbidden him, to lay hold of actuality, for once actually to be. With
what success? That is easy to guess" (GM; III; 4). The "success" is
his "velleity" and his corruption.

In Book 5 of The Gay Science, the book he added in the second
edition (1887), Nietzsche's attitude is equally deprecating, though

his target is not so much the artist as the modern age that is molding art. Section 356, "How things will become ever more 'artistic' in Europe," is a critique of the culture of modern Europe, where art is not considered the precondition to making life "bearable." Nietzsche's critique focuses on the tendency to compel everyone to make a living, to play a role, and to have an occupation.[9] He decries the fact that individuals lose sight of the many accidents involved in their "vocation": "the role has actually *become* character; and art, nature" (GS; 356). But his argument changes; it is no longer a critique of the naive faith that one is predestined for a particular occupation. Rather, it is a critique of hubris. In modernity, the individual "becomes convinced that he can do just about everything and can manage almost any role, and everybody experiments with himself, improvises, makes new experiments, enjoys his experiments; and all nature ceases and becomes art" (GS; 356). Nietzsche's sympathy for a hierarchical and stratified social order leads him to claim that a "rigid" belief in the "predestined" character of one's occupation allows honesty and loyalty, thus creating optimum conditions for stable institutions. An honest individual will treat as a duty his compliance with the rules and expectations of his role.

The possibility that such honesty and loyalty are products of self-deception is unimportant. What is significant is that the acceptance of a role within a social hierarchy constitutes a fertile ground for "nature," namely, for institutions that reflect the unequal character of individuals. When "all nature ceases and becomes art," the moorings that kept each person in place are swept away. "Art" thus has a corrosive influence on the crucial principle of rank among people; it opens the gates for the chaos of human equality. Art is thus both a balm and a poison. One is tempted to draw the conclusion that the cacophony of a more artistic Europe would fit perfectly with Nietzsche's own preference for the reveling Dionysius, as opposed to the reflecting Apollo. But this is not the case. He finds instead an "artistic" façade, an excuse for that dishonesty and antinature that the principle of equality epitomizes, and he warns of the dangers of too much acting.[10]

Art, however, is exactly what he advocates in *Beyond Good and Evil* (1886), and in the preface to the 1887 edition of *The Gay Science:*

to be "[a]dorers of forms, of tones, of words . . . [a]nd therefore—
artist" (GS; P; 4). Philosophers are experimenters and, as such, artists. The idea of experiment is defined as "the great liberator,"
namely, "the idea that life could be an experiment of the seeker for
knowledge—and not a duty, not a calamity, not trickery" (GS; 324).
No deception is intended by the person who seeks knowledge. He
is probably playing the role of a reluctant actor. His philosophy of
desecration, of playing with holy things, leaves no room for doubt
(GS; 382), and even less so his call to believe in "the whole Olympus
of appearance" (GS; P; 4).[11]

As an artist, Nietzsche presents himself as the aleph, that point
in which all time is contained, and as one who is able to observe it.
He intends (and he certainly thought he succeeded) to experience
"the history of humankind as a whole as *his own history*," as the person "whose horizon encompasses thousands of years past and future, being the heir of all the nobility of all past spirit" (GS; 337).
"For the human being carries around with him the memory of all
previous generations."[12] But Nietzsche appears to be the only person
aware of this historical memory. He describes himself as the dreaming vessel, through which the entire past of humanity continues and
makes claims on the living.[13] The "human and animal past, indeed
the whole primal age and past of all sentient being continues" and
runs through him. "I suddenly woke up in the midst of this dream,
but only to the consciousness that I am dreaming and that I must go
on dreaming lest I perish" (GS; 54).[14] But somehow in Book 5 of *The
Gay Science* the dream became reality or reality became the dream,
or in any case the boundaries of these two territories melted away,
and Nietzsche woke up. His aesthetic project was still the same: he
was still the aleph, who wanted to see European morality from a
distance and needed "to create for oneself eyes to survey millennia"
(GS; 380). In this alephian survey, he must "first of all 'overcome'
this time in himself—this is the test of his strength—and consequently not only his time but also his prior aversion and contradiction *against* this time, his suffering from this time, his un-timeliness,
his *romanticism*" (GS; 380).

Did Nietzsche accomplish this goal? Or did he fail to overcome
his "suffering from his time"? Nietzsche's stories are like a castle

with closed doors; only when one approaches does one notice that the doors are unlocked and, in many cases, ajar.

HONESTY AND SELF-KNOWLEDGE: THE NEED TO BE MISUNDERSTOOD

Nietzsche specified two kinds of suffering: suffering from an over-flowing of life and suffering from an impoverishment of life (GS; 370).[15] The former leads to a Dionysian forest, to an altar of flowers where half-creatures—"poetizing philosophers and philosophizing artists" (H; I; 110)—celebrate nature, and the latter leads to guilt. If Nietzsche overcomes his suffering, he destroys the most important component that makes him a unique individual, among other things an individual who abhors Kantian universalism and treats it as a sign of bad taste. For Nietzsche, suffering is a training ground as well as an opportunity to show self-control, which is one of the signs of a higher spirituality. "But [the individual] is at the height of his powers when he resists the flood of his emotions and virtually de-rides it; only then does his spirit emerge fully from its hiding place—a logical, mocking, playful, and yet awesome spirit" (GS; 96). Self-control can also appear in pedestrian ways; Nietzsche gives as an example his complete composure in taking care of a man who had suddenly collapsed in front of him one morning (D; 119).[16]

The individual should remain faithful "to what is true and au-thentic" in him (GS; 99). This is the test of his honesty. This is the only thing that is "needful: that a human being should *attain* satis-faction with himself, whether it be by means of this or that poetry and art; only then is a human being at all tolerable to behold" (GS; 290). Dissatisfaction is the predicament of modern man. "The man of 'modern ideas,' that proud ape, is immoderately dissatisfied with himself: that is certain" (BGE; 222). And honesty, satisfaction with oneself, is the virtue of the free spirits.

> Honesty—granted that this is our virtue, from which we cannot get free, we free spirits—well, let us labour at it with all love and malice and not weary of 'perfecting' ourselves in *our* virtue, the only one we

> have. . . . It is probable that we shall be misunderstood and taken for
> what we are not: but what of that! . . . Our honesty, we free spirits—
> let us see to it that our honesty does not become our vanity, our
> pomp and finery, our limitation, our stupidity! (BGE; 227; see also
> D; 370, 556)

This honesty is the cornerstone of Nietzsche's very personal morality, a morality in which the individual owes a reckoning only to
himself (AOM; 179).[17] It is the limit to the dangerous game that the
philosopher is expected to play with himself, the boundary to his
experiments, or the one unacceptable danger in a life meant to be
lived perilously.[18] Schopenhauer's honesty, for example, greatly attracted Nietzsche (SE; 2). The "last pope" praises Zarathustra's honesty, a virtue that will lead him "beyond good and evil" (Z; IV;
"Retired"). Nietzsche even praises the ascetic ideal, as long as it is
honest (GM; III; 27).[19] "Your enemy you shall seek, your war you
shall wage—for your thoughts. And if your thoughts be vanquished,
then your honesty should still find cause for triumph in that" (Z; I;
"War"). Honesty requires that the individual "must organize the
chaos within him by concentrating on his genuine needs." These
"genuine needs" always stand against imitation (ULH; 10). A person
who wants to promote the culture of a people ought to remove the
damaging effects of history and restore its health, which means that
he has to rediscover the people's "instincts and with them its honesty" (ULH; 4).

Nietzsche's morality stands in an elusive relationship to both
deception and self-knowledge. He admits to possessing "an unconquerable mistrust of the *possibility* of self-knowledge" (BGE; 281),
and at times explicitly describes self-knowledge as an impossible
goal (D; 115). "There must be a kind of aversion in me to *believing*
anything definite about myself" (BGE; 281). Once this aversion is
registered, one can understand why Nietzsche treats the taste for
the unconditional as the "worst of all tastes." "[T]he slave wants the
unconditional," that state in which the dishonesty or delusion about
the world leads him to deny his world and to hope for an afterlife
(BGE; 31, 46). In the *Genealogy*, Nietzsche is more emphatic. "We
'men of knowledge' have gradually come to mistrust believers of all

kinds" (GM; III; 24). These believers are proud of their strong faith and present it as the proof of their beliefs. They, along with the counterfeit "free spirits" Nietzsche has discovered, are still imprisoned within the "unconditional will to truth" (GM; III; 24). They do not want to recognize what they see, which is, not by accident, Nietzsche's definition of a dishonest lie. "I call a lie: wanting *not* to see something one does see, wanting not to see something *as* one sees it: whether the lie takes place before witnesses or without witnesses is of no consequence. The most common lie is the lie one tells to oneself; lying to others is relatively the exception" (AC; 55). The same principle—to perform a deed without the presence of witnesses—applies to courage (Z; IV; "Higher Man"), as well as to the tests the individual must submit himself, those tests in which he is the only judge and witness (BGE; 41).

The individual can and may engage in deception, dissembling, and cunning, but he must be careful to avoid misunderstanding and deceiving himself.[20] This is why both Thucydides and Machiavelli are special to Nietzsche: neither attempted to deceive himself.[21] This is also the place to draw an important line regarding the use of masks and the art of disguise. No matter how many masks an individual may wear, Nietzsche's arguments suggest an important distinction between hiding and denying. Hiding is a show of cunning and mastery. It is a strategy to reveal, in the dark alleys of one's spirit, what one is or thinks one is (for Nietzsche, there is no difference between these two states). Denying is quite different; it is to suppress both in private and in public what one is. This is the trait of the Socratic and the ascetic type. A Nietzschean mask is a strategy of hiding; it is a way of concealing one's spirit in order to protect it. It is an act not of denial, which is a sign of dishonesty, but of affirmation.

But deception, like the will to power, is sewn into the very fabric of life. Human beings have a certain perception of reality, which is not necessarily more accurate than the perception other creatures might have. But we also have words, which are illusory bridges to a reality that, we imagine, becomes stable in the words that we utter. But in fact, reality is like an elusive web, or like a goblin who can take a thousand shapes and who inhabits a forest of infinite dimensions. Words are the illusory bridge to what is not there (Z; III; "Convalescent"). The so-called "thing in itself" was never a "thing," never "in," and never "itself." Words are the vehicles of knowledge, which is the attempt to bring the unfamiliar closer and to make it familiar, and fear may be the root of knowledge (GS; 355). If knowledge of the "thing in itself" is ruled out, as it was by Kant, then truth and falsehood also disappear, good and evil are fictions, and knowledge itself is brought into question. Nature is neither true nor false; the world is neither good nor evil. The "will" too is a fiction, and we lack an organ for knowledge (GS; 354). The "honest old 'I' has evaporated into" an "it" (BGE; 17). Yet, nothing of this dissuades Nietzsche from also talking about "facts." As late as 1886, he refers to facts, not in the ambit of historical events but in the sphere of interpretations: "I shall never tire of underlining a concise *little fact* which these superstitious people [the logicians] are loath to admit—namely, that a thought comes when 'it' wants, not when 'I' want; so that it is a *falsification* of *the facts* to say: the subject 'I' is the condition of the predicate 'think'" (BGE; 17, first and third emphases mine).

Nietzsche argues, further, that "even with this 'it thinks' one has already gone too far; this 'it' already contains an *interpretation* of the event and does not belong to the event itself" (BGE; 17). Faithful to an argument that he will make explicit in the *Genealogy,* namely, that man is a "valuating animal," Nietzsche asserts four propositions here: (1) that the entity that faces the event (thinking) is an "it"; (2) that this "it" offers an "interpretation"; (3) that this "interpretation" is *independent* of the event itself; and (4) that there is something which can be called the "event itself." These are open to at least three objections. First, by separating the *interpretation* from the *event,* isn't Nietzsche stipulating an "I" who interprets, in that an interpretation implies an interpreter? Second, by presenting the event as independent of interpretation, the event reappears as the "thing in itself," which Nietzsche is committed to debunking. Third, by making such judgments, Nietzsche at least suggests that there is an agent who can make those judgments, and this agent might well be the "honest old 'I'" he seeks to leave behind.

In other words, Nietzsche shows no intention of jettisoning his status as a seeker of knowledge, even while asserting that the objects of knowledge are inaccessible, that humanity's truths are *"irre-futable* errors" (GS; 265), and that the central means of knowledge—words—bear the imprint of deception from their very creation.[22] Thus, his self-characterization as the first tragic figure is accurate. He is a seeker of knowledge, a seeker of an illusion, or, in the worst-case scenario, the seeker of a truth that would be too dangerous for life. But tragedy is not the last word. The search for knowledge is also an opportunity for Nietzsche to deploy his Dionysian disposition. For knowledge, according to Nietzsche, "is a world of dangers and victories in which heroic feelings, too, find places to dance and play" (GS; 324).

Yet (a "yet" is always a sign of icy conditions on the slippery roads of language), he does not want to be deceived, and sees himself as a truth seeker still drinking from the metaphysical fountain that envisions truth as divine (GS; 344). At first sight, Nietzsche appears inebriated by the bright prospects that open before him: man is the sphinx that speaks, the one who perceives and who describes himself. Hence the need for a chemistry of moral sensations (H; I; 1). But language is inviting and alluring, and we are bewitched by sounds promising a decipherment of what those sounds will never apprehend. We are destined to self-deception. But we can turn the tables by realizing that such a deception is part of what we are. This is far from being a paradox: realizing this self-deception is the first step toward honesty, just as realizing that we are a war of instincts is a necessary stage toward self-overcoming.

This leads to a twofold predicament. First, the individual faces the daunting and impossible task of organizing his inner chaos in order to ascertain his genuine needs (ULH; 10). Second, misunderstanding is both a need and a boundary of his moral horizon. Despite Nietzsche's occasional insistence that he and the "new philosophers" do not "want to be misunderstood or taken for what [they are] not" (BGE; 44),[23] no philosopher in the Western canon has given more attention than Nietzsche to the intricacies and inevitability of misunderstanding. "Every profound thinker is more afraid of being understood than of being misunderstood" (BGE; 290).[24] The new philosophers *"want* to remain a riddle in some respects" (BGE; 42). Nietzsche writes, not to be understood, but to produce the opposite effect. He writes about masks, dances, and abysses. Artists ought to be actors; so, too, philosophers. Plato had a copy of Aristophanes under his pillow (BGE; 28). For the wanderer he is, Nietzsche wants, not one, but two masks (BGE; 278). In the case of *serious opera,* "[a]ll of its masters take pains to prevent anyone from understanding their characters" (GS; 80). Misunderstanding is a radical need in Nietzsche's philosophy. For if he is understood, this shows that his fellow human beings are getting close, too close! to his secret citadel (BGE; 26), to the cave where he consorts with his eagle and serpent. Understanding can even spoil his good writing, he claims. "Most thinkers write badly because they communicate to us not only their thoughts but also the thinking of their thoughts" (H; I; 188).[25] In *Thus Spoke Zarathustra,* the hunchback voices aloud his lack of conformity with Zarathustra's double-talk. "But why does Zarathustra speak otherwise to his pupils than to himself?" (Z; II; "Redemption"). Nietzsche seems to exude joy in describing the "not altogether innocent readiness of the spirit to deceive other spirits and to dissemble before them . . . in this the spirit enjoys the multiplicity and cunning of its masks, it enjoys too the sense of being safe that this brings for it is precisely through its protean arts that it is best concealed and protected!" (BGE; 230)

There is no danger here for Nietzsche, since he might be misunderstanding himself, and others' understanding of him would merely amount to apprehending one of his fictional characters, that is, the fleeting or enduring errors he happens to believe at any given moment. The real danger lies elsewhere: if Nietzsche is understood, even if his audience or pursuers are only ensnared by his errors, this means that he is living in the present; and what does philosophy have to do with today? "We children of the future, how could we be at home in this today?" (GS; 377).[26] If he is understood, he would no longer be "the bad conscience" of his age (BGE; 212), nor would he inhabit past and future centuries. "Live in *ignorance* about what seems most important to your age. Between yourself and today lay the skin of at least three centuries" (GS; 338).

The first act of the tragedy, in the search for knowledge, is that one does not want to be deceived, one seeks truth, but one knows, or (if knowing is too demanding a verb) somehow senses, that one might well be misunderstanding oneself. As Michel Haar observes,

The man of knowledge, the conquering and faithful one, is an artist who does not know himself. To know means simply to rediscover schemas that the artistic instinct has already cast over things. . . . if art has to become the highest value, it is because art corresponds best to, is most adequate to, the essence of the Will to Power as permanent growth of the self, as unfathomable depth of beneficent and exalting illusion, and as reinforced affirmation.[27]

Yet, the affirmation to which Haar refers above could signify that although one ought not to judge life, one also ought to be honest with oneself, engage in self-creation, and learn to acknowledge one's nature: this is a sign of nobility. It "will always be the mark of nobility that one feels no fear of oneself, expects nothing infamous of oneself" (GS; 294). And how could one fear oneself, when we "want to be the poets of our life"? (GS; 299; see also 302). "We, however, *want to become those we are*—human beings who are new, unique, incomparable, who give themselves laws, who create themselves" (GS; 335).

The artist, as a good individual, shows self-control, but only a narrow line separates self-control from the annihilation of self-creation. When an individual's self-control builds a barricade between him and the world of errors, from which he learns, the narrow line vanishes. The individual himself turns "into a castle," whose eternal guardian he is. This castle becomes a prison for the individual who is unwilling to accept that one "must be able to lose oneself occasionally if one wants to learn something from things different from oneself" (GS; 305; D; 271).

This, however, is the predicament of Nietzsche's individualism. Nietzsche's philosopher is like an arrow that is frozen, but at least pointing toward the infinite darkness of solitude. It is the artist's predicament as well: he is prejudiced against human beings. Nobility requires the citadel of solitude,[28] and this citadel reveals that Nietzschean individuals are "virtuosos of contempt," who "love nature the less humanly it behaves, and art when it is the artist's escape from man, or the artist's mockery of man, or the artist's mockery of himself" (GS; 379).

ART, SCIENCE, AND DIONYSIAN INTOXICATION

Tragedy, as I mentioned above, is not the last word for Nietzsche, and neither is acting. Deception is a part of life, but Nietzsche is far from enthusiastic about the road the ancient Greeks once traveled, for example. *"They really became actors."* And in this role, he asserts, they conquered Rome. Nietzsche confesses to what he sees as a frightening prospect: we moderns are following the same path that the Greeks trod, "and whenever a human being begins to discover how he is playing a role and how he *can* be an actor, he *becomes* an actor" (GS; 356; see also AOM; 221). When dissimulation is practiced over a long period of time, it becomes nature (D; 248, 306). Founders of religions prepare their act with such a degree of care and confidence that they end up believing in themselves (H; I; 52).

In an intriguing section of *The Gay Science* (356), Nietzsche protests against a view of art that destroys any possibility of lasting constructions. This view pits the actor against the architect. Acting is a fleeting moment; the actor's concern is to play an ephemeral role, even though he devotes his life to this. In contrast, the architect, like the philosopher, is a builder of society, and for Nietzsche, there is no longer any material left for building. The architect is always influenced by power, and the "highest feeling of power and security" requires a *"grand style"* (TI; "Expeditions"; 11; see also AC; 58). In other words, today he is a vanishing species. For the architect needs sound foundations; he demands a type of power that is unheard of in modernity; and he needs to carve out both a place and the individual who will occupy it. This requires a dual perspective of time and greatness, the same one that the Romans displayed when they saw themselves as members of a project that was worth preserving and expanding, either in its republican or imperial form. Modernity has erased this kind of perspective. "For what is dying out is the fundamental faith that . . . man has value and meaning only insofar as he is *a stone in a great edifice;* and to that end he must be *solid* first of all, a 'stone'—and above all not an actor!" (GS; 356). Shortly after writing this, Nietzsche would put in Pascal's mouth his own words: "How you have bungled and botched my beautiful stone!" (BGE; 62).

Modernity has the stones but lacks the edifice. And even the stones are weakened by utilitarian and religious concerns. This argument of Nietzsche's in *The Gay Science* was short-lived, though it is revisited in *The Anti-Christ* when he expounds his pyramidal view of society.[29] Books 4 and 5 of *The Gay Science* are poetic utterances, at times almost a Delphic mosaic of words. Their dominant theme is the centrality of the individual and his relation to art. Art is the conduit to a higher form of suffering, which is present when the individual, like Homer, invents his own gods (GS; 302).

There is no better way, for Nietzsche, to conjure up the idea of an individual as an aesthetic project than by comparing life to a poem. Art, like religion, allows the individual to impose a pattern of beauty on things which, in themselves, distill only ugliness. But when one follows the Homeric pattern and writes one's own epic, invents one's own gods, and thus reverses the wrong detours taken by humankind, one does not fall into a god—that is, one does not invent a god to whom one is accountable. Rather, all the magnified powers of multiple divinities, namely, the rich polytheism of the will to power, revert back to their originators—the alephian artists and actors who dance on the brink of a new thirst, their search for knowledge. Inadvertently, they may turn out to be philosophers. The poet whose life has not become a "fine poem" cannot be a teacher of men (H; I; 172).

Or, the artist could become a valet, a mere servant to the effusive but shallow fame of the age. The kind of art that an artist practices shows his type as a unique individual. This is the justification of a "monological art," one that, like the tests the philosopher endures before himself, proves whether the artist can stand firm and exclaim without blinking, "My art does not need an audience; it does not need a witness." This is the ideal of art for the sake of art, which is removed from, but parallel to, Nietzsche's early view of science as a pursuit of knowledge for the sake of knowledge. "I do not know of any more profound difference in the whole orientation of an artist than this, whether he looks at his work in progress (at 'himself') from the point of view of the witness, or whether he 'has forgotten the world,' which is the essential feature of all monological art; it is based *on forgetting*, it is the music of forgetting" (GS; 367). This is art in the labyrinth of solitude; art as Zarathustra; art as the new philosopher would portray it.[30]

The Nietzschean artist is the warrior who crushes his nemesis—the scientist—and then is ashamed that he ever considered him an opponent worthy of a contest. In his earliest formulations, however, Nietzsche treated art as a primitive atavism, which is shrouded in magic and images of deception. The scientist was the further step of humanity, after the artist. But even this earlier view includes the idea that the artist brought consolation. "Art makes the sight of life bearable by laying over it the veil of unclear thinking" (H; I; 151). As usual, the Greeks set the right example: "They do not deceive themselves, but they deliberately and playfully embellish life with lies. . . . and they knew that even misery could become a source of enjoyment solely through art (H; I; 154).[31] The struggle between artist and scientist continues in Nietzsche's late writings; he wants to scrutinize himself with the same rigor he expects from a scientific experiment. But he is already pushing science to the background of his meditations, until it too becomes an enemy.

The evolution of Nietzsche's assessment of art shows a labyrinthine relationship, which finally triumphs in defining his identity. In his last published works, he represents himself, not only and not primarily as a philosopher, but as Dionysus, the god of orgiastic intoxication—which is one of the traits of the artist. In *The Birth of Tragedy*, Nietzsche presents a metaphysics of music, and he is enamored of the artistic explosions that he finds in Greek tragedy. This line of thinking was interrupted by his short-lived affair with science in *Human, All Too Human,* where Nietzsche offers a complex picture of art as an enterprise that is closer to nature than is science, and of artists as individuals who throw over reality a veil of unclear thinking. "Art begins from the natural *ignorance* of mankind as to his interior (both bodily and as regards character): it does not exist for physicists or philosophers" (H; I; 60). Our knowledge of ourselves is superficial, and "[t]here is much illusion involved in [the] created characters of the artists; they are in no way living products of nature, but, like painted people, a little too thin, they cannot endure inspection from close to" (H; I; 160). The artist is a deceiver who is always at pains to make his audience think that his works do not gradually "become" but spring into existence from nowhere, revealing the work of a genius. "The artist knows that his work produces its full effect when it excites . . . a belief that it came into being with a miraculous suddenness" (H; I; 145, 155; see also AOM; 176). This is also Nietzsche's characterization of monumental history, which could be called "a collection of 'effects in themselves'" without regard for their causes (ULH; 2).

The artist is still in the realm of the "fantastic, mythical, uncertain, extreme, the sense for the symbolical, the over-estimation of the person, the belief in something miraculous in genius." He "does not wish to be deprived of . . . profound interpretations of life and guards against simple and sober methods and results" (H; I; 146). The "science of art" has to counter the illusion that the perfect emerged instantaneously (H; I; 145). And the scientist, the one who shows "devotion to the true in any form," enters the scene as the artist's adversary (H; I; 146).

Much more than an adversarial relationship is involved here. It is one of replacement, followed by the gradual effacement of the artist. "The scientific man is the further evolution of the artistic" (H; I; 222). Artists are doomed. "The artist will soon be regarded as a glorious relic, and we shall bestow upon him, as a marvellous stranger upon whose strength and beauty the happiness of former ages depended, honours such as we do not grant to others of our own kind." However, we experience nostalgia for the nourishment that has been lost. "The best in us has perhaps been inherited from the sensibilities of earlier ages to which we hardly any longer have access by direct paths; the sun has already set, but the sky of our life still glows with its light, even though we no longer see it" (H; I; 223).

But the sun did not set, in fact. Even in *Human, All Too Human*, Nietzsche argues that an individual who has within himself the two conflicting powers of "the spirit of love with the plastic arts or music" and the "spirit of science" is in a position to make "the finest discoveries" in the realm of culture. This individual must accommodate the two conflicting powers of art and science; in his soul there must "reside mediating powers with the strength and authority to settle any contention that might break out" (H; I; 276). Nietzsche, however, did not say what these "mediating powers" were. In *The Gay Science,* science suffers a gradual reversal, while art is reevaluated and declared an ally. Here Nietzsche treats science as still trapped within the metaphysics of truth, a metaphysics that, by his own confession, is also his own prison (GS; 344). But he increasingly takes from the artist and the scientist the activity that will later define his new philosopher: all of them are experimenters. The scientist has to test the validity of his hypotheses through experimentation. The artist in his sphere does the same: "All the great artists have been great workers, inexhaustible not only in invention but also in rejecting, sifting, transforming, ordering" (H; I; 155). Nietzsche comes to see life as an experiment, for the seeker of knowledge (GS; 324; see also 319). Science is obsessed with certainties, and art is suspicious of knowledge. Nietzsche, ultimately, treats the demand for certainty as an expression of an instinct of weakness (GS; 347). In contrast, he is willing to take the risks associated with the artistic mood: "To lose firm ground for once! To float! To err! To be mad!" For these states were "part of the paradise and the debauchery of bygone ages" (GS; 46). Yet the individual ought to practice the rigor of the scientist in evaluating his own experiences: "But we, we others who thirst after reason, are determined to scrutinize our experiences as severely as a scientific experiment—hour after hour, day after day" (GS; 319).

In *Human, All Too Human,* Nietzsche did not hide his enthusiasm for the encroaching nature of science and its eventual defeat of metaphysics. Artists are criticized because they insist on bestowing a higher significance on life, one that does not measure up to the cold scrutiny of science. In *The Gay Science,* however, the former account of the evolution of the artistic is assailed on the opposite grounds, and scientists are derided for their inability to bequeath any meaning to life. "A 'scientific' interpretation of the world . . . might therefore still be one of the *most stupid* of all possible interpretations of the world, meaning that it would be one of the poorest in meaning" (GS; 373).[32] Artists, by contrast, make "everything healthy by making everything *run!*" (BGE; 28). For art rejects dogmas and abhors Egyptianism.

In 1888, in *Twilight of the Idols,* art is fully reintegrated into Nietzsche's philosophy, while scientific pursuits are deprecated.[33]

But only a year before this reconciliation, in *On the Genealogy of Morality*, Nietzsche offered valuable insights concerning his need for art, especially in its relation to tragedy, and made no secret of his mixed feelings about the artistic nature. His insights reveal the full extent to which his aestheticism was much more than a play between different styles and genres.[34] It was for him a refuge. The inner desperation felt by artists, by the young who discover the falsity of metaphysics in *Human, All Too Human* (see H; I; 17), and by Nietzsche himself, who yearns to find a meaning for his own life and a role for himself in the stories he narrates, explains why his aestheticism is his last refuge. For artists, after all, are not trustworthy; they are not independent enough to stand *"against* the world"": ""artists never stand apart; standing alone is contrary to their deepest instincts"" (GM; III; 5).[35] Again, he presents Wagner as the exemplary case of this failing. But a great tragedian—and Nietzsche, as we have seen, envisions himself in the light of tragedy—is one who comes to realize that history and the world have been a tragedy, and this is a necessary step to leaving behind the age of tragedy. A great tragedian ""arrives at the ultimate pinnacle of his greatness only when he comes to see himself and his art *beneath* him—when he knows how to *laugh* at himself"" (GM; III; 3).

Life is not a laughing matter, however. After describing the Dionysian intoxication of the artist's psychology, Nietzsche depicts art as the link between individuality and power: ""This *compulsion* to transform into the perfect is—art. Even all that which he is not becomes for him none the less part of his joy in himself; in art, man takes delight in himself as perfection."" The genuine Christian, in contrast, displays an ""anti-artisticality of instinct"" (TI; ""Expeditions""; 9; see also BGE; 62).

We thus approach a perplexing problem, but not one, according to Nietzsche, that a reader of souls will be unable to decipher. Intoxication, as one of the trademarks of the Dionysian state, ""must first have heightened the excitability of the entire machine: no art results before that happens."" ""All kinds of intoxication,"" Nietzsche insists, possess the power to explode as an artistic creation (TI; ""Expeditions""; 8). The Dionysian state intensifies ""the entire emotional system""; this state ""discharges all its powers of representation, imitation, transfiguration, transmutation, every kind of mimicry and play-acting, *conjointly*." In this state the facility of metamorphosis reaches one of its highest expressions, "in a similar way to certain types of hysteric, who also assume *any* role at the slightest instigation." The Dionysian man is in a process of constant transformation (TI; "Expeditions"; 10, first emphasis mine). Though it is worth noticing the association Nietzsche makes between "hysterics" and the "Dionysian man," it is more important, for my purposes, to focus on the idea of a continuous transformation, namely, in the facility to play any role, "conjointly," under conditions of intoxication.

"The facility of metamorphosis" is important, and should be understood in connection with the way Nietzsche treats his multiplicity of literary styles as reflections of the multiplicity of his inner states. Each inner state requires a particular style, and he was able to make the right fit. (This is why, in his judgment, he could use the German language in a way that nobody had ever done.) The perplexity, referred to above, arises because Nietzsche describes the "modern soul" as a "chaos" produced by the mixing of classes and races that takes place in the age of democracy, and he includes himself as part of this "chaos." Although he is celebrating this "chaos" and interprets it as an "artistic refinement" (BGE; 224), he is not oblivious to his own indictment of the age of modernity and democracy as an age of decadence (BGE; 203). "Democracy has always been the declining form of the power to organize" (TI; "Expeditions"; 39). In other words, describing the modern soul as a chaos is another way of describing a multiplicity of inner states. If Nietzsche too, partakes of a multiplicity of inner states, then he shares the decadence of his times—the same era that he wants to contemplate from a safe distance of at least three centuries. The Dionysian person, according to Nietzsche, can change into different forms "conjointly," and this description fits the idea of chaotic transformations of the modern soul. It is likely that Nietzsche noticed the tension in his thought here; in any event, he made a distinction between the chaos of modernity and the multiplicity of states that *he* experienced. An explanation of the perplexing problem, however, is simpler. Nietzsche was not afraid to admit the truth to himself: he was a decadent, but his difference from other decadents is that he has always found, instinctively, the *"right* means" to combat his decadence (EH; "So Wise"; 2).

Aaron Ridley asserts that Nietzsche, in his glorification of the Dionysian, does not adhere to his own standard of honesty. Here he expands on Julian Young's argument that a Dionysian acceptance of becoming is the opposite of courage, since the Dionysian individual plunges into the whole flux of becoming and thus "achieves immunity to the penalties of being *part* of that flux."[36] "Indeed, so completely has [honesty] gone missing that we are here squarely back in the territory, not of making life *'bearable'* by turning it into 'an aesthetic phenomenon' (GS 107), but of claiming that 'as an *aesthetic phenomenon* . . . existence and the world are eternally *justified'* (BT 5). The Dionysian art of 'becoming', then, to which Nietzsche accords the highest status of all, represents a travesty of the intellectual conscience."[37]

The plausibility of Ridley's interpretation lies in two assumptions: first, that there is an inconsistency between one's willingness to see oneself intoxicated, through the Dionysian, in the whole of becoming, and one's disposition not to flinch in the face of the incessant variability of becoming; and second, that there is an inconsistency between making life "bearable" and seeing life as "justified" as an aesthetic phenomenon. These assumptions are seriously compromised, however, when one takes stock of the fact that intoxication by its nature cannot extend beyond some ephemeral moments. No one, not even the Greek discoverers of the Dionysian, is able to engage in acts of permanent intoxication. Firm grounds are indispensable. In the form of culture and all its conceptual measuring rods, they are the starting points for anyone surveying himself and his values, as well as those of others. It is reasonable to interpret Nietzsche's reference to intoxication as one of those instances where he encourages his reader to be willing to err, to float, and to leave behind, at least for certain moments, the certitude of their beliefs (GS; 46). Since Dionysian intoxication is bound to be ephemeral, how could this Dionysian marker be seen as a lack of honesty? Nietzsche has not abandoned his view that art seeks to beautify life: this Apollonian impulse is inextricably associated with art. Nor has

Nietzsche changed his position that one ought to examine oneself in order to know what one is. This is not a previous step but part of a fluid process toward becoming what one is. This is what Nietzsche calls giving "style" to one's character, which involves concealing the ugly that cannot be removed or making it "sublime" through reinterpretation (GS; 290).

But the *Genealogy* opens up a new horizon, in that Nietzsche is no longer the detached observer of morality of *Daybreak* and *The Gay Science*. Seemingly, in *Beyond Good and Evil* he engaged in a dangerous game (exploring the possibility that the good originated in evil); in the *Genealogy* he came too close to the abyss (as discussed in the previous chapter); and a sense of urgency dawned on him, one that was not present in his previous books. The *Genealogy* is Nietzsche's full-fledged realization that one form of morality, the Christian morality of self-denial and the ascetic ideal, created new opportunities for the human species, but at the same time sickened the animal man in such a way that this adventurous creature became a pitiful shadow ashamed of its own nature. The ascetic ideal makes human beings delicate, cunning, and self-disciplined, but the cost is too high: the earth has become a madhouse populated by wounded beasts, which, molded by the idea of sinfulness, tear themselves apart. Against the realization that European culture is enslaved by resentment, guilt, and self-directed nausea, Nietzsche sides with the innocence of becoming and becomes deeply conscious, as he believes, not only of missed opportunities—the Roman Empire, for example—but of whether tests to measure his own strengths are still available. His description of Dionysian intoxication in *Twilight of the Idols* occurs in a passage in which he is defending, with a renewed sense of urgency, one's belonging to a whole from which one cannot remove oneself. This truth, regardless of how many moments of intoxication one indulges in, may lead to despair. But Nietzsche is not in a despairing mood: his duel with truth, with actuality, and his belief that he is still standing once this duel is over, are his courage and intellectual honesty.

The second assumption of Ridley's interpretation, that it is inconsistent to treat life as both "bearable" and as "justified" as an aesthetic phenomenon, creates no actual conflict. Most people will always stand in need of art: their quantum of the will to power requires the deceptive tricks of art in order to carry on through a life mired in goallessness and meaninglessness. For them, life will always need to be justified as art. And for Nietzsche? On his view of self-creation, he himself is a work of art. This means that he is an artistic phenomenon justified both by "actuality" (what justifies man is his reality) and by his own art. This artistic phenomenon is the work of his instincts and their peculiar struggles. It is the work of that fragile web called consciousness, and that special awareness that his philosophy, as a biography of his founder, has brought to the European culture. The current that informs his artistic creation is different from other philosophers, but the outcome is the same: he is a work of art. This is a truth that, as Ridley points out, he makes explicit in *Ecce Homo,* and it suffices to show that making life bearable and justifying it are not contradictory.

Let us grant that Nietzsche, as a work of art, is able to withstand life without any artifice or subterfuge—or so he believes. But if he is in no need of subterfuges, then he does not need art to make his life *bearable.* This objection could be addressed from two standpoints. First, who can say that, in his artistic creation of affirming, removing, and concealment (GS; 290), there is no element whatsoever of self-deception? If there can still be areas of self-deception, no matter how insignificant one thinks they are, could not these areas be considered artistic consolations, that is, they help one bear life? We might respond that self-deception is not necessarily a consolation aimed at making life bearable; however, it is also reasonable to argue that self-deception is, more often than not, infused with consolation. Indeed, in Nietzsche's philosophy, self-deception as consolation has the upper hand. Second, Nietzsche is consistent in his claim that a second nature could become a first nature. If this is so, the artistic proclivities of human beings may be already part of what they are: these proclivities would be necessary to us, not something that could be shed at will. As such, Nietzsche's intellectual honesty demands from him a clear acknowledgment of what he has become. This is something he does, I think, in his insistence that one is part of a whole and—as he says in *Ecce Homo,* echoing words first uttered in *Human, All Too Human*—that nothing is dispensable.

Our inextricability from the whole is central to Nietzsche's idea of *amor fati*, which according to Ridley, should be construed "as an ethical attitude towards the world, rather than as a (disguised) metaphysical thesis about how much of the world is necessary."[38] It is true that *amor fati* is an ethical attitude. But this is only so to the extent that Nietzsche's epic spirituality requires an affirmation of everything in life. If Faust is the spirit that always denies, Zarathustra is the spirit that *never* denies. Nothing is dispensable, and everything is necessary. This affirmation is a metaphysical need, that is, an essential and therefore indispensable component of the meaning of life for Nietzsche.

In 1888, in explicit passages in *Twilight* and *Ecce Homo*, Nietzsche returns to an ethical principle that he had spelled out in 1882 and called, aptly enough, "personal providence." A "certain high point in life," he wrote in *The Gay Science*, confronts the individual with the idea of "a personal providence," which is "the greatest danger of spiritual unfreedom." Why unfreedom? Because he now realizes that "everything that happens to us turns out for the best. . . . it proves to be something that 'must not be missing'; it has a profound significance and use precisely for us" (GS; 277). This universal affirmation, however, should be distinguished from merely accepting all experiences and treating them as equally important for us. Although everything that happens to us is necessary, it is still incumbent on us to display "our own practical and theoretical skill in interpreting and arranging events" (GS; 277). Nietzsche's philosophy of reconciliation in 1888 relies on the interpretation and arrangements of events that define all his theoretical endeavors, together with his principle of giving "style" to his character (GS; 290). It is worth noticing that Nietzsche composed his autobiography as an artistic event that begins with a dramatic title—*Ecce Homo*; that follows with a certification of his wisdom, immediately juxtaposed to his cleverness; that recounts and summarizes all his books; and that ends in a cataclysmic crescendo with the section entitled "Why I Am a Destiny."

A concern expressed by Ridley is that *Ecce Homo* might be seen as a "self-help manual" that does away with the honesty required by the intellectual conscience. "One is, it appears, opportunistically to reinterpret one's past in a way that makes it seem providential. And one is to take seriously the thought—the fantasy, surely—that one might regard one's life as a work of art, and oneself as its moment-by-moment creator." Ridley himself hastens to reject this idea, since Nietzsche was still writing about courage, truth, and honesty in 1888. Nietzsche's words about courage in *Ecce Homo* "are not the words of a witting fantasist, or of one bent on falsifying the past."[39] I have already argued, however, that Nietzsche's philosophy requires a dose of misunderstanding, which is a mask he may wear for self-protection. In light of this reading, there is no problem in detecting an inconsistency in Nietzsche's arguments; namely, in accepting that although Nietzsche wrote about truth in *The Anti-Christ* and *Ecce Homo,* he is not always telling the truth about himself. Furthermore, the test of consistency that Ridley applies to Nietzsche's conception of honesty stands on fragile grounds, especially when we consider that Nietzsche shunned systematizers and hardly worried himself about consistency. But, even accepting that Nietzsche is telling the truth as he sees it, it is not clear why interpreting *Ecce Homo* as a therapeutic construction is an objection to it. After all, one can argue that every philosophy is a memoir of its founder, and this memoir arranges the world—the theoretical framework for interpreting reality—that is of concern to the philosopher. And since falsehood is necessary for life, falsifying one's past in order to deal with one's present and future would be an acceptable strategy.

I propose that Nietzsche's interpretation of his life as an aesthetic phenomenon is compatible with self-therapy. And my most persuasive argument for this view does not lie in the personal memoir model of philosophy, nor in the necessity of falsehood. To put it simply, the boundaries between consciousness and the instincts are not, and cannot be, clearly demarcated for Nietzsche. The impossibility of knowing one's dominant instincts and the way in which they wage their secret and unavoidable war counts against any talk of falsification. How can Nietzsche know that he is or is not falsifying his past, since what he now is has been the *unknown* work of his instincts? Since Nietzsche himself was not aware of what was going on in him, how could he know whether his instincts were falsifying his past? More important, what does falsification mean, if interpreting, arranging, and even molding the events in one's life are tasks that are always infused with some falsehood?

To be sure, Nietzsche's description in *Ecce Homo* suggests that the individual, in interpreting his life as an artistic artifact, somehow acquires an awareness of what happened in his life, though he will not know *how* this happened. "To have turned out well," Ridley observes, "is to be able to interpret one's development as the *unconscious* unfolding of one's latent potential, as the gradual, invisible piecing-together of a coherent self."[40] But how can one know that the final result is a "coherent self" when one does not know the particular configuration of one's instincts, and even less the way that these instincts have shaped the material (the physiological and psychical constitution) upon which they worked? Ridley comes from a different direction but concludes that, yes, Nietzsche is articulating a fantasy: "nothing could correspond to living one's life, from moment to moment, as if it were a work of art. So in this sense, Nietzsche's self-presentation does have the air of fantasy about it. . . . Nor is it very troubling to think that [*Ecce Homo*] might be taken as a self-help manual, as a promoter of positive thinking."[41]

In *Ecce Homo,* Nietzsche distances himself from the theme of Dionysian intoxication and, in describing how he crafts his life as an artistic event, appeals to a distinction between chaos and multiplicity: "a tremendous multiplicity which is nonetheless the opposite of chaos—this has been the precondition, the protracted secret labour and artistic working of my instinct" (EH; "So Clever"; 9). However, this claim presupposes, first, a certain ranking or structure in that multiplicity, which is why it is distinguished from a chaos; and second, a knowledge about how his instinct arranges this ranking. As I will demonstrate in the next chapter, both presuppositions have no place in Nietzsche's philosophy. No one knows the hierarchical ordering of his own instincts, and even less how those instincts would organize a multiplicity of inner states. Nietzsche must posit his own awareness of the variety of his inner life, lest he fall into the habit he abhors in Plato. Plato "mixes together all forms of style; he is therewith in the matter of style a *first décadent*" (TI; "What I Owe"; 2). But, again, this awareness of his inner life furnishes him with the self-knowledge that he considers to be impossible.

If Nietzsche's assertions about his inner states place him in the realm of decadence, another contention returns him to a stance he had dismissed in *Human, All Too Human*. After confessing "the artistic working of [his] instinct," he offers a beautiful description of his inner life. "The magnitude of its [his instinct's] *higher protection* was shown in the fact I have at no time had the remotest idea what was growing within me—that all my abilities one day leapt forth suddenly ripe, in their final perfection" (EH; "So Clever"; 9). This is, precisely, the deception that the artist works on others, by presenting himself as a genius: the artist is intent on denying that his work is the result of a normal process of development. Instead it marvelously springs into existence. Nietzsche does the same. After all, he does not worry about the possibility of being deceived (BGE; 34).

In those moments when Nietzsche claims to be a Dionysian man, he cannot be a philosopher, and vice versa. In the Dionysian state, philosophy is not merely brought to a standstill but is expelled from the space where intoxication is the supreme sensation. But when Nietzsche surveys the variety of states in his soul, he can choose to be a philosopher and something else, at intervals of his own (that is, his *instincts'*) choosing. As such, he is both the poeticizing philosopher and the philosophizing poet—a half-creature, perhaps.

For Nietzsche, the quest for knowledge, treated as an inner drive, joins the quest for artistic consolations as an instinctive need to make life bearable. The unavoidable nature of deception is joined with the desire to avoid self-deception. Self-misunderstanding might even be part of any deliberate attempt to be misunderstood by one's interlocutors. All of these are different dimensions of the role that the unconscious plays in Nietzsche's philosophy. I turn to these topics in the next chapter.

Chapter Five

THE SECRET WAR
OF THE INSTINCTS
Knowledge and the Unconscious

In *Twilight of the Idols,* Nietzsche is "telling a story about how we in the West became who we are."[1] But this story, riddled with knowledge claims, faces an important lacuna. How is this knowledge possible in light of the prominence that Nietzsche ascribes to the unconscious? Surprisingly, although his view of the unconscious explains his natural morality of innocence and unaccountability and undermines the ingrained dichotomies between slaves and nobles, it does not appear to have a significant place in the secondary literature.[2]

In this chapter I examine Nietzsche's understanding of knowledge and the unconscious in terms of his description of himself as an explorer of the inner world. I proceed by identifying some of his shifting and contradictory evaluations in areas in which he himself calls for precision, such as culture and morality; by locating these evaluations in the inner journey that is part and parcel of his philosophy; and by closely examining his ideas on the structure of knowledge and the secret war of the instincts. His inner journey is understood here, first, as a darkening of Nietzsche's theoretical horizon, in which he portrays an increasingly pessimistic and, at times, hopeless evaluation of both the condition of modernity and the causes underlying this condition; and second, as a decipherment of history that, in important ways, is also a projection of the turbulence of his philosophical endeavors.[3]

The darkening of the theoretical horizon is manifested in the differing descriptions and analyses he offers from 1878 to 1888. Nietzsche himself acknowledged the evolution of his thoughts on morality (GM; P; 4) and concluded that the internalization of man was a deeply damaging event in the history of humankind (GM; II; 16). In emphasizing his inner journey, I do not deny that Nietzsche recognizes the importance of both depths (going into his soul) and heights (affirming and celebrating life). But it is clear that, in his philosophy, an inner journey may produce either the wrong type of spirituality, as in the case of the ascetic priest, or the right type of spirituality, as the one that marks off the new philosophers from their predecessors.

SHIFTING EVALUATIONS

Between 1887 and 1888, Nietzsche's suffering, induced by his philosophical conclusions, expressed itself in his genealogical accounts of Western history. In a kind of symbiotic relationship, his sense of the debacle of Western culture produced inner lacerations, which in turn molded, in subtle or open ways, his cultural analyses. In other words, Nietzsche's genealogies of Western history decipher historical characters and events, but in the process he is describing a substantial portion of himself.

I suggest, moreover, that despite all the lyric declamations about eagles, mountains, climbing, and flying, Nietzsche's theoretical journey was subterranean in the sense explained in chapter 2; namely, a journey into historical origins to "uncover" physiological maladies and psychological traits. The "fatality of the heights, *our* fatality" (GS; 371), is hardly the best image. Consider instead: "Thus Zarathustra began to go under" (GS; 342); "I descended into the depths" but "returned safe and sound" (D; P; 2); "In this book you will discover a 'subterranean man' at work" (D; P; 1); "I come from heights no bird has ever soared to, I know abysses into which no foot has ever yet strayed" (EH; "Good Books"; 3). His struggle against dominant values was an underground struggle, and, as he wrote in 1888, he "had become, imperceptibly . . . something like a lair."[4] These confessions apply to most of his texts.

I will first trace some of the evolving arguments in Nietzsche's philosophy, before examining how his description of the instincts ambushes other claims of his own philosophy.[5] In following these shifting premises and emphases I am not attempting to imitate what Robert C. Solomon describes as *ad hominem* arguments.[6] My discussion is based on the turns and, at times, dramatic evolution of Nietzsche's theoretical reflections. The purpose is to spell out how his philosophical horizon darkened, especially in his post-Zarathustran texts, and how his understanding of the instincts disabled his critique of slaves and their morality.

My starting point is *Human, All Too Human* (1878), a text that expresses tremendous confidence in the emergence of a new moral order and provides anticipations of a philosophy of reconciliation (discussed thoroughly in chapter 9). In *Human, All Too Human,* Nietzsche portrayed the support of, or opposition to, customs, that is, the adherence or rejection of common agreements on rules of conduct for the community, as the standard to measure good and evil (H; I; 96). Good and evil refer here to the *external* sphere of persons' relationships to one another. But Nietzsche also turned inward and followed (whether consciously or unconsciously is not important) the program he suggested for the "serious workman": "one should, finally, reflect on the motives of human actions, disdain no signpost to instruction about them and be a collector of these things by day and night. One should continue in this many-sided exercise some ten years: what is then created in the workshop, however, will be fit to go out into the world" (H; I; 163). In a self-fulfilling prophecy, nearly a decade later, he claimed in the *Genealogy* that he knew enough about "the motives of human actions" to depict their minutest details. By the time his ideas on morality come to fruition in the *Genealogy,* good and evil no longer characterize external actions presupposing external social agreements. First, there is no single community, but rather two groups, the nobles and the slaves, each one striving to impose its own interpretations. Common customs do not exist. Second, the noble-slave duality leads to two opposing moralities. Third, the nobles define what is good, while evil is, initially, a causal connection that takes shape in the emerging soul of the slave.[7]

In *Human, All Too Human*, Judaism is described as nothing less than the *"continuation of the Greek."* The Jewish "freethinkers, scholars and physicians" held high the banner of intellectual freedom and protected Europe from Asia. Not only that, they also offered "a more natural, rational and in any event unmythical elucidation of the world," so much so that the bond uniting European culture with "the enlightenment of Graeco-Roman antiquity" remained "unbroken." "If Christianity has done everything to orientalize the occident, Judaism has always played an essential part in occidentalizing it again: which in a certain sense means making of Europe's mission and history a *continuation of the Greek*" (H; I; 475).

This evaluation, as I discussed in chapter 2, did not last. In *Beyond Good and Evil* (1886) the Jews are seen negatively as the precursors of Christianity, and in the *Genealogy* Nietzsche's historical perspective undergoes a dramatic change. The ties between Europe and "the enlightenment of Graeco-Roman antiquity" are no longer "unbroken"; a chasm separates them. The Jewish freethinkers, scholars, and physicians are expunged from Nietzsche's account, and the Jewish priests take center stage. Judaism is now portrayed as a culture designed by the priests, who in turn are sworn to oppose nature and rationality. Judaism, *in toto*, is described as the only soil in which Christianity could grow, and Judea is the dark and decaying moment that prevailed against Rome.

This movement from positive to negative evaluation of Judaism occurs in other works. In *Daybreak* (1881) the priestly people *par excellence*, the Jews, are described as a powerful race that may hold the key to a regeneration in Europe. The Jews act like the nobles that Nietzsche depicts in the *Genealogy*: patient, confident, self-assured. The Jews are confident because they "also know that at some future time Europe may fall into their hands." To accomplish this, Nietzsche counsels, they need "to distinguish themselves in every domain of European distinction and to stand everywhere in the first rank: until they have reached the point at which they themselves determine what is distinguishing." From the variegated motley of

Jewish history, there will arise "great men and great works!" (D; 205). It is true that an "eternal vengeance" still darkens the bosom of Jewish intentions, but this vengeance will be transformed into an "eternal blessing" (D; 205). It is also true that "their souls have never known chivalrous noble sentiments nor their bodies handsome armour," but they will "ally themselves with the best aristocracy of Europe" and "will soon have created for themselves a goodly inheritance of spiritual and bodily demeanour." In the span of a century, they will be victorious: "they will appear sufficiently noble not to make those they dominate *ashamed* to have them as masters. And that is what matters!" (D; 205).

If the Jews already have the genetic endowment to become nobles and to set the standards of "what is distinguishing," in *Daybreak* the workers are not far behind. They, too, possess the primal attributes of the nobles, but they require a new environment to thrive: "Let Europe be relieved of a fourth part of its inhabitants! . . . Outside of Europe the virtues of Europe will go on their wanderings with these workers; and that which was at home beginning to degenerate into dangerous ill-humour and inclination for crime will, once abroad, acquire a wild beautiful naturalness and be called heroism" (D; 206). "Spiritual and physical transplantation" was a remedy that Nietzsche had spelled out in *The Wanderer and His Shadow* (1879) to bolster his call for physicians:

> *History* as a whole, as knowledge of the various cultures, is *pharmacology* but not the science of medicine itself. The *physician* is still needed who will avail himself of this pharmacology to send each person to the climate favourable precisely to him—for a period of time or for ever. . . . In the end, the whole earth will be a collection of health resorts. (WS; 188)

In *Beyond Good and Evil*, however, the workers and the herd are inseparable. The herd is governed by utility, and is thus the yardstick of mediocrity and the average. One book later, in the *Genealogy*, Nietzsche's universe is even more somber, and the health resorts are bankrupt. The Jews are still strong, but they now embody the sickening hatred of the ascetic priest, a hatred that, in Nietzsche's script, welled up until it exploded in the sick physiology of the Christian church. The workers and the masses are no longer potential heroes who happen to live in the wrong place. They are now the sick, anaesthetized, and hypnotized herd that follows the ascetic priest on the road to nothingness as the alleviation for physiological inhibition. The workers, the herd, and the weak are a failure from the start, and no amount of geographical therapies will change their nature. Segregation, not emigration, is the urgent policy called for by Nietzsche.

In *Daybreak*, the "fable of a loving god" overtook the ancient world because "this fable represented so bold an inversion and so daring a paradox that the ancient world, grown over-refined, could not resist it" (D; 130). The advocates of the "loving god" defeated antiquity not out of timidity but out of their audacious paradox. In the *Genealogy*, the "fable" is still an inversion, but Nietzsche never says that the nobles grew "over-refined," and, in fact, he never explains why the nobles' morality succumbs.[8]

In *Beyond Good and Evil*, Nietzsche's account of the slave morality is spiritually different from the final version he will offer in the *Genealogy*. In Nietzsche's first account, slave morality seeks, not to enjoy life, but to endure it. It is predicated on a narrow calculus that values survival at any cost—hence, the virtues of piety, kindness, and humility, which are means toward self-preservation. The fundamental goal of the slave is self-preservation, while the overriding concern of the noble individual is life, and these are not the same. "It is their instinct for preservation which teaches [men] to be fickle, light and false" (BGE; 59). Life as the will to power accepts dangers and regards death as part of its own nature, while self-preservation is a truncated will to power. It is a will to power that took a detour toward a safe cavern or some other hiding place, instead of directing its steps straight toward the battlefield. In Nietzsche's terms, when perils abound and the possibility of one's destruction only elicits a glance of contempt (by the nobles), there is neither space nor patience for the concept of evil. Their contempt at death is short-lived and reveals the way that the nobles look at things. Staring, in contrast, is a long-term commitment; it characterizes the slaves, who stare at the battle from the safety of their cavern.

Nothing can be considered evil, Nietzsche argues, if a living organism sees, or better still, does not even see its own destruction as part of nature. Things can still be "bad": the prey escapes, the beasts succeed in ambushing the warriors, rain interrupts the battle, a wound puts a halt to a fight, and so on. This is why the noble individual makes a distinction between "good" and "bad," while the slave puts forward something different: it distinguishes between "good" and "evil" (BGE; 260). Though this distinction will be present in his later version, in *Beyond Good and Evil*, the slave morality, as the morality of utility, leads to a certain "disdain" of the good man (BGE; 260). More important, slave morality arises from its *own* predicament; it is a prudential but well-intentioned calculation to ease the miseries of existence and to assuage pain.

> The slave is suspicious of the virtues of the powerful; . . . Slave morality is essentially the morality of utility. Here is the source of the famous antithesis 'good' and '*evil*'—power and danger were felt to exist in evil, a certain dreadfulness, subtlety and strength which could not admit of contempt. Thus, according to slave morality the 'evil' inspire fear; according to master morality it is, precisely the 'good' who inspire fear and want to inspire it, while the 'bad' man is judged contemptible. The antithesis reaches its height when, consistently with slave morality, a breath of disdain finally also comes to be attached to the 'good' of this morality—it may be a slight and benevolent disdain—because within the slaves' way of thinking the good man has in any event to be a *harmless* man: he is good-natured, easy to deceive, perhaps a bit stupid, *un bonhomme*. (BGE; 260)

In the *Genealogy*, the slave is not presented as primarily suspicious, nor is he motivated by a "benevolent disdain" toward the good man or the noble individual. He is now *resentful*. His leitmotif is hatred. He does not regard the powerful men as harmless, but as oppressive. His morality is not one of utility, but of resentment, and he is no longer the original source of his morality, which is now seen as a reactive deed, a negation of the values of the nobility. It is the nobles who now show disdain toward those below them, although Nietzsche does not explicitly abandon his claim that the nobles are probably, in the slaves' eyes at least, a bit stupid.

Just as Nietzsche spells out two conceptions of the slaves, similarly, it is possible to distinguish two concepts of the nobles in the evolution of his thought. In discussing the "striving for distinction," he opposes the ascetic and the martyr, on the one hand, and the barbarian, on the other. The ascetic imposes suffering and pain upon himself in order to obtain distinction. The barbarian seeks the same goal by inverting the ascetic's strategy; that is, the barbarian, who can be seen as a fresh and raw version of the nobles, imposes suffering "on others on whom and before whom he wants to distinguish himself" (D; 113). The barbarian thus needs the presence of others to feel distinction; his feeling of superiority is dependent upon the suffering of his victims. In the *Genealogy*, the psychological constitution of the nobles is different. They gain distinction through deeds performed in the company of equals, namely, other noble individuals. They create their own sets of values for themselves and do not depend on the slaves' suffering in order to be convinced of their own superiority. As argued in *Beyond Good and Evil* (sections 257, 259, and 260), the nobles require the presence of slaves in order to develop the pathos of distance from them. But the nobles' striving for distinction is achieved by defeating people like themselves, people who are worthy enemies; the slaves are not worthy of the warrior's attention.

In *Human, All Too Human*, asceticism is motivated by "vanity": the ascetic type fights boredom by waging an imaginary war, inventing an "enemy within," and interpreting "his life as a continual battle and himself as a battlefield upon which good and evil spirits wrestle with alternating success" (H; I; 141). In the *Genealogy*, asceticism is driven by the impotence and hatred of the priest. The ascetic ideal still has an inner dimension, but it now occupies a narrower space. The ascetic priest is not so much concerned with the "enemy within" as before; actually, in some cases he is able to free himself from depression (GM; III; 17). His overriding goal is to wound and then to prescribe remedies. He now demands dominion over a suffering external to himself, the suffering of the herd.

In *Human, All Too Human,* Nietzsche interpreted "the victory of Christianity over Greek philosophy" as proof that "the coarser and more violent . . . conquered the more spiritual and delicate" (H; I; 68). In *Beyond Good and Evil* and the *Genealogy,* the weak are still violent (against themselves), but they are no longer coarse: they possess cunning and are trained in the sophisticated arts and weapons of the soul. The strong are neither spiritual nor delicate. They are simply strong, and their strength makes them violent agents who act with cheerfulness. They are beasts of deeds. It is worth noticing here that Nietzsche first describes a conflict between Christianity and Greek philosophy; later on, the conflict becomes one between Christianity and Rome. The opponents change, but the need for opponents remains a constant.

In *Beyond Good and Evil,* Nietzsche identifies a threefold advantage in the pathos of modernity and democracy. This pathos is the foundation for a coming age of tyrants; it will produce a slave "in the subtlest sense"; and in some cases, the strong individual will become stronger and richer "than has perhaps ever happened before—thanks to the unprejudiced nature of his schooling, thanks to the tremendous multiplicity of practice, art and mask. What I mean to say is that the democratization of Europe is at the same time an involuntary arrangement for the breeding of *tyrants*—in every sense of the word, including the most spiritual" (BGE; 242).[9]

Nietzsche even claimed to find in modernity a ground for the nourishment of a richer culture. He extolled "the mad and fascinating *semi-barbarism* into which Europe has been plunged through the democratic mingling of classes and races" (BGE; 224). "The past of every form and mode of life, of cultures" is running through the modern soul, and "our instincts now run back in all directions, we ourselves are a kind of chaos." Through this "semi-barbarism in body and desires," the modern soul has "secret access everywhere such as a noble age never had, above all the access to the labyrinth of unfinished cultures and to every semi-barbarism which has ever existed on earth" (BGE; 224). But these hopes of his were shattered. By the time he wrote the *Genealogy,* his perspective had changed dramatically. The strong were infected, and no one would turn out well. The ascetic priest was triumphant. The earth had become a madhouse, a hospital, and an abattoir. The "semi-barbarism" was burned out, and its ashes now covered the masses as a mantle of guilt. The "secret access" was locked, and the "chaos" of the modern soul was reprogrammed through the hypnotics of the priest.

In *Human, All Too Human,* Nietzsche could write a section with the title "Future innocuousness of metaphysics" (H; I: 10). In *Daybreak,* still bathed in the optimism of *Human,* he prophesied that people like him were "making the first attempts to organise themselves and therewith to create for themselves a *right.*" He anticipated that "the inventive and productive men shall no longer be sacrificed," and "a tremendous burden of bad conscience shall be expelled from the world" (D; 164). In *Assorted Opinions and Maxims,* a text published in 1879 and reprinted in 1886 as part of the second volume of *Human,*[10] Nietzsche wrote about the "good" of his age, namely, the opportunity to enjoy all the cultures that had existed along with their productions, making it possible to "nourish ourselves with the noblest blood of every age." Now, "for the first time in history, the tremendous far-flung prospect of human ecumenical goals embracing the entire earth" was within reach without any need of "supernatural assistance" (AOM; 179). He imagined an era in which daily lectures and hours of meditation would be available for all adults, who would receive this education without compulsion, rather, "as a command of custom." These edifying lectures would be given in churches, which, as the places "richest in memories," were also "the worthiest venues" for such lectures. The lectures would constitute a daily "festival" on behalf of the "dignity of human reason." This education, in which the dualities of nobles and slaves, sick and healthy, and so forth, play no role, would be offered by "the ideal of the teacher," who is a fusion of the virtues of the priest, the artist, and the physician (AOM; 180).

One of the most dramatic twists in Nietzsche's journey toward a darkened spiritual horizon was the fate of this ecumenical "vision" of 1879. Again, such hopes collapsed. In the *Genealogy,* as we have seen, Nietzsche described bad conscience as a universal illness, and metaphysics as the last step before nihilism. The "noblest blood of every age" was tainted, and the "human ecumenical goals" were scattered under the iron grip of the priest and the Christian theologian. The vision of public lectures and meditation in churches disappeared, and *The Anti-Christ* ended with a decree to destroy all churches. According to *Assorted Opinions and Maxims*, "mankind can do with itself whatever it wishes" (179)—but it could not.

In *Beyond Good and Evil*, Nietzsche made a list of the things that had strengthened the European spirit. He mentioned, among others, "the protracted spiritual will to interpret all events according to a Christian scheme and to rediscover and justify the Christian God in every chance occurrence—all these violent, arbitrary . . . and antirational things have shown themselves to be the means by which the European spirit was disciplined in its strength, ruthless curiosity and subtle flexibility" (BGE; 188). Barely a year later, in the *Genealogy*, the spiritual will of Christianity plays the opposite role. It is now an instrument that has disciplined the European spirit *in weakness* and, through its insistence on a single viewpoint, has squandered all the achievements of Western culture.

The darkening of Nietzsche's theoretical horizon culminated in a cultural revaluation that displaced Greece and exalted Rome. Greek culture introduced the idea of the tragic, and Nietzsche thought that he was the first to understand it. In *Daybreak*, Thucydides was "the last glorious flower" of "*that culture of the most impartial knowledge of the world*" (D; 168). But in *The Anti-Christ*, Nietzsche declares that he learned nothing from the Greeks. His gaze was set on Rome, Imperial Rome, to be accurate. Rome is not only the highest expression of right institutions, namely, those that bred nobility; it is, above all, a style, an aesthetic pleasure in the right use of words, which is "*noble par excellence.*"[11]

The above comparisons are by no means an exhaustive survey of Nietzsche's shifting evaluations. However, they are important clues to his philosophical path. One might add that his early interest in being understood, in communicating, and in assisting "towards making all good things common property and freely available to the free-minded" (WS; 87; see also H; II; 122) has also vanished and has been replaced by a longing for misunderstanding (BGE; 230) and a contempt for communication (GS; 354) (as discussed in chapter 4).

I am not in a position to find a cause or the causes of these shifting evaluations. In light of his own philosophy, with its emphasis on instincts, Nietzsche cannot explain them either. Clearly, however, some of the evaluations described above, especially those that deal directly with a genealogy of morality, do not rise to the level of precision and self-knowledge that Nietzsche explicitly sought (GM; P). It is necessary to consider the structure of knowledge in Nietzsche's philosophy and ask whether this can explain the darkening described above.

The Structure of Knowing

The web of human knowledge, for Nietzsche, is agonistic and complex. It is marked by the struggles and ephemeral truces of our instincts. In this arena, relaxation can be costly, since vanquished instincts are always in the background, as if permanently plotting a return to dominance. In the architecture of knowing, first, there are the senses, the instruments for perceiving the images of the world. Second, there are the instincts, which, as the second component in the cognitive endeavor, seize sensory images and fight about how to examine and interpret them, according to the nature of each instinct.[12] "Every drive is a kind of lust to rule; each one has its perspective that it would like to compel all the other drives to accept as a norm" (WP; 481). In this inner struggle, the vanquished instincts still remain as subordinated shadows, as it were, waiting for any possible shift in the total configuration of a person's drives: "The struggle fought among ideas and perceptions is not for existence but for mastery: the idea that's overcome is *not annihilated* but only *driven back* or *subordinated. In matters of the mind there is no annihilation.*"[13]

We do not understand how our perceptions occur or are processed: "Sense perception happens without our awareness: whatever we become conscious of is a perception that has already been processed."[14] We thus find two sets of filters between "reality" and the way it is "known" by human beings.[15] The senses are the first, and the instincts the second. The so-called secret war of the instincts produces emotions, which are, in turn, expressed in thoughts. "Thoughts are the shadows of our feelings—always darker, emptier, and simpler" (GS; 179). The instincts, however, can also create thoughts without using the pathway of the emotions. Thoughts are *reinterpreted images* until language is invented. As Nietzsche states in *The Will to Power:* "First *images*—to explain how images arise in the spirit. Then *words*, applied to images. Finally *concepts*, possibly only when there are words—the collecting together of many images in something nonvisible but audible (words)" (WP; 506). With the development of linguistic utterances, our thoughts and emotions can then use language as an outlet to express to oneself or to others whatever the dominant instincts seek to communicate.

As Nietzsche also claims, in *Thus Spoke Zarathustra*, linguistic utterances—our words—are a bridge that is destined to never successfully establish a link with reality (Z; III; "Convalescent").[16] This is, precisely, the significance of language: "that mankind set up in language a separate world beside the other world, a place it took to be so firmly set that, standing upon it, it could lift the rest of the world off its hinges and make itself master of it" (H; I; 11). But there is no mastery, in the sense that all "our words refer to fictions" and "the bond between man and man depends on the transmission and elaboration of these fictions" (WP; 676), a position that Nietzsche took from Friedrich Albert Lange and Eduard von Hartmann and developed further.[17] This important caveat narrows considerably the prospect of apprehending "actuality." Not only do our words refer to fictions, but our thoughts and words depend on one another in a relationship in which each attempts to make do with its deficiencies: "we have at any moment only the thought for which we have to hand the words" (D; 257), but thoughts cannot be "entirely" reproduced by words (GS; 244), and ossified words are a hindrance to knowledge (D; 47). That is, thoughts are constrained by the straightjacket of words, which cannot reproduce thoughts in their totality. Thus, aspects of the thinking process remain unknown and are permanently deaf to the realm of utterances. Perhaps, music, gestures, and stares sometimes express them.

"Speaking is a beautiful folly: with that man dances over all things" (Z; III; "Convalescent"). The ideas of depths and surfaces are thus intertwined: "depths" spread their net over instincts, emotions, and thoughts, while "surfaces" are the domain of words and the senses. In the conflict of our instincts, some may lie dormant while others are always on the qui vive. The most likely scenario with respect to our perceptions is clear enough, however: our initial perceptions are subject to a plurality of interpretations. "The material of the senses adapted by the understanding, reduced to rough outlines, made similar, subsumed under related matters. Thus the fuzziness and chaos of sense impressions are, as it were, logicized" (WP; 569). The initial perceptions first become images, which are, in themselves, interpretations by the senses; then they fall prey to the instincts and may be torn to pieces by them, before they reach a level of abstraction in the form of an emotion or in the form of thoughts, which are further interpretations. "The 'external world' affects us: the effect is telegraphed into our brain, there arranged, given shape and traced back to its cause: then the cause is *projected*, and *only then does the fact enter our consciousness.*"[18]

Perceptions, then, are the primeval food that nourishes the instincts, and words attempt to manifest the shreds or the embroidered sensations that the instincts send to the domain of our thoughts. We "have senses for only a selection of perceptions" (WP; 505). And, just as the senses and the instincts are filters through which the images are transformed, so also thoughts and words are additional filters of that chunk of "reality" that was originally perceived.

Knowledge emerges as the constitution of that part of reality that is of concern to us (WP; 521), and this constitution is the work of the instincts. As late as the spring of 1888, Nietzsche argued that "we have learnt that the sense impression naively posited as conditioned by the outer world is actually conditioned by the inner world: that every real action of the outer world *always* takes its course unconsciously."[19] The labyrinthine play of instincts, senses, and thought projects the ideas of logic and causality onto things:

> In this mirror—and our intellect is a mirror—something is taking place that exhibits regularity, a certain thing always succeeds another certain thing—this we *call*, when we perceive it and want to

call it something, cause and effect—we fools! . . . For we have seen
nothing but *pictures* of 'causes and effects'! And it is precisely this
pictorialness that makes impossible an insight into a more essential
connection than that of mere succession. (D; 121)

The conclusion is not difficult to draw: what human beings perceive; what they think or feel; and what they express through words
will be different and, at times, conflicting manifestations of that first
encounter of the individual's senses with what Nietzsche calls "actuality."[20] These relationships evince a complex predicament, which
results from the changing boundaries of power and shifting configurations of the instincts in the body.

> *Every thought,* every feeling, every will is *not* born of one particular
> drive but is a *total state,* a whole surface of the whole consciousness,
> and results from how the power of *all* the drives that constitute us is
> fixed at that moment—thus, the power of the drive that dominates
> just now as well as of the drives obeying or resisting it. The next
> thought is a sign of how the total power situation has now shifted
> again.[21]

The body is in a constant state of becoming, in which its smallest
parts are "struggling, reproducing, and dying off," and its moments
of fixity are episodic, to the extent that they reflect "the total power
situation" of the drives at a given point in time. A "fluid setting of
the boundaries of power is a quality of life."[22]

This fluidity, taken together with Nietzsche's understanding of
consciousness, compounds his view of "actuality." Consciousness
emerges through the need to communicate with others, and this
need is predicated on utility. It follows, Nietzsche claims, that it is
"only as a social animal that man acquired self-consciousness" (GS;
354). Words envelop the inner experience in the net of familiarity
and bring this experience into consciousness. "The 'inner experience' only enters our consciousness after it's found a language that
the individual *understands* . . . i.e., a translation of a state into states
more familiar to the individual."[23] Thus, the thinking process that

reaches the level of consciousness is "the smallest part" that arises from the inner states of man. It is also "the most superficial and worst part—for only this conscious thinking *takes the form of words, which is to say signs of communication*" (GS; 354). Indeed, consciousness "is a subsidiary role, almost indifferent, superfluous, perhaps destined to vanish and give way to a perfect automatism" (WP; 523).[24] The need to communicate, which is one of the roots of consciousness, forms habits that will also play a role in the "apprehension" of "actuality."[25] As Michel Haar observes,

> the schematizing and assimilating activity of knowledge is not even the work of consciousness. This activity emerges already at the level of the body, and from there enters onto the conscious level. . . . Philosophy has never ceased to show disdain for the body; it has not wished to recognize that it is the body that whispers thoughts to the 'soul,' and that consciousness is only a superficial and terminal phenomenon.[26]

And further,

> Consciousness . . . is the instrument that executes choices and decisions that have already been made in our depths. Everything that emerges to consciousness is the reflection of a temporary equilibrium in the interplay of the impulses.[27]

Interpreted in this light, Nietzsche's insistent idea that our souls possess inner caves and unknown hiding places is a very accurate description of the plurality of struggles that he identifies in each individual. The senses could fight in their "apprehension" of images; thoughts may struggle with one another; and the same predicament holds in the realm of emotions. This architecture does not have clearly delineated boundaries, however. Domains overlap and are frequently reconfigured. Nietzsche's claim that we lack an "organ for knowledge" appears now as persuasive. What we have, instead, is a plurality of processes vying to impose a final interpretation and thus seal a view of "reality."

THE SECRET WAR OF THE INSTINCTS

The processes described above and the "reality" they seek to apprehend, however, lie in unknown regions of our inner world. The
structure of knowing that has been described exposes a problem
in a duality that is possible to discern in Nietzsche's reflections.
Throughout his work we find dualities, not only between nature and
morality, nobles and slaves, the strong and the weak, the healthy
and the sick, but also between a legitimate will to power (the noble's)
and an illegitimate one (the ascetic priest's), and between a healthy
suffering and a perverted one (GS; 370). Life is the will to power, but
this will can take a wrong turn by torturing the body in the attempt
to guarantee entrance into another world after this life. Suffering is
a precondition of nobility and greatness, but the wrong type of suffering leads to illness, guilt, and nihilism. A lie could pursue the
"right" purpose as expressed in a higher culture, but it could also be
the result of a falsifying and dishonest attitude.

These dualities collapse, however, as soon as we follow through
with Nietzsche's own reasoning and conclude, as he does, that
people are what they are by nature. Everyone "*is* what he has been
made by decree from above!" (D; 166). Life is the will to power, and a
person's rank in the order of nature is determined by "the quantum
of power you are" (WP; 858). By nature, some people are presumably endowed with a lower quanta of power and primeval energies;
they presumably exist to nourish a stronger species. This notion
suggests a teleological view in an otherwise purposeless world. The
key issue here is that people are not responsible for the quantum of
power each one contains. It is not within the scope of the nobles'
actions to control what they are, and, accordingly, they should not be
seen as accountable to the slaves. But in Nietzsche's theoretical universe, the slaves bear responsibility for being what they are: they
glorify the instinct for self-preservation; they shun war and settle for
peace; and they want all people to be like them. The slavish second
nature—the state in which responsibility and the distinction between good and evil are introduced—becomes the first nature, a

transformation he attests to even in his earlier writings.[28] But, as I argued in chapters 2 and 3, if life is the will to power, it is reasonable to expect that the oppressed energies of the slaves will seek new outlets to relieve their inner pressures.

This apparent inconsistency in Nietzsche's position could be taken as a valid objection, but, as I have already argued in chapter 2, an appeal to "medicine" seems to offer him a way out: resentment is certainly an expression of the will to power, but it is a sick, perverted one. It is, most likely, an illegitimate form of suffering—suffering as the impoverishment of life (GS; 370).[29] Nietzsche thus wants there to be sick people, to the extent that the nobles' pathos of distance necessitates their existence, but he does not want contagion between them. This is a metaphysical blunder: he separates life from its holders. That is, he envisions "life" on one side and the slaves on the other side of an unbridgeable divide. He evaluates life through philosophy and morality, and he dismisses what he takes to be its negation—the slave morality and the herd instinct—through physiology and medicine. This distinction is prone to collapse as soon as we take into consideration the consequences of his naturalism, as discussed in chapters 2 and 3. Since the slaves' illness is a natural reaction to conditions of protracted oppression and, therefore, the slaves do not bear any responsibility for their illness, it follows that slaves and their morality are part of the permanent and fluid becoming of nature. Nietzsche explicitly states that "we cannot do without sickness, and even less without the passions. We *need* the abnormal, we give life a tremendous *shock* with these great sicknesses."[30] Once the slaves' illness is understood as a natural event, we should understand this illness as part and parcel of becoming, and no one can accuse nature of injustice. Nature is chance; becoming is innocence. If, on the contrary, the slaves' illness is a *conscious* choice, then the very chain of connections that Nietzsche wants to debunk (the self—free will—intention—responsibility—accountability), in a word, morality, reappears.

Granted, when people arrive at certain moral, religious, or political concepts that deny or alleviate their first nature as slaves, those concepts might bring about spiritual, intellectual, and even physical transformations that become their "second" nature. But if everything is impermanence and becoming, how can one determine that the first nature is the "real" nature, since it was never meant to remain static? It is part of a permanent process of becoming, with continual metamorphoses and even abrupt changes that leave no trace or recollection of previous states. On Nietzsche's view of becoming, morality and religion could be seen as two of these transformations. But he does not accept this conclusion, and his arguments cannot be made consistent. He interprets morality, religion, and metaphysics as the negation of becoming. They are conceptual interruptions of the innocence of nature, which are bound to spawn physiological mutations (the ascetic priest, for example). A conceptual interruption denies the facts of becoming, but the danger of this was also inscribed in nature. Here, Nietzsche appears as overprotective: he wants the new philosopher to live perilously, but he also wishes to keep becoming at a safe distance: a becoming that does not alter in any way the philosopher's physical and spiritual constitution.

If danger is part of life, perishing is part of it, too. If, as Nietzsche claims, there is an instinct for causality and an instinct that "constantly needs lies,"[31] it follows that morality, religion, the ascetic priest, and the slaves can trace their ancestry back to the instincts, namely, to nature. Is Nietzsche trapped by his own logic? In a pattern that is by now familiar, he relies on the physician to free him. He argues that there is a difference between perishing as a life-affirming consequence of becoming, which is a common occurrence in the nobles' endeavors, and perishing as a negation of becoming, which is what takes place when morality and religion take over. But the trap remains: the negation of becoming is one of the consequences of becoming itself. "From the standpoint of morality," Nietzsche asserts, "the world is false. But to the extent that morality itself is a part of this world, morality is false" (WP; 552). To paraphrase him: From the standpoint of nature, sickness is false. But since sickness is part of nature, nature, too, would be false.[32] And Nietzsche in fact states that sickness is false, and his statement implies causality, in that something is false "because" it is sick (AC; 52).[33]

In Nietzsche's stories and his philosophy, the innocence of becoming turns out to be a labyrinth of fictitious boundaries. Life appears as an abstract value, completely independent of the majority of its embodiments—the herd; and suffering is understood as spiritually and experientially different from the sufferers when they happen to be the wrong type of sufferers (i.e., neither the nobles nor the new philosophers).

There is, then, no way out for the slaves. When they seek relief in an inner world, the Nietzschean physician diagnoses them as sick. When they carve out the notion of evil in this inner world, the illness is full-fledged. If they choose, literally, to battle the nobles, it is because they are driven by resentment. In Nietzsche's universe, they are both haunted and hunted. When the ascetic priest follows Nietzsche's own advice and adopts a commanding posture in order to convince his enemy that an attack would be futile (AOM; 354), he is accused of dishonest dissembling. Evil, then, is a one-way experience. It is what the slaves do to the nobles, not what the nobles do to them. The nobles are not fit to stand any kind of trial; their stupidity explains them, whereas the slaves enter the sphere of responsibility when they express their pent-up resentment in the form of a refined pity and humility that *consciously* disguise their hatred. This is why the nobles are the genuine victims of evil, of the hatred of the ascetic priests and the eerie smiles of the sick. And yet, Nietzsche holds that deception is more central to life than truth; namely, that the will to untruth is more relevant than truth. If the weak are deceptive and treacherous, why are these features *illegitimate?* A passage from his notebooks of 1899 deepens the quagmire. Even the "release of *ressentiment* in the judging, rejecting, punishing of egoism" (i.e., in the judging of the noble morality) is also "an instinct of self-preservation on the part of the underprivileged" (WP; 373). This suggests that the instincts of the downtrodden, of the "failures," are flawed. When Nietzsche claims, in *Twilight of the Idols,* that everything good flows from the instincts, he is referring to the instincts of a specific group of individuals who ought to occupy the highest rank of society, because by nature they already possess that rank in themselves.

To put this criticism differently, when Nietzsche postulates and decries the duality of self-preservation and of life as the will to power, his concept of life reflects the very same error that he criticizes in logicians and philosophers. He is taking the effect (the will to power) as the cause (life) and presenting that effect as the *essence* of life (H; I; 13).[34] Will to power is an idea, a concept he imposes on life; and to the extent that it is an external imposition, if we follow Nietzsche's reasoning, it is an interpretation that may well be the outcome of an erroneous process of thought. Thinking, Nietzsche suggests, could well be a hoax (BGE; 34).[35] If the individual "always discovered in things only *that which he had put into them!*" (TI; "Errors"; 3), then he "discovered" the will to power in life because he was the one who put that will into life in the first place. We lend life its predicates (D; 210).

The dualities between nobles and slaves, the right type of suffering and the wrong type, and the right type of will to power and the wrong one, presuppose, of course, that the choice Nietzsche is making is, at least, the right interpretation. But this presupposition is a dead end. The secret war of the instincts forbids it.[36] The secret war leads Nietzsche to a standpoint that redeems the priests and the slaves and returns him to the predicament of *Human, All Too Human,* that is, the unconditional necessity of all actions and the complete innocence of all persons, slaves and women included (H; I; 107).

In a crucial section in *Daybreak,* where Nietzsche discusses "six essentially different methods of combating the vehemence of a drive," he concludes:

> *that* one *desires* to combat the vehemence of a drive at all, however, does not stand within our own power; nor does the choice of any particular method; nor does the success or failure of this method. What is clearly the case is that in this entire procedure our intellect is only the blind instrument of *another drive* which is a *rival* of the drive whose vehemence is tormenting us: whether it be the drive to restfulness, or the fear of disgrace and other evil consequences, or love. While 'we' believe we are complaining about the vehemence of a drive, at bottom it is one drive *which is complaining about an-*

other; that is to say: for us to become aware that we are suffering from the *vehemence* of a drive presupposes the existence of another equally vehement or even more vehement drive, and that a *struggle* is in prospect in which our intellect is going to have to take sides. (D; 109)[37]

In subsequent sections, he discusses the impossibility of self-knowledge by noting the incapacity of language to describe "inner processes and drives" and emphasizing the prison in which our senses have locked us (D; 115, 117). Words are instruments of our consciousness; they are used to communicate "superlative" states of the inner processes, while the states of "middle degree" and "lower degree" "elude us, and yet it is they which weave the web of our character and our destiny." Not surprisingly, "[w]e are none of us that which we appear to be in accordance with the states for which alone we have consciousness and words" (D; 115). More important, Nietzsche issues an eloquent indictment of Plato's allegory of the cave when he discusses how our world is formed by our senses, thus leaving us in a prison without any "bypath into the *real world!*" (D; 117). Plato builds his cave allegory to show the limits of our perception and why it is important to ascend from the cave toward the sun, as that which represents "real" knowledge; Nietzsche stands at the opposite end. For him, we are fated to be prisoners. "The habits of our senses have woven us into lies and deception of sensation: these again are the basis of all our judgments and 'knowledge'— there is absolutely *no escape*" (D; 117, emphasis mine).[38]

Further, Nietzsche argues that a person's knowledge "of the totality of *drives* which constitute his being" is bound to be incomplete. After posing a difference between waking life and the world of dreams, he asserts:

Waking life does not have this *freedom* of interpretation possessed by the life of dreams, it is less inventive and unbridled—but do I have to add that when we are awake our drives likewise do nothing but interpret nervous stimuli and, according to their requirements, posit their 'causes'? . . . that our moral judgments and evaluations too are only images and fantasies based on a physiological process *unknown to us,* a kind of acquired language for designating certain nervous stimuli? that all our so-called consciousness is a more or less fantastic commentary on an unknown, perhaps unknowable, but felt text? (D; 119, second emphasis mine)[39]

As quoted above, "our moral judgments and evaluations too are only images and fantasies based on a physiological process unknown to us." In section 129 of *Daybreak,* he returns to these issues and claims that the struggle between the motives of actions is "hidden from me."[40] In *Beyond Good and Evil,* he repeats the same argument: "The will to overcome an emotion is ultimately only the will of another emotion or of several others" (BGE; 117).[41] The claim in *Daybreak* that our intellect has to take sides is probably the view that such a "decision" is determined by something unknown. Finally, in *The Gay Science,* he offers a more categorical description of the unknown world and the secret war of the instincts.[42]

> For the longest time, conscious thought was considered thought itself. Only now does the truth dawn on us that by far the greatest part of our spirit's activity remains unconscious and unfelt. But I suppose that these instincts which are here contending against one another understand very well how to make themselves felt by, and how to hurt, *one another.* This may well be the source of that sudden and violent exhaustion that afflicts all thinkers (it is the exhaustion on a battlefield). Indeed, there may be occasions of concealed *heroism* in our warring depths. (GS; 333)[43]

For Nietzsche, in other words, the instincts do not rise to the level of consciousness, but they are, as it were, conscious of what they do to one another; they "understand very well" how to gain other instincts' attention and how to hurt them.[44] In the *Genealogy* Nietzsche mentions "the noise and struggle of our underworld of utility organs working with and against one another" (GM; II; 1). In two fragments written in 1888, he was more explicit: "*In summa:* That which becomes conscious is involved in causal relations which are entirely withheld from us" (WP; 524). The "*real* process of inner 'perception', the *causal association* between thoughts, feelings, desires is absolutely hidden from us. . . . *Between* two thoughts there are, in addition, *all sorts of affects* at play: but they move so fast that we *mistake* them, we *deny* them."[45] "The most universal and basic instinct in all doing and willing has . . . remained the least known and most hidden, because *in praxi* we always follow its commandments, because we *are* this commandment" (WP; 675). Our consciousness and purposefulness are "the smallest part of us" (WP; 676; see also 707, 985).[46] As Haar observes, "There is "a plurality of elementary 'wills'—which is to say unconscious impulses, forever in conflict, alternately imposing themselves and subordinating themselves. . . . Seen with regard to these impulses, the whole of our conscious motivation comes down to a fiction—or rather a *symptom*."[47] Gemes goes further: "[W]e contain within us hidden affects and drives," which "are not part of any integrated whole. . . . That is to say, we have strangers *within* ourselves, so that, in fact, our self is no genuine self. We are nothing more than a jumble of different voices/drives having no overall unity."[48] In *Ecce Homo* (1888), Nietzsche answers what is, probably, one of the most important questions of his philosophy: how one becomes what one is. The precondition to succeed, he claims, requires "that one does not have the remotest idea *what* one is." The answer would be given only by "the protracted secret labour and artistic working of my instinct" (EH; "So Clever"; 9).

All of these passages reveal a consistent pattern concerning the unknowable character of a person's inner domain,[49] and this pattern points to something more fateful, which is the impossibility of self-knowledge, as well as the impossibility of knowing other people's morality. "The best that one is one does not know—one cannot know." No one "can behold how and where he goes astray" (BGE; 249, 29). "To know the strength of a man's moral nature one has to know the best and the worst he is capable of in thought and deed. But to learn that is impossible" (AOM; 35).[50] An "unconquerable mistrust of the possibility of self-knowledge . . . is almost the most certain thing I know about myself" (BGE; 281). "I know that I know nothing of myself" (WP; 594). The "greatest portion" of one's life, that portion that includes "our thinking, feeling, and willing life," takes place without the awareness that consciousness provides (GS; 354). Early in his philosophical journey, Nietzsche shows an awareness of the "veiled thing" a person is, and the danger of inner explorations:

> How can the human being get to know himself? He is a dark and veiled thing; and if the hare has seven skins, the human being can shed seven times seventy skins and still not be able to say: "This is really you, this is no longer outer shell." Besides, it is an agonizing, dangerous undertaking to dig down into yourself in this way, to force your way by the shortest route down the shaft of your own being. (SE; 1)

One of the best exemplars of the secret war of the instincts, according to Nietzsche, is the personality of Wagner. Wagner was pulled in conflicting directions by two drives, one creative and innocent, which led him toward love, and the other dark, which led him to please the prevailing moral tastes of his audience. The "interrelation of these two most profound forces . . . was the only thing that *was not within his own power*"; he could do nothing, but "to observe and accept" (RWB; 3, emphasis mine).

The dense and obscure maze of instincts, as I have suggested above, strips Nietzsche of any solid ground to criticize those he has chosen as his enemies. Ultimately, the dispositions of the slaves, the priests, and the theologians can be traced to that realm of unaccountability, namely, the sphere of instincts that are always beyond a person's knowledge. "To appraise being itself! But this appraisal itself is still this being!—and if we say no, we still do what we *are*" (WP; 675). A person's deeds are beyond intention, purposes, consciousness, and knowledge. Thus, no one is responsible for the wars that the instincts wage, and even less for the victory of some instincts over others.[51] We do "what we *are*." The nourishment of some instincts is the work of chance (D; 119), and their victory is hidden (D; 129). We are fated to live in a world of deception built by our senses (D; 117). Our instincts arrange and simplify the world that we see as "true for *us*" (WP; 568). Individual happiness "springs from one's own unknown laws" (D; 108). "*The true world of causes is hidden from us.*"[52] And the mind has its own processes of "sorting and storing" and of providing for "the care and protection accorded the co-ordination of the bodily functions." However,

> [t]here can be no doubt that a highest authority exists for these processes: a kind of managing committee where the various *chief desires* assert their votes and power. . . . *In sum:* what becomes conscious is subject to causal relations entirely concealed from us—the succession of thoughts, feelings, ideas in consciousness tells us nothing about whether the succession is a causal one: but it gives the *illusion* of being so, in the highest degree. Upon this *illusion we have founded our whole notion of mind, reason, logic,* etc. (none of these exist: they are fictitious syntheses and unities). . . . And these, in turn, we have projected *into* things, *behind* things![53]

The same ideas appear, forcefully, in *Twilight of the Idols.* "The 'inner world' is full of phantoms and false lights: the will is one of them." The ego "has become a fable, a fiction." This means that the will and the ego, posited as causes outside the body, that is, as spiritual causes, are false through and through. "There are no spiritual causes at all." But man has "projected his three 'inner facts,' . . . will, spirit, ego, outside himself" (TI; "Errors"; 3). Alas, these "inner facts" are fictions.

Nietzsche's critique and his genealogical inquiries are the play or the war of *his* dominant instincts against other people's dominant instincts. This view of the role of the instincts might well suggest that Schopenhauer's characterization of religion as a metaphysical need, for example, is unassailable. This view does not invalidate Nietzsche's interpretations or diminish the pain of his suffering, but it introduces a sense of proportion and modesty in his own suffering. His genealogies, his stories, are what his dominant instincts see, or more accurately, what they want to see. Instincts act in the unconscious; the actions they engender are "unknowable" (GS; 335; D; 116). It is not possible to know either the origins or the consequences of our actions (WP; 291).[54]

THE NIETZSCHEAN SOUL

Leslie Thiele, in commenting on Nietzsche, observes that "[c]on-sciousness in general, and conscious moral judgment in particular, is the registration of instinctual strife."[55] He also claims, more questionably, that the "politics of the soul is laudatory, not because it gives equal voice to every drive, but because all of one's drives are exploited in the creation of a powerful regime embodying beauty and order."[56] In Nietzsche's reflections, however, it is difficult to find any such emphasis on order and harmony. As shown by the secret war of the instincts, the Nietzschean soul is constantly shifting its inner configurations, always exposed to dangers, and always experiencing the aftershocks of struggles that occur beyond the purview of consciousness. We "are, all of us, growing volcanoes that approach the hour of their eruption" (GS; 9). The image of a volcano is one of a person ruled by unknown drives, which point to a region beyond self-knowledge. This person is not in a position to exploit these drives toward the creation, for example, of an aristocratic regime.

In contrast to this idea of inner struggles beyond a person's will, Thiele refers to a soul that is "well-ordered," "harmonious," and possessing "organic unity."[57] These are attributes of an Apollonian soul, not to a Dionysian one. And although both the Apollonian and the Dionysian are part of life, Nietzsche explicitly expresses his preference for, and devotion to, the Dionysian. The soul as Thiele depicts it comprises materials that are "organized and exploited" by the individual, a view that presupposes a willing subject who consciously decides to organize its soul and to arrange its passions in a particular way. This is a picture of the liberal self; it is even reminiscent of the Platonic soul as described in the *Republic;* but it is not the Nietzschean soul that is rife with an inner war, whose ravages it must suffer, and for which a controlling ego is a fiction. It is worth repeating: the precondition for one to become what one is demands "that one does not have the remotest idea *what* one is." The idea of a "harmonious" and "balanced" soul is what Nietzsche describes, in 1888, as "juxtaposition without antagonism and collaboration." To be sure, this stage is "harmonious"; it is seen as "healthy," and it is where the "most interesting men, the chame-leons" find their home. It is also worth noticing that Nietzsche re-fers here to the "most interesting men," not to the highest spiritual beings. The "most interesting men" could well be the artists and the actors. These interesting men "are not in contradiction with them-selves, they are happy and secure, *but they do not develop*—their dif-fering states lie juxtaposed, even if they are separated sevenfold. They change, they do not *become* (WP; 778, first emphasis mine).

In Nietzsche's view of the soul as a battleground of instincts, his philosophy, which is so insistent on self-creation and on opening new vistas for individuals, appears disturbingly closed. It also ap-pears as a labyrinth, which displays a clear pattern that can be re-constructed in the following statements, all of them important in understanding Nietzsche's arguments about thinking, drives, and interpretation:

There are no moral phenomena, only interpretations (BGE; 108).
"*[T]here are no moral facts whatever*" (TI; "Improvers"; 1).
There are no facts, only interpretations (WP; 481).
Moralities [are the] sign language of the emotions (BGE; 187).[58]
Emotions [are the] sign language of drives/instincts (BGE; 117).
Instincts . . . are part of the granite stratum of man and are unknowable
    (BGE; 231; D; 109, 119).
Actions are unknowable (GS; 335; D; 116; WP; 676).
Causes are unknowable.[59]
Thinking [is] the relationship between (unknowable) drives (BGE; 36).
"Thinking" is "a quite arbitrary fiction, . . . an artificial arrangement for
    the purpose of intelligibility" (WP; 477).
In the landscape of "thinking," "both the deed and the doer are fictions"
    (WP; 477).[60]

Thus, we might refer to the "Euripidization" of Nietzsche. The idea of self-control and responsibility emerges as a *deus ex machina* in his stories and his philosophy, in much the same way that Euripi-des certified the validity of a plot by invoking the authority of "divine truthfulness" (BT; 12, 17, 18). Although, in the *Genealogy*, Nietzsche puts forward a detailed story about the origins of responsibility, this responsibility is deployed as an external imposition. It is the outcome of social expectations, not the end result of instincts. In the face of warring instincts, Nietzsche never explains how self-control and responsibility could emerge. A backdoor is always open: self-control and responsibility could be presented as the offshoots of a *dominant* instinct. But this poses, squarely, a tension between necessity and self-awareness: namely, a secret war expressing what we are and determining what we do conflicts with any idea of self-awareness. It also points toward the problem of self-reference; self-awareness must be present in order for us to understand, at least, that we are a raging war of instincts and that we lack control of the instincts that will eventually triumph, even if this triumph is a transitory one. We are fated to become what we are, and we cannot will the outcome since the will is a fiction.

I suggest that Nietzsche had theoretical resources to address this problem, although he ascribes more importance to the unknown war than to any degree of consciousness. Consciousness, he believes, is a small part of our constitution, but it is an important part. With the small consciousness we have at our disposal, some people may reach a level of self-awareness that may dictate what they want to become. Nietzsche is not particularly concerned about contradictory statements, but, in this case, I think, his reasoning is coherent. A self-awareness that can dictate something *is already part* of what the individual is. The self-awareness is not that person's will; it is inscribed in the configuration of his genetic endowment, and destined to rise to a level where the individual can obtain a glimpse of certain patterns that have coalesced into his personality. As I discuss in chapter 9, in some cases, for Nietzsche, these patterns are the fruits of seeds planted in the remote past.

In light of the subterranean war of the instincts, it is worth asking whether Nietzsche himself is suffering from unknowable actions and interpretations, which are incited by unknowable instincts that aim at nothing and achieve nothing.[61] I will address this issue in the next chapter, but for now it suffices to pose a series of related questions: Is Nietzsche suffering from two unknown entities (actions and instincts); from a realm of fictions (interpretations); and from the abyss of nothingness, which is, after all, not a fact but an interpretation of his that must also be a fiction? Is he suffering from his own "thinking," which, as he states in *The Will to Power*, is an "arbitrary fiction"? Or, to return to one of his finished texts, is he suffering from a process of thinking that, most likely, played on us "the biggest hoax ever" (BGE; 34), with no guarantee that another kind of thinking would not be another hoax? What are the differences between Nietzsche's shipwreck and the ascetic priest's self-mortification?

If a flash of awareness, a lightning bolt of conscience, could arise in us, this would be a ground, however slight, for positing an agent, an "I" whose self-awareness would be independent of his instincts. This route is closed for Nietzsche, however. As discussed above, self-awareness is, most likely, the sophisticated mask of another instinct (or several instincts) striving for dominance. People, Nietzsche avers, are accustomed to lying. He might well add that they are completely unaware that they are also accustomed to be lied to by their own drives. Self-awareness has its limits.

Again, Nietzsche is in a corner. In his notion of "restored reason" (TI; "Errors"; 2), everything good comes from the instincts, which might lead the ascetic priest and the slaves to put forward their moral claims as blameless. But in order to maintain the tempo of his own suffering, Nietzsche must posit that religious or moral inclinations are independent of the instincts. Or else, they are the consummate expressions of a *sick* instinct, and the suffering they engender is the wrong type of suffering. This is how, as a philosopher/physician, he can continue with his intoxications and his genealogies, while reflecting on the "concealed *heroism*" of his own "warring depths" (GS; 333). Poets, after all, "always know how to console themselves" (H; I; 33).

Chapter Six

THE METAPHYSICS OF
MEANING

I would speak here first of an idea which, so far as I know, has never before come into anyone's mind—we must have a new mythology, but this mythology must stand in the service of the Ideas, it must be a mythology of reason.

Until we make the Ideas aesthetic, i.e. mythological, they have no interest for the people; and conversely, until the mythology is rational the philosopher must be ashamed of it. So the enlightened and the unenlightened must finally join hands, the mythology must become philosophical and the people rational, and the philosophy must become mythological in order to make the philosophers sensuous.

—Hegel, "The Earliest Programme for a System
of German Idealism"[1]

The senses, instincts, thoughts, and use of language that constitute the unique individual form a complex array of traits caught in an endless cycle of competition, interpretations, reinterpretations, and changing alliances. But this complexity does not deter Nietzsche from his quest for knowledge. Clearly, knowledge can be pursued for its own sake, independent of a moral framework. But, in Nietzsche's case, knowledge has a moral dimension. He does not want to be deceived. Avoidance of deception, to be sure, can be merely a prudential strategy to cope with the world. Nietzsche's philosophy, however, treats knowledge as a necessary condition for arriving at principles one *ought* to live by. His view of honesty demands "our will not to deceive *ourselves*."[2]

Despair and the Philosophy of Destruction

One of Nietzsche's most powerful declarations appeared in *Human, All Too Human* (1878), when he asks where knowledge of the "untruth" of life might lead us. The individual, Nietzsche observes, cannot come face to face with the possibility that the "whole of human life" is buried and sunk in untruth, without becoming "disillusioned" about his past, present, and future. Here Nietzsche posed a perennial question: "Is it true, is all that remains a mode of thought whose outcome on a personal level is *despair* and on a theoretical level a *philosophy of destruction?*" (H; I; 34, emphasis mine).

In *Beyond Good and Evil* (1886), Nietzsche openly advocated the idea that truth and falsehood were inextricably linked, and he seemed to be reconciled to the prospect of a "philosophy of destruction." He even used this type of philosophy as a first way to test one's independence and ability to digest one's own experiences (GM; III; 16). Explicitly rejecting the utilitarian views propounded in *Human, All Too Human*, Nietzsche argued that something could be both true and dangerous; "indeed, it could pertain to the fundamental nature of existence that a complete knowledge of it would *destroy* one." "[T]he strength of a spirit" would be measured by how much "truth" it could take or whether it "*needed*" truth "attenuated" and "falsified" (BGE; 39, first emphasis mine). "Severity and cunning" could constitute conditions for the formation of strong individuals.[3]

Earlier, in *Thus Spoke Zarathustra*, Nietzsche had referred to the crushing duty of those who are fated to command. Zarathustra, having stated that the nature of the living requires obedience and that the one "who cannot obey himself is commanded," declares the "third point" he has heard about the living: "commanding is harder than obeying; and not only because he who commands must carry the burden of all who obey, and because this burden may easily crush him. . . . Indeed, even when [the living] commands *itself*, it must still pay for its commanding. It must become the judge, the avenger, and the victim of its own law" (Z; II; "Self-Overcoming"). Seemingly, Nietzsche divined in himself the burden of commanding, which he takes to be one of the attributes of genuine philosophers (BGE; 211). The archaeological and genealogical instincts were such strong drives in him, he states, that he has despaired of discerning "the entire history of the soul *hitherto*," and regretted that in such a demanding task he could count on no one. Everything had to be done by himself. His "curiosity," or what he could also term his thirst for knowledge, was a "pleasurable vice" and, for this very reason, a strong incentive (BGE; 45). But as soon as the metaphysics of meaning enters the picture, this "pleasure" showed its true colors: it was entwined with pain, a pain that was "profound" (GS; P; 3). As physician, archaeologist, and soul reader, he had divined all the lies behind the modern ideas and, "in a single glance," had understood all under favorable conditions, everything "could be *cultivated out of man.*" The character of this drama—Nietzsche himself—"knows even better from *his most painful memories* against what wretched things an evolving being of the highest rank has hitherto usually been shattered and has broken off, sunk and has itself become wretched" (BGE; 203, emphasis mine). That is, Nietzsche has learned, from his "most painful memories," the traps and perils threatening an individual of "the highest rank," and the fact that this individual, more often than not, has perished. These are "painful" memories for anyone who sees himself either as an actual higher being or as a potential one. Such an individual looks into a dark horizon or, to use Nietzsche's words, a dark abyss, which reciprocates in kind and turns its gaze on him (BGE; 146).

Thus, the question that Nietzsche had posed in *Human, All Too Human* and the "despair" and "the philosophy of destruction" that he had intimated in 1878 continued to haunt him. He was honest enough to provide the standard of his strength, namely, how much "truth" he could take, or better still, how much "truth" he could withstand.[4] He was burdened by the weight of it, even granted that this "heaviness" was produced by the web of senses, instincts, thoughts, and words that always fall short of "reality." The person who had mocked the martyrs of truth was now suffering, not from interpretations, but from truth. We can understand in this light his statement, "We all *fear* truth" (EH; "So Clever"; 4). We may take this statement, despite its patina of self-mockery, as expressing one of his most important beliefs about himself.

The metaphysics of meaning, for Nietzsche, encompasses the festering feeling that, notwithstanding all one's critique of the dichotomies of truth and falsehood and all one's cheerfulness, one does not want to recognize the truth, yet, as an honest warrior, one will not run away from it, either. It encompasses the belief that the world could have taken another turn; the excruciating idea that one was born in an age—modernity—that epitomized one of those wrong turns, and that one's whole life was a missed opportunity; and the conviction that one is still groping in the dark, attempting to ascertain the role one plays in the drama of life. This metaphysics of meaning also encompasses the suffering induced by what Nietzsche saw as his unique personal burden: to be the crossroad, at which human history divided itself into two halves. "We all *fear* truth." It was the painful realization that in the struggle against his age, the great human being engages in "a senseless and destructive struggle against himself" (SE; 3), followed by an awareness that is almost unbearable: "usually we do not transcend animality, we ourselves are those creatures who seem to suffer senselessly" (SE; 5).[5] In *Beyond Good and Evil*, Nietzsche longs for the new philosophers, the ones who will leave behind the many chances that history has been so far (BGE; 203). The meaninglessness of history and human life must be overcome. Everything could not be necessity.[6] There must be a will somewhere, and it must be taught by the new philosophers: they must "teach man the future of man as his *will*, as dependent on a human will" (BGE; 203).

The metaphysics of meaning appears in many guises in Nietzsche's writings: in the need for artistic creations; in the art of dissecting the human soul; in the concomitant need to interpret one's personal life as a set of hieroglyphs to decipher human life in general; and in the despair of a philosophy of destruction. Even in Nietzsche's early reflections on Wagner's music, the problem of the meaning of life was for him a deeply emotional one. Wagner's music, Nietzsche claims, discloses nature by making the invisible world visible and forces the individual who has seen the nakedness of nature to ask himself: "'What does this nature want from you? Why do *you* actually exist?'" (RWB; 7).

The new philosophers may provide a hint to answer this question. We must remember that Nietzsche always claimed to possess a keen foresight, and in his description of the new philosophers it is not difficult to see what he is already doing; that is, what he already claims that he is. Who are these new philosophers to whom we now have to turn?[7] They are "spirits strong and original enough to make a start on antithetical evaluations and to revalue and reverse 'eternal values'"; they are "heralds and forerunners," as well as "men of the future who in the present knot together the constraint which compels the will of millennia on to *new* paths" (BGE; 203).

Nietzsche, of course, meets all these criteria. He is providing a fresh start on "antithetical evaluations"; he is revaluating "eternal values"; and, above all, he is a man of the future "*who in the present*" is attempting, with all his powers, to steer clear of the abyss of modernity and turn humankind toward a new path. He is a member of a group of "free spirits" who "are already a 'revaluation of all values,' an *incarnate* declaration of war and victory over all ancient conceptions of 'true' and 'untrue'" (AC; 13). That he is a man of the future should be in no doubt: "My time has not yet come, some are born posthumously" (EH; "Good Books"; 1). He needed meaning for his own life, and he constructed this meaning by narrating a set of stories about the past that had spawned him. If, as he claimed in *Twilight of the Idols,* no one is accountable for what he is,[8] he at least intended to become aware of who he was.

But this goal demanded that he know *why* he had become the individual he was, and this nagging "why" kept sending him back to the genealogy of deeds and concepts until he thought he had found a solution: namely, whole millennia were unfolding in him and through him (GS; 54; AOM; 223). He sought in tragedy a means to strengthen his spirit. The first expression of this unfolding—*in* him—gave Nietzsche a glimpse of awareness of his life's meaning. The second dimension—*through* him—made him responsible for both the present and the future. A passage written in 1882 turns out to be an uncanny premonition of the fate awaiting him, a premonition mixed with the growing pain that Nietzsche, apparently, had felt since he concluded that everything was innocence and chance, that is, human existence had no meaning. In this passage he referred to persons as the "emerging late ghosts of past cultures and their powers," and "whoever feels these powers in himself must . . . defend, honor, and cultivate them" against the world that resists them. A person who regards himself as carrying the ghosts of past culture may become a great human being, but he may also be forced into madness or perish early (GS; 10). Nietzsche conceived of the past as a repository that never ends and, accordingly, he was aware of what it was in his own bosom; the ghosts struggled in himself. As a result, he was able to identify Napoleon as a figure of antiquity and to know the driving motivations of the Athenian aristocracy (D; 247)—he, after all, had "seen" it all before (SE; 7). But if he had "seen" it all before, it was because the metaphysics of meaning provided him with an epistemological and privileged standpoint from which he could assess life and his own role and value within it.

At this point, it is appropriate to specify in more detail how I understand the metaphysics of meaning in Nietszche, and why I regard it as central to an understanding of his philosophy. It is clear that Nietzsche's concept of the will to power is a metaphysical claim; that is, the will to power is meant to refer to the distinctive feature of all forms of existence. It is also an undemonstrable claim. Furthermore, his idea of "eternal recurrence" is also an undemonstrable metaphysical claim. But another key element in his philosophy qualifies the importance accorded to the will to power. There is no will to power without its embodiments, in the same way that there is no life without particular living bodies. In other words, it is not enough to claim that the will to power is the "essence" of life. Nor is it enough to declare that the will to power is "not a being, not a becoming, but a *pathos*—the most elemental fact from which a becoming and effecting first emerge" (WP; 635).[9] This "essence" and this "pathos" always need specificity,[10] which is why the will to power expresses itself in valuations and the creation of meanings (WP; 675, 590), in establishing justice (WP; 375), in interpretations and the will to truth (WP; 534, 552, 556, 585A), in self-preservation, in health and sickness, in life-affirming possibilities, and even in decaying forms of life. Valuations, interpretations, and the will to truth are all expressions of meaning. This view is more compelling when we take stock of an important qualification that Nietzsche makes in his appraisal of man. Namely, of all living creatures, man is a valuating animal, which means that the creation and revaluation of values—that is, the ascription of meaning—are part of human nature.

In this sense, valuation and the will to power are defined by a symbiotic relationship. The will creates and shapes valuations, but this act of the will to power is, at the same time, an expression of the valuating character of our humanity. Nietzsche's philosophy suggests that the creation of values and therefore of meaning is the highest expression of the will to power. And, I will argue below, eternal recurrence is the highest meaning bestowed on life. It is through the creation of meaning that the will to power empowers itself, in a case of self-enactment.

THE METAPHYSICS OF MEANING AND THE JUSTIFICATION OF LIFE

The components of Nietzsche's metaphysics may be outlined as follows:

(1) Life has no intrinsic meaning. This is best expressed in *Human, All Too Human*. The "deeper one looks, the more our valuations disappear—meaninglessness approaches!" (WP; 602).

(2) Four questions follow:
   (a) Why does life have no meaning?
   (b) Why do I need to give meaning to life?
   (c) Why do I need to answer questions (a) and (b)?
   (d) How could I give meaning to my life?

Only question (d) is consistent with a philosophy that acknowledges the thoroughly accidental character of nature. Accordingly, it is the only question that one imbued with Nietzschean theoretical concerns may attempt to answer. However, instead of accepting statement 1 above, Nietzsche attempts to answer questions (a), (b), and (c) through the stories he tells and the origins he seeks.

(3) Life and suffering are entwined, as I discussed in chapter 2. This presupposition goes back to the idea of primal suffering in *The Birth of Tragedy* (BT; 3, 7–9).

(4) Suffering requires meaning. This explains why the ascetic ideal is central to Nietzsche's revaluation of Western culture. It gave meaning to suffering, even though it promoted the wrong suffering and furnished the wrong meaning. A similar problem still accompanies dominant values, moralities, and religions, which all lead to a dead end by offering wrong meanings.

(5) Suffering, as the condition of demanding meaning, is entwined with morality, which is a creation predicated on the false assumption that human beings possess a higher nature. By 1886, Nietzsche had asked and answered what, by then, was a familiar question in his philosophy: "*Why have morality at all* when life, nature, and history are 'not moral'"? (GS; 344). Because the "beast in us wants to be lied to; morality is an official lie told so that it shall not tear us to pieces. Without the errors that repose in the assumptions of morality man would have remained animal" (H; I; 40). He "*has* to believe, to know, from time to time *why* he exists" and he would not grow without a special faith, "without faith in *reason in life*" (GS; 1).[11] The imperative to know why he exists is a fundamental part of his spiritual horizon. The answers arising from man's valuations and his need to justify life may be false and, more likely than not, they are false, but, still, they are necessary. At a certain stage, knowledge is no more than the identification of the falsehoods that make life possible, and knowledge could even be a conscious effort to hide or to run away from truth.

(6) The juncture of the principle that life is meaningless with our need to know why we exist transforms truth into a frightening

duty. "We all *fear* truth." "For truth is ugly" (WP; 598). For Nietzsche, as for Hobbes, truth begins as a quality given by language, not by independent objects. But this view is later abandoned, and truth appears as independent of the interpreter's perspective, thus opening the way for certain absolute truths. Once we take stock of this evolution, it is possible to identify several stages in Nietzsche's view of truth:

(a) At a certain stage, truth is antithetical to life. (Life cannot withstand truth.)

(b) Falsehood thus provides sustenance to life (the principle of its utility, as presented in *Human, All Too Human, The Gay Science,* and the *Genealogy* (see GM; I; 3; WP; 583A).

(c) The meaninglessness of life is too heavy a weight for us to bear—this is implied by (a) above.

(d) Statements (b) and (c) imply that man needs consolation, an idea consistent with Nietzsche's view of art and the importance of finding a meaning for suffering.

(e) The depth provided by religion, morality, and art allows us to regard truth as the measure of the spiritual level of a person, that is, how much truth he can bear.

(f) A historical past consisting of errors creates the conditions both for nihilism and for a new sensibility and awareness, whose best exemplars are the new philosophers, the ones who can bear the heaviness of truth. This view was expressed in *Human, All Too Human* when Nietzsche argued that "men are capable of consciously resolving to evolve themselves to a new culture, whereas formerly they did so unconsciously and fortuitously" (H; 24). It is also expressed in *Daybreak* (D; 108; see also WP; 605). As late as the Spring–Fall of 1888, Nietzsche wrote: "The belief that the world as it ought to be *is*, really exists, is a belief of the unproductive who do *not desire to create a world* as it ought to be." Thus the will to truth is equated with *"the impotence of the will to create"* (WP; 585A).

The six components discussed above comprise a metaphysics, not because they constitute an ontology of life, but because they are an ontology that *transcends* life. Meaning is elevated to the point of becoming the standard to judge the validity of life and the goal toward which life should strive. It is obvious that life can go on, without a quest for meaning. But when this quest turns into the center that defines one's identity, it appears as transcendental. That is, meaning is understood as a value that is *above* life. Meaning is also an antecedent goal, in the sense that the individual finds himself in a meaningless void with a moral duty to escape from that void by bestowing meaning on life. Life is understood as surrounded by a fundamental lack, and this lack *needs* to be filled. The underlying premise is that a life without meaning would be truncated, and life instead needs to be justified.

In a fragment dated Spring–Fall 1887, Nietzsche volunteered an eloquent comment on his spiritual biography. In 1876, he stated, he felt "terrified to see all I had desired hitherto *compromised*." He felt imprisoned in his philology and teaching. "At the same time, I grasped that my instinct went into the opposite direction from Schopenhauer's: toward a *justification of life*, even at its most terrible, ambiguous, and mendacious; for this I had the formula 'Dionysian'" (WP; 1005). Nietzsche's move toward a "justification of life" here is tantamount to saying that he intends to justify nature. His angst reached an unknown depth in the summer and fall of 1888, when, in *The Will to Power*, he argued that virtue must be understood and justified as "part of the fundamental immorality of all existence" (WP; 328). "For this existence is immoral—And this life depends upon immoral preconditions: and all morality *denies* life" (WP; 461). Hence the need to justify life, which is a task that requires, as a precondition, the abolition of the "real" world (WP; 461).

Thus, in the double sense of being above life and in providing a justification of life, the quest for meaning emerges as metaphysics. As I understand it, in Nietzsche's philosophy, something could be placed above life, but nothing is *outside* life. Even "the condemnation of life by the living is after all no more than the symptom of a certain kind of life" (TI; "Morality"; 5). God, sin, moral responsibility, guilt, and so forth are all human valuations, and in "valuations are expressed conditions of preservation and growth" (WP; 507). Similarly, human beings invented the "real world," that is, the world of being, in order to prosper. "We have projected the conditions of *our* preservation as predicates of being in general" (WP; 507). But there "are no spiritual causes at all!" The "other world" is a case of idolatry, a case in which human beings worship their own causal and conceptual inventions. Man invented his "three 'inner facts'"—will, spirit, ego—and then projected them into the outside world. He "posited 'things' as possessing being according to his own image, according to his concept of the ego as cause. No wonder he later always discovered in things only *that which he had put into them!*" (TI; "Errors"; 3).

For Nietzsche, such "idolatry" is the denial of one's life. It is my contention that the quest for meaning, too, should be understood as a denial of life, to the extent that this quest looks for a transcendental anchor to save life from its emptiness and to explain, as a moral duty, why life is sick and how it could find redemption. It is possible to argue that the will to power constitutes the central anchor that characterizes Nietzsche's metaphysical paradigm. But, as I have argued above, for Nietzsche, the will to power alone is not enough. This will is valued for its particular embodiments and deeds. The will to power interprets, creates values, seeks truth, establishes justice, and so on. But after defining life as will to power, Nietzsche continues to refer to the bewilderment of existence and the "riddle of life" (GM; II; 7; III; 25) and places a high premium on knowing correctly the cause of one's suffering and in avoiding self-deception. Nietzsche goes so far as to argue that one needs to suffer from the events and characters who are responsible for the mediocrity and barrenness of modernity (AC; 8). He criticizes the anarchist who, due to his lack of culture, is unable to understand "*why* he is really suffering" (TI; "Expeditions"; 34). The socialist, too, does not understand why he suffers (WP; 373). And, in contrast to the slaves—who at least received an explanation for their suffering from the ascetic priest—neither the anarchist nor the socialist will have this consolation.

Nietzsche is thus right in emphasizing the centrality of the tragic. For although he rejects the Socratic formula that virtue equals happiness, he embraces another formula that is at the heart of the tragic sensibility, namely, that life is suffering, and that suffering is a prerequisite to obtain wisdom.

> Zeus, who guided men to think,
> who has laid it down that wisdom
> comes alone through suffering.
>
> (Aeschylus, *Agamemnon*, 175–80)

This formula is joined, in tragedy, both to the figure of the suffering wanderer who does penance for his deeds, and to the question of identity. Odysseus, Orestes, and Oedipus are all wanderers, and Oedipus pays a high price for his ill-conceived obsession with finding out who he is. The question "Who am I," a question also present in Nietzsche's philosophy, is Greek through and through.[12]

This portrayal of Nietzsche's thought is incomplete without an important caveat. The emphases of his philosophy suggest the possibility that Nietzsche wished to turn the quest for meaning upside down; that is, the possibility that in the process of providing the "right" meaning to both life and suffering through a revaluation of all values, the metaphysics of meaning will be superseded. Indeed, in a note from *The Will to Power*, Nietzsche describes nihilism as signifying a sign of either "*increasing* strength or *increasing* weakness." It is a sign of strength when the will to impose meanings has increased to such a level that the creation of meaning is no longer needed. It is a sign of weakness when, due to the lack of strength to form new meanings, "disappointment becomes the dominant condition." The latter is a sign of exhaustion, and this nihilism of weakness is incapable of believing in a "meaning" (WP; 585B). Nietzsche, however, did not retain this view of nihilism, even though he asserted that nihilism could be a transitional stage in the process of overcoming the world and the philosophy of being (WP; 585A). On the contrary, he presented the doctrine of eternal recurrence as the highest meaning, one that determined one's value and one's role in history.

THE OVERMAN: A REINTERPRETATION

How could a doctrine of eternal recurrence provide the highest meaning for life, however, given that Nietzsche presents the "overman" as the gift that brings meaning to life? "I bring men a gift,"

Zarathustra proclaims in a prologue fraught with omens. "*I teach you the overman,*" who, Zarathustra goes on, is "the meaning of the earth." This issue must be addressed before turning to Nietzsche's doctrine of eternal recurrence. For Zarathustra, man is a "polluted stream," and one "must be a sea to be able to receive a polluted stream without becoming unclean" (Z; P; 2, 3). The overman is "this sea." The characterization of man as "polluted," as something filthy that needs cleanliness, is precisely the view held by the first version of the ascetic priest, of the priestly aristocracy (GM; I; 6). The "polluted stream" is a presage of both hope and tragedy. "Man is a rope, tied between beast and overman—a rope over an abyss" (Z; P; 4). It should not escape our attention that both Zarathustra and the ascetic priest describe man as a bridge. But the ascetic priest conceives of life as a bridge toward another mode of existence, which will redeem that life. Life is a "wrong turn," and it is necessary to "walk back to the point where it begins" (GM; III; 11). For Zarathustra, by contrast, there is no turning back. Man must walk forward. Man is a bridge between the past (the beast) and the future (the overman), and it is in this sense of "bridge" that man's greatness lies. Thus is Zarathustra's teaching, after he abandons his cave, walks through the forest, runs away from the saint, and comes to the marketplace where the mob waits for the tightrope walker.

Who is this tightrope walker? He is not the overman, but he is the project toward the overman. He crosses over a bridge that may lead toward a future but that also shivers over an abyss. The tightrope walker begins his journey, which is disguised as a public performance, but a jester, who is none other than a representative of the mob, a character who comes out of the same small door from which the tightrope walker stepped toward his fate, trips him and makes him fall. Before the tightrope walker's fall, Zarathustra has described himself as a herald, who comes before the advent of lightning and before the advent of the overman. As a herald, he knows that he, and not only he, must perish. The tightrope walker, as the symbol of the project toward the overman, perishes too. Zarathustra brings him consolation in the last moment of his dangerous journey. The walker is not the overman. It is worth noticing, however, that he is destroyed only when he reaches the exact midpoint of the rope. Zarathustra promises to bury him, places the dead body on his back, and is admonished by the jester to leave town, which he does. As Zarathustra vows, "Human existence is uncanny and still without meaning: a jester can become man's fatality. I will teach men the meaning of their existence—the overman, the lightning out of the dark cloud of man" (Z; P; 7). And so Zarathustra becomes the gravedigger who carries the corpse of the one who attempted to become the overman. Like Nietzsche, the tightrope walker was born posthumously. He was Zarathustra's first companion, who stood in the background when Zarathustra made the crucial commitment that he would no longer talk to the dead, nor be a gravedigger, nor speak to the people. "I shall join the creators, the harvesters, the celebrants" (Z; P; 9). And immediately, an eagle and a serpent appear, who will be his animals and his companions. His goal of joining the creators and celebrants is thus stillborn. Much later, in the section "On the Higher Man," Zarathustra remembers this first moment and regrets it. "I committed the folly of hermits, the great folly: I stood on the market place." In the evening, "tightrope walkers and corpses were my companions; and I myself was almost a corpse."

On this reading, not only is God dead, but the first person who tries to reach the stage of the overman suffers a humiliating death. Zarathustra's first, unconscious act that will alter the direction of his life is to carry a corpse on his back, leave the marketplace, and bury his first companion. Zarathustra's awareness of life thus comes through his encounter with death. He will join the harvesters and the celebrants; that is, he will join those who create and enjoy life. But he is destined to solitude: neither the people nor his disciples understand him. Thus, he emerges as an anti-Plato, who puts forward his own allegory of the cave. In Plato's account, the cave is underground. Zarathustra's cave is located on a mountain. In Plato's account, one of the prisoners dwelling in the cave gets loose and walks toward the sun, going up. For the latter, the sun goes to his cave, and he is nobody's prisoner. "For ten years you have climbed to my cave: you would have tired of your light and of the journey had it not been for me and my eagle and my serpent" (Z; P; 1). In Plato's account, the upward road is an incentive that spurs the recently freed prisoner to keep walking. For Zarathustra, he and his animals are the incentives, and the sun needs to visit them.

Zarathustra, as the monk who witnesses the tragedy of the tightrope walker, learns that the overman is a possibility that will overcome man. But even the overman is the will to power, and as such, he will be obsessed with overcoming something more than man. The overman will need to overcome the "it was" in order to ascend to the highest dimension of the will to power and, in Nietzsche's view, come closest to the stage of being. This means that the overman, the tightrope walker who actually succeeds in reaching the tower on the other side of the rope, will then have to retrace his steps and walk back, over and over. "What is great in man is that he is a bridge and not an end: what can be loved in man is that he is an overture and a going under" (Z; P; 4). Thus the idea of an eternal recurrence offers the conditions for the greatness of man, as well as the requirements for loving him. On Nietzsche's concept of the eternal recurrence, the bridge will always be present, and there will be no end to crossing it. Man will always be both an "overture" and a "going under."

Eternal Recurrence and the Whole

The contours of Nietzsche's idea of eternal recurrence are well known. The world, he claims, contains a definite quantum of force that exists in infinite time, from which he concludes that all possible combinations of lives are destined to recur eternally (WP; 1066, 1067). Nietzsche, not surprisingly, did not develop this idea, much less attempt to prove it in any systematic way. For our purposes, the doctrine is important because it establishes a direct link to his metaphysics of meaning. As Karl Löwith states, "to Nietzsche himself the doctrine of eternal recurrence was the fundamental issue of his philosophy."[13] When it made its debut in *The Gay Science*, Nietzsche presented it as a mere thought experiment, proposed by a demon (GS; 341). In *Thus Spoke Zarathustra*, he was more emphatic. In *Beyond Good and Evil* the thought experiment is now presented as the "ideal . . . of the most living and world-affirming man," one "who has not only learned to get on and treat with all that was and is but who wants to have it again *as it was and is* to all eternity, insatiably calling out *da capo* not only to himself but to the whole piece and play" (BGE; 56). In *The Will to Power*, Nietzsche sums up the meaning of the doctrine.

The idea of eternal recurrence is Nietzsche's response to the spiritual catastrophe produced by the death of God, a death that leaves us permanently adrift. To use some of his metaphors—there is no longer a sun around which to revolve; there are no guardrails to protect us on our journey toward nowhere. For there are no goals to life. "Are we not plunging continually? . . . Are we not straying as through an infinite nothing?" (GS; 125). With a tinge of irony, Nietzsche introduces the parable of the madman, who in all likelihood prefigures himself. The madman announces to the complacent crowd of modernity the heartrending news that God is dead. At first, the crowd's attitude is one of jest and laughter. They already know it and are willing to go along with it. The madman is the only person who is aware of the *implications* of the death of God, which have never entered the mind of the crowd. However, when he proceeds to recite these implications, the crowd's mood changes, and jest gives way to silence and astonishment. The tables are turned, and the madman emerges as the only figure who is in complete control of his wits. It is the crowd that is in the grip of madness. They have lost any sense of reality, and they lack knowledge of the darkness that lies ahead. They even fail to realize that they were the doers of the deed (of destroying God), whose consequences will reach them in a distant future. For his part, the madman, like the tightrope walker and Nietzsche, realizes that he is a posthumous person. "I have come too early . . . my time is not yet." By breaking his lantern, he, too, returns to darkness. He, too, lacks a consolation for the death of God (GS; 125).

This consolation appears in section 341 of *The Gay Science*, titled "The greatest weight," but an anticipation is given in an earlier section, beginning, "*The most dangerous point of view.*—What I do or do not do now is as important for everything that is yet to come as is the greatest event of the past: in this tremendous perspective of effectiveness all actions appear equally great and small" (GS; 233). In section 341, a demon utters a new knowledge: the individual will live his life "innumerable times more; and there will be nothing new in it." Everything will be repeated identically. The individual will be changed or crushed by this thought, since it is the new yardstick to measure himself against eternity as a responsible agent. "The question in each and every thing, 'Do you desire this once more and innumerable times more?' would lie upon your action as the greatest weight" (GS; 341). Or, as Nietzsche would state in 1888, Do you want to say "Yes to all things"?

The idea of eternal recurrence encapsulates the "most dangerous point of view," as well as the "greatest weight." In section 233, Nietzsche is referring to responsibility toward the future, but given the idea that human existence is a circular sequence of events recurring eternally, responsibility cuts both ways: it addresses both the past and the future, and it redeems human existence. Nietzsche applies his scales of valuation to Zarathustra and finds a human being who experiences the present and the past as "most unendurable." Would he be willing to be an advocate [*Fürsprecher*] and redeemer [*Erlöser*] of existence? The answers lie in the future. But if the now and the past are unendurable because of their failures, the will to power is also gnawed by melancholy. The will is impotent before the invincible "it was." "The will cannot will backwards; and that he cannot break time and time's covetousness, that is the will's loneliest melancholy" (G; 233).

Hence Nietzsche defines the revenge of the will to power as "the will's ill will against time and its 'it was.'" In other words, this will, which is the will to power, realizes that the past is beyond its reach, and this realization produces wrath and the desire for revenge. Nietzsche here anthropomorphizes the will to power, as if it were a person who must will a reconciliation with time and a reconciliation with "something higher than any reconciliation." This "higher" stage is the ability "to will backwards" (Z; II; "Redemption"). The predicament is one of despair, which brings the metaphysics of meaning to its limits. How "could I bear to be a man if man were not also a creator and guesser of riddles and redeemer of accidents?" (Z; II; "Redemption"). The idea of eternal recurrence, however, opens up a vast horizon of possibilities. It means that the will to power can go backward, and thus it frees man from the desire for revenge. The riddle of life is solved. Life is more than the will to power; it is the eternal recurrence of the same life, which, in its circularity, exists in the infinitude of time. "Must not whatever *can* happen have happened, have been done, have passed by before? . . . and that this moment draws after it *all* that is to come?" (Z; III; "Vision"; 2). Time can go backwards, and life will accompany it. The "it was" has been conquered. The "accident" of life is now redeemed because the will has become "his own redeemer and joy-bringer" (Z; II; "Redemption"). Or, as Pierre Klossowski points out, "The Eternal Return is a necessity that must be willed."[14] To express this differently, eternal recurrence is the supreme wish of the will to power. This is why, in my judgment, eternal recurrence for Nietzsche is the highest meaning imprinted on life.

Ivan Soll argues that if the doctrine of eternal recurrence entails that our actions, in the life we are living now, are destined to be perpetually repeated, this is a determinism that leaves no room for choice. Our actions have been determined by our previous and identical actions. And if eternal recurrence refers, not only to the particular life a person lives, but to all possible variants of his life, then there is no significance in the choices he makes. "But this version of the doctrine," Soll argues, "commits you to repeat *ad infinitum* all the logically possible alternative choices in every decision situation, *no matter how you now choose*, with the result that one's choices, instead of being invested with greater significance, as Nietzsche intended, would be robbed of significance."[15] The "undermining of the significance of the concepts of choice and action," he concludes, "is particularly problematic for a theory one of whose purposes is to increase our sense of the significance of the choices we make."[16]

These objections can be dealt with if we integrate Nietzsche's conception of the whole with his view of eternal recurrence. The idea of the whole or the totality of human existence places Nietzsche's apparently conflicting claims in a new light. In *Schopenhauer as Educator*, Nietzsche had propounded the ideal of seeing in one individual's life the codes to decipher all possible lives (SE; 3). This person carries, indeed, "the greatest weight." The doctrine of eternal recurrence signifies not only that one's life will determine all one's future lives, but also that, due to the circular movement, it will determine all past lives as well. The past and the future are thus implicated in the present. Yet, the idea of eternal recurrence should not be confused with historiobiography, as I have defined it. Historiobiography refers to the philosophical and psychological conviction that the past is always present in all human beings and that some individuals become aware of this presence. Eternal recurrence refers to a finite, but eternal, quantum of power that exists in an infinite time. This quantum of power, which is present in both organic and inorganic processes, is then destined to repeat itself. One's life will be relived in an eternal cycle of return. The question is whether a person who knows this can withstand this fatality. Since, in Nietzsche's view, the idea of eternal recurrence imposes an obligation, in that the individual must act in such a way that the best possibilities he can envision will be fulfilled, the idea of eternal recurrence establishes a moral imperative.

In discussing the rehabilitation of the chaotic character of nature through life in this eternal cycle, Haar states that "there are the requirements of the imitation of the cycle: they urge us to become cyclical beings, to identify with existence, to be capable of experiencing several contrary points of view, several opposite philosophies, to view health from the perspective of sickness, and *vice versa*."[17] Although Nietzsche's argument is that the cycle occurs regardless of our choices, Haar's argument is convincing: the eternal recurrence is a call to affirm, cheerfully, human existence. "If we affirm one single moment, we thus affirm not only ourserves but all existence" (WP; 1032). Furthermore, since eternal recurrence is not reincarnation, people do not know the details of the life they are now repeating, but they should be aware of the best achievements of human history so far.[18] Thus, they should act in a way that affirms a healthy life.[19] If their instincts and their quantum of power prevent them from such an affirmation, in knowing that what they are is what they have been and will be, they could be changed or crushed. But, at least, they ought to know the injunctions of Nietzsche's philosophy.

This mode of ethical reasoning makes people responsible agents who are also reconciled with the total innocence of becoming. The fact that they may be wrong, in what they think is the most appropriate choice to achieve the best possibilities that the future may hold, does not diminish their moral obligation. But this moral obligation is one that realizes and confirms, in an eternal recurrence, one of Nietzsche's most cherished goals, namely, the theory of the total unaccountability of nature.[20] The innocence of becoming is restored. Responsibility and necessity are reconciled: "event and necessary event is a *tautology*" (WP; 639). And the will to power reaches its supreme height when the character of being is imposed on becoming.

How can "being" be imposed on "becoming"? This is meaningful in the sense that becoming is compatible with states of relative stability that permit thought. Or, to express it metaphorically, becoming for Nietzsche contains portions or chunks of being, an assertion that obtains its full significance in the idea of eternal recurrence. An act, as something that begins at point A and ends at point B, has specific boundaries. It does not matter if, in the movement toward point B, the act undergoes inner changes. From the perspective of an eternal circle, this act will repeat itself *identically*, and its inner changes in the motion from A to B will repeat themselves in an identical fashion (WP; 1066). From the viewpoint of eternity, which is the view that Nietzsche adopts by enclosing human history within the circle of eternal recurrence, the perpetual repetition of the same act or the same series of acts is bound to be the closest possible approximation of being. That is, it is a fixed set of occurrences that repeats itself *ad infinitum*. "To impose upon becoming the character of being—that is the supreme will to power. . . . That *everything recurs* is the closest *approximation of a world of becoming to a world of being*" (WP; 617). Nietzsche had already claimed that the only way he could justify philosophy was by using it "to describe Heraclitean becoming and to abbreviate it into signs (so to speak, to *translate* and mummify it into a kind of illusory *being*)."[21]

Nietzsche, however, has forgotten some important pieces of the puzzle. Nature is chance, but time is not. Time simply is. The will to power does not impose any meaning on life, because this will does not create the eternal recurrence. Rather, the will to power discovers a cosmos whose fundamental feature is an eternal recurrence. Thus, there is, after all, a purpose to life, and this purpose is the desire and courage to live life once more without flinching at the pain one must endure. Soll's critique, described above, can thus be answered. Taken together, the idea of eternal recurrence and the idea of the whole impose on the individual the choice of rejecting or accepting, *cheerfully,* his fatality. The significance of this choice, which entails a defense and a reconciliation with life, is not diminished by the fatality.

Eternal recurrence is, in Nietzsche's well-known phrase, *amor fati,* which is the formula that measures the greatness of human beings: "that one wants nothing to be other than it is, not in the future, not in the past, not in all eternity" (EH; "So Clever"; 10). "Was that life? . . . Well then! Once more!" For "all joy wishes eternity, deep, deep eternity" (Z; IV; "Song"). It is not surprising that Nietzsche called the idea of eternal recurrence a part of his "first solution: Dionysian wisdom," and why he placed it in opposition to "the paralyzing sense of general disintegration and incompleteness" (WP; 417). We thus reach the point at which it is necessary to propose a "small" correction to the way Nietzsche conceived the eternal recurrence. Either as the repetition of one's life or as repetition of all the options inscribed in one's life, eternal recurrence is much more than the closest approximation to being. When one's life is repeated or when all the possible variants of one's life are exhausted, the perpetual repetition of the same is something that *is;* it is something *immutable.* Chance morphs into necessity, and becoming turns into being.

The climactic character of Nietzsche's view of the whole should not be underestimated. The whole is the key to the acknowledgment of a new morality based on the innocence of becoming.[22] The whole becomes historiobiography in the fundamental tasks Nietzsche sees himself carrying on. In *Twilight of the Idols,* Nietzsche puts forth the principles needed to restore the innocence of becoming. The "fatality of [the individual's] nature cannot be disentangled from the fatality of all that which has been and will be. . . . one *is* in the whole . . . *nothing exists apart from the whole.*" Only by accepting that there is no accountability in the whole "is the *innocence* of becoming restored" and the world redeemed (TI; "Errors"; 8). Nietzsche had presented this principle earlier in *Thus Spoke Zarathustra:* "And are not all things knotted together so firmly that this moment draws after it *all* that is to come?" (Z; III; "Vision"). Goethe, the "last German," whom Nietzsche revered, aspired to achieve totality, one in which "everything is redeemed and affirmed" (TI; "Expeditions"; 49). Within Nietzsche's vision of totality, "to condemn and think away anything means to condemn and think away everything" (WP; 584). "For nothing is self-sufficient" (WP; 1032). "Every individual consists of the whole course of evolution (and not, as morality imagines, only of something that begins at birth)" (WP; 373). And, just as the individual determines past and future possibilities, the idea of God should be seen through the same lens. God should be understood as "a point in the evolution of the will to power by means of which further evolution just as much as previous evolution up to him could be explained" (WP; 639; see also 672). Evolution and the past and the future are found in every person and even in some concepts. As Kathleen Higgins observes, "Nietzsche identifies all phenomena as aspects of a single whole, although he does not call this 'God'; and he urges full appreciation of the necessity of all that is."[23]

I have argued that the metaphysics of meaning receives its highest expression in the doctrine of eternal recurrence. This doctrine is the insurance that Nietzsche provides for the strong individuals and the best accomplishments of human history. He knows that the relatively few strong individuals can be no match for the many weak ones, but thanks to the idea of an eternal recurrence, the strong will always return. Becoming and unaccountability rule within the compass of an eternal circle. Being, according to him, has come the closest it can to becoming. Life has been justified through the meaning of the circle, and Nietzsche has passed his own test. He is not crushed by the "greatest weight."

In Nietzsche's own stories, unfortunately, the metaphysics of meaning can only go so far. After all the journeying through abysses, recesses, and the secrets of the soul (his own and other people's souls), the end of the journey seems to be nihilism. I will examine this topic in more detail in chapter 9. For now, it suffices to say that any reader who has followed Nietzsche's journeys and suspected the cause of his suffering and, accordingly, his need to explain it, will not find Nietzsche's reflections on nihilism surprising. Nihilism is, first, a deep discouragement "when we have sought a 'meaning' in all events that is not there." Nihilism, as a psychological state, is the awareness of "the long *waste* of strength, the agony of the 'in vain'" (WP; 12[A]), this "in vain" that is going to torment him, as it did in the case of the Roman Empire (AC; 58–60). It is the even more distressing realization that this waste of strength is tantamount to "being ashamed in front of oneself, as if one had *deceived* oneself all too long." In other words, Nietsche's own individuality, as a person who is unashamed of anything, is compromised. Nihilism is thus akin to the slave morality and its quest for meaning to assuage its suffering. This time, however, there are no external consolations. And nihilism is not content with merely contemplating the "in vain." Just as the slaves are not content until they bring the nobles to their level, similarly, nihilism is not "merely the belief that everything deserves to perish: one helps to destroy" (WP; 24).

This "in vain" is extremely disconcerting to Nietzsche. "Duration 'in vain,' without end or aim, is the most paralyzing idea, particularly when one understands that one is being fooled and yet lacks the power not to be fooled" (WP; 55). When the philosopher is pierced by this "in vain," by the world he has to "endure," and when denial is not a way out, he reaches for his stores of medicines and finds or concocts a consolation. Faithful to his notion of honesty, Nietzsche had already admitted in 1886 that he had been forced to invent his own fictions to endure his life. In the preface to the edition of *Human All Too Human* published in 1886, he wrote, "Where I did not find what I *needed* I had, artificially, to force, forge, and invent for myself (—and what have poets ever done differently?") (translation mine).[24] In a note, presumably written in 1885, he volunteered the same remedy. Claiming that he was "a few centuries ahead in Enlightenment," he confessed that he could not bear alone the tremendous weight or responsibility of this awareness: "to live alone 'without God and morality' *I had to invent a counterpart for myself.* Perhaps I know best why man alone laughs: he alone suffers so deeply that he *had* to invent laughter. The unhappiest and most melancholy animal is, as fitting, the most cheerful" (WP; 91, first emphasis mine).

Why must Nietzsche invent a "counterpart" for himself? This invention only makes sense for a philosopher who is trapped within the metaphysics of meaning. It is only when life is deemed groundless and meaningless, and when these characterizations elicit anguish, that the individual must cope with what Nietzsche himself describes as an all too human need: the need to justify existence. In meeting this need, Nietzsche takes on himself the redeeming task of designing a device—the eternal recurrence—to infuse his life with meaning. This meaning is the conviction that he possesses the strength to cheerfully shoulder the emptiness of life for all eternity. He is a Sisyphus satisfied.

In providing companionship and solace, the "counterpart" that Nietzsche invents is part of the justification that, according to him, life needs. And, in sculpting this "counterpart," he had an opportunity to dig the deep furrows that marked his individuality. Yet, despite his sense of despair or, at times, resignation at the prospect of nihilism, in his last published books he fought his way forward until he stood on the side of the same values he had criticized and mocked with so much fervor. This is the topic of the next chapter.

Chapter Seven

TRUTH AND REASON
The Dangerous Game Is Over

The year 1888 was a watershed in Nietzsche's life and philosophy, as I stated at the beginning of this book. It was his last year of sanity, as well as the last year in which he completed for publication his final books: *Twilight of the Idols, The Anti-Christ, Nietzsche contra Wagner, The Case of Wagner,* and *Ecce Homo.* These works are more than an eloquent summary of Nietzsche's philosophy. They furnish proof of the philosophical problems with which he was grappling and the "solutions" or new paths he thought he had found. We deny a crucial dimension of Nietzsche's reflections if we ignore his writings on nihilism as they appear in *The Will to Power.* But, I suggest, we make another serious interpretive error if we fail to pay attention to what Nietzsche writes about nihilism in the books finished in 1888. Clearly, nihilism was a ghostly and, perhaps, ghastly vision throughout Nietzsche's philosophy. But his final books can be understood as a fight against nihilism.

The archaeological, genealogical, psychological, and physiological drives intensify in 1888. But for the first time in his published works, he seems to be tormented by the prevalence of lies in modernity, and he emphasizes the importance of truth. The argument presented in *Beyond Good and Evil* that life is sunk in untruth, or that truth is a lie one tells to oneself, vanishes. Instead we witness a powerful struggle, in which he is pulled in different directions and subject to conflicting demands. The script we have described thus far has not changed, as is made clear in his assessment of tragedy.

That is, the philosopher, like the noble, is a warrior. "The most spiritual human beings" are "the most painful tragedies," and they honor life "because it brings against them its most formidable weapons" (TI; "Expeditions"; 17). But this struggle is, in itself, a tragic encounter. We consist of our instincts; and the world of appearances is the only world. Dominant philosophies and religions posit the existence of a different world, the "real one," and codify rules to guarantee admission into that world. Nietzsche accepts the world of appearances, but he is not content to stay there; he turns to the instincts for ultimate explanations. The important issue here is that both these philosophers and priests, on the one hand, and Nietzsche, on the other hand, *need* an explanation of the existing world. Notwithstanding Nietzsche's claim to the contrary, he must go "underneath" to explain the world of appearances. As he argued in *Schopenhauer as Educator* (1874), a great human being "must descend into the depths of existence" and pose to himself clear-cut questions: "'Why am I alive? What lesson is life supposed to teach me? How did I become what I am, and why do I suffer from being what I am?'" (SE; 4).

In the world of appearances, our senses are "subtle instruments," and the nose is a "delicate tool" (TI; "Reason"; 3). Nietzsche assures us that he is able to smell bad blood running through the veins of his contemporaries. Yet he is driven to pick up the old and rusty, but still powerful, weapons of truth and reason and to say a few things against modernity. "'Reason' is the cause of our falsification of the evidence of the senses." As long as the senses show the reality of becoming and how nature is chance, "they do not lie." "The 'apparent' world is the only one: the 'real' world has only been *lyingly added*" (TI; "Reason"; 2). Not only are the senses truthful, but they have been the condition *sine qua non* for our scientific knowledge (TI; "Reason"; 3). That is, science has advanced when the evidence provided by the senses escapes the cover-up of reason. Nowhere does Nietzsche explain why we have a "prejudice" in favor of reason, unless we take, as his explanation, the claim that man is a "valuating animal" who, whether moved by vanity or a will to untruth, seeks for divine origins of his existence. Along similar lines, following arguments first presented in *Human, All Too Human*, he stresses the fact of unaccountability and that man is a product of fate (TI; "Errors"; 8). But in an ironic twist, in *The Anti-Christ* Nietzsche seems to need the weapons he has abhorred. It is true that he offers powerful arguments about the futility, or the "in vain," that he discusses both in *The Anti-Christ* and in *The Will to Power,* that "in vain" that succeeded in shattering the best potentialities of the Roman Empire. But it is equally true that, in a book devoted to express a despairing plea against morality and Christianity, Nietzsche somehow decided to take up the task of the old philosophers. The "revaluation of values" is more irony than reality. He is now fighting for truth because, after all, he was drinking from the same metaphysical fountain that posited the divinity of truth (GS; 344).

His arguments about falsification and lies in both *Twilight of the Idols* and *The Anti-Christ* rest on the dichotomy of truth and falsehood. In *Twilight of the Idols,* Nietzsche not only writes about falsification, as he had done in previous books, but also claims that, for the first time in human history, his age—the age of modernity—knows that it lies and falsifies (AC; 38). The same thing happens with religious belief. Modernity is an age in which the transparent awareness of lying comes to the fore: people lie, knowing full well that they are lying. Hence, modernity is an age without shame. Consider, for example, this contemporary description by Jonathan Raban of the churchgoers who attended his father's church.

> Like most sixteen-year-olds, as I was then, I could see inside people's heads. None of the churchgoers actually believed. They might go through the motions, singing the hymns, crossing their hands to accept the Communion wafer, covering their eyes in the performance of public prayer, but they didn't really think that the world had been created by a Palestinian peasant, or that a personal paradise of harps and angels awaited them on the far side of their last visit to Lymington hospital.[1]

Nietzsche would nod approvingly at Raban's description and would add that the minister, priest, or theologian is no longer the self-deluded character the ascetic priest was, the same priest who elicited genuine outbursts of admiration for the honesty of the ascetic ideal. The theologian, Nietzsche asserts, knows that he is lying and goes along with his lie.

IN THE SERVICE OF TRUTH

Truth is, after all, extremely important, so important that Nietzsche is willing to sacrifice "everything" for it. His incursion into the history of Israel in *The Anti-Christ* is not another one of his archaeological explorations. He describes genuine suffering at the loss of a "correct" relationship with God, when the notion of divinity was "falsified" by the priests. This all-encompassing "falsification" stemmed from a choice made by the Jewish priests between being and nonbeing. They chose "being *at any price*." This "at any price" implied the falsification of "all nature" and "all reality." They invented their own history. Christianity did the same in devising a history that was "[*n*]ot the reality, *not* the historical truth" (AC; 24, 25, 42). Christianity then had the temerity to sap and finally destroy "the instinct for *realities*" that was firmly and confidently established in that cultural and political event represented by the Roman Empire. If Rome, this most lasting architecture, could be demolished by a secret conspiracy of deception, it is not surprising that the "whole of mankind, even the finest heads of the finest epochs (with one exception who is perhaps merely a monster—) have allowed themselves to be deceived" (AC; 44; 58). (An exception to this universal deception, according to Nietzsche, is Heraclitus [TI; "Reason"; 2].) Nietzsche, in *The Anti-Christ*, emerges as one of the champions of truth, which he had ridiculed in the *Genealogy*. One can no longer find references to a will to deception and untruth. "[A]ll profound intellects" learned that "everything" has to be sacrificed for the sake of truth. He asserts, "Truth has had to be fought for every step of the way, almost everything else dear to our hearts, on which our love and our trust in life depend, has had to be sacrificed to it. Greatness of soul is needed for it: the service of truth is the greatest service" (AC; 50).

At the same time, one should not dismiss Nietzsche's critique of the martyrs of truth in *The Anti-Christ*. "Martyrs have *harmed* truth," and "one never needs to refute a martyr" (AC; 53). The emphasis here is different and even subdued: it is on the contrast between the fictional "truths" of martyrs and the process of "disciplining the intellect and self-overcoming" that is "necessary for the discovery of any truth, even the very smallest" (AC; 53). Barely a year earlier, in the *Genealogy*, this distinction had emerged in a dramatic way, in Nietzsche's description of the philosopher: "He thinks it in bad taste to play the martyr; "to *suffer* for truth"—he leaves that to the ambitious and the stage heroes of the spirit . . . (the philosophers themselves have something to *do* for the truth" (GM; III; 8). The distinction, apparently, is between those who are willing to suffer for their "truth" and those who "have something to *do* for the truth." The idea of truth that Nietzsche associates with traditional philosophers is one without qualification, namely, the idea of certain, unconditional truth. The truth that he associates with himself is uncertain and also frightening. He is afraid of this truth, though he does not and cannot know why. He finds some comfort in the belief that his healthy instincts will not betray him. But this belief is a matter of faith, not truth, which is a convincing reason why Nietzsche honors so much the tragic.

Nietzsche in the *Genealogy* went beyond his assertions about the martyrs of truth and claimed that it was necessary to criticize "the will to truth": "let us thus define our own task—the value of truth must for once be experimentally *called into question*." He posited that in his philosophy, for the first time in human history, "the will to truth becomes conscious of itself as a *problem*" (GM; III; 24, 27). The adverb "experimentally" is essential here. Questioning truth is an "experiment" that might either lead to new understandings or leave intact the value so far ascribed to truth. In *The Anti-Christ*, however, Nietzsche is not in the mood to call into question, even experimentally, the value of truth. Nor is he interested in proclaiming how truth became a problem that was, in turn, conscious of being a problem. He seems to be willing to suffer for the sake of truth, to sacrifice everything to it, and to announce that its service was the "greatest" service. The year 1888 was, indeed, a watershed year.

In *The Anti-Christ*, Nietzsche laments the imposition of second meanings on a text. Even closer to his constant vocation of philology, he now seems to forget that the notions of second meanings and of right interpretations presuppose the ability to discern the author's true intention in writing his text; and he seems to forget that, on his own account, when one enters the sphere of intention, one is in the domain of morality. To be sure, the latter was not a new development. The idea of philology as a method that can establish value had been presented as early as 1878 in *Human, All Too Human*. In *The Anti-Christ* he depicts its methods as yielding the "most valuable insights" (AC; 13). In *Human, All Too Human*, he criticizes metaphysics for its tendency to presuppose "a *second* meaning" in a text, but he claims that the elucidation of texts "has now finally discovered the correct methods. . . . It was only when the art of correct reading, that is to say philology, arrived at its summit that science of any kind acquired continuity and constancy" (H; I; 8, 270).[2] Philology was indispensable because even though humankind had learned to draw "correct conclusions"—such was the optimistic view presented in *Human, All Too Human*—it was still mired in false interpretations (H; I; 271).[3]

Nietzsche did not eschew his concerns about "secondary meanings" in the books following *Human, All Too Human*. In *Beyond Good and Evil*, for example, he derided physicists for indulging in a "distortion of meaning . . . to meet the democratic instincts of the modern soul!" (BGE; 22). In more categorical terms, he described the *homo natura* as an "eternal basic text," over which "fanciful interpretations and secondary meanings" had been scribbled. He called for the discernment of that "basic text," and, following his instinct to look beneath the surface, he confidently claimed that "at the bottom of us, . . . there is, to be sure, something unteachable, a granite stratum of spiritual fate, of predetermined decision and answer to predetermined selected questions." So powerful and impervious to external influences was this "granite stratum," that a thinker could not "relearn but only learn—only discover all that [was] 'firm and settled' within him" on particular subjects and cardinal problems (BGE; 230, 231). In *The Anti-Christ*, he claimed to find in the Christian theologian an *"incapacity for philology,"* and defined philology as follows: "Philology is to be understood here in a very wide sense as the art of reading well—of being able to read off a fact *without* falsifying it by interpretation, *without* losing caution, patience, sublety in the desire for understanding. Philology as ephexis [undecisiveness] in interpretation" (AC; 52).

Nietzsche's insistence in this definition on not "falsifying" a fact by an interpretation sounds very odd, in light of his view of interpretation in the *Genealogy,* namely, his claim that falsification is part and parcel of, and belongs to the "essence" of, interpretation (GM; III; 24). But, again, in 1888, Nietzsche has dropped or toned down his theme of the ambiguity of life. Instead, he lists five things that he, as an honest thinker, would prefer to know, even if he did not know anything else (AC; 53). As the above definition of philology illustrates, he distinguishes between "facts" and falsification through "interpretation," which means that Nietzsche is here fighting on the side of facts and truth. With this move, I emphasize, Nietzsche places himself in the stage of intention, which is, by his own account, a stage in the development of morality; namely, it is the stage in which the value of an action is judged by the intention that motivates the doer, not by the consequence of the action (BGE; 32). Morality, Nietzsche argued in *Human, All Too Human,* only looks at intentions (H; I; 60), and intentions come into the open when the interpreter "reads well"; that is, when he is willing to see the "facts" that the author wants to communicate and does not falsify them. As Volker Gerhardt argues, "Nietzsche himself was not able to get away from intentions and therefore also not able to break free from the will, its aims, purposes and ideals, although he demands this time and again."[4]

Philology and morality thus turn to be entwined in a manner that demolishes Nietzsche's own view of intention. Nietzsche, the philosopher of the mask, the explorer of inner corridors, is also the experimenter who wants to go beyond the first two stages of morality (the first emphasizing the consequences of actions, the second emphasizing the intentions behind actions). In *Beyond Good and Evil* he stood for a new stage that he called the "extra-moral," a stage that lent further credence to the secret war of the instincts. The "extra-moral" is characterized by the "suspicion" that "the decisive value of an action resides in precisely that which is *not intentional* in it." What is intentional is what "can be seen, known, 'conscious,' still belongs to its surface and skin—which, like every skin, betrays something but *conceals* still more. In brief, we believe that the intention is only a sign and symptom that needs interpreting, and a sign, moreover, that signifies too many things and which thus taken by itself signifies practically nothing" (BGE; 32).

Alas, the intention was so crafty that it kept appearing in Nietzsche's reflections in the guise of meaning. He wants to disabuse physicists of their "interpretation and 'bad philology.'" The claim that nature acts in conformity to law "is not a fact, not a 'text', but rather only a naive humanitarian adjustment and distortion of meaning with which you go more than half-way to meet the democratic instincts of the modern soul!" (BGE; 22). Psychology has not done better than physics; it, too, showed its lack of philology when it "*believed* in antithetical moral values and saw, read, *interpreted* these antitheses into the text *and* the facts" (BGE; 47).[5] Much earlier, in *Human, All Too Human*, Nietzsche had emphasized the need to imitate good philologists in avoiding "second meanings": "It requires a great deal of understanding to apply to nature the same kind of rigorous art of elucidation that philologists have now fashioned for all books: with the intention of comprehending what the text intends to say but without sensing, indeed presupposing, a *second* meaning" (H; I; 8).[6]

The same issue is addressed in *Daybreak,* when Nietzsche criticizes the Christian church for its interpretation of Jewish history (D; 68, 84; see also H; I; 135). It reaches its climax in *The Anti-Christ* in the definition of philology quoted above (AC: 52). As Blondel comments,

> Nietzsche recommends philology as a way of returning to the text itself. . . . Philology is, therefore, a discipline that refines intelligence and probity, and so there is no doubt that its valorization by Nietzsche is a legacy of his rigorous Protestant past in which he was an assiduous reader of the Bible. Out of respect for the text, there is good reason to differentiate, if possible, between the *Deutung* or *Auslegung* (exegesis, interpretation in the strict sense) and *Interpretation,* a more or less free commentary or unfaithful gloss that is added to the text.[7]

The problem is that the enterprise of reading well, of "returning to the text itself," and of avoiding second meanings presupposes a twofold intention: the reader's conscious intention of finding the author's intention that is embedded in the text. This is, at the level of both texts and actions, precisely the stage of morality that Nietzsche wishes to leave behind (BGE; 32).[8] Philology thus gets the best of Nietzsche: first it eschews second meanings in favor of "first" meanings, then it goes back and forth between avoiding interpretations for the sake of facts (facts should not be falsified by interpretations) and exiling facts for the sake of interpretations (there are no facts, only interpretations).

The Anti-Christ is not merely a summary of Nietzsche's critique of Christianity and modernity. It is also a work in which Nietzsche explicitly adopts a moral position in light of his own definition of morality (reading well an author's intention), advocates truth, and stands out as a defender of reason. The Anti-Christ is a defense of reason against the false methods of the triumphant religion. The "reason" of the "intellectually strongest natures" has been depraved; Protestantism is the "half-sided paralysis" of reason (AC; 5, 10). To use one of his many journey metaphors, Nietzsche has called off his circumnavigation. When Ferdinand Magellan, whose search for the Spice Islands accidentally led to the first circumnavigation of the globe, realized that his maps were useless, he threw them overboard.[9] He was literally, from the European perspective, in unknown regions. Nietzsche, as we have seen, ventured into new areas of thought, and he may have sailed through many dark nights, but he never strayed too far from the shore to return. Nietzsche called for a revaluation of truth, morality, and reason, but not for their complete destruction. That is, the old values stayed with him. And this closes off for him the terra incognita represented by nihilism.

His 1888 works keep nihilism at bay and suggest that nihilism disappears as a philosophical problem. As a possible reply to his views in The Will to Power on the lack of goals, in Twilight of the Idols Nietzsche summed up his formula for his happiness: "a Yes, a No, a straight line, a goal" (TI; "Maxims"; 44). Furthermore, he destroyed the grounds sustaining nihilism and even his own indictments, by arguing for the impossibility of judging life. The value of life is "inaccessible." Thus, "[o]ne would have to be situated outside life, and on the other hand to know it as thoroughly as any, as many, as all who have experienced it, to be permitted to touch on the problem of the value of life at all: sufficient reason for understanding that this problem is for us an inaccessible problem" (TI; "Morality"; 5). He was even more straightforward than this:

> Judgments, value judgments concerning life, for or against, can in the last resort never be true: they possess value only as symptoms, they come into consideration only as symptoms—in themselves such judgments are stupidities. One must reach out and try to grasp this astonishing *finesse, that the value of life cannot be estimated.* Not by a living man, because he is a party to the dispute, indeed its object, and not the judge of it; not by a dead one, for another reason. (TI; "Socrates"; 2)

In a fragment from *The Will to Power,* Nietzsche had argued, "It must be shown to what extent everything conscious remains on the surface; . . . how essential fictions and conceits are in which we dwell consciously; how all our words refer to fictions (our affects, too), and how the bond between man and man depends on the transmission and elaboration of these fictions" (WP; 676). In *Beyond Good and Evil,* he claimed that there is an "order of rank of states of soul" that accords with "a rank of problems," and "the supreme problems repel without mercy everyone who ventures near them without being, through the elevation and power of his spirituality, predestined to their solution" (BGE; 213). In *The Anti-Christ,* however, he saw the same issue in an entirely different light. "[A]ll the supreme questions, all the supreme problems of value are beyond human reason. . . . To grasp the limits of reason—only *this* is truly philosophy" (AC; 55). The "supreme problems" of life had repelled him.

Such a view should have given Nietzsche pause, but apparently he did not grasp or did not want to grasp its implications. He continued talking about an affirming form of life versus a decadent way of life. However, once we accept that the problem of the value of life is "inaccessible," that judgments about life are impossible, and that the "supreme questions" and "supreme problems of value" are beyond reason, then one must ask why any individual should suffer from the prospect of nihilism or the realization of the meaningless-ness of life. Why should there be suffering or a sense of despair about values that are merely "symptoms," to recall the passage from *Twilight of the Idols* quoted above, especially "symptoms" that one considers "stupidities"? Or, to put it differently, why should suffer-ing be a result of enduring a life in which "fictions" are prevalent?

This is the tragic stance: life cannot be evaluated, and yet human beings cannot escape their nature as "valuating" animals. Religion, in particular, is a two-edged sword. It made possible the discovery of an inner realm and, through asceticism, gave depth to human life, yet its consequences have been far more painful than its balms. Man "is a reverent animal" (GS; 346), so reverent, indeed, that he is the only animal that needs to find meaning for his life (GS; 1). When this meaning is lost or found to be an illusion, nihilism knocks at the door.

TWO CONCEPTIONS OF NIHILISM

In contrast to his idea of eternal recurrence, for which there are scattered and coherent references in his published texts, Nietz-sche's thoughts on nihilism are found primarily in his unpublished manuscripts. In a long passage from his notebooks dated Novem-ber 1887–March 1888, he identified different stages of nihilism from the standpoint of psychology. First, nihilism comes from the deep disappointment an individual feels when he discovers that he has been looking for a meaning that does not exist. 'Nihilism is then the becoming conscious of the long *squandering* of our strength, the torment of the 'In vain.'" This discovery leads to shame at the fact that one has been deceived. The meaning sought may take the form of any goal, and the process toward that goal "aims to *achieve* something:—and now it is realized that becoming aims for *nothing*, achieves *nothing*."[10] Second, nihilism is the belief in a whole that is superior to, and gives value to, the individual. But since there is no whole, this leads to the devaluation of man. Man "loses his belief in his own value" because he "conceived of such a whole *in order to be able to believe in his own value.*"

The search for an escape from these two forms of nihilism leads to the condemnation of the world of becoming and the invention of the idea of a "true" world. The third stage of nihilism is reached when one realizes that this "true" world is also a fiction. One admits that becoming is the only reality, "but *cannot endure this world which one yet does not want to deny.*"

—What, at bottom, has happened? The feeling of *valuelessness* was reached on understanding that neither the concept of *'purpose'*, nor the concept of *'unity'*, nor the concept of *'truth'* may be used to interpret the total character of existence. Nothing is aimed for and achieved with it; . . . the character of existence is not 'true', is *false* . . . one simply no longer has any reason to talk oneself into there being a *true* world.[11]

These three stages share a disenchantment with meaning, the idea of the whole, and the realm of being, respectively, but the third stage adds a new and fateful dimension. It is both an inability to endure the world and an unwillingness to deny it. This predicament brings Nietzsche to the limits of his strength. This passage, along with other scattered and fragmentary passages, shows that Nietzsche vacillated between and wrestled with at least four different ideas of nihilism, each conveying different assessments. He interpreted nihilism, first, as the upshot of the will to self-destruction that animates those who are weak and leads them to look for their executioners;[12] second, as the realization by the weak that they do not possess a superior moral standpoint, in the sense that they, just like the strong, are moved to satiate their will to power;[13] third, as the consequence of a twofold attitude of disgust and compassion for humanity (GM; III; 14); fourth, as a cleansing process that will sift and segregate the physiologically deranged from the strong. This cleansing process, this crisis, is presented as a willingness to destroy "everything which lacks aim and meaning."

The **value** *of such a crisis* is that it *cleanses,* that it crowds related elements together and has them bring each other's destruction, that it assigns common tasks to men with opposite ways of thinking—

bringing to light the weaker, more uncertain of them as well and thus initiating *an order of rank among forces,* from the point of view of health: recognizing those who command as commanders, those who obey as obeyers. Of course, outside all existing social orders.[14]

Nietzsche's notebooks make it clear that he developed and changed his ideas on nihilism in 1886 and 1887, in the same period that his notions about slave morality and the ascetic priest came to full fruition in the *Genealogy,* before settling on two major and opposing conceptions. On the first conception, nihilism as a denial of life followed by a flight from "actuality" to a transcendental sphere. Since this sphere stems from the denial and hatred of "actuality" and presupposes a nonexistent entity, the outcome is the abyss of nothingness. Nihilism here stands for values that are decoys for emptiness and nothingness. In this sense Nietzsche regards Christianity as a nihilistic religion.[15]

His second conception of nihilism, however, is completely different. It is not the flight into nothingness but, on the contrary, the painful and shattered state in which one is left when an interpretation of morality, which happens to be the only interpretation of morality, collapses. In other words, this nihilism is birthed by the death of God. Instead of ascribing "meaning" to evil, people cling to the belief that nature is immoral.

> Nihilism appears now *not* because unpleasure in existence is greater than it used to be, but because we have become more generally mistrustful of a 'meaning' in evil, indeed in existence itself. *One* interpretation has perished; but because it was regarded as *the* interpretation, there now seems to be no meaning at all in existence, everything seems to be *in vain.*
>
> *Continuing* with an 'In vain,' without aim and purpose, is the *most paralyzing* thought, especially when one realizes one's being fooled and yet has no power to prevent oneself being fooled.[16]

When the God of this morality succumbs, which means the loss of purpose, intention, and meaning, human beings are disoriented and conclude that existence is a void. This nihilism is despair from the "in vain." And who despairs from the "in vain"? The person who needs a God, namely, who needs purposes, intentions, and meaning. He is the one who becomes a nihilist. He is not sufficiently strong to deal with the effacement of God and to bear, alone, the burden of existence. Ironically, the priests of modernity do not need God. They are cheerful in their lies and keep their good consciousness. Platonism, Christianity, and the dominant morality spawned the first conception of nihilism. But the second arises from Nietzsche's metaphysics of meaning.

In the first conception, nihilism is a denial of life through the affirmation of nothingness. In the second, nihilism is the anguished recognition that life is nothingness and leads to nothingness. This second version is not an acceptance and even less an affirmation of life. It is an intermediate stage.[17] It is not sufficently cowardly to flee to the ideal world, but it is also not sufficently courageous to celebrate life, much less feel joy in it. Nietzsche rails against the first conception, but he seems to consider the second one more dangerous. The first is less dangerous because it still needs and relies on the consolation of a transcendental domain to ascribe meaning to life. The greater danger lies in the second idea of nihilism, since it is a type of suffering without the strength to face the pain of a meaningless existence and without the will to seek consolations. In the first conception, another form of nihilism could be used to deny transcendence. Although this would amount to an opposition of nothingness to nothingness (transcendence), it would still be a sign of strength.

> —that the **measure of force** is how far we can admit to ourselves *illusoriness,* the necessity of lies, without perishing.
>
> *To this extent nihilism, as the* **denial** *of a true world, of a being, might be a divine way of thinking.*[18]

In the second conception, however, a nihilistic attitude toward becoming constitutes a fatal weakness. This is the nihilism that shackles the individual to the "in vain," representing a "great paralysis: *working in vain,* struggling *in vain.*"[19] For this "in vain" destroys the possibility of philosophy and lands the individual in the state that Nietzsche fears the most, that of being unable to give himself a goal.[20] Nietzsche's strategy against the first form of nihilism is his genealogical method, which leads to an epic spirituality of redemption. His strategy or, better, his remedy against the second form of nihilism is his idea of eternal recurrence.

Although Nietzsche often conflates his two conceptions of nihilism, he dissects and attacks the first in the texts he prepared for publication in 1887 and 1888. At the same time, he seems to struggle with the second, until he feels he has come out victorious. The victory is achieved through his belief that he possesses the strength to affirm every moment of life in the idea of eternal recurrence, which in one passage he characterizes as "the most extreme form of nihilism."[21]

But Nietzsche also paints himself into a logical corner. For he, too, consistently concedes that a meaningless life is painful to bear. In this sense, the choice of anguish (nihilism) or joy through a Dionysian celebration of life (Nietzsche's remedy) is a choice between two equally valid options. The former accepts the torture and shuns all consolations; the latter celebrates and rejoices in the pain. Both are honest, but the latter comes in handy to measure an individual's strength.[22] It is tempting to regard Nietzsche's joy as pain masquerading as joy, but is not necessary to go this far. The joy that Nietzsche describes can be seen as both an affirmation of life and a reconciliation with the torture that life is. "Was that life? . . . Well then! Once more" (Z; IV; "Song").

My arguments above notwithstanding, Nietzsche's nihilism is hard to grasp. It presupposes that human beings finally arrive at a stage of awareness of the truth or reality of the world. Their cherished beliefs collapse, and they realize that they have been in their own epistemological prison. Their concepts, of morality, religion, knowledge, and goals, are all in error. Their situation is an inverted case of the prisoners in Plato's cave. Their awareness of falsehood leads to discouragement, while for Plato's prisoners the awareness of truth acts as an incentive to seek knowledge. Nietzsche's gives a beautiful analogy of the butterfly that falls short of its hopes:

The butterfly wants to get out of its cocoon, it tears at it, it breaks it open: then it is blinded and confused by the unfamiliar light, the realm of freedom. It is in such men as are *capable* of that suffering— how few they will be!—that the first attempt will be made to see whether mankind could *transform itself from a moral to a knowing mankind.* (H; I; 107)

The similarities between this and Plato's analogy of the cave are striking, but, at the same time, the analogies stand on opposite ends. The heralded "realm of freedom" that Nietzsche announced in *Human, All Too Human* is shipwrecked, not by the new knowledge that made it possible to leave morality behind, but by the knowledge that becoming has no goal and can achieve nothing. To be sure, this knowledge is also a form of freedom, but the confusion it brings is not what Nietzsche expected in 1878.

And yet, if people follow Nietzsche's lead, instead of suffering confusion and discouragement, they might accept error as part of life, or as the truth of life, and go on living in illusions. They might conclude that they are already accustomed and even addicted to living with falsehoods. If they have done so successfully for millennia, what prevents them from wallowing in errors for another thousand years? Nihilism, then, is the logical outcome of the loss of an ultimate aim, truth, and unity in people's perceptions of the world. The disappearance of an aim sweeps away any idea of teleology. The debunking of truth destroys any prospect for traditional understandings of morality and religion, not to mention Western metaphysics. The negation of unity sends logicians to the company of the unemployed. Concepts of aim (teleology), truth (morality), and unity (logic) are no longer tenable, and, accordingly, the path to a world beyond, as intimated by these categories, is closed.

Nihilism in the late works bears the same descriptions it had in *Human, All Too Human* (1878), but its significance is much greater. In the series of notes compiled as *The Will to Power*, nihilism is the same goallessness Nietzsche described vividly in *Human* (H; I; 33), but increased one-thousandfold. As he wrote in his unpublished

notebooks, the ideals spurring the imagination and deeds of humankind were at least goals, and "any goal is still a meaning. What
all these kinds of ideas share is that the process aims to *achieve*
something:—and now it is realised that becoming aims for *nothing*,
achieves *nothing*."[23] This statement—"and now it is realised"—is
perturbing, since this possibility was already present in *Beyond Good
and Evil*. Were not appearances there, after all, the only "reality" one
could hope for?

The Nihilism in the unpublished notebooks is the nausea identified
in *The Gay Science*, but without the consolation of art. It is the meaningless of suffering that tortures the herd in the *Genealogy*, but without the balms and ointments of the ascetic priest. In one of its
dimensions, nihilism is "a symptom of the badly off" when they have
lost all consolation.[24] In the nihilistic state, the individual realizes
that he cannot endure the world of becoming, but he does not deny
it either. Nihilism is thus the zenith of the virtue Nietzsche requires
most, namely, honesty. Nietzsche had already stated that the most
dangerous tests are those that one experiences without the presence
of witnesses. The lack of witnesses is what constitutes the heroic: it
"consists in doing a great thing (or in *not* doing a thing in a great
fashion) without feeling oneself to be in competition *with* others *before* others. The hero always bears the wilderness and the sacred,
inviolable borderline within him wherever he may go" (WS; 337). In
facing nihilism, Nietzsche will not seek cover under a dishonest attitude, nor will he make any compromise. His warlike soul prevents
both (GS; 32).

The archaeologist/physician longs for the transparency of origins and the physiological causes of concepts, but once this transparency manifests itself, it is too painful for the sick to bear. The
story takes a Platonic twist: Nietzsche's seekers despair and sink
into nihilism, just as Plato's prisoners, who are habituated to their
condition, do not want to give up the chains that are the only "true"
reality they know. The heirs of Christianity and Western metaphysics do not want to flow with, or *in*, the flux of becoming.[25] Like Martin Luther, they are too sick for alternatives. The only ones left standing are the Platonic philosopher (when the cave was the analogy)
and Nietzsche (when illness was closing in). For he is "the first per-

fect nihilist of Europe," one who has gone through that stage and already left it behind (WP; P; 3). This is, perhaps, a clue to conceiving of philosophy as a messianic syndrome: there is always one philosopher standing, either as a gadfly (Plato's Socrates) or as "the bad conscience" of his age (Nietzsche) (BGE; 212).

Is Nihilism Possible?

Let us now face the cruelty that is part of life—or actuality—and examine nihilism from this standpoint. What is actuality, given Nietzsche's arguments?[26] As my discussion suggests, actuality for Nietzsche is the external world that is perceived by the senses, read and interpreted by our inner drives, and then goes through the two additional filters of thinking and language. Thus, four levels of interpretation are involved: the portion of the external world grasped by the senses, the interpretation imposed on sense perception by the drives, that registered through the thinking process, and that expressed through language. It would be difficult to assume that the version molded by the thought process and the one that is couched as a linguistic statement are exact replicas of the "reading" already done by the inner drives. Moreover, all the dominant categories we use to define "actuality," such as form, space, motion, and time, may well be, according to Nietzsche, the products of a "false conclusion." And thinking itself could be a hoax (BGE; 34).

Viewed through this lens, nihilism seems to occupy an epistemological vacuum. All values are created by human beings. In the first version of nihilism, the escape toward the ideal involves constructing a transcendental sphere ("nothingness") as a human value. In the second conception, the affirmation of life through the idea of eternal recurrence is unable to obliterate the simple fact that this affirmation, too, is a human value. It does not matter whether these values affirm or deny life, since the "fact" is that everything we believe in has been filtered by our senses, instincts, thoughts, and words. Our senses are our net for capturing reality, and everything we thereby catch will be in our net already (D; 117). On these grounds, Nietzsche would be hard-pressed to justify the very concept of nihilism—a term that, according to the first conception specified above, he understands as the belief in nothingness when the individual abdicates his "reality," that is, when he flees from the actual, treats life as a torment, and seeks solace in the embrace of a merciful God. The solace could be real in the sense that it could act as an effective hypnotic, but the merciful God is a fiction contrived by a sick priest as a balm for a wounded and sick herd. This picture takes a turn for the worse when the individual makes himself accountable to his own fictions, and when we are reminded that "actuality" is a very unstable reconfiguration of images, perceptions, and interpretations.

The human net of sense-perception and the individual's physiological constitution are givens. This means that, regardless of whether they are life-affirming or life-denying, human values are fictions. They are never truly a bridge to the "actual," because the bridge (our thoughts and words) consists of our own illusions. Even the concept of "actual" is an invention, created and recreated through our interpretive filters. Fictions are illusions, and in their most artistic forms, they are myths. But fictions are not nothingness.[27] Nor do they lead to nihilism, when nihilism is understood, as Nietzsche sees it, as the will to believe in nothingness.

In Nietzsche's view, the ideas of Christianity, equality, the afterlife, democracy, and so forth are all nihilistic values. In light of Nietzsche's metaphysics, discussed in chapter 6, a life without meaning or without a goal will fall into nothingness. This claim of his, however, is not convincing. Just as the materiality of the body curtails and extinguishes any enthusiasm for the idea of the soul, understood as an imprint of the transcendental realm, so also the materiality of life should lead Nietzsche to posit the impossibility of nothingness. A meaningless life is still a life.

Thus, based on his own scales of measurement, all of the values that he identifies as nihilistic are human values. And the only objection that he can raise against them is that they are sick values. The priest "is false *because* he is sick: his instinct *demands* that truth shall not come into its own at any point" (AC; 52). Sickness, however, is not nothingness. That is to say, Nietzsche's view of nihilism is an epistemological impossibility. "False" and "sick" values might well be false and sick, but they are not a will to nothingness. They may protect, as Nietzsche claims, the wrong type of life, the life of the weak and the sick, but they always *preserve* a type of life. Even given Nietzsche's premise that sick values deny life by imposing a poisoned will to power, these values, like all values, are human creations.[28] If individuals want to worship their own infirmities, this is their problem. After all, it takes courage or stupidity or both to feel obliged to offer an account of one's actions to one's fictions. We should keep in mind, moreover, that the man of modernity knows what he is doing (AC; 38). *He is not deceiving himself. He is just acting dishonestly.*

Nihilism, then, is not an invisible danger or an undetected error. It is a conscious choice. This is an abyss that Nietzsche faces. One "must be profound, abyss, philosopher" (EH; "So Clever"; 4). In his attempt to understand the abyss of a nihilistic modernity, he confirms what he says about the nobles: being naive or dumber than the slaves, they follow their passions toward traps from which they never return (GS; 3). Nietzsche, however, does return because, like Houdini, his traps are prepared by himself. He chains himself to his stories, and when the audience expects the climax of a vanishing act, Nietzsche announces that such an act is another expression of a false conclusion and a flawed causality. In fact, he is not trapped. It is his audience, educated in the falsifying concept of causality, that *interprets* his predicament as trapped. He, by contrast, is well aware that his self-therapy comes from interpretations which might well be fictions, and he is not deterred. For with those fictions he is setting up his own act, his debunking of tragedy in favor of comedy (GS; 1). And in the process, he is waging his own war and having fun at the expense of venerable symbols and beliefs of the Western tradition. This is the privilege he reserves exclusively for himself: to desecrate through laughter and to make a mockery of everything holy (GS; 382).

Apparently, Nietzsche persevered against the despair he first discussed in *Human, All Too Human,* his despair at the goallessness and emptiness of life. He sought a remedy in the quest for meaning through art, storytelling, and his belief that he was the harbinger, if not the embodiment, of a new philosopher. He was, in all likelihood,

212 NIETZSCHE AND THE DRAMA OF HISTORIOBIOGRAPHY

the "sentinel" he announced in 1873, namely, a person who would take upon himself the task of watching over the "inalienable" and "sacred treasures amassed" by past generations and threatened by the dangers of the modern age (SE; 3). But the despair stubbornly remained, and Nietzsche sought another palliative process: to engage in the cycle of intoxication, to lose himself in imaginary wars against inner torments and real culprits while dreaming that he yearned for the infinite, and to follow this with an awareness of his self-control as a test of independence and self-responsibility; this stage, in turn, was followed by exhaustion, veiled as a fleeting cheerfulness and the dreadful prospect of nihilism. It was his own, futile Pickett's Charge against the enemy Union lines. "Becoming," for Nietzsche, played the role of a cycle of intoxication and exhaustion, which always stopped short of the abyss. For him, the "battle" was no longer a match between Dionysus and the crucified Christ, and never was. It was the predicament of the trapped Dionysus, of the individual who seeks refuge in origins while longing for "time-lessness," and who despairs of artists yet turns out to be an artist himself (GS; P; 4).[29] It is the same predicament as that of one of Jorge Luis Borges' characters, in the story "The Circular Ruins." He dreamed that he birthed a man; the sign that this son of his was only a dream was his inability to feel flames. But one day a fire broke out in the jungle and crawled to the ancient temple where the dreamer, an old man, had resigned himself to die. It was then that he discovered what he was. The fire caressed him rather than burning him, and he realized that he too was an illusion, and someone else must be dreaming him.

Modernity, however, was not a dream to Nietzsche but rather the universality of a decay that had been at work for centuries. The priests rule the masses, and the masses rule culture. Wagner is sick; everybody is sick. The philosopher is "only the further development of the priestly type" (AC; 12). Where is Europe heading? Nietzsche believes that he is the only witness to its debacle. He is the defeated "sentinel," who, like Socrates, will not abandon his post. He is both the first and the last individual; he is the self-awareness that is finally produced after centuries of blind alleys in human history. His storytelling has met the "demand of every great philosophy, which as a totality always says: 'This is the picture of life; learn from it the meaning of your life.' And conversely: 'Just read your life and decipher on the basis of it the hieroglyphs of life in general'" (SE; 3).[30] Nietzsche has deciphered these "hieroglyphs" and therefore can announce that he is the last philosopher and "the last man in the universe," a character completely different from the "last man" he describes in *Thus Spoke Zarathustra*.[31] This is a case of a self-fulfilling prophecy, since he had announced this "destiny" as early as 1872: "'I call myself the last philosopher, because I am the last man. No one speaks with me but myself, and my voice comes to me like the voice of a dying man!'" (PRS; 87).

In rehearsing this scene again and again, the new philosopher is testing his independence and making ready to enter his own secret citadel. His is not the solitude of a dreamer but the solitude of the wanderer. But it is also a deep need to invent something in answer to what he found lacking. This was, perhaps, his metaphysical consolation. And he was too honest to hide his own strategies of survival. Nietzsche coped with his metaphysics of meaning by writing a script and specifying a role in which he had to fulfill his self-appointed task: the creation of conditions for the production of genius, free spirits, and new philosophers, not to mention the reading and dissecting of the souls of slaves, priests, and the Germans. In *Human, All Too Human,* he invented fictions because this is what poets do. In 1888, in *Ecce Homo,* he wrote: "The great poet creates *only* out of his own reality—to the point at which he is afterwards unable to endure his own work." And he confesses that he could no longer endure reading his *Zarathustra* without sobbing (EH; "So Clever"; 4). Could it be that Nietzsche, as a philosopher/poet, created a story meant to soothe himself and then could not endure it?

Incepit tragoedia: the tragedy begins. He "knew" that the world was not "true" (GS; 346) and had no meaning. He suffered from the cultural past and its origins (H; I; 249), but he had to endure them to measure his strength. "It is a measure of the degree of strength of will to what extent one can do without meaning in things, to what extent one can endure to live in a meaningless world *because one organizes a small portion of it oneself*" (WP; 585A). "The terrible loneliness of the last philosopher! . . . Vultures hover above him. And so he cries out to nature, 'Grant me forgetfulness! Forgetfulness!' *No, he endures suffering like a Titan until he is offered reconciliation in the highest tragic art"* (PRS; 85). Forgetfulness was not available to him, yet, as we will see, reconciliation was in the offing. He believed that he had to endure life without any illusions or consolation. But his own claim that man, as the "vainest of all creatures," had a "proud and tragic way" to display his suffering and possessed an unequalled "spiritual inventiveness" should have given him pause (WS; 14).

Is Nietzsche's willingness to suffer from a life bereft of illusions in fact another form of sickness, an inverted form of the ascetic ideal? The ascetic suffers from too much falsehood and seeks a palliative in denying this world. Nietzsche suffers from too much "truth" and uses that "truth" to size himself up and to measure his strength, while assuring us that we should not pity him. The ascetic priest suffers from nothingness (the illusions of "sin," "gods," and the like) and turns to nothingness (the belief in a transcendental world, where he will spend his "eternity"). Nietzsche suffers from the goallessness of life and from the fact that the world has consistently been interpreted falsely (GS; 346; BGE; 34), and soothes his pain with the belief that he, at least, is not being deceived by actuality or by himself. Truth and belief, he warns us, are two different things.

Nietzsche's suffering, compared to the priest's, is tantamount to suffering from another form of nothingness: the absence of meaning in life and the realization that "becoming" achieves nothing. The ascetic priest is able to cover his suffering with the mantle of meaning, and this cover-up is his main contribution to life. Furthermore, he is frequently able to cure himself from his depression with his "system of hypnotics, which thus counts among the most universal facts of ethnology" (GM; III; 17). Nietzsche, despite his assurances to the contrary, suffers from the meaninglessness of life, but his honesty saves him from straying into a transcendental paradise. He claims to accept the lack of meaning of existence (GS; 346) and is content with enduring life in order to learn how much "truth" he can digest. But is not *enduring* life precisely what the slave does?

"We no longer believe that truth remains truth when the veils are withdrawn; we have lived too much to believe this" (GS; P; 4).

But neither truth nor "truth" was ever there. Still, why should the absence of truth or, more accurately, enduring the absence of "truth" lead to suffering? What is the fundamental difference between martyrs for "truth" and a sufferer for "truth"? And, since Nietzsche would certainly argue that his suffering belongs to the healthy kind of suffering, what are the differences between a healthy and a sick form of suffering? One should resist any rush to judgment here, especially when one keeps in mind Nietzsche's question of whether the thirst for knowledge and self-knowledge requires both the sick as well as the healthy soul (GS; 120). In defense of Nietzsche, one can say that both he and the ascetic priest suffer from fictions. But Nietzsche's fictions, or so he believes, are within the realm of human possibilities, while the fictions of the ascetic ideal are nihilistic. "A nihilist is a man who judges of the world as it is that it ought *not* to be, and of the world as it ought to be that it does not exist" (WP; 585A). Alas, this defense must be overruled. Nietzsche leaves the door open for the realization that this world of ours could lead to an inescapable dilemma, which Nietzsche calls a "terrifying Either/Or," of the kind that is running throughout Europe. The dilemma is that either the reverences that made it possible to endure life are destroyed, or individuals destroy themselves. "'Either abolish your reverences or—*yourselves!'* The latter would be nihilism; but would not the former also be—nihilism?—This is *our* question mark" (GS; 346).

What is at stake in both the ascetic ideal and Nietzsche's philosophy, however, remains unchanged. Like the ascetic priest, Nietzsche suffers from a sense of nothingness. Worse, he suffers from a life that, in his own categorical words, cannot be evaluated, such that any judgment about life can never pass beyond the status of "stupidities." In 1888, Nietzsche understood courage "in the face of reality" as the distinctive mark of certain people. He treated Plato as a coward because Plato was unwilling to withstand "reality" and preferred, instead, to flee "into the ideal." In direct contrast to Plato, Thucydides "retain[ed] control over things" (TI; "What I Owe"; 2; see also D; 448). Goethe, too, "did not sever himself from life, he placed himself within it" (TI; "Expeditions"; 49). It is Thucydides' company, not Plato's, that Nietzsche eagerly seeks, but he was also

216 NIETZSCHE AND THE DRAMA OF HISTORIOBIOGRAPHY

too honest not to acknowledge that Plato, in his hands, was a "caricature" (WP; 374). In 1888 the mood of Nietzsche's texts is somber, and his delight in cheerfulness seems to be hidden. In *The Anti-Christ*, Nietzsche reconciles himself with the ascetic ideal for philosophers. The philosophy of the mask, appearances, and the dangerous "perhaps" is gone. The zeal to live dangerously is no more. The idea that the thinker does not recognize a duty to see and to tell the truth has vanished (WS; 43). The dangerous game is over. Nietzsche was gasping for air and, for once, he sought solid ground.

I posed the question in chapter 5 of whether Nietzsche was suffering from two unknown entities (i.e., actions and instincts), and from the realm of fictions (interpretations). Now, as a conclusion to this chapter, I want to place this question squarely at the center of Nietzsche's main concern, that is, one's attitude toward actuality. If Nietzsche is suffering from his "moral fact"—the "fact" that he has to endure a meaningless life,[32] a "fact" invented by deceptive senses that are governed by the secret war of the instincts—then he is suffering *from what he is*. Does this mean that he, like the ascetic priest, is denying life and thus denying actuality? The sinner, Nietzsche declares in the *Genealogy*, is like a "hen trapped by a chalk line" (GM; III; 20). Could it be that the sinner was not alone, and that Nietzsche, too, drew an unnecessary chalk line around himself?

Chapter Eight

MODERNITY, PLATO, AND THE PERSIAN TURN

Nietzsche saw modernity as both abyss and opportunity. The abyss was nihilism, and, in Nietzsche's view, the abyss had prevailed. The weak had won. The opportunity was the advent of new philosophers and the possibility of learning from what Aeschylus once did. In *Human, All Too Human,* Nietzsche had described Aeschylus's task as one that resembled his own. Aeschylus had to educate the Greeks in order to be understood by them (H; I; 170). Probably Nietzsche imagined this as his project before despairing of its futility.

MODERNITY: THE INDUSTRIAL ORDER AND INAUTHENTICITY

How does Nietzsche envision "modernity"? He sees it as the epitome of restlessness (H; I; 285), where even reflection has lost its dignity. "We think too fast," (GS; 6), he complained. Modernity stands for a concept of "freedom" that portends the degeneration of instinct (TI; "Expeditions"; 41). It is a realm of costumes, masks, and artificiality that parades, as a great triumph, the legal principle of equality. Even worse, the modern rich do not even want to increase their powers, since their only concern is to protect their possessions, and, in so acting, they have given strong incentives to the socialist "pestilence" spreading throughout Europe (AOM; 304). The modern age imposes the faith of industriousness, that is, faith in a fanatical acceptance of work as the means to achieving wealth and honor. But industriousness is a denial of individuality; it is the virtue of instruments at the beck and call of the general good (GS; 21).

Nietzsche despises and reviles the "industrial culture," which "in its present shape is altogether the most vulgar form of existence that has yet existed." The industrial culture is the empire of need; people have to sell themselves to survive; and those who traffic in other people's needs bear no resemblance to the nobles (GS; 40). Though he is a harsh and perceptive critic of the socialist and nationalist movements of his age,[1] Nietzsche employs the socialist's vocabulary in criticizing the impersonality of work in the industrial age (WS; 288), a feature that Rousseau, too, had criticized in his description of the transition from the age of independent producers to the stage of utter dependence.[2] Perhaps because he was deeply concerned about the economic misery fueling socialism, Nietzsche advocated an Aristotelian remedy: let the accumulation of wealth be moderate, and thus there will be no basis for the poor to hate the rich. In *The Wanderer and His Shadow* (1880), he even thought that this strategy might allow property to "become more moral" (WS; 285).[3]

> [W]e must keep open all the paths to the accumulation of *moderate* wealth through work, but prevent the sudden or unearned acquisition of riches; we must remove from the hands of private individuals and companies all those branches of trade and transportation favourable to the accumulation of *great* wealth, thus especially the trade in money—and regard those who possess too much as being as great a danger to society as those who possess nothing. (WS; 285)

Aristotle had defended the same principle in his discussion of the mean, and Rousseau explicitly warned of the dangers of accumulated wealth for a society built on the principles of *The Social Contract*.[4] We should note Nietzsche's suspicion of bankers ("the trade in money"), and though he criticized those who worship the state, he also defended a policy of removing economic activities that promote the sudden accumulation of great wealth (presumably through speculation and high interest rates) from the hands of private individuals and companies (WS; 285) and placing them, most likely, under the state's jurisdiction, thus making the state stronger—just as both Plato and the socialists wanted. What makes this argument especially intriguing is that it is presented in a section devoted to criticizing the socialists and mocking Plato's utopia for a "defective knowledge of man."

The economic configuration of modern European society was not one of Nietzsche's primary concerns, but his critique was one of his ways of attacking the artificiality of the modern age. He described modern society as a zero-sum relationship, in which suspicion becomes a central virtue. The strong oppress the weak, and the weak try to take advantage of the strong. Why this zero-sum character, and how does it come about? The explanation, like nearly everything else in Nietzsche's stories, requires the genealogical instinct and a journey into the origins of the modern soul and its institutions. Modern society, according to Nietzsche, replaced an earlier hierarchical order, in which people belonged to different spheres and each person knew what the other expected of him. But a leveling tendency led to the principle of equal rights, an idea already prefigured in the religious notion of the equality of souls. The communality that a legal equality is supposed to bring about, however, is a fiction. In fact, people are more suspicious of one another than ever before. In earlier times, a person knew what to expect from another based on social status. Unequal, hierarchical relations made possible what could be called a stability of expectations, a stability that crumbles in the context of equality. The end result is a condition of universal disguise, and hence suspicion. "The phenomenon of the modern human being has become nothing but semblance; he himself is not visible in the image he now presents; instead, he is hidden" (RWB; 5). "The need to disguise and conceal itself appears to this age more urgent than the need to keep from freezing" (RWB; 6). This situation heightens the importance of being able to interpret the intentions and motives of all persons. The transparency of a hierarchical ranking of people, as sanctioned by customs and legal institutions, stands in stark contrast to the opacity of the modern age, in which all people find themselves equals before the law. They also find that an inherited title or rank is no longer a marker of a social, much less a spiritual, difference. Equality of rights overruns social titles and ranks. If we believe Nietzsche, it took centuries for the old markers and rankings to develop and to create a "pathos of distance" between people. A glance sufficed to show one's place and expectations in society, as in the clearly demarcated lines between nobles and slaves (or nobles and peasants). These lines are erased in the boisterous, chaotic marketplace of modernity. Chaos affords the opportunity to wander aimlessly.

However, modernity overran the limits of good taste when, in addition to its chaos, it became a carnival of disguised beings, in which everyone is hiding something. It was the age of the mask. I propose here the difference between portraiture and photography as two modes of representation that separated the age of ranks so dear to Nietzsche from the ethos of modernity. By its very nature, portraiture once signaled a social identity. A person commissioned a painter to represent his countenance. He posed for the painter and looked directly at him. The painter, with his subject's active or implicit acquiescence, would interpret his character. The painting of the portrait was a serious matter that required slow and painstaking labor. The ensuing portrait was meant not as a display of vanity but as a legacy to one's descendants. It was meant to provide clues to one's character, and those clues would be judged by posterity. Portraiture was a private enterprise, in which the subject knew all too well the public implications of his posing. Now compare this to nineteenth-century photography. It is still an art and a trade, but it pales in comparison to portraiture. The technology behind it is more complex than the techniques of painting, but the act of taking a photo is quicker and simpler. If the photo is meant to take the place of a portrait, the subject is dressed up for the occasion and looks firmly at the camera. But when the same subject is photographed as part of a group, the situation tends to be significantly different. A look at a typical nineteenth-century group photo reveals a consistent pattern in the way people reacted to the camera lens. It was customary *not* to look at the lens. The eyes look east or west, but not at the photographer, as if the subjects are afraid of revealing something, or prefer to show their humility by not looking as though they were posing. It could also be that they want the photo to hide something, to conceal what their eyes might have revealed. Portraiture can be deceiving, but it is less opaque than photography. The early photos of the modern age, by contrast, show subjects whose character is elusive.

When this elusive character is translated into the terms of legal citizenship, we find a condition of universal philology: the self becomes a text that needs to be deciphered in order to ameliorate fear. "Fear has promoted knowledge of men more than love has, for fear wants to divine who the other is, what he can do, what he wants: to deceive oneself in this would be disadvantageous and dangerous" (D; 309). Thus a mistake could be fateful; it could lead to contagion, or one could become the victim of "confidence men," a term that evolved into "con artists." And, in Nietzsche's hands, philology soon evolves into physiological and psychological diagnoses.

The "uncivilized" hordes who were inundating the great European cities sent tremors through the "educated" sensibilities of thinkers such as John Stuart Mill, Alexis de Tocqueville, and Nietzsche. These hordes, for Mill, would become the vessels of dominant prejudices; for de Tocqueville, a tyrannical majority; and for Nietzsche, a sick herd. The big city was the realm of deception *par excellence,* where "con artists" flourished and where, for Nietzsche, philological acumen and practice are essential. As one historian has described New York of the late nineteenth century, for example,

> [It] was a city of strangers—of men and women who reveled in the opportunity to escape a dull, constricting, or unwanted past and to become new people. If the dream of self-invention was profoundly democratic, it was also an open invitation to fraud. A well-bred widow from Kansas City might have been a notorious prostitute, just as a Russian count might really have been a serf, or a so-called Western gold mine might be a heap of worthless rocks. With the telegraph still in its infancy, and with few central sources of personal or financial information available, it was impossible for anyone to be sure.[5]

Nietzsche, always a philologist, epitomizes this predicament: he does not want to be deceived, a principle that dates back to his

Schopenhauer as Educator.[6] But "the art of psychological dissection and computation is lacking above all in the social life of all classes, in which, while there may be much talk about people, there is none at all about *man*" (H; I; 35).

The "will of the spirit," Nietzsche assures us, strives toward cunning and deception, but when this peculiar idiosyncrasy of "the spirit" is universalized in the modern age, the new philosopher senses his approaching redundancy. The universality of actors, of people who know how to produce the effect of truth with untruth and who lie with a good conscience, has made new philosophers pointless. The universality of actors is a physiological mutation (probably, for Nietzsche, due to a mixing of races and classes) that turns the Nietzschean philosopher into an antiquarianism. He will never be able to decipher or dissect the other person. When he thinks he is roaming through another person's soul, he is merely wasting his time in a chamber built with the explicit purpose of alluring and deceiving him. He is experiencing, with all human beings, what the hermit knows firsthand when he doubts "whether a philosopher could have 'final and real' opinions at all, whether behind each of his caves there does not and must not lie another, deeper cave—a stranger, more comprehensive world beyond the surface" (BGE; 289). The Nietzschean new philosopher sees (his far sight is still intact) his coming irrelevance and names it: the approach of nihilism. At one minute he thinks he is ushering in a new era, but at the next he is sent unceremoniously into early retirement. The advent of nihilism is one of the ways that he describes his sudden awareness of his own disposability.

As I have argued, Nietzsche sought to dissect the modern soul and to reveal its secrets. He proclaims his cheerfulness and despises vindictive sentiments. Yet he shows a strong resistance to the idea of genuineness in individuals. When he is not a physician discerning a chemical imbalance, a psychologist discovering hidden motives, or an archaeologist who is planting his own evidence, he is always on the lookout for the dishonesty and deceptive zeal that he takes to be the true dimensions of a person's actions. In most of the events and characters he describes, he detects a lack of authenticity.[7]

Behind love, he sees egoism (GS; 14); behind the slaves' resistance, he sees resentment; behind the ascetic priest, he sees hatred; behind the centrality of self-preservation, he sees decay; behind peace, he sees bad conscience.[8] Behind virtue, he sees the denial of individuality (GS; 21). Behind praise, there could be the subtle traits of revenge (D; 228; see also 273). And behind an act of courage, there might be "a sign of cowardice" (D; 299). We seek to benefit others because it is an opportunity to display our power. We attempt to rescue a drowning person only if there are witnesses who lack the courage to do it (H; I; 325). "Even if we offer our lives, as martyrs do for their church, this is a sacrifice that is offered for *our* desire for power or for the purpose of preserving our feeling of power" (GS; 13). In the feeling of pity, "we are, to be sure, not consciously thinking of ourself but are doing so *very strongly unconsciously*" (D; 133; see also 224). The advocacy of selflessness is self-serving. "The 'neighbor' praises selflessness *because it brings him advantages*" (GS; 21). The "man of renunciation . . . wants to conceal from us . . . his intention to soar *beyond* us" (GS; 27). The magnanimous person is moved by revenge and egoism (GS; 49). The person who shows self-denial is at the same time egoistic: he uses other people to relieve the tensions of his own heart (H; I; 138). The prisoner who goes through the ordeal of physical torture returns to his cell relishing every moment of it: he now has a strong motive to feel pride in himself (D; 229).[9] "Goodness has mostly been developed by the protracted dissimulation which sought to appear as goodness" (D; 248; see also 315).

The person who pours contempt upon his neighbor and then asks for forgiveness is performing a scene for the sake of himself (D; 219). The saint practices, among other things, self-idolatry, and invents stimulants to fight his boredom (H; I; 141, 142).[10] The people who preach and practice the "sacrifice of oneself" should know better: "The truth," Nietzsche informs them "is that you only *seem* to sacrifice yourselves: in reality you transform yourselves in thought into gods and enjoy yourselves as such" (D; 215). Philosophers, who are "a different kind of saint," swear their allegiance to truth, but "their entire trade demands that they concede only certain truths; namely those through which their trade receives *public* sanction"

(TI; "Expeditions"; 42). Everything about Socrates was "exaggerated, *buffo,* caricature, everything [was] at the same time hidden, reserved, subterranean" (TI; "Socrates"; 4). Many of the men of ancient times who acquired fame for their virtue just *"play-acted before themselves"* (D; 29). Play-acting is present in those who try to cover their lack of charm with a mask of "strict virtue." It is also present in those for whom a "noble intimacy is impossible" (D; 266, 288). A person could be trustful, but this is due to a lack of trust in his ability to hide his hypocrisy; that is, "he does not trust his acting talents and prefers honesty, 'playing at truth'" (D; 418; see also AOM; 56). Indeed, in modernity, not even hypocrisy is genuine (TI; "Expeditions"; 18).

The invalids and the mentally afflicted moan and complain in order to hurt "those who are with them." The pity that invalids receive shows that "they possess at any rate *one power;* the *power to hurt.*" The unfortunate man feels superior because "in the conceit of his imagination he is still of sufficient importance to cause affliction in the world" (H; I; 50). Little does the invalid know that, in the presence of any unfortunate person, "we always play a little comedy" (D; 383). In social life, "three-quarters of all questions are asked, three-quarters of all answers given, in order to cause just a little pain to the other party" (H; I; 50). Most human relations are a matter of looking for opportunities to display superiority or to gain ascendancy over others.[11] In short, people "lie unspeakably often, but afterwards do not remember it and on the whole do not believe it" (D; 302). In *Human, All Too Human,* Nietzsche sums up the lack of genuine individuals and the overwhelming evidence of the conceit behind our actions: "One will seldom go wrong if one attributes extreme actions to vanity, moderate ones to habit and petty ones to fear" (H; I; 74).

Many more examples could be given here.[12] These suffice, however, to show that Nietzsche's persistent proclivity for discovering secret intentions and denying authenticity bodes ill for a philosopher who seeks the company of his equals, namely, people who possess the highest virtue of free spirits, which is honesty. Honesty is in short supply in modernity, the age of the "perfect herd animal," the plebeian instinct, and the *"collective degeneration of man"* (BGE; 203).

Modernity is the realm of the mob, which is the realm of the atom. "We live in the age of the atom, the age of atomic chaos." And this chaos brings to the surface "the most profound of all modern tendencies—the tendency to implode or explode" (SE; 4), which, not by accident, is the same tendency that marks the souls of the slaves. Modernity is the age of democracy, which is inherited Christianity; it is the age of the "uglification" of Europe (BGE; 202, 203, 222); it is a stage of decadence in which individuality falls into desuetude. Democracy mixes together masters and slaves. Unlike the noble individual, the "vain man" of modernity subjects himself to the opinions of other people (BGE; 261), a concern powerfully expounded by Rousseau a century before Nietzsche. The philosopher suffers from a greater degree of disgust than others because he realizes that "this animalization of man to the pygmy animal of equal rights and equal pretensions is *possible*" (BGE; 203; see also 201). Modernity is the antithesis to the return to nature and the continuation of the Renaissance that Napoleon, according to Nietzsche, had epitomized.[13] (It is easy to imagine Nietzsche's grimace of pain and shame at John D. Rockefeller's remark that Napoleon's greatness was the consequence of his origins as a man of the people; or at Ralph Waldo Emerson's comment, "I call Napoleon the agent or attorney of the middle class of modern society; of the throng who fill the markets, shops, counting-houses, manufactories, ships, of the modern world, aiming to be rich.")[14]

Nietzsche's account of the role of the artist in 1876 could well be applied to the relationship between the philosopher and modernity. Much like the intoxicated artist, the philosopher "probably feels as though he is suffering from chronic insomnia" and dwelling among "confused and tormented sleepers," who are "nothing but dreamers and sufferers." The philosopher emerges as the only wakeful person, "the only one with a sense for the truth and the real" (RWB; 7).

MINIATURISTS AND ACTORS

The modern world, according to Nietzsche, represents not only the diminution of man but also the diminution of philosophy. There is no longer a place for royal characters or the "hermits of the spirit" of antiquity.[15] Greatness is no longer possible (BGE; 213). But since it is "quite impossible" not to inherit the preferences of one's ancestors, modern ideas and modern education are only able to deceive us with respect to their plebeian origins, now dressed up in the costume of "progress" (BGE; 264). Even worse, the modern decay is depicted as "toleration" (TI; "Expeditions"; 18), which is one of the first things that a noble morality denies: "every aristocratic morality is intolerant" (BGE; 262). Tracy B. Strong claims that, in Nietzsche's view, the "democratization of the modern world makes it possible . . . for there to be conditions such that new values could be impressed on a whole people."[16] But Nietzsche, I submit, harbors no such hopes about the capacity of modernity to create new values. Modernity is not even able to create strong institutions. Democracy is the political representation of man in decay, and modernity is one step away from the abyss of nihilism.

The intrinsic inability of the modern age to understand its decay, along with the lack of "genuineness" that Nietzsche ascribes to it, are the probable end result of a phenomenon deeply disturbing to Nietzsche: the arrival of a new mode of being, in which the theatrical stage takes center place.[17] This is what he calls a "theatocracy," referring not only to the precedence but the lording of the theater over the other arts (CW; Postscript). Modernity involves universal play-acting and deception, as we have already seen. Here again we notice the importance of philology to Nietzsche, which he transforms into psychology when he turns to the sphere of human relations. One is tempted to interpret Nietzsche's critique of modernity as a defense of his own trade, namely, the deciphering of other people's souls. This "trade" is derailed in an age in which behind every mask, the self-avowed archaeologist of transparency will find yet another mask, and another, and so on *ad infinitum*. Nietzsche's critique is more complex than this, however.

Nietzsche's critique of Wagner, for instance, is a critique of the aesthetics of modernity, the aesthetic of decay.[18] Modernity is an age that diminishes things: it relishes small parts, existing in a chaos of separate units. The idea of a grand unity or wholeness has disappeared. A word is sovereign in a sentence, and a sentence is sovereign in a page. This is a "sign" of literary decadence (CW; 7). Wagner is "our greatest *miniaturist* in music" (CW; 7). As Nietzsche intimated in *The Gay Science,* the age of great architecture has passed. There are no building materials for great works any more—everything built is on a small scale. "What can be done well today, what can be masterly, is only what is small" (CW; Second Postscript). Modernity opened the gates to theatocracy, which is decay expressed in a single formula: "the musician now becomes an actor, his art develops more and more as a talent to *lie*" (CW; 7). Wagner is "a first-rate actor" (CW; 8). Modernity is an age without shame: "a 'good conscience' in a lie is actually *modern par excellence,* it almost defines modernity" (CW; Epilogue; see also BGE; 263).

If truth is associated with morality, then Nietzsche adopts a moral stance against what he calls the chaos of modern aesthetics. "Wagner's music is never true." Nietzsche, in contrast, stands for a "higher lawfulness, *style,*" which he claims that Wagner did not respect. Wagner wants "nothing but effect," whereas Nietzsche demands "substance above all else" (CW; 8). "One is an actor by virtue of being ahead of the rest of mankind in one insight: what is meant to have the effect of truth must not be true" (CW; 8). Wagner, the "protagonist" of European decadence (CW; 5), who caters to the masses, is the antithesis of authenticity. "Victor Hugo and Richard Wagner—they signify the same thing: in declining cultures, wherever the decision comes to rest with the masses, authenticity becomes superfluous, disadvantageous, a liability. Only the actor still arouses *great* enthusiasm" (CW; 11).

These reflections of Nietzsche's are baffling if one attempts to fit them into an aesthetic project that identifies the use of deception and illusion as what makes life endurable. It is still more baffling if one ventures to define authenticity within Nietzsche's philosophy. These difficulties suggest that, in Nietzsche's universe, only the new philosopher is authorized to wear a mask—only he is allowed to be an actor. Plato might be relevant here, since only the philosopher kings are permitted to lie.[19]

Once again, Nietzsche as philosopher/physician is on call to diagnose the illness and issue his verdict. By now, his formula is familiar. The name of the first patient is crossed out and Wagner's name put in its place. The first patient was the ascetic priest. Wagner may suffer from a different illness, but in terms of the symptoms, the ones the physician sees, he is the latest version of the ascetic priest. Wagner "makes sick whatever he touches—*he has made music sick*—." "He is a master of hypnotic tricks" (CW; 5). And he is an actor, a "first-rate actor," to be accurate. Sickness, hypnotics, and acting are the three specialties of the ascetic priest, who is also clever, like Wagner. Both, too, are seducers of the masses and especially of women, though admittedly they have different goals in mind. The ascetic priest is a good actor who adopts a "bearlike seriousness and feigned superiority" (GM; III; 15). But here the affinities between priest and Wagner end, to the extent that the ascetic ideal is a form of perverted nobility that "believes in its own predominance over every other power, in its absolute *superiority of rank* over every other power" (GM; III; 23). In contrast to the nobles, those "surface creatures," the ascetic ideal gives a deep meaning to life (GM; III; 28). It therefore creates new values, even when those values are the fruits of sickness. Wagner, according to Nietzsche, neither gives meaning to life nor creates values. Artists, in general, are mere valets of the masses, and actors are even worse.

In diagnosing culture and cultural artifacts, Nietzsche develops another duality in his script. He is either the first or the last: he is the first immoralist (EH; "Destiny"; 2); the first tragic philosopher (EH; "Birth"; 3); the first who discovered the tragic (a feast that not even the Greeks accomplished) (WP; 1029); the first who understood Socrates as representative of Hellenic disintegration (EH; "Birth"; 1); the first nihilist (WP; P; 3); the first who saw truth as a problem (BGE; 1); the first who saw the antithesis between the Dionysian and the "degenerated" instincts behind Christianity (EH; "Birth"; 2); and "the first decent human being" (EH; "Destiny"; 1). He is also "the last disciple and initiate of the god Dionysus" and the last of the Stoics (BGE; 295, 227). Probably, he is also the last warning before the advent of universal nihilism.

WHERE IS THE GUILT?

Nietzsche's characterizations as the first and the last are the costumes he designs for his stage appearances, the masks he wears even when his suffering is genuine. But, by his own account, his suffering is not credible. He objects to those agitators and actors (i.e., old philosophers) who were disposed to die for the truth. Nietzsche, who claims to have better taste, is instead suffering for his own *interpretations,* which are not even the truth. This is, perhaps, an appropriate moment either for Nietzsche to invoke the famous doctrine of equivocation or for a more than welcome recantation. As I argued in chapter 7, Nietzsche, who scorns truth-seekers and the improvers of mankind, ends up, in *The Anti-Christ,* on the side of truth (true interpretations that do not falsify history) and morality (he does not want to be deceived). Leaving aside these conflicting perspectives—after all, for Nietzsche, consistency is a sign of decadence—the topic that led Nietzsche to his jarring indictments of Christianity and the madhouse of modernity is that of guilt. Nietzsche attacked the ascetic priests for infecting the masses with the concept of sin, yet the masses seem to be surviving and enjoying themselves with little attention to priests of any kind, much less to the flames of hell. Consider a description of a famous "French Ball" celebrated in New York in 1869:

> One of the women is caught up by the crowd and tossed bodily into a proscenium box, where she is dragged by half a dozen brutes in over the sill and furniture in such a manner as to disarrange as much as possible what small vestige of raiment there is on her. The feat awakens general merriment. . . . There is not a whisper of shame in the crowd. . . . It whirls in mad eddies round and round.[20]

Such scenes, little different from the combination of squalor and a lively social life in European cities, are anything but expressions of "guilty," suffering masses. Or consider historian Christopher Haigh's description of these scenes in England from the late sixteenth and early seventeenth centuries:

On Shrove Tuesday 1586, Joan Agar of Little Bardfield, Essex, climbed into the pulpit and delivered a mock sermon, as if she were a minister—and Willian Cooke egged her on, handing her a Bible to provide her text.

Philip Callion of Steyning, was cited in 1617 for 'acting the person of a clergyman upon Ascension day last past, in a profane morris dance, with a book and spectacles and other apish and ridiculous gestures of eyes, hands and countenance, to the public scandal of the ministry and vilifying of that sacred function.'

Thomas Smith of Backwell, Somerset, regarded overmuch praying as rather a joke, telling Richard Hiscox in 1619, 'I will buy thee a fool's coat and write the Paternoster in the back.'"[21]

In addition to mock sermons, some engaged in mock wedding ceremonies and mock baptisms.[22] "God," Haigh concludes, "mattered to the less-godly as well as to the godly, though he was a different sort of God. Their world was as it was because God had made it so, *not because men had rebelled against him and ruined it.* The ordinary ways of the world were good ways, even God's ways. So Christians should do as their neighbours did, and take the world as they found it."[23] Haigh does not underestimate the Christian ideas of sin and the importance of godly living in the period, but obviously the depth of these ideas varied widely. And the "ungodly" were, by far, the average Christian believers. Such notions contrast dramatically with Nietzsche's idea of guilt as an inescapable presence in European culture.

Where is the guilt that Nietzsche finds, not merely as a reference point, but as *the* defining feature of European culture? Where is the mob throbbing and sobbing with guilty feelings? One might even adopt for a moment a genealogical standpoint and ask, point-blank, where is the guilt in the fundamental texts that underpin the Judeo-Christian tradition, namely, the Old and New Testaments? It is possible to argue that there is not a single manifestation of guilt, as an immediate feeling of wrongdoing, in the Old Testament, and that only two expressions of guilt appear, fleetingly, in the New

Testament—Peter's torment after his denial of Jesus and Judas's guilt after betraying his teacher. Nietzsche himself stated in *Daybreak* that the Christian gospel had abolished the notion of guilt—and then proceeded, as an archaeologist of the soul, to explain how guilt came about thanks to the "tormented" soul of St. Paul, the "first Christian" (D; 68).[24]

Nietzsche's silence is also telling in two other areas of the Judeo-Christian tradition. One is the message of the Old Testament prophets, who railed against the Jewish priests. Another is the Arian controversy arising from the teaching of Arius that Christ was a deeply human figure, a view that implies a strong sense of individuality in the Christian believer. Nietzsche was silent on both topics.[25]

The conspicuous absence of guilt in the Old Testament and the relative indifference toward it in the New Testament are an important contrast to the torments, guilty feelings, and ideas of wandering as a form of expiation in the Greek tragedies (as with Orestes and Oedipus). But tragic Greek wanderers are glossed over in Nietzsche's stories. Even the preeminence he ascribes to the concept of guilt in his later works (*Genealogy of Morality, Twilight of the Idols,* and *The Anti-Christ*) undergoes unexpected twists. In his own account, the "stupidity" that explains "every" other stupidity of the modern age is the question of labor—the idea that the worker ought to fulfill a role for which nature never intended him. The worker is allowed to vote, to organize unions, and even to wear a military uniform. In consequence, workers ask for rewards "more and more impudently" (TI; "Expeditions"; 40). A key element, however, is missing; if Nietzsche's own categories are applied, the labor question must be explained by the resentment of the masses. And resentment, as a stage in which explosive materials accumulate, is *antecedent* to guilt. Resentment is an explosion waiting to happen until the ascetic priest alters its direction and turns it inward, where it becomes guilt. But the labor question, precisely, is the opposite: it is a resentment that goes outward and attacks the principle of rank that is so praised and precious in Nietzsche's universe. That is, the labor question is the manifestation of a resentment that bypasses guilt. It is one more piece of Nietzsche's larger picture of the tolerance and pluralism characteristic of modernity.

NIETZSCHE AND PLATO'S REPUBLIC

Ultimately, the question of the truth of Nietzsche's "facts" about modernity is not important to understanding his thought. As I demonstrate in chapter 1, the philosopher, in Nietzsche's view, relates a story that has to do more with his own standpoint than with the facts about the people and deeds he describes.[26] But regardless of the "facts" of modernity, he saw in this age the enervation and evaporation of many possibilities for humanity, and he intended to close the floodgates by presenting the ideal social structure, a structure that modernity adamantly opposes. Nietzsche's thought thus took a sudden turn to Persia for its inspiration and returned with a version of Platonism, although without the Platonic Forms.

The project he spells out in *The Anti-Christ* for the new philosopher and the ideal society is modeled on the Platonic paradigm, as delineated in the *Republic*. Like Plato, who changed the content of Greek education while leaving intact its traditional structure (music, poetry, and gymnastics), Nietzsche too transforms the content of the education required by his new species of humanity. This transformation, moreover, occurs within a Platonic structure that is not questioned.

The first legislative act of the *Republic* with respect to the education of the young is to forbid traditional stories about the gods and the netherworld: "The young can't distinguish what is allegorical from what isn't, and the opinions they absorb at that age are hard to erase and apt to become unalterable. For these reasons, then, we should probably take the utmost care to insure that the first stories they hear about virtue are the best ones for them to hear" (*Republic* 378d–e, translations mine). Plato is the first philosopher who enacted laws for his city, for the divine realm of the polis, and for the afterlife. He proposes new stories about the afterlife and the deletion of lines from traditional poems that might instill the fear of death in the future guardians of the polis (*Republic* 386b–c). Not even words depicting Hades as a dreadful place will be allowed (*Republic* 387b–c). The enactment of laws about the divine realm even precedes legislation for citizens. Plato contends that religious laws are the most important ones in his republic, yet also expresses a subtle derision of the gods. The enactment of religious laws, considered "the greatest and finest and the first of the laws," is left to the oracle at Delphi. Their objects are "[t]he building of temples as well as sacrifices and other honors for gods, daemons and heroes. Furthermore, the burial for the dead and whatever service for those who are there [buried] since it is necessary to have their propitious favor" (*Republic* 427b). The "finest laws," then, are those devoted to the ritual owed to the dead and to the service owed to the gods. But Plato's claim that he does not know anything about these things, especially the service to the gods, is hardly persuasive. He makes this statement in Book 4, long after he has established, in Book 1, that justice is the function of the soul and that the just person can count on the favors and friendship of the gods. In other words, Plato eviscerates religion of any meaning relevant to life, by converting it into a set of rituals for *the dead*. He has another agenda for the living, which is his educational program. It is difficult not to conclude, in passing, that the members of the Athenian jury had good reason to execute Socrates for corrupting the youth.

Nietzsche explicitly suggests that genuine individuals create their own gods. Although he invokes Homer (H; I; 125) on this matter, not Plato, it is clear that he too wants the gods to derive their authority from him, not the other way around. Plato introduces order in an otherwise chaotic conception of warring gods, and he uses religion (his own view of religion) as a powerful incentive for socializing ordinary citizens. Nietzsche follows the same path. Not only does he want to create his own gods, who will be accountable only to him, and not only does he chastise "the strong races of Northern Europe" for their blatant failure in this area—"they have failed to *create* a God" (AC; 19)—but also, and more importantly, he specifies the best religion for the masses. And this turns out to be Buddhism, a religion that plainly rejects the principle of equality and posits a hierarchical ordering of mankind, justified as a natural one. Both Buddhism and Christianity, in Nietzsche's view, are decadent religions, but Buddhism is more "realistic" than Christianity (AC; 20–23) and thus to be preferred.

But Nietzsche goes further than Plato, in the sense that religion is an important part of the training of the Nietzschean new philosophers. For Plato, the divine realm is for all citizens, but especially the masses. The educational program for his philosophers is more comfortable with geometry and dialectics than with religion. Nietzsche, too, has an advanced program for himself and the new species of which he is the first representative. But he argues that religion plays a necessary part in the training of the individual. It is religion that makes possible the emergence of the inner domain, the realm of the sublime (H; I; 130). Metaphysical ideas, moreover, "have been responsible for the advancement of mankind." Thus, an archaeology of metaphysics is necessary, that is, an investigation into the historical and psychological justifications of metaphysical ideas. Without this archaeology, the individual "will deprive himself of the best that mankind has hitherto produced" (H; I; 20; see also 17). Philosophical reflection on religious needs is a way of learning metaphysical illusions, of swallowing the bitter pill of the emptiness of existence, and thus of hardening the new type of man. Better still, religious training gives the individual "a hunger and thirst for *himself*" and allows him "to find satisfaction and fullness in *himself*" (GS; 300).

Like Plato, Nietzsche believes that only a few people have a philosophic nature. Following the Platonic model, he also depicts the philosopher as a fragile creature, who needs the proper environment to blossom (BGE; 276).[27] "For the corruption, the ruination of higher human beings, of more strangely constituted souls, is the rule: it is dreadful to have such a rule always before one's eyes" (BGE; 269). This notion is taken directly from Plato's arguments in the *Republic:*

> I think that when, by any chance, this way of learning for the philosophic nature arrives, this nature necessarily develops into a virtuous one. But without this way of learning, the philosophic nature turns into its opposite once it is sown, planted, and nourished, unless, through good fortune, some of the gods come to the rescue. (492a)

> None of the constitutions of the existing cities is worthy of the philosophic nature. For these cities twist and alter this nature. It is like sowing a foreign seed in an alien land, a seed that turns out to be of fading strength when confronted by the native species. Similarly, in the existing cities the philosophic nature is not strong in its proper authority and power, but degenerates into a foreign character. (497b–c)

In other words, without a favorable environment, neither Platonic nor Nietzschean philosophers will ever achieve their potential.

Hence the importance of training, discipline, and exile. Plato wants his potential philosophers to live in exile, removed from the temptations of flatterers who offer them the glittering but shallow trappings of power (*Republic* 492–496). Nietzsche constructs his own exile, whether he calls it a desert or the masks that hide his identity. Plato dwells on the centrality of war as a means of training, and, as early as Book 2 of the *Republic*, he equates a future guardian with a "young pedigree dog" (375a–e, 376c).[28] Nietzsche, too, treats ideas of war and battlefields as necessary to the development of his own philosophical nature. Plato wants only the right kind of music in his city (398–400a). "Rather, we should try to discover what are the rhythms of someone who leads an ordered and courageous life and then adapt the meter and the tune to his words, not his words to them" (399e–400a). Nietzsche is well aware of the importance of sounds (GS; 104). Plato does not want the confusion of different styles of music, which might bring a chaos of conflicting emotions into the soul (397d–e). Nietzsche, while enthusiastic about music and poetry, sternly forbids the mixing of styles and accuses Plato of mingling "all forms of style"—in this respect, Plato was a *"first décadent"* (TI; "What I Owe"; 2). Plato stands for a noble lie; Nietzsche, too, advocates a lie when its purposes are clearly attuned to a higher telos: "Ultimately the point is to what *end* a lie is told" (AC; 56). Plato abhors imitation to the extent that, if the character imitated is a slavish one, this vice will become the imitator's real nature. Nietzsche shares the same belief. The person who intentionally experiments with himself by allowing pity in his life will "inevitably grow sick and melancholic" (D; 134).

Plato's and Nietzsche's philosophies find a common ground when Nietzsche uses the metaphor of a butterfly emerging from its chrysalis to describe the process of acquiring knowledge. "The butterfly wants to get out of its cocoon, . . . [and] then it is blinded and confused by the unfamiliar light, the realm of freedom." Only a few men are capable of this suffering, which is the means for mankind *"to transform itself from a moral to a knowing mankind"* (H; I; 107). The Platonic philosopher faces a similar challenge when he decides to leave his chains and his prison and ascend from the cave to the bright light of genuine knowledge. He, too, will suffer and will be blinded (*Republic* 514–517a). But he is blinded by sunlight that he willingly seeks, whereas the prisoners left behind do not want to see that light. Nietzsche applies the same description to the masses of modernity: "they do not *want* light, but only blindness; indeed, they *hate* light—when it is cast on themselves" (RWB; 6).

Plato designs strict rules for his philosophers, which range from a prohibition against a family life to one against touching silver and gold (*Republic* 416d–417a). He also makes testing the central yardstick of the philosophic soul. Nietzsche, too, designs his own rules, and they rely on suffering, tests, and dangerous games that the philosopher plays with himself. Plato begins the process of testing in childhood, but this process continues until the individual reaches adulthood (413c–414a). Nietzsche does not advocate the Platonic requirement of exposing children to the sights of war, but his tests, once they begin, seem to be permanent. Through tests, "a soul could grow to such height and power it would feel *compelled* to these tasks," namely, the tasks of revaluating values, of superseding history as the "gruesome dominion of chance" it has been so far, and of living as new philosophers (BGE; 203). He is not content, however, with putting an end to "the dominion of chance" in history. His philosophers must "*subdue* the entire past" and legislate for the future. In this conquest, Nietzsche drinks from the Platonic cup to the very last dregs. "*Actual philosophers . . . are commanders and law-givers*" and use "the preliminary work of all the philosophical labourers, of all those who have subdued the past" (BGE; 211).

Nietzsche, however, introduces an element of urgency that is not present in Plato. It is true that Plato treats the disrepute that philosophy suffers at the hands of illegitimate practitioners as a cause of searing pain (*Republic* 495c–e). His ideal city, however, is a geographically confined area that is bound to fail eventually, no matter how rigorous the philosophers are in their breeding techniques and their marriage arrangements. All great things fall (497d). Plato never treated the rule of the philosophers as one that would radically change human history. Nietzsche, however, treated his new protagonists of history, namely, the new philosophers, in line with nineteenth-century sensibilities and expectations. His new philosophers are supposed to be a major turning-point in history. Hence his sense of urgency, and his sense of "the terrible danger they might not appear or might fail or might degenerate—these are *our* proper cares and concerns, do you know that, you free spirits?" (BGE; 203).

Plato stressed that the core of a successful new philosophical and political project was nothing other than the breeding of individuals, particularly philosophers. Nietzsche, without giving credit to his predecessor, also insisted on a politics of breeding. "For every elevated world one has to be born or, expressed more clearly, *bred* for it: one has a right to philosophy—taking the word in the grand sense—only by virtue of one's origin; one's ancestors, one's 'blood' are the decisive thing here too" (BGE; 213; 262; D; 150; 151). Hence the danger of religion taking over the right of philosophers to rule: "it costs dear and terribly when religions hold sway, *not* as means of education and breeding in the hands of the philosopher, but in their own right and as *sovereign,* when they themselves want to be final ends and not means beside other means" (BGE; 62).

The Platonic philosopher uses religion and marriage regulations to maintain proper order in the city and to breed the right species. Nietzsche follows in his footsteps. Religion is necessary for the masses, and marriages should not be left to chance. For "'chance in marriage makes a grand rational progress of mankind impossible'" (D; 150). A new species of man must be a result of our willing to create it: "To create a new responsibility, that of the physician, in all cases in which the highest interest of life, of *ascending* life, demands the most ruthless suppression and sequestration of degenerating life—for example in determining the right to reproduce, the right to be born, the right to live" (TI; "Expeditions"; 36).

Plato advocates a rational, carefully constructed curriculum to train the intellect of his future rulers. Nietzsche advocates the study of science as a training ground in discipline. The pursuit of a rigorous science "will eventuate an increase in energy, in reasoning capacity, in toughness of endurance; one will have learned how *to achieve an objective by the appropriate means*" (H; I; 256).

From the arrangement of marriages to the influence of musical sounds, Nietzsche is deeply indebted to the Platonic paradigm. His mimesis of Plato reaches its zenith in the advocacy of a natural hierarchy of individuals. He literally copies the same hierarchy that Plato invented in the *Republic* (guardians, auxiliaries, and workers) and identifies three types of people—those who are most spiritual, the soldiers, and all the rest—who know their specific place in society. Every ideal society, Nietzsche avers, has a pyramidal form (AC; 57).[29] In contrast to the soldiers of the Platonic city, the Nietzschean soldiers act, not primarily as the city's defenders, but as a buffer zone to keep the masses at a distance and thus prevent them from coming close to the spiritual rulers. "Cleanliness," after all, together with fear of contagion, seems to have been one of Nietzsche's obsessions. In this sense, the Platonic comparison fails, and Nietzsche's society would seem alien to the ancient Greek taste.

Plato's three classes of people correspond to his idea of the three parts of the soul: the guardians correspond to reason, the auxiliaries/warriors to our spirited part, and the workers to the passions. Nietzsche follows a similar pattern, with one crucial difference. He does not seem to appreciate the full importance of Plato's configuration of the soul and thus society. By locating the passions in the soul, Plato indicated that they are eternal. The role of reason was to moderate the passions; it was not to *deny* them.

NIETZSCHE'S ASCETIC SOCIETY

The pyramidal society that Nietzsche builds, as we will see, resembles an ancient Persian society or an Asian caste system more than it does the Platonic ideal city. Any high culture and any healthy society, Nietzsche argues, is a pyramid in which the supreme law of nature—the natural ranking—is represented in three types of people: the most spiritual, the muscular, and the masses. "The *order of castes,* the supreme, the dominating law, is only the sanctioning of a *natural order,* a natural law of the first rank over which no arbitrary caprice, no 'modern idea' has any power." These three types "mutually condition one another": "Nature, *not* Manu, separates from one another the predominantly spiritual type, the predominantly muscular and temperamental type, and the third type distinguished neither in the one nor the other, the mediocre type—the last as the great majority, the first as the elite" (AC; 57). The most spiritual "rule not because they want to but because they *are;* they are not free to be second in rank."[30] The second in rank are the warriors, who are responsible for maintaining order, security, and, above all, for protecting the rulers from "everything *coarse* in the work of ruling." This "order of rank," as expressed in the three types, "only formulates the supreme law of life itself; the separation of the three types is necessary for the preservation of society, for making possible higher and higher types—*inequality* of rights is the condition for the existence of rights at all" (AC; 57).[31] Note that this is a far cry from *The Gay Science,* where Nietzsche declared that there were no laws in nature: "There are only necessities: there is nobody who commands, nobody who obeys, nobody who trespasses" (GS; 109).

As in the Platonic polis, "the supreme law of life itself," the ranking, ought to reflect the principle of specialization in a pyramidal society. "To be a public utility, a cog, a function, is a natural vocation, it is *not* society, it is the kind of *happiness* of which the great majority are alone capable, which makes intelligent machines of them" (AC; 57). This makes sense in terms of Nietzsche's philosophy. In 1882 he had claimed that the masses would willingly submit to the nobles, provided that these nobles were genuine representatives of nobility and not the counterfeit individuals who hold economic power in the modern age; that is, provided that "the higher-ups [would] constantly legitimize themselves as higher, as *born* to command—by having noble manners" (GS; 40).

A paradox, given Nietzsche's indebtedness to the Platonic model, is that Plato, the presumably anti-nature philosopher who, Nietzsche claims, was perverted by Socrates, requires his rulers to excel in both philosophy and war (actual war) and rewards those who prove their military prowess with sexual pleasure (*Republic* 468c). Nietzsche, the bard of the instincts who seeks a total faithfulness to nature, has the meager consolation of waging inner wars, exactly like the ascetic priest, and claims to prefer his solitude to the temptations represented by women. Thus, there is an important and disturbing irony at the core of Nietzsche's philosophy. The philosopher who supposedly derides the instincts and seeks a flight from actuality, among whom Plato is one of the best representatives, can also be a genuine warrior, who indulges in the pleasures of sexual intercourse as the state-sanctioned recompense for his or her exploits on the battlefield. Plato recommends that "the best men sleep together with the best women as frequently as possible, but the opposite with the worst men and the worst women" (459e); further, the "authority of sleeping with women must be given to those who, among the youth, are the best at war or in other things as well as gifts of honor and prizes [but] without envy, so that this is the cause of them fathering as many of the children as possible" (460a–b). "The kings of them are those who have become the best in philosophy and war" (543a). It is clear that, in Plato's account, the "best men" are the philosophers-guardians. Plato even allies himself with Homer in giving the most meat and wine to the best men and women (468c). In Book 4 he states that the guardians have nothing to give to their mistresses (420a), but, still, they do have mistresses, although this view is abandoned when the communality of women is introduced in Book 5. All these examples point to the fact that the Platonic philosopher, the one who wants to prepare his soul for eternity, is very much engaged in the sensual delights of *this* world.

Plato, perhaps, was unknowingly playing a dangerous game; this engagement could ruin the virtue of moderation that he sought for his ideal city. The Nietzschean philosopher, however, looks more like a member of a band of monks that Nietzsche describes as the "most spiritual order" in a natural system of rank. The monk is protected by the muscular type in society while he strives to reach the highest level of spirituality and keeps a safe distance from the masses. As Nietzsche wrote in 1879, "It was up to you, and is up to us, to *take from* the passions their terrible character and thus prevent their becoming devastating torrents" (WS; 37). The philosopher/ monk discovers in himself the work of one or more dominant instincts exercising control over some of his passions. Nietzsche insists that the subtle and more select human beings, namely, the new philosophers, "are liable to remain alone . . . and seldom propagate themselves" (BGE; 268). In contrast to the Platonic philosopher, the Nietzschean new philosopher will supervise the breeding in his society, but he himself will not be a breeder. He is too aloof, too obsessed with his cleanliness, and too conscious of the "pathos of distance" that he needs to maintain. After all, he possesses in himself, but in a very spiritualized manner that the nobles lacked, the trait of the vanquished nobility: "the lofty glance that rules and looks down, the feeling of being segregated from the mob and its duties and virtues" (BGE; 213).

Nietzsche's ideal philosopher, ruler, and legislator thus embodies the ascetic ideal without the ideas of the herd, of a world beyond, guilt, or reliance on gods. But, as I have already suggested in chapters 2 and 3, it is clear that the new philosopher is not free from sickness. Spirituality always requires some form of sickness and entails the sacrifice of certain of our instincts. And how does one know that the suppressed instincts are the ones that, for a particular philosopher, ought to be crushed? Perhaps Nietzsche was following the Greek attitude toward sickness. The Greeks "were certainly not possessed of a square and solid healthiness;—their secret was to honour even sickness as a god if only it had *power*" (H; I; 214).

NIETZSCHE'S REVALUATION OF THE MASSES

In constructing his pyramidal society, Nietzsche in 1888 suggests a radical revaluation of the masses. In contrast to his portrayal in the *Genealogy*, in *The Anti-Christ* he does not depict the masses of modernity as vindictive. Their resentment comes from without rather than within. The workers, the herd, are infected by the socialists. "Whom among today's rabble do I hate the most? The Socialist rabble, the Chandala apostles who undermine the worker's instinct, his pleasure, his feeling of contentment with his little state of being—who make him envious, who teach him revengefulness" (AC; 57). Thus, a certain circle in Nietzsche has been closed. In 1874, the proper role of the masses is to realize that their significance hinges upon their assistance in the production of genius (SE; 6). In *The Anti-Christ*, the role of the masses is similar: it is now the acceptance of a natural hierarchy that makes possible the best environment for the philosopher to flourish. The idea of the ruler-monk, who occupies the highest echelon in Nietzsche's pyramidal society in 1888, is thus joined with the idea of the genius that was prominent in 1874.

The theoretical and political significance of these two moments should not be underestimated. At both ends of the spectrum—1874 and 1888—we have the same argument: the majority of human beings instinctively know that they are a means to the accomplishment of something higher. In *Schopenhauer as Educator*, the "seductive voices" of a "modish" culture are intended to alienate the mob "from their instincts" (SE; 6), the same instincts that led them to obedience. In 1888 the danger came from another quarter with a similar goal, namely, from all the political tendencies preaching moral and social equality throughout Europe. It is worth emphasizing here that the portrayal of the masses as spiteful conspirators intent on bringing down the strong first appears only in *Beyond Good and Evil* (1886), in preliminary strokes, and then, in a detailed account, in the *Genealogy* (1887). These two works serve as an interregnum between earlier views about the innocence of all actions in *Human, All Too Human* (1878) and the reconciliation offered in *The Anti-Christ* and in *Ecce Homo* (1888). Nietzsche's idea of the conspiracy of the weak, which is central in defining the slave morality, was not present in 1874 and was abandoned in *Twilight of the Idols* and *Ecce Homo*. In *The Anti-Christ*, Nietzsche's central targets are the alleged Christian hatred of actuality and its war against instincts and higher human beings. The emphasis is not on a sick herd that found relief and reprieve in the hypnotic tricks of the ascetic priest, but on the Jewish priestly caste, the Christian theologians and priests, and the church's "misunderstanding of an *original* symbolism" (AC; 37).

These new emphases should not go unnoticed. The story told in the *Genealogy*, of a sick herd that wanders through life until it finds the ascetic priest and thereby lays the foundation for a conspiracy of the weak, has been radically altered. First, we no longer find a sick herd or of an ascetic priest on the lookout for sufferers. We find the argument that the Christian church misunderstood the message of the redeemer, and that this misunderstanding led it to exact revenge. Second, the herd described in the *Genealogy* seeks alleviation for the pain of its suffering, while the first Christians in *The Anti-Christ* seek vengeance. Third, in the *Genealogy* the herd finds guidance in the ascetic priest, but the ascetic ideal presented in *The Anti-Christ* plays no significant role. Fourth, in the *Genealogy* the ascetic ideal is praised for its honesty. Since the ascetic priest is sick but does not understand his own sickness, let alone the illness of his patients, he does not lie on purpose. By contrast, the Christian priest of modernity is sick and *knows* that his teachings are false. "The priest knows as well as anyone that there is no longer any 'God,' any 'sinner,' any 'redeemer'—that 'free will,' 'moral world-order' are lies—intellectual seriousness, the profound self-overcoming of the intellect, no longer *permits* anyone *not* to know about these things" (AC; 38). Fifth, in 1888 the story that had been presented in the *Genealogy* takes a new detour: the demise of antiquity is no longer the end result of a conflict between the slaves and the nobles. It is a struggle between the particularity of the Christian church and the universality of the Roman Empire, which encompassed the highest achievements of human culture. It was a struggle between one institution—the church—and the greatest symbol of a grand architecture that perished at the hands of Christianity.

Hence, a circle closes. It is as if Nietzsche ransacked his memory (or, as if certain instincts once again got the upper hand) and returned to ideas he had originally advanced in *Human, All Too Human*. In *The Anti-Christ* he attains a reconciliation with the idea that both ants and cyclops, both workers and geniuses, are all deemed to be necessary in society:

Next to the cult of the genius and his force there must always be placed, as its complement and palliative, the cult of culture: which knows how to accord to the material, humble, base, misunderstood, weak, imperfect, onesided, incomplete, untrue, merely apparent, indeed to the evil and dreadful, a proper degree of understanding and the admission *that all this is necessary;* for the harmonious endurance of all that is human, attained through astonishing labours and lucky accidents and as much the work of ants and cyclops as of genius, must not be lost to us again: how, then, could we dispense with the common, deep and often uncanny groundbass without which melody cannot be melody? (H; I; 186)

This is a portent. It is, in effect, Nietzsche's formulation of society as a collective individual—or else his version of pluralism as a natural ranking. In contrast, in the *Genealogy* Nietzsche did not treat the emergence of guilt and the slave morality as necessary, and ants and cyclops are separated as if they had completely different natures. Guilt and the slave morality are anti-natural detours in history, which have infected humankind and buried its best possibilities.

In an early essay, "The Greek State," in which his emphasis was on war and the creation of military genius, Nietzsche also described a pyramidal society: "Here we see as the most general effect of the war tendency, the immediate separation and division of the chaotic masses into military castes, from which there arises the construction of a war-like society in the shape of a pyramid on the broadest possible base: a slave-like bottom stratum" (TGS, p. 184). But here Nietzsche was writing about the military profession and the quasi-poetical link between genius and the state. He did not mince words in expressing his awe at the Platonic project. Leaving aside the exclusion of inspired artists from Plato's republic—a policy that was, after all, "a rigid consequence of the Socratic judgment on art"— Nietzsche confidently announces that "in the total concept of the Platonic state," it is possible to discern "the wonderfully grand hieroglyph of a profound *secret study of the connection between state and genius,* eternally needing to be interpreted: in this preface we have said what we believe we have fathomed of this secret script" (TGS, p. 186). After all of Nietzsche's inner wanderings, his training with eagles and lions, and his meditations in his secret citadel, he thought he was able to fathom a bit more of that secret script. The result is the twist to the Platonic pyramid in section 57 of *The Anti-Christ*, as quoted frequently above. The script was deciphered, the class structure was modeled after Plato's polis, but the hierarchy was Persian, and so, too, was Zarathustra.

Modernity, for Nietzsche, opened the gate to a cosmic self-consciousness that abolished the dualities of all past history:

> If genius consists, according to Schopenhauer's observation, in the connected and lively recollection of experience, then in the striving for knowledge of the entire historical past—which ever more mightily distinguishes the modern age from all others and has for the first time demolished the ancient walls between nature and spirit, man and animal, morality and the physical world—it may be possible to recognize a striving for the genius of humanity as a whole. History perfect and complete would be cosmic self-consciousness. (AOM; 185)

This defense of an idea of unity, however, came tumbling down in the dualities that Nietzsche began to recognize in his own stories and plots, which he had devised to explain the unfolding of his individuality. The "genius of humanity as a whole"—Nietzsche's genius—will wither away in the fog of guilt, resentment, and sickness characteristic of modern man, Nietzsche argues, unless he drinks the bitter cup of "actuality" and, as I will show in the next chapter, reaches the moment of reconciliation that is expressed in *Ecce Homo*.

Chapter Nine

THE TRAPPED DIONYSUS
Historiobiography, Epic Spirituality, and Reconciliation

Our conjecture that metaphysics is a substitute, albeit an inadequate one, for art, seems to be further confirmed by the fact that the metaphysician who perhaps had artistic talent to the highest degree, viz., Nietzsche, almost entirely avoided the error of that confusion. A large part of his work has predominantly empirical content. We find there, for instance, historical analyses of specific artistic phenomena, or an historical psychological analysis of morals. In the work, however, in which he expresses most strongly that which others express through metaphysics or ethics, in Thus Spoke Zarathustra, *he does not choose the misleading theoretical form, but openly the form of art, of poetry.*

—Rudolf Carnap, "The Overcoming of Metaphysics through Logical Analysis of Language"[1]

In this book my intent has been to show that Nietzsche is a story-teller, whose stories bear the imprint of his metaphysics of meaning. I have paid close attention in my arguments to his genealogical and physiological explanations, which amount to his continuation of a tradition in which philosophers/physicians have excelled ever since Plato appointed himself the physician of the polis. In Nietzsche's case, the metaphysics of meaning appeared, at times, to be a painful reality that required a stoical approach, an approach that neither affirms nor denies (GM; III; 24), although he, the self-proclaimed "last of the stoics," in fact does plenty of both. In this chapter, I return to some of his stories and then weave together my reflections on Nietzsche's epic spirituality and philosophy of reconciliation.

FRAGMENTED GENEALOGIES

Although Nietzsche's stories display a consistent pattern overall, there are important moments in which his thinking zigzags off course, until he reaches the conclusions that satisfy him. I offered some examples of his changing assessments in chapters 4 and 5. Here I consider some additional areas of shifts in this thought, which, to the best of my knowledge, have not been explored to the extent that they deserve. This lack of attention is disconcerting once we notice that these areas encompass three key themes in Nietzsche's philosophy: the dominant morality, the concept of guilt, and the role of Christians in the ancient Roman world.

In his earlier formulation of the origin of the dominant morality of his age, for example, Nietzsche asserted that it grew in the soil of "*ruling* tribes and castes" (H; I; 45). This position is not necessarily a radical departure from the later view that attributes it to the slaves' resentment. Already in *Human, All Too Human,* he treats the ideas of mistrust and evil as arising in the souls of those who are subjected. But in 1878, mistrust and evil lack the element of hatred that he will portray in later texts. The crucial point here is that, according to his 1878 account, the morality of modernity arose in the spiritual environment of "ruling" groups. This is a far cry from the morality described ten years later in the *Genealogy,* which is born of hatred and is the outcome of a conspiracy orchestrated by the weak and oppressed.

Even more revealing of shifting evaluations is the fact that in 1876, Nietzsche had discussed guilt and bad conscience—well before the appearance of the ascetic priest. The modern age, he claimed, needed to find reasons to defend its principles in the face of the trial that lay in store for it. But there was only one accuser in this trial: "our own bad conscience." It took Nietzsche eleven years to invent another story purporting to explain the alleged bad conscience of modernity. And this story took a dramatic turn. In his reflections on Wagner's music, Nietzsche argued that the task of modern art was "to stupefy or intoxicate! To drug or deaden. To make one's conscience unconscious, one way or the other! To help the modern soul escape its feeling of guilt . . . rather than help it return to innocence! To defend the human being against himself by forcing him to remain silent and by plugging his ears!" (RWB; 6). But in the *Genealogy*, Nietzsche reallocated this task and put the ascetic priest in charge of what once he understood to be the humiliating function of modern art.

In 1878, moreover, both the saint and the ascetic are described as possessing a lust for power, and the ascetic is depicted as one who surrenders his will to another. "The ascetic . . . seeks to make his life easier for himself," but in pursuing this goal, Nietzsche writes, the ascetic's "own willfulness and passions are not in any way involved; after one has acted there is no feeling of responsibility and therefore no pangs of remorse" (H; I; 139). In other words, this is an asceticism without mortification and torture of the body and, even better, it is an asceticism without responsibility or remorse. It is akin to the asceticism of a utilitarian, who looks for a way that, in his judgment, will make his life easier. This is not the ascetic character that Nietzsche presents in 1887. His portrait of the ascetic priest, sometimes drawn with broad strokes, sometimes with detailed ones, is the very opposite. The ascetic priest is so consumed by the will to power that he wants control, not over particular aspects of life, but over life itself. He is a character that is sick and needs torture as part of his sickness; a character that is drowned in the airless chamber of responsibility, remorse, and sin.

The emphases in these two stories clearly are very different. The shift, I suggest, that leaves the reader reeling for at least a hint of explanation involves the origin of the saint. In the 1878 story the saint/ascetic, a character who mystified and confused the people of the ancient world, was "the last *pleasure antiquity invented* after it had grown apathetic even to the sight of animal and human combats." The saint/ascetic provided people of antiquity with a spectacle, and with him they recovered "the attraction of the spectacle" and used this spectacle as a stimulant for a bored soul (H; I; 141). The saint/ascetic was thus a pleasurable stimulant to life, not the expression of a weary life. One might say that the saint/ascetic was "invented" by antiquity as a "pleasure." In 1887 and 1888, there are no longer any traces of this story or of an era that got tired of gladiatorial fights and craved a substitute. An even more dramatic shift in thought occurs. In *Assorted Opinions and Maxims,* written in 1879 and published in 1886 as the second volume of *Human, All Too Human,* Nietzsche described Christianity as "the evening-bell of good antiquity, a bell broken and weary yet still sweet sounding" (AOM; 224). Christianity even saved the Greek and Roman cultures, which otherwise would have been overrun by the youthful barbarians. By weakening the barbarians, the Germans, for example, Christian doctrines acted as a poison for them and a "balm" to the Graeco-Roman world. And what, Nietzsche asks, "would have been left to us of Greek culture! of the entire cultural past of the human race!" if the barbarian hordes had been able to maraud freely? Nietzsche's answer to this question could not be more revealing: "one comes to respect the quiet Christian community and is *grateful that it overran the Graeco-Roman world*" (AOM; 224, emphasis mine).

In the *Genealogy* (1887) and in *Twilight of the Idols* and *The Anti-Christ* (1888), the ascetic individual and Christian individuals, in general, are part of a conspiracy plotted by the weak to suck the blood of the strong. As such, they worked in secret, not in the public theaters of the Roman Empire, and took advantage of the "frivolous tolerance" of Roman culture (BGE; 46). The "balm" that Nietzsche identified in 1879 is nonexistent, and the earlier "weary antiquity" that found solace in Christianity was in 1888 the towering Roman Empire, which satisfied the "*first* principle of grand architecture," that is, the ability to withstand "the accident of persons," just as it survived its bad emperors (AC; 58). In the story told in 1879 and repeated in 1886, Christians were "benevolent" and "undemanding" figures, while most of the people of the Roman world "were born as though with the souls of slaves and the sensuality of old men" (AOM; 224). In the story told in 1888, the same Christians are described as the *"corruptest* form of corruption," and Roman citizens are no longer presented as bearers of the "souls of slaves." They are now "those manly-noble natures who found . . . their own pride in the cause of Rome" (AC; 58). In 1879, the Roman culture of late antiquity was weary and already distilling the scent of the flowers of mourning. In 1888, the same Roman culture was the imposing empire eviscerated by weak, but clever, creatures.

Plainly, Nietzsche's first genealogies were erased and new ones took their place, or at least were a layer placed over the previous accounts. It is worth emphasizing again that these differences in stories do not have a significant impact on Nietzsche's philosophy as a whole, especially given that he regarded consistency as a symptom of a decadent modernity.[2] These different stories are worth mentioning because they provide different snapshots of a philosopher and poet who is defining his own identity through his writings, despite his assurance that the purpose of writing is concealment. These stories are his own attempt at becoming what he thinks he is, through a selective rummaging of the past that he believes is somehow flowing through him. This is Nietzsche's version of historiobiography. In this process toward self-awareness, two features help us to understand why solitude plays a central role in his system of self-training. The first, already mentioned in chapter 8, is his unwillingness or inability to see authenticity in other people's actions. His tendency is to locate authenticity in practices (the ascetic ideal, for example) or in a few individuals who are already gone (Thucydides is a case in point) or who exist as future potentialities. Authentic individuals are either in an irretrievable past or, depending on his changing perspectives, in a distant or near future, that future when the new philosophers, he hopes, will arrive. The second feature is entwined with the first. Nietzsche criticizes resentment and abhors people who are always on the lookout for imaginary or real slights, as a way of satiating their thirst for suspicion and vengeance. Yet he himself, who despises the "indignant man," is very reluctant to give credit to other people for the beliefs they hold or the causes or ideals for which they are willing to suffer. In these two areas, Nietzsche is, surprisingly, stingy. He is always surrounded by enemies, and he cannot stand the man of today (AC; 38).

OPPOSITION TO, VERSUS DENIAL OF, THE WORLD

For a thinker who claims the capacity to deduct an attitude from a single word (AC; 44), Nietzsche's tendency to confuse *opposition* to the world with its *denial* is even more puzzling. Yet he consistently confuses the two. Section 344 of *The Gay Science* is a good example of this tendency. Here, he acknowledges that as a "godless antimetaphysician" he is inflamed by the desire to seek truth because truth seems to be divine. Science, he claims, rests on two principles that are driven by different justifications. The first is the will "*not to allow oneself to be deceived.*" The second is, "I do not want to deceive." But since we lack the knowledge to decide, in advance, that truth is more advantageous than mistrust, it follows that when science chooses truth over mistrust, it is making a determination about the harmful effects of deception, mistrust, and falsehood. Nietzsche concludes that, in so choosing, science is standing on moral grounds; it takes the side of truth for moral reasons, without even considering all the evidence of the importance to life of both truth and untruth. Given this, Nietzsche draws what he takes to be the necessary and logical conclusion. That is, when science or an individual chooses truth as a moral value and does not want to see the proofs that "life, nature, and history are 'not moral,'" this choice presupposes the affirmation of "*another world*" and the denial of this world, "*our* world." Indeed, the will to truth "might be a concealed will to death." He ascribes this view to all dominant moralities, religions, and philosophies.

Here, however, one encounters a flawed reasoning. First, the choice of truth could be seen—and in Nietzsche's universe, it must be seen—as an expression of the dominant instincts that form that aggregate of drives constituting the will to power. In preferring and even fighting for truth, the will to power is not denying nature, life, or history. It is making an evaluation, a selection, which is an activity that, Nietzsche claims, marks human beings as valuating animals. Truth as an expression of the will to power would not be a total negation of this world; it would be, at best, a partial negation, to the extent that it excludes falsehood from life. And all interpretations, which is what the will to power represents, entail "forcing, adjusting, abbreviating, omitting, padding, inventing, falsifying, and whatever else is of the essence of interpreting" (GM; III; 24).

Second, Nietzsche clearly implies that the affirmation of another world refers to the transcendental domain of God and the afterlife. Both, he holds, are fictitious, and, accordingly, such affirmation is an urge toward nothingness. The "other world" is a place where the dichotomies from which human beings have suffered disappear into a long-sought unity. Truth vanquishes untruth; the soul is freed from the body; being is no longer threatened by becoming. But is this other world a "denial" of "our" world, or is it only a denial of *some aspects* of the world in which we live? Is this "other" world in fact an intrinsic part of "our" world, that is, a need of *our* world as we *interpret* it? Nietzsche's philosophy contains an explicit answer: the "real" and "true" world, on the one hand, and the "apparent" world, on the other hand, are different expressions of life. That is to say, the "other," "real," and "true" world is just another manifestation of *our* nature.

> The apparent world, i.e., a world viewed according to values; ordered, selected according to values, i.e., in this case according to the viewpoint of utility in regard to the preservation and enhancement of the power of a certain species of animal. . . . The 'apparent world,' therefore, is reduced to a specific mode of action on the world, emanating from a center. (WP; 567)

This argument can be equally applied to the "real" and "true" world, namely, the world that claims to be outside life. The "real" world is one created according to something's quantum of power, for the sake of the preservation of a certain kind of life. In a passage dated March–June 1888, Nietzsche insists that "every center of force—and not only man, construes all the rest of the world from its own view," which means "according to its own force" (WP; 636). Interpretation is then a matter of the quantum of power inherent in each organism, and reality is nothing more than the action and reaction of every center of force toward the whole (WP; 567). The Christian struggle against nature "*is nature against something that is also na-*

ture" (WP; 228, emphasis mine). Nietzsche's argument that placing something "beyond" life entails, by necessity, a negation of life and a flight into nothingness is thus contradicted by his own naturalistic philosophy. An argument I presented in chapter 6 is worth repeating here: nothing is outside life. On these terms, Nietzsche's obsession with debunking the "real" world invites puzzlement, the more so when he concedes that the "real" world could well be something that makes *"this* world possible for us"* (WP; 586B).[3] His reasoning that the "true" world has been created by "the instinct of life-weariness, and not that of life" is deeply flawed (WP; 586C). A weary life is a manifestation of a sick life, but it is still life.

Nothingness is an impossibility for man qua valuating animal. The valuating animal may fly toward fictions and falsehood, and he may even be sick, but, as argued in chapter 6, none of these conditions is equivalent to nothingness. As long as there is life, that is, the will to power, the gate to nothingness is closed. Nietzsche himself argues that nihilism, which is the belief in nothingness, could be a sign of either strength or weakness (WP; 585B). This is another way of saying that the real problem turns on the type of will to power creating that "nothingness." In his role as a physician, Nietzsche even claims that the philosopher "recuperates with nihilism" (WP; 598).

Our world, seen from another perspective, is organized by our instincts as a space in which "we are able to live," and this ability is turned into "proof of [this world's] truth for us—" (WP; 568). But this "truth" is completely alien to the traditional moral view. In 1882, Nietzsche described truth as man's *"irrefutable* errors" (GS; 265). In 1885, he asserted that truth is not necessarily "the antithesis of error, but in the most fundamental cases only the posture of various errors in relation to one another" (WP; 535). On these assumptions, both "our" world and the other world are configurations of errors.

Nietzsche asserts that both truth and untruth "constantly prove to be useful," but nobody knows whether there exists a fixed arrangement in favor of one or the other, or whether this arrangement is constantly shifting. Putting aside for now Nietzsche's final conclusion that the value of life cannot be estimated, the only thing one can do is to acknowledge the existence of *both* truth and untruth in

254 NIETZSCHE AND THE DRAMA OF HISTORIOBIOGRAPHY

life. But this acknowledgment must include the recognition that even if the existence of another world is false, this falsehood is still part of our life as we understand it. The belief in another world is thus not necessarily a "denial" of our world, especially when "our" world, in light of Nietzsche's philosophy, is the peculiar arrangement of errors that give us comfort. Furthermore, the acknowledgment of both truth and untruth cannot passively accept the idea of an immutable stratum in the form of fixed human types, which somehow are immune to the process of becoming. For if this were the case, then the will to power would become a timid replica of the "tolerance" so praised by modernity and so abhorred by Nietzsche. It would also become a glorification of the passive individual, who is merely a sick animal. Nietzsche himself proclaims his lack of patience with tolerance and proudly announces his own "intolerant taste" and his warlike nature (EH; "So Wise"; 7).

Let us follow Nietzsche's daring questions and ask, What if the affirmation of another world were a means to discipline ourselves and to become what we are? As I have already mentioned, Nietzsche does not underestimate the importance of religion in providing discipline to the human spirit. Yet on the path he takes, morality is opposed to nature, or is "anti-nature"; anti-nature becomes a denial of the instincts; and this denial leads, inexorably, to the affirmation of another world that is free of nature—the world where the eternal soul dwells.

PERSPECTIVES, DIONYSUS, AND ZARATHUSTRA

Nietzsche's responsibility for all future millennia requires him to eschew the flight into the world of the eternal soul, that is, into nothingness, a flight that is rooted in a misunderstanding of the body. Reality must be endured because endurance is man's only justification. But this conclusion is far from being a pleasant one, even when we accept the opportunities it affords for training in warlike activities and for the inner journey into Nietzsche's own soul. On the contrary, reality is a bitter drop to swallow. This is precisely what the tragic artist understands and communicates of himself.

> *What does the tragic artist communicate of himself?* Does he not display precisely the condition of *fearlessness* in the face of the fearsome and questionable? . . . Bravery and composure in the face of a powerful enemy, great hardship, a problem that arouses aversion— it is this *victorious* condition which the tragic artist singles out, which he glorifies. (TI; "Expeditions"; 24)

And this is also what Nietzsche chose to do, or, as he would express it, this is what his nature and his instincts drove him to choose. His fate was to become aware of the fundamental errors of mankind; to be the first who saw truth as a problem; to know that the most spiritual human beings are also "the most painful tragedies"; that "they honour life because it brings against them its most formidable weapons" (TI; "Expeditions"; 17); and to know that he had to accept the meaningless of life just as the Spartans faced the Persians—as a tragic fate but one from which they chose not to turn their backs. For they, unlike Plato, were not cowards in their duel against reality. Ultimately, "[w]hat justifies man is his reality—it will justify him eternally" (TI; "Expeditions"; 32). When Nietzsche was playing his dangerous game and flirting with a dangerous knowledge, he dared to ask: "Why could the world *which is of concern to us*—not be a fiction?" And if someone replies that the fiction belongs to an author, "could he not be met with the round retort: *why?* Does this 'belongs' perhaps not also belong to the fiction?" (BGE; 34). It was time to abandon the unconditional line between subjects and predicates.

These questions, seemingly, took their toll. When Nietzsche squared off against the ascetic ideal, he ran headlong toward "actuality" in accusing the ascetic priest of denying "the world *which is of concern to us.*" The possibility that this world was a "fiction" did not reappear in any forceful way. Nietzsche embraced "actuality" and argued that the body was our "firmest possession," that our "instincts" were a superior form of intelligence, and the senses our best guides (BGE; 10, 134, 218). He tied all of these claims to his concept of the Dionysian, and he clothed that solitary monk, Zarathustra, in a Dionysian garb. The Dionysian mode of life is one of intoxication and orgy, but, above all, it is "the profoundest instinct of life," which "is in this world experienced religiously." It is procreation. It is "*to realize in oneself* the eternal joy of becoming—that joy which also encompasses *joy in destruction*" (TI; "What I Owe"; 4–5). In open contrast, Christianity dwells on a set of causes, a natural science, a psychology, and even a teleology that are all purely imaginary. "[T]his entire fictional world has its roots in *hatred* of the natural. . . . Who alone has reason to *lie himself out* of actuality? He who *suffers* from it." This is an "abortive actuality" (AC; 15; see also 62). This interpretation, however, leads to the crux of the matter: What is "actuality," if it is composed of multiple perspectives determined by the different configurations of a person's instincts? If actuality requires fictions, and if illusions may heal people, then beliefs in a world beyond this one and in the accountability of human beings before a God would be part of this actuality; they would be an extension, not a denial, of this world. It is completely irrelevant whether these beliefs are better interpretations than the one Nietzsche offers. Interpretations are the products of the dominant instincts and, as such, express what we are. We are already familiar, however, with Nietzsche's consistent way of getting out of a conceptual conundrum: he summons the physician in himself, and a diagnosis of sickness follows. Some interpretations portend a sick nature, while others are proofs of healthy instincts, the same instincts that are present in the ideal of the Dionysian.

The concept "Dionysian" is the *"supreme deed."* Here is the crossroad at which Dionysus and the monk Zarathustra discover their affinity. "The psychological problem in the type of Zarathustra is how he[,] . . . a spirit bearing the heaviest of destinies, . . . can nonetheless be the lightest and most opposite" [of a spirit of denial]. Zarathustra has the same disposition as that of the pagan priests who say "Yes to life" and "to whom 'God' is the word for the great Yes to all things" (AC; 55). The monk does not find objections to existence, and *"that is the concept of Dionysos once more"* (EH; "Thus Spoke"; 6).

"Reality," or "actuality," seems to be an anchor that keeps Nietzsche afloat when he struggles against his inner storms and creates, as a unique individual, his own sun (GS; 320). It led him to define nihilism as follows: "If a philosopher could be a nihilist, he would be one because he finds nothingness behind all the ideals of men.

Or not even nothingness merely—but only the worthless, the absurd, the sick, the cowardly, the weary, dregs of all kinds from the cup of his life *after he has drained it*" (TI; "Expeditions"; 32). And that poses a predicament for Nietzsche. As I argued in chapter 8, modernity, for Nietzsche, is the first age of mankind that chooses nihilistic values, though men know quite well that those values express and lead to nothingness. The man of modernity, not merely the theologian, knows the fraudulent character of the values he so enthusiastically praises. "Everyone knows this: *and everyone none the less remains unchanged*" (AC; 38). No wonder the depth of Nietzsche's despair and his belief about the responsibility he had on his shoulders. Given this perspective, he can assert that he is "the first *tragic philosopher*" (EH; "Birth"; 3). He is also the first psychologist. "To be the first here can be a curse" (EH; "Destiny"; 6). All of human history rests, as it were, on the warnings uttered by Nietzsche and on his success in turning back the enormous tide coming toward mankind. Nietzsche had drained the bitter cup, and was now keenly aware that the ascetic ideal was more sinister than anyone had ever imagined. His archaeological proofs were the evidence; modern science was another version of that ideal; and the philosopher was a further development of the priestly type (GM; III; 25; AC; 12). Nietzsche himself was destiny because he understood what history had misunderstood (AC; 36).

In his quest for meaning for himself, Nietzsche had recognized the nihilism behind the values of humankind, and he was prepared to say that, although he was "the first perfect nihilist of Europe," he had already overcome that stage (WP; P; 3). He was now sailing on a new sea. Through the last book he prepared for publication, he continued exploring and reflecting on the meaning he personally would have, not only in the stories he narrated, but in other people's stories. His good conscience, or rather the cornerstone of his honesty, was his belief that he never opposed and never denied life. The same attitude distinguished his character Zarathustra, who "has thought the 'most abysmal thought,'" but "finds in it no objection to existence." Rather, he sees in existence "one more reason *to be himself* the eternal Yes to all things" (EH; "Thus Spoke"; 6). Zarathustra stands for a species of man who "delineates reality *as it is*." This type of man "is *reality itself,* he still has all that is fearful and questionable in reality in him, *only thus can man possess greatness*" (EH; "Destiny"; 5).

Dionysus and Zarathustra are allies. Dionysus celebrates life, and Zarathustra represents the affirmation of reality and existence. But what, exactly, is the reality that Nietzsche/Dionysus/Zarathustra affirms? According to Nietzsche, our needs determine our interpretations and, consequently, different needs require different "realities" (WP; 481). At the same time, Nietzsche does not allow an interpretation that recognizes equal rights for all mankind, on the ground that there is an inequality of rank dictated by nature. There is also, he holds, a granite stratum impervious to teaching, and he even claims that all philosophies return to "a primordial total household of the soul" (BGE; 20).

To affirm existence by saying "yes to all things" or to affirm reality "as it is" was, of course, wishful thinking. Nietzsche did not say "yes to all things," and he seems to forget that reality "as it is" and "reality itself" are, by his own account, fictions. But this is how the teacher/poet/monk Zarathustra dealt with his "reality" in the world he invented for himself. Nietzsche needs to talk about a reality that is no longer refracted through a multiplicity of perspectives. He needs to appeal to the "thing in itself," or "reality itself," in order to feel at home with the immense tasks before him. Yet if one takes seriously his claim that philosophy creates the world in its own image, it is unreasonable to exclude Nietzsche from this claim (BGE; 9). A person's evaluations "betray something of the *structure* of his soul" (BGE; 268). Nietzsche's texts are no exception. He, too, is creating the world in his own image, but his storytelling is particularly demanding because he sees himself and his writings as signposts for understanding the past, as well as warnings to guide the future. He claims to be the first seer who can look both ways: he can see how the past could have turned out and what is in store in the future. Man, he wrote in 1872, "carries around within himself the memory of all previous generations" (PRS; 92; see also GS; 54, 377). The awareness he had achieved is not one of transparency, however. The seer wrestles with a world of signs that constantly disguise themselves, to the extent that every work of an artist or philosopher, in a sense, invents its author. Hence a distinction must be made between the author and his work. The work turns out to be an independent entity and even has the temerity of re-creating its author (BGE; 269). In light of this distinction, Nietzsche emerges as a fiction chiseled by his own works. "I am one thing, my writings are another" (EH; "Good Books"; 1). The characters created by the artist are one thing, and the artist is something else. As Nietzsche warns in Wagner's case, however, a close scrutiny of these characters makes it possible to discern the development of the artist's soul (RWB; 2). With warnings such as these, it is difficult to resist the temptation of thinking that Nietzsche creates an effigy of himself and then holds a mock funeral for the "fiction." This could be another strategy of concealment and misunderstanding, but it might also reveal something of Nietzsche's soul. His contemporaries, especially the German idealists, he argued, could not possibly comprehend what he knew.[4]

Many questions posed in Nietzsche's writings are left hanging, like a mysterious rope dangling over a cliff. No one knows whether the rope once was used to save someone's life or is a reminder that an executioner is nearby. Nietzsche never explains, for example, why the herd instinct—the instinct of self-preservation in opposition to the will to power—has been dominant in the history of humankind. Nor does he say why man is a valuating animal. He does not explain why human valuations include "low" and "high" actions (H; I; 132). Nor does he offer any hint as to why human beings act on the urge to be in harmony with something greater than themselves. This urge is explained as a piece of "vanity," but where does this "vanity" come from? There is no answer for this (AOM; 50; WS; 31, 181).

A lack of answers to certain questions does not deter Nietzsche's sacrificial quest for truth. "I do not want to be taken for what I am not—and that requires that I do not take myself for what I am not" (EH; "Good Books"; 1). But the demand he makes to us—"do not take me for what I am not"—and the strict exigency of self-knowledge he places on himself are meaningless when one factors in both the labyrinthine nature of knowledge and the instincts and their tricks. His devotion to "truth," "reality," and "nature," as displayed in the *Genealogy, Twilight of the Idols,* and *The Anti-Christ,* conflicts with his reflections on interpretation and the secret war of the instincts, as shown in chapter 5. His epistemology does not furnish grounds either for the tasks he envisions for himself or for his suffering. His devotion in 1888 to "truth" and "reality" is also at variance with the multiplicity of perspectives that he appears, at times, to propose. This multiplicity cannot obscure the fact that Nietzsche puts forward some truths. Equally important, in the many dualities he puts forward in his philosophy, there is always a better or "more true" pole. Thus, of the following pairs of opposites, the first is generally "more true":

nobles	slaves
will to power	self-preservation
truth	appearances
individuals	the herd
strength	weakness
inequality	equality
instincts	reason
body	soul
war	peace
lack of accountability	morality
innocence of all actions	guilt
Roman culture	Jewish culture
becoming	being
intolerance	tolerance
life-affirming possibilities	life-denying possibilities
chance	will
nature	anti-nature
this world	a transcendental world
health	sickness
suffering as training	suffering as sickness
aristocracy	democracy

Certain passages in Nietzsche's texts call for caution in this interpretation, since they explicitly argue for the interrelation of opposites. The quest for knowledge and self-knowledge, for instance, requires both the sick and the healthy soul (GS; 120). Sickness should not be discounted altogether, because the will to health alone would be a piece of barbarism (GS; 120). Indeed, there are different types of physical and spiritual constitutions and, accordingly, "innumerable healths of the body" (GS; 120), so much so that the philosopher is even in a position to use nihilism to restore his health. In a passage dated March–June 1888, the boundaries separating health and sickness all but vanish: "For by now we have learned better than to speak of healthy and sick as an antithesis: it is a question of degrees" (WP; 812).[5] In short, "[w]e must discover the *hero* no less than the *fool* in our passion for knowledge" (GS; 107). Yet in the texts after *The Gay Science,* it is possible to detect a hardened attitude when Nietzsche deals with the components listed in the two columns above. In each of these dualities, he chooses the principles, practices, events, and institutions of the first column. In certain cases, he posits principles, not merely as his personal interpretations, but as universalizable truths.

Two issues here require an explanation. First, it is possible to make a distinction between a *universal perspective* and a *universalizable perspective.* Nietzsche rejects the possibility of a universal perspective; every perspective is fated to be the interpretation of a particular person or group. But he accepts the possibility of perspectives that are universalizable; that is, they reflect the reality of, and can be applied to, particular epochs, persons, groups, and even all of life. A universalizable perspective represents a higher epistemological standpoint, and, Nietzsche seems to believe, this standpoint is on a par with truth. Second, Nietzsche's writings clearly treat truth on two levels. At one level, truth is an interpretation or the existing agreements in a community, and in either case, "truth" could well refer to errors that are accepted as truth. Guilt and sin, for example, are errors, but the *existence* of these errors and the *suffering* they produce are true. At another level, however, truth for Nietzsche consists of a set of a few facts, among which the will to power is one. Finally, Nietzsche's philosophy suggests a distinction between truth and the *value* of truth. Nietzsche believes in some truths, but he insists that the value of truth is overrated. Untruth may well have been more useful than truth or, at least, may have possessed the same value as truth. His philosophy combines all of these dimensions, but the second level of truths/facts is the one that we need to recognize in order to understand his sense of destiny and fatality.

Solomon has argued that "[i]f Nietzsche made us aware of anything in ethics, it is the importance of *perspectives,* the need to see all concepts and values *in context.*"[6] This leaves unanswered several questions about the meaning of "perspectivism." What does it mean to see something "in context?" Does this mean that the context *explains* a perspective, or that it *justifies* a perspective? How could seeing something in a context differ from a relativistic stance? Solomon is right in denying that Nietzsche is a relativist, but he fails to show why this is so. In another essay he argues that Nietzsche "believes that there is a single psychologically justifiable standard, and that differences in the ways of acting upon that standard are not differences in basic moral principles, but only differences in character. The weak cannot exercise their power in the same ways as the strong."[7] Unfortunately, he does not identity what this "single psychologically justifiable standard" is, and the adverb—"psychologically"—dooms the coherence of the claim. For Nietzsche does not attempt to produce a single psychology. The further claim that Nietzsche has his sight on "differences of character" does not lead us very far. Solomon, morevoer, argues that

> Nietzschean nihilism consists of the attack upon and rejection of all those *conceptions* of morality which do not recognize the will to power and personal needs and desires as primary. These would include . . . every conception which finds its source in a historical tradition or in a society or group rather than in personal character. They would include every conception of morality which would insist that its commands be universal, an explicit rejection of the interests of the individual.[8]

"Personal character" and "the interests of the individual," however, are as relative as a "historical tradition" or a society. In each case, there are particular definitions with no external source to justify them. Yet, in contrast to such relativism, Nietzsche does posit some facts that transcend any individual perspective. He is not a relativist.

Nor is he the pluralistic perspectivist that some interpreters take him to be.[9] Relativism entails a context of interpretation and the absence of an independent ground for evaluation outside of the observer/interpreter's context. It is precisely because relativism depends on a context that there is no independent ground to decide whether one view is better than another. The criteria to decide "better-ness" are inscribed in the context. Perspectivism partakes of the same features.[10]

In his published texts, Nietzsche uses the term "perspectives" sparingly (D; 170; GS; 162, 374; BGE; P; 188; GM; III; 12). His philosophical reflections, however, are imbued with perspectivism. I propose to divide Nietzsche's perspectivism into five categories:

(1) Perspectives that arise from power relationships (e.g., rulers and ruled, nobles and slaves, strong and weak, eagles and lambs)
(2) Perspectives pertaining to a person's identity (e.g., the ascetic priest, the saint, the artist, the invalid)
(3) Perspectives that reflect stages in the evolution of human history (e.g., the way primitive men interpreted their dreams, the invention of logic, the invention of religions)
(4) Perspectives that stem from and project the culture of a particular group and epoch (e.g., the ancient Greeks, the Jews, the Romans, the men of modernity)
(5) Perspectives that arise from gender differences.

These five categories of perspectives do not exclude the possibility of truths/facts that would be valid for all people and, in some cases, for every historical age.[11] Under the heading of Nietzsche's universal truths/facts, one ought to include the following: the will to power, which he sees as "the essence of life" (GM; II; 12); the body, nature, chance, becoming, sickness, and the natural law of selection (BGE; 62); the "unalterable innate order of rank" (BGE; 263; see also 219, 221); the *"order of castes"* as the "sanctioning of a *natural order*" (AC; 57); and the lack of accountability.[12] At this point it is hardly necessary to point out that in an earlier presentation of his view of nature, Nietzsche claimed that in nature no one commands (GS; 109). But, as I already argued, in important areas Nietzsche's ideas coalesce to the point of fixity, especially in the texts after *The Gay Science*. In the domain of truths/facts, Nietzsche also finds a lack of authenticity in most individuals, a lack that takes on the sick and ugly form of resentment. He is convinced of a fundamental error in the way we usually understand the world. "Whatever standpoint of philosophy we may adopt today: from every point of view the erroneousness of the world in which we believe we live is the surest and firmest thing we can get our eyes on" (BGE; 34). Our "mind" has produced a "falsified" world, and this calls for a healthy dose of suspicion in our assessment of "reality," not to mention in our evaluation of ourselves. The "right place" to inaugurate culture is the body. Morality rests on a psychology of error (TI; "Errors"; 6; "Expeditions"; 47). Apart from Nietzsche's critique of falsification, in the case of the priest he even equates sickness with falsehood. The priest "is false *because* he is sick: his instinct *demands* that truth shall not come into its own at any point" (AC; 52). I have already discussed Nietzsche's many assertions of his dexterity in reading other people's souls. And in *Twilight of the Idols,* he describes the "will to life" as "the *fundamental fact* of the Hellenic instinct" (TI; "What I Owe"; 4). The Jewish nation represented "the toughest national will to life" that has ever existed, but this nation chose being, even at the price of falsifying "all nature" and "all reality" (AC; 24, 27). The Greeks followed suit. They became actors, that is, false to whatever "nature" they had.

NIETZSCHE'S EPIC SPIRITUALITY

Intriguingly, the evaluation for which Nietzsche calls, of reality and of ourselves, should not be possible. For our actions are always ambiguous, unfathomable, and inexplicable (BGE; 287; GS; 335; WP; 676). "The best that one is one does not know—one cannot know" (BGE; 249). "One hears only those questions for which one is able to find answers" (GS; 196). Is there a way out of this dilemma for Nietzsche? The answer to this question must acknowledge that, by his own admission, he is in the moral domain of those who do not want to be deceived, and who might tell lies but at least want to know the truth that is relevant to *them*. Why do they want to know this truth? And what do they do if the truth they need is nowhere to be found? The answers to these questions go to the heart of Nietzsche's epic spirituality, since knowing the truth is a requirement of inner strength. What is the truth that he finds and has to deal with?

Nietzsche, as we have seen, claims to find only ruins in the world he faces. European culture is decadent and nihilistic. Christianity is the dominant religion, and four Jews reign in Rome (Jesus, Mary, Peter, and Paul) (GM; I; 16). Resentment, which formerly was at least restricted to the slaves, is gaining a universal foothold through democracy. Hatred is rampant in the socialist and the anarchist, and in those who call for universal suffrage, the most recent product of the idea of an equality of souls that Socrates had the nerve to present as a fact. Democracy is Platonism for the masses, Christianity is Platonism for the priests. The pathos of distance is gone, modernity is an age without shame, and the notion of rank is the object of derision. "[W]e no longer possess rank!" (D; 203). "Things are bad generally. Decay is universal. The sickness goes deep" (CW; Second Postscript). The nobles have vanished, and only the prey have survived.

Western civilization, he argues, had three opportunities for greatness and squandered each one of them. It had the Greeks, until Socrates, an ugly son of a mason, started to ask questions. It had the Roman Empire (BGE; 46), until Saint Paul began preaching the resurrection. Finally, it had the Renaissance, until a German monk, a mere peasant's son, went to Rome. Three opportunities, and the three of them missed. How could nature, he asserts, have been more generous? And on further examination, he claims to find one more lost opportunity, as personified by Napoleon, who embodied the greatest moment of the nineteenth century only to perish in utter ignominy (D; 245; BGE; 199; GM; I; 16).[13] It is difficult to imagine a more nefarious deed, Nietzsche claims, than Napoleon's defeat by the British.

The storyteller—Nietzsche—is the only reliable witness to these debacles and to the dark future ahead. His experience is a battleground for an epic spirituality that will also provide a significant amount of self-therapy. Nietzsche suffers his own suffering, wages his own wars, and finds his own enemies. He is fated to solitude: "the desert and the cave are always with him" (SE; 3). The sick philosopher offers a highly stylized portrait of the kind of philosophy he approves and consorts with, and this portrait appears to be coherently derived from all of his previous stories. The philosopher is the last remnant of the vanquished nobles. This is Nietzsche's vanishing-species syndrome at its best: "I, the last disciple and initiate of the god Dionysus"; "we last of the Stoics" (BGE; 295, 227). Like his spiritual predecessors, he needs to practice discipline and harshness on himself and to create an environment of cruelty and deception that will nourish his destiny. "Perhaps severity and cunning provide more favourable conditions for the formation of the strong, independent spirit and philosopher" (BGE; 39). Since the pathos of distance has vanished, he must rebuild it himself. He needs his own isolation, his own asceticism, and his "secret citadel" (BGE; 26). Here, I submit, Nietzsche is following the recommendations of a work he admired, Machiavelli's *The Prince*.

> There is no doubt that rulers become great when they overcome difficulties and the attacks directed against them. For this reason fortune, especially when it wants to increase the power of a new ruler (who has more need to gain a reputation than an hereditary one) encourages the growth of enemies, and makes him fight against them, so that he will be able to vanquish them, and thus rise higher, as if by a ladder that his enemies have provided him with.[14]

The new philosopher should not wait for fickle Fortuna, and he must test himself to see whether he "is destined for independence and command" (BGE; 41). He "affirms *his* existence and only *his* existence" (GM; III; 7); like Schopenhauer (SE; 3), he lives "*imprudently*"; "he risks *himself* constantly, he plays the dangerous game" (BGE; 205; see also 224).[15]

What exactly is "the dangerous game"? It is exploring deep, unknown regions, where he might find a truth that he will not be able to bear and have to rush for escape to the surface: "let no one doubt that he who *needs* the cult of surfaces to that extent has at some time or other made a calamitous attempt to get *beneath them*" (BGE; 59).

It is entering a labyrinth from which he may never return. In this enterprise, he is not in a position to choose. He is impelled by the drive
to knowledge and the need to measure his strength. Strength for a
society is contingent on how many parasites it can endure (D; 202).
Strength for the physical body is established by how much sickness
it can endure and overcome, thus showing its great health.[16] And
strength for the individual is determined not by the number but
by the *kind* of truths he can face without self-destruction. Strength
requires answers to questions such as these:

> how far to approach *truth* and contemplate its most dubious
> aspects?—how far to go forward to meet *suffering*, self-contempt,
> pity, sickness, vice, with the question mark over whether one will
> master them? . . . (what does not kill us makes us *stron-
> ger* . . .)—finally, how far to make concessions in one's own mind to
> the ordinary, the mean, the petty, good, decent, the average nature,
> without being vulgarized by them?[17]

The dangerous game is taking on oneself the problem of life
and feeling the problem of morality as a "personal distress" and torment (GS; 345); it is experimenting with the paralyzing thought that
the "in vain" is a genuine possibility and that self-deception is unavoidable. In his reflections on European nihilism in June 1887,
Nietzsche left no room for doubt about the weight represented by
the impossibility of reliable knowledge. "*Continuing* with an 'In
vain', without aim and purpose, is the *most paralysing* thought, especially when one realizes one's being fooled and yet has no power to
prevent oneself being fooled."[18] This was an apt description of his
own state of mind. He thus conceived of the dangerous game as a
spiritual test that begins as an individual endeavor and is transformed into a process of redemption. His philosophy bore the burden of life as a duty on behalf of himself and humankind, and his
success or failure, he thought, would determine the fate of future
millennia. This situation was determined, he concluded, by destiny,
by the necessity of his particular past.[19]

In the fall of 1887, Nietzsche wrote a passage that is representative of the way he understood the dangerous game.

My new path to 'Yes'

My new version of *pessimism:* willingly to seek out the dreadful
and questionable sides of existence: which made clear to me related
phenomena of the past. 'How much "truth" can a spirit endure and
dare?'—a question of its strength. The *outcome* of a pessimism like
this *could be* that form of a Dionysian *saying Yes* to the world as it is,
to the point of wishing for its absolute recurrence and eternity:
which would mean a new ideal of philosophy and sensibility.[20]

As I have shown in chapter 7, in the area of exploring and experimenting with the "questionable sides of existence," this dangerous
game came to a halt in 1888. In the area of affirming life as it is,
Nietzsche's thought arrived at a philosophy of reconciliation, which
is mentioned in *Human, All Too Human* and developed, albeit frag-
mentarily, in the texts he prepared for publication in 1888.

Since the dangerous game is carried on in a culture that abhors pain and is thoroughly dominated by the instinct for self-
preservation, the philosopher must find his own way by means of
war, pain, and suffering. "Live at war with your peers and yourselves" (GS; 283). Humankind courts danger when it unlearns "how
to wage war" (H; I; 477).[21] Nietzsche goes so far as to claim that war
is "the normal condition" and peace is the exception.[22] War is, incidentally, another principle extolled in *The Prince* as the antidote to
the enervating tendency of peace.[23] When the Romans of the imperial era became bored, for instance, they resorted to gladiators and
moved the killing of animals from the wilderness to the circus; and
when modern Englishmen become bored, Nietzsche observes, they
turn to mountain climbing and other perilous travels (H; I; 477; see
also AOM; 187).

War, for Nietzsche, also purifies and hardens the individual's
spirituality; pain contributes to the enhancement of the species (GS;
318); and suffering is the scale by which the individual's standing in
the order of human rank is weighed.[24] "Profound suffering en-
nobles; it separates" (BGE; 270; D; 18). "The discipline of suffering,
of *great* suffering" has contributed to the elevation of mankind
(BGE; 225).[25] The "highest type" of man has been "the type that has
suffered most" (BGE; 62).[26] And the ones who suffer most are the

idle (H; I; 439). Suffering purifies Nietzsche of the decadent notion that life is a moral attribute, not a natural fact. Through suffering he discharges his own will to power and hardens himself as a warrior, his true nature. And as a warrior, who faced suffering from his early childhood, he became the father of Zarathustra.[27]

Nietzsche's epic spirituality develops through suffering, solitude, war, and having the right type of enemies. These are three important signposts in the path toward self-discipline. "It follows that some people need open enemies if they are to rise to the level of their own virtue, virility, and cheerfulness" (GS; 169). "You should have eyes that always seek an enemy—*your* enemy" (Z; I; "War"). In *Ecce Homo*, Nietzsche categorically states, "I am by nature warlike. To attack is among my instincts" (EH; "So Wise"; 7). The three traits mentioned above mirror the previous ones: a person shows his virility in war, his cheerfulness in solitude, and his virtue in suffering. Nietzsche took his own advice to heart: "The mood in which we usually exist depends upon the mood in which we maintain our environment" (D; 283).

A passage from his notebooks sums up this idea of spirituality in Nietzsche's philosophy. "A full and powerful soul can not only cope with painful, even terrible losses, privations, dispossessions and disdain: from such hells it emerges fuller and more powerful and—the crucial thing—with a new growth in the blissfulness of love."[28] Hence his spiritual discipline requires an increase in suffering. A state of well-being makes one "ludicrous and contemptible" (BGE; 225), and the obsession with the avoidance of suffering is one of the traits that distinguishes modernity from ancient times.[29] The "man of antiquity, under the educating spell of his morality, was a stronger and more profound man than the man of today—he was the only 'well-formed' man there has been."[30]

As Nietzsche argues, suffering is more challenging when there are no reasons to suffer. His "own utopia," as he describes it early on, is his constant companion during his wandering into the depths and heights of his philosophic soul:

> *My utopia.* — In a better ordering of society the heavy work and exigencies of life will be apportioned to him who suffers least as a

consequence of them, that is to say to the most insensible, and thus
step by step up to him who is most sensitive to the most highly sublimated species of suffering and who therefore suffers even when
life is alleviated to the greatest degree possible. (H; I; 462)

Admittedly, suffering from the absence of suffering seems a puzzling idea.[31] But, for Nietzsche, philosophy defined as epic spirituality must magnify the suffering and hyperbolize its enemies. If
suffering is not in sight, it needs to be created. The wildcat must
turn into a tiger before the philosopher/warrior will battle it, since
the tiger, not the wildcat, is the enemy that fits his nature. "If a
man wants to become a hero the serpent must first have become a
dragon: otherwise he will lack his proper enemy" (H; I; 498). The
philosopher/warrior needs worthy enemies, which is why the
nobles' victory over weaker foes signals their inevitable demise.
When the bow relaxes, the arrow languishes on the ground, and
man turns inward.

As a warrior who needs a permanent war, Nietzsche finds his
worth not in negation but in the realization that he has discovered
what others have missed. His genealogical missions thus took on
the form of retrieval: out of the traces of defeated opportunities—
the Greeks, the Romans, the ancient nobles—he contrived his own
version of the nobles, the Greeks, and the warriors. The new philosopher is a precarious mosaic, in which the primal energies and
indeed the whole history of mankind still sweat and breathe in an
agent saddled with two conflicting drives. He is both the philosopher of self-responsibility and also the intoxicated Dionysian artist
who creates perfection through art, even when this art is a destructive deed that he will never remember once he is sober again. The
new philosopher is always transforming himself (TI; "Expeditions";
10). The problem is that this constant transformation leads to
exhaustion—which might explain why Nietzsche clung to facts in
the *Genealogy* and why, in the texts he wrote in 1888, the dangerous
game was over.

Nietzsche wages his personal war by devising a psychological
method based on the belief that he can ascertain and feel what other

people experience. This method operates in the larger realm of history and culture, as well as in the smaller theater of a given individual's soul. In *Human, All Too Human,* Nietzsche described a program of study as a path toward wisdom, in which he explicitly mentions the need for genealogical investigations. "Turn back and trace the footsteps of mankind" through its past: "thus you will learn in the surest way whither all later mankind can and may not go again" (H; I; 292). That is, knowledge of the past will be "the surest way" to avoid past mistakes and to know where humankind should direct its steps. This process of retrieving the past can be accomplished through the study of history, through the understanding of origins and their evolution (D; 197), and also by feeling in oneself what past creatures felt (H; I; 379; D; 61; GS; 337; GM; II; 3). The individual soul may harbor strong impulses of plastic arts or music and those of science; if he is unable to suppress one of these two powers, his only option is "to turn himself" into an enlarged hall of culture, in which both powers will be accommodated. Nietzsche hopes that unidentified "mediating powers" will come into play and settle any possible conflicts between art and science. A soul such as this will "bear the strongest resemblance to the cultural structure of entire epochs and provide continual instruction regarding them by means of analogy" (H; I; 276).

On a smaller scale, Nietzsche proposes "empathy" as necessary to understanding people, an understanding that is best revealed to us by music.[32] We need to imitate a person's *"feelings in ourselves,"* and this includes an imitation of his voice, eyes, body movements, and so forth. This method, Nietzsche claims, will produce a similar feeling in us (D; 142). From this method of understanding, he designs a strategy in which the philosopher relives past cultures and acquires knowledge through suffering (D; 114) and through taking on himself the way of life of others, including those "below" him. In order to judge all past evaluations, "one has voluntarily to live through them once again, and likewise their antithesis—if one is at last to possess the right to pass them through the sieve" (D; 61). Nietzsche was referring here to the men of the future, but it is clear that he endeavored to act like them. The historical sense is the ability to reconstruct in oneself past ideas and sensations, just as one might reconstruct the plan of an entire temple by studying the few pillars still standing (H; I; 274). The philosopher cannot lock himself up in his secret citadel; he must go down and engage in the study of the "*average* human being," a task that is unpleasant and rife with disappointment, yet a necessary part of every philosopher's biography (BGE; 26). This is a clue as to why Nietzsche commiserates with princes: they are not allowed "to vanish into society from time to time," and thus always have to observe other human beings from a distance (D; 526). Only in taking on himself the feelings and experiences of humankind is the philosopher in a position to know himself and others. This is not an experiment for the sake of experimentation. It is a test of strength and a means toward the unity of knowledge and self-knowledge, so much so that self-knowledge makes it possible to know future cultures. When you are "strong enough to see to the bottom of the dark well of your nature and your knowledge, perhaps you will also behold in its mirror the distant constellations of future cultures" (H; I; 292). It is worth noticing that in the same passage, Nietzsche refers to knowledge of the past as the "surest way" to know the roads that are open for future humanity, but when this knowledge is mixed with one's nature and is thereby refracted, he thinks it necessary to introduce the "perhaps." Perhaps the individual, by knowing himself, will rise to a position in which he will know the structure of future cultures.

But how can one discipline oneself when the times are not propitious to one's spirituality? How can one train oneself in the context of modern lassitude? It is not unreasonable to suggest that Nietzsche, like the saint he describes in *Human, All Too Human,* "rejoices in the wild riot of his desires" and "knows how to lay a trap for his affects" (H; I; 142). This gives way to a philosophical asceticism that demands cleanliness of thought, solitude, suffering, and the need for enemies. Here, the idea that Nietzsche constructed the slave morality as an external enemy that he needed in order to wage his own inner wars appears less far-fetched than it might otherwise.

In any new creation, Nietzsche concluded, war and enemies are more important than friends; the more solitary the struggle, the higher the individual climbs. "A new creation in particular, the new *Reich* for instance, has more need of enemies than friends; only in opposition does it feel itself necessary, only in opposition does it *become* necessary" (TI; "Morality"; 3). The existence of opposition proves that the new creation is necessary. This places the new creation in the realm of a reactive deed, namely, in the realm of the slave morality. Nietzsche's main occupation, as he himself describes it, is to overthrow ideas, which is another reactive deed.[33] The soul ought to shun inner peace and to seek war instead. The soul needs to do battle and to be at war even if that war is imaginary. The soul, we should not forget, is an extension of the body; it is the dark tunnel that is dug up when man turns inward. And what kind of war does an immoralist, a "free spirit," wage? He fights to achieve self-mastery and, most likely, to reach a level of awareness in which a plurality of drives struggles for dominance. "We adopt the same attitude towards the 'enemy within': there too we have spiritualized enmity, there too we have grasped its *value*. One is *fruitful* only at the cost of being rich in contradictions; one remains *young* only on condition the soul does not relax, does not long for peace" (TI; "Morality"; 3).

This war seems to be key. However, if the soul needs opposition to remain young, is that a symptom of sickness or of health? Is the quest for opposition, which could be an external or internal opposition, what justifies the philosopher? Nietzsche's philosophy suggests that he must will a reason or cause for opposition, and in virtue of this cause, he becomes necessary. He is thus walking in the footprints of the ascetic priest and the saint whom he describes in *Human, All Too Human*. He is establishing an imaginary connection between a *cause* (external or internal) and the *need* to oppose it. And this is exactly the type of defective reasoning that he finds behind the notion of causality (TI; "Errors"; 1–6).

It is disturbing that the spiritualization of enmity is precisely what the slaves do best. The material enemy, in Nietzsche's stories, becomes a spiritual enemy, whom the slaves fight with love and compassion. The saint needs an opponent to fight his boredom, and Nietzsche, as the anticipator of new philosophers, needs an enemy, probably for the same reason. He, however, couches it in a higher language: he needs an enemy to test whether he is destined for independence and self-control. The "perfect sage," Nietzsche wrote in *Daybreak,* "without knowing it elevates his opponent into the ideal" and transforms him into "a god with shining weapons." Only then does the sage fight his enemy (D; 431). Nietzsche did not do this. He never claimed to be a "perfect sage," either.

The need for an external resistance, an external enemy, was a powerful one for Nietzsche. In 1887, the year he wrote the *Genealogy,* he advocated a politics of physical segregation to save the strong from the weak, proclaimed his disgust at the victory of a weak ideal, and profiled the nobles as individuals who did not care about the slaves. Yet in the same year, he depicted Christianity in quite different terms: "The continuance of the Christian ideal is one of the most desirable things there are—even for the sake of the ideals that want to stand beside it and perhaps above it—they must have opponents, strong opponents, if they are to become *strong*" (WP; 361).[34] In the 1888 works, there is no trace of this wish, but it is a powerful proof of Nietzsche's need to make do with whatever enemy is put in his way, even Christian theologians.

Nietzsche's definition of "what is noble" in *The Will to Power* turns out to be deeply revealing of his own spiritual needs. "*What is noble?*—That one constantly has to play a part. That one seeks situations in which one has constant need of poses. . . . That one knows how to make enemies everywhere, if the worst comes to the worst even of oneself. That one constantly contradicts the great majority not through words but through deeds" (WP; 944). Acting ("to play a part"), masks (the "need of poses"), and war ("to make enemies everywhere"): this is close to a definition of Nietzsche's epic spirituality. As he wrote, "One day, however, bigger dragons will come into this world. For in order that the overman should not lack his dragon, the overdragon that is worthy of him, much hot sunshine must yet glow upon damp jungles. Your wildcats must first turn into tigers, and your poisonous toads into crocodiles; for the good hunter shall have good hunting" (Z; II; "Prudence").

Nietzsche's philosophical journey, he hopes, will hasten the arrival of that "day." The "free spirits" of the future, he claims, loom on the horizon. "I see them already *coming*, . . . and perhaps I shall do something to speed their coming if I describe in advance under what vicissitudes, upon what paths, I see them coming?" (H; I; P; 2). Nietzsche envisioned a "warlike age" that was "about to begin." This age would "carry heroism into the search for knowledge" and "*wage wars* for the sake of ideas and their consequences" (GS; 283). It requires us to redirect our hopes toward the new philosophers, for "we have no other choice." In the same way that he foresaw "free spirits" in *Human, All Too Human* (1878), he foresaw the new philosophers in 1886. "It is the image of such leaders which hovers before *our* eyes—may I say that aloud, you free spirits?" And he goes on, as he did earlier, to specify the "circumstances one would have in part to create, in part to employ, to bring them into existence" (BGE; 203).

This is an individualism in the Platonic sense: the individual, like the Platonic ruler, ought to do something for the sake of himself and for humankind. In saving himself, the Platonic guardian saves the polis. And so too with Nietzsche, who will save all human beings. He wants to redeem life from a morality that fails to recognize the prevalence of chance in our natural and cultural constitution. But he also wants to free the world from chance and to flow, *consciously,* toward a goal (ULH; 9; D; 108; H; I; 24). Zarathustra endures man to the extent that man is "the redeemer of chance" (EH; "Thus Spoke"; 8). In 1887 Nietzsche refers to "the *redeeming* man," whose solitude "will be misunderstood by the people as though it were flight *from* reality," when, in fact, he needs to immerse himself in reality in order to redeem it "from the curse which its ideal has placed on it up till now" (GM; II; 24).

This idea of redemption, and the unique awareness of possessing a soul whose structure bears the "strongest resemblance" to different cultural epochs and the entire human past, are the salient traits of his epic spirituality. For all his insistence on a revaluation of all values, Nietzsche was still bound up with the Christian idea of redemption. For all his critique of the weak, Nietzsche wanted to redeem all existence and all people from the inherited errors of millennia. He perceived the greatness as well as the heaviness that this task represented. He sensed that he was destiny and, though the responsibility of freeing human beings from chance was a crushing one, he thought he could endure and fulfill it. He provided himself with a cosmological conscience. His training and suffering led him to believe in his redeeming powers.

The title of his autobiography is enigmatic and, at the same time, so transparent that it shuts the door to possible misunderstandings. *Ecce Homo:* this is the phrase that a puzzled Pontius Pilate uttered to the crowd and to himself. The Roman prefect was at a loss in front of the Redeemer. Nietzsche appropriates the phrase and applies it to himself. Nietzsche acts as both Pilate and the soon-to-be-crucified Jesus. *Ecce Homo:* Nietzsche is still bewildered by what he is, but has also figured out, in distinct terms, his role as a turning point in history. And he is certain that he is fated to be crucified to a responsibility that he cannot avoid. He takes this as a sign of tragedy and also a sign of strength.

Yet, although the philosopher must harden himself through discipline, suffering, war, and enemies, his epic spirituality arises from his inner strength, from the fictions he must create in order to nourish his environment, and from historiobiography. He builds around himself a fortress that will protect his individuality, as well as the ghosts he has chosen as his companions. "I want to have my lion and eagle near me so that I always have hints and omens that help me to know how great or small my strength is" (GS; 314). Nietzsche's genealogical journeys allow him to claim that, finally, he had "a country of my own" (GM; P; 3). Both his philosophical investigation into the origin and evolution of morality and the consolations he concocts for himself are outlets for his artistic nature, and these outlets will eventually raise him up to a state of health: "where I could not find what I *needed*, I had artificially to enforce, falsify and invent a suitable fiction for myself (—and what else have poets ever done? And to what end does art exist in the world at all?)" (H; I; P; 1).

Knowledge serves as a script for self-protection in this spiritual drama, in which Nietzsche is both playwright and actor. In the *Genealogy*, Nietzsche explains that the first philosophers on earth resorted to asceticism because, in a frightful age, they had to become actors and use frightful means in order to survive (GM; III; 10). But, suddenly, Nietzsche, the narrator, walks onto the stage himself and crosses over to the action. The storyteller is now an actor. Temporal distance is erased, and another drama ensues. The ascetic philosopher might well be one living in his own desert—a hotel room, preferably—moving aloof among his contemporaries, wearing multiple masks for self-protection, and avoiding the heaviness of today. What does philosophy have to do with the present? (GM; III; 8). The reply is that the first philosophers are effaced, and Nietzsche takes their place. The philosopher, Nietzsche wrote in *Schopenhauer as Educator*, "will wisely refrain from reading the newspapers every day, and above all from serving in a party, although he will not hesitate for a single moment to take up his position if his fatherland is threatened by a real danger" (SE; 7). The philosopher's isolation is, too, a strategy for survival. But this time, it is Nietzsche's acting and survival that are at stake. He is now in his desert, so alone that he no longer has a fatherland. What is this "desert"?

> A voluntary obscurity perhaps; an avoidance of oneself; a dislike of noise, honor, newspapers, influence; a modest job; an everyday job, something that conceals rather than exposes one; . . . perhaps even a room in a full, utterly commonplace hotel, where one is certain to go unrecognized and can talk to anyone with impunity—that is what "desert" means here: oh, it is lonely enough, believe me! (GM; III; 8)[35]

Time, moreover, is abolished in Nietzsche's story of himself because, as he confesses in *The Gay Science,* the spirit of past and future ages intersects in him (GS; 54; H; I; 452). And when time disappears, a reflection on primeval philosophers quickly evolves into historiobiography.

Nietzsche had to invent a fiction for himself. As he remarks, what else have poets ever done? What else have philosophers ever done? These are relevant questions because the genealogist who finds evidence of origins, and the physician who diagnoses the evidence, discover themselves in the predicament Nietzsche attributes to the ascetic and saint in *Human, All Too Human.* The saint makes his life enjoyable by "waging war and in the alternation of victory and defeat. To this end he requires an opponent, and he finds him in the so-called 'enemy within'" (H; I; 141). And this is not a trifling matter when the "enemy within" is the whole animal and human past, as well as the height potentially reachable, and when this "enemy" demands a type of dangerous knowledge that may paralyze the philosopher, leaving in his eyes the glimpse of a desired future (D; 45). The predicament of the saint and the new philosopher may be the same, but the "enemy" is completely different.

By leading his life as his philosophy spurs him to live, the new philosopher obtains access to a dimension that was not available to the nobles, let alone the slaves: that of taking responsibility for the self. The philosopher is sick and is aware of his spiritual condition, which is based on physiological misfortunes. He must take sides against his own times and his own sickness through "a special self-discipline: to take sides against everything sick in me, including Wagner, including Schopenhauer, including all of modern 'humaneness'" (CW; P). Against the weariness of his own time, "[t]he philosopher in me resisted" (CW; P). However, in pursuing knowledge, he separates himself from nature and chisels out his own character as a unique individual. Philosophy is the sickness that pulls itself out to health, thereby mesmerizing any potential audience with a feast denied by logical causality. The philosopher is *causa sui.*

The new philosopher is able to bear this responsibility, which is owed neither to an external code of nature nor to a transcendental command. It comes from our own tests, the ones the individual should not avoid, "although they are perhaps the most dangerous game one could play and are in the end tests which are taken before ourselves and before no other judge" (BGE; 41). This responsibility is not even moral, if by morality we refer to a code of conduct, even one self-imposed, that demands consistency. *Self-responsibility is the will to power's awareness of itself through knowledge.* Self-responsibility is only possible through sickness, self-examinations, and war. This awareness allows the will to power—which is what life is—to constrain itself and to go deeper into the soul, not as an internalization that reeks of bad conscience, but as an opportunity to sharpen one's sense for deceit, and as a new battlefield for waging war and living dangerously. War "is a training in freedom. For what is freedom?

That one has the will to self-responsibility. That one preserves the distance which divides us. That one has become more indifferent to hardship, toil, privation, even to life" (TI; "Expeditions"; 38). "The free man is a *warrior*," and the battlefield is his own as well as other people's souls. Self-responsibility, thus conceived, is an aesthetic dimension available only to artists and philosophers. Nietzsche's conception of art and music as either a constrained will to power or as a proof of strong individuals makes sense in this context.

And yet, at least once in the *Genealogy*, the type of radical spiritual "vivisection" that Nietzsche enthusiastically extolled as part of his physiological and philosophical project provoked in him either a deceptive move or a genuine call toward reexamination. Only one year after his discussion of this art of vivisection in *Beyond Good and Evil*, he described it in a different way, almost as if he repented it: "our attitude toward *ourselves* is *hubris*, for we experiment with ourselves in a way we would never permit ourselves to experiment with animals and, carried away by curiosity, we cheerfully vivisect our souls: what is the 'salvation' of the soul to us today?" (GM; III; 9).

Through the knowledge condensed in the stories he tells and in the causal links he establishes, Nietzsche can redirect the will to power. Instead of being used for a crude oppression of the herd, he puts that will to a better use on the *higher* plane of history and culture. His self-characterization as a "subterranean man" (D; P; 1) refers to his role in the former. His self-characterization as a "physician of culture" describes his task in the latter (see PCP). Even though he claims that history is not "definable" (GM; II; 13), he defines it in the meanings that unfold when he analyzes European culture and human vicissitudes since the invention of morality.

Nietzsche's stories, ultimately, are the script in which he writes his own biography as a man of destiny. The script is much more than a personal one, and the stakes are high. He is writing *historiobiography*, a genre in which, as I mentioned in chapter 1, history and the individual are entwined and express one another. Nietzsche's scripts lay bare the magnitude of his self-appointed task as the last soothsayer reading the signs of the advent of nihilism, or, if we allow an optimistic twist, as the last harbinger of the philosophy of the future.[36] But he is more than a harbinger, for he is already a philosopher of the future.[37] "The philosopher of the future? He must become the supreme tribunal of an artistic culture, the police force, as it were, that guards against all transgressions."[38] This view, presented in 1872–1873, coalesced and took its final form in the ideal society described in 1888 in *The Anti-Christ* (AC; 57). By that time, Nietzsche believed that he had "divined" what lies behind modern ideas (BGE; 203). But the endeavor had been costly: one side of his epic spirituality turned into a mock battle against imaginary foes. Nietzsche had to fight a war, to make enemies, and, if real enemies were not in sight, battle against their shadows.

The genealogist/archaeologist/physician deciphers history, religion, and morality and identifies the physiological roots of the religious type, the ascetic type, and the noble type. The only task remaining is to define the higher stage awaiting humankind—that of the new philosopher—and Nietzsche provides it in a grand nineteenth-century fashion. He is "the man of the most comprehensive responsibility who has the conscience for the collective evolution of mankind" (BGE; 61). Nietzsche's introspection in one of his genealogical journeys sheds a new light on this passage. In distinguishing between the artistic genius and the genius of knowledge in regard to their unique suffering, he claims that the sufferings of the artistic genius

> are felt to be exaggerated because the sound of his lamentations is louder, his mouth more persuasive; and *sometimes* his sufferings really are great, but only because his ambition and envy are so great. . . . In very rare cases—when the genius of ability and of knowledge is amalgamated with moral genius in the same individual—there is added to the sufferings referred to a species of suffering that one must take to be the most singular exception in the world: an extra- and supra-personal sensibility attuned to a nation, to mankind, to a whole culture, to all suffering existence: which acquires its value through its connection with very difficult and remote forms of knowledge (pity in itself is of little value). —But by what standard, on what scales can we measure whether or not it is genuine? Is it not almost obligatory to mistrust all who *speak* of possessing sensibilities of this sort? (H; I; 157)

This is an important question, particularly if one understands Nietzsche as a philosopher who combined, or at least believed that he combined, "the genius of ability and of knowledge" with the "moral genius," and who certainly was convinced that he possessed a "supra-personal sensibility" attuned to the prospects of European culture and the human race. Unfortunately, Nietzsche quickly forgot this important question. In *The Gay Science* he dreams of being the incarnation of the nobility of the past (GS; 54, 337), and in all his books after *Human, All Too Human*, he presents suffering as the standard to judge and to determine who is of noble stock. One might pose the question: Is Nietzsche's characterization of the founders of religions as self-deceived individuals a fair assessment of his own condition? (H; I; 52). Could it be that, like the founders of religion, he too never emerged from his self-deceptive belief that he possessed a "supra-personal sensibility" attuned to the entire history of humankind? In *Ecce Homo*, he explains why he is destiny as follows: "Self-deception has to exist if a grand *effect* is to be produced" (H; I; 52).

Though history has been deciphered, the body dissected, and the mind revealed, the end result of Nietzsche's philosophy is not inviting. It is the hubris of an illusory transparency. In an 1885 fragment he described philosophy as follows: "Philosophy in the only way I still allow it to stand, as the most general force of history, as an attempt somehow to describe Heraclitean becoming and to abbreviate it into signs (so to speak, to *translate* and mummify it into a kind of illusory *being*)."[39] As the most general force of history, philosophy thirsts for an abbreviation and translation of an inapprehensible being, a being that the genealogist wishes to demarcate. The problem is that the story can easily turn into a process of manufacturing its own evidence.

Do Nietzsche's genealogies fabricate a past that is then transformed into a setup for his conclusions? Does Nietzsche, for instance, plant resentment in the soul of the slave? Not only did he fail to follow his own advice to look at origins ironically (H; I; 252),[40] but he went after these origins with a bludgeon. We should recall that the archaeologist of the soul wears a mask for self-protection. "Everything profound loves the mask" (BGE; 40); "the fundamental will of the spirit . . . ceaselessly strives for appearance and the superficial—in all desire to know there is already a drop of cruelty" (BGE; 229). Nietzsche is not impervious to that cruelty, but he knows that he needs to know, and thus he seeks some degree of transparency among his friends and all those who come close to him. The archaeologist of the soul "*wants* a mask of him to roam the heads and hearts of his friends in his stead" (BGE; 40). As I have shown, although Nietzsche does not want to be taken for what he is not, there is an important sense in which his genealogy of the past and archaeology of the soul require at least a subtle dimension of misunderstanding.

"Flee away and conceal yourselves! And have your masks and subtlety, so that you may be misunderstood!" (BGE; 25). Nietzsche is most revealing when he is interpreted as the genealogist of transparency, who seeks misunderstanding as part of his philosophical plots or, one might say, *ploys*.

HISTORIOBIOGRAPHY AND RECONCILIATION

Throughout this book I have argued that Nietzsche, as a philosopher and poet, sought and found his way to answer those and only those questions "for which one is able to find answers" (GS; 196) through the stories he told to himself and his potential audience. In these stories he sculpted himself as a character who knew the depth of the meaning of tragedy; who believed that he was "bearing a responsibility for all the coming millennia" (EH; "So Clever"; 10); and who, like the poet he had described in 1879, acted "*as though he had been present at the weaving of the whole nexus of the world*" (AOM; 32, emphasis mine). The highest men, after all, of which he is one, "bear the *greatest responsibility*" without collapsing under it" (WP; 975). Nietzsche's belief in his responsibility elicited a suffering that made him wonder whether "any man has ever suffered so. Who, indeed, feels as I do what it means to feel with every fiber of one's being that the 'weights of all things must be decided anew.'"[41] Storytelling was a reordering of the past, and this reordering was possible because, according to his philosophy, the past never disappears from the individual's life. The past is always flowing and leaving its marks on and through us.[42] This idea is, once again, that of historio-biography. But this standpoint cuts both ways: it applies to both the past and the future. As Nietzsche wrote Franz Overbeck, unless whole millennia "make their loftiest vows in my name, then in my eyes I shall have achieved nothing."[43] And this is stated in the same missive in which he described the distress produced by his task of inventing new ways of measuring the weights of all things. Historio-biography, then, cannot be confined to Nietzsche's own turmoil, fears, and hopes in his philosophical texts. Historiobiography is supposed to be much more than Nietzsche's life. It is, above all, an event: a sudden awareness that one's life contains the code to deci-pher all previous events and to foresee future occurrences, a task that the notion of the eternal recurrence of all things makes easier. As early as 1883, Nietzsche called himself "the victim of a terrestrial and climatic disturbance, to which Europe is exposed."[44] That is, he sensed in himself the same inner currents and tremors that were reverberating through his own times and culture, and he first had to overcome those in himself.

In his archaeological quest, the philosopher is able to recon-struct the past and to pinpoint the events that were ladders for climbing to new heights, as well as the ones where wrong turns were taken. We "require history, for the past continues to flow within us in a hundred waves; we ourselves are, indeed, nothing but that which at every moment we experience of this continued flowing" (AOM; 223; see also GS; 54). The storyteller uses history as a spring-board to acquaint himself with a "*subtler* art and object of travel," an art in which the philosopher can set sail without leaving his cave and desert. With the required training, the individual "will redis-cover the adventurous travels of [his] *ego* in process of becoming and transformation in Egypt and Greece, Byzantium and Rome, France and Germany." The ego will go to the age of nomadic and settled na-tions, to the Renaissance and the Reformation. "Thus self-knowledge will become universal knowledge with regard to all that is past" (AOM; 223). This is the unity—of self-knowledge and universal knowledge—that Nietzsche defined as the task of any great philo-sophical enterprise: to read one's life and to decipher "on the basis of it the hieroglyphs of life in general" (SE; 3). This, I submit, is one of the finest achievements of his philosophical storytelling. His conception of the ego as a hundred-eyed Argos, as the aleph, or as that which contains all past history gave credence to his stories of the past and to his belief in the heavy weight he was carrying for himself and for all future humanity.

Storytelling, thus defined, shows the communion between the philosopher's soul and the totality of history. Anyone "who is destined for history in the broadest sense will never see things for the first time and never himself be something that is seen for the first time" (SE; 7). I suggest that here, Nietzsche shows his fidelity to the idea that his personal life can be a way to decipher life in general. This idea becomes cohesive and coherent when he insists that all past human history runs through him like a stream. He himself contains the traces and stories of past events, deeds, and individuals. He has seen it all already. His life is like a small grain of sand that contains iridium, the evidence of a cataclysmic collision between an asteroid and our planet, and the memory of this collision therefore lives on in him. The idea of the eternal recurrence of past and future makes it impossible for the philosopher *to see* things "for the first time." The same past will not allow him *to be* "something that is seen for the first time." He has been in Greece, Rome, and Byzantium, and in both settled and nomadic nations. The contemporary world is not new to him, and "those who know history must increasingly have the feeling that they are recognizing the features of an old familiar face" (RWB; 4). The philosopher is "a compendium of the entire world" (SE; 7). "Higher natures have their origins infinitely farther back, and with them much had to be assembled, saved and hoarded" (EH; "So Wise"; 3). Nietzsche *is* all the names and people in history.[45]

Historiobiography is interpretation, which is not only a process of selection and falsification, but also an expression of the will to power (WP; 556). The relationship between interpretation and the will to power becomes more fruitful, as well as fateful, once one also opens the door to another link. In *The Will to Power*, Nietzsche establishes the unity of meaning and the will to power: "All meaning is will to power (all relative meaning resolves itself into it)" (WP; 590).

Interpretation is the introduction, or rather, the imposition of meaning on the world (WP; 604). Nietzsche argues that a fact becomes a fact only after a meaning has been imposed on it:

> The question 'what is that?' is an imposition of meaning from some other viewpoint. 'Essence,' the 'essential nature,' is something perspective and already presupposes a multiplicity. At the bottom of it there always lies 'what is that for *me*?' (for us, for all that lives, etc.) . . . One may not ask: 'who then interprets?' for the interpretation itself is a form of the will to power, exists (but not as a 'being' but as a process, a becoming) as an affect. (WP; 556)

Thus, all interpretations express, seek, and construct meanings, which are in turn reflections of the will to power. And this will to power is the crystallization of our needs (WP; 481).

Once interpretation is equated with meaning, and this meaning is the stamp of the will to power, we return to the familiar question: How does one determine whether one will to power is better than another? Since all wills to power are the symptoms of unknown instincts, Nietzsche has only one way out: to become the physician and surgeon, or to divine the entrails of other people's souls. In his role as physician, Nietzsche diagnoses the "diseased reason" of the priest (TI; "Morality"; 6) and gives himself the authority to certify one will to power as sick and the other as healthy. It does not matter that this is an old trick he learned from Plato, and even less that the "diagnosis" itself is the work of his unknown instincts. His consolation is to believe that he is a *décadent* whose instincts fortunately always choose the right means to combat his decadence (EH; "So Wise"; 2). Nietzsche thus is forced to reach out for the old "I" he had rejected in *Beyond Good and Evil* in order to give his reflections some semblance of credibility. But he is not always sure of himself. He ruminates painfully about whether he is a buffoon, which clearly he is not (TI; "Destiny"; 1). Rather, as he wrote in 1872, he is "the philosopher of tragic knowledge."

> He masters the uncontrolled knowledge drive, though not by means of a new metaphysics. He establishes no new faith. He considers it

tragic that the ground of metaphysics has been withdrawn, and he will never permit himself to be satisfied with the motley whirling game of the sciences. He cultivates a new *life;* he returns to art its rights. . . . One must even *will illusion*—that is what is tragic. (PRS; 37)

The philosopher of tragic knowledge is the "last philosopher," the "'last' for our world. He demonstrates the necessity of illusions, of art, and of that art which rules over life" (PRS; 38). He must will illusions because "nature needs knowledge, and it is horrified at the knowledge it actually needs" (SE; 5). Truth is ugly, not soothing.

THE EPISTEMOLOGICAL PRISON

I have already argued that Nietzsche's philosophy displays an unflinching commitment to avoiding a denial of the world. In 1876, Nietzsche had offered a picture of Wagner's life that matched his own, in that Wagner's life required him "to be unsettled and not at home in the world, and yet to have to speak with it, to have to make demands of it; to despise it, and yet not to be able to get along without it" (RWB; 10). This type of life suffers in the world but does not deny the world. In *Ecce Homo,* he describes his invention of the Dionysian as a *"supreme deed"* (EH; "Thus Spoke"; 6) and describes Zarathustra as one who does not deny. The ideal world that promises the realization of our true essence is the lie that he battles and wants humanity to leave behind in order to reach for its future (EH; Foreword; 2; WP; 583B, 586A). The lie of the ideal world has made our world appear false and mendacious, and Nietzsche abhors the lie. But in the last book he prepared for publication, *Ecce Homo,* he surprises his audience with a gesture of reconciliation, and stands for the *"profoundest* . . . insight most strictly confirmed and maintained by *truth and knowledge"* (EH; "Birth"; 2, second emphasis mine). This insight, "confirmed" by "truth and knowledge," is a "Yes to life," which is an "affirmation without reservation even of suffering, even of guilt, even of all that is strange and questionable in existence." It is precisely the acceptance of "actuality," of this "Yes to life," that requires courage and strength: "precisely by this measure of strength does one approach truth" (EH; "Birth"; 2).

The reconciliation is complete, or at least it is presented in categorical terms. "Nothing that is can be subtracted, nothing is dispensable" (EH; "Birth"; 2), which I take to mean that nobles and slaves, priests and theologians, democracy and churches, the sick and the herd, and guilt and resentment all play a part in what Nietzsche calls "actuality." "In the actual world, in which everything is bound to and conditioned by everything else, to condemn and think away anything means to condemn and think away everything" (WP; 584). Thus, the reconciliation that Nietzsche affirms in *Ecce Homo* echoes his words in *Human, All Too Human:* "everything that happens is inextricably knotted to everything that will happen." Herein is the immortality of motion: "what has once moved is enclosed and eternalized in the total union of all being like an insect in amber" (H; I; 208). This is not the final word of an exhausted warrior. The storyteller/philosopher makes peace with "actuality," namely, with the vast tapestry of his own reflections, experiences, fears, and fictions.[46] The reconciliation found in *Ecce Homo* is presented, not as a premonition, but as part of a philosophy that weaves coherent patterns. As I quoted in chapter 7, the last philosopher *"endures suffering . . . until he is offered reconciliation in the highest tragic art"* (PRS; 85). Could it be that the "highest tragic art" was the obligation to create a world that would be the womb from which he would be born, even if posthumously? This is what his philosophical investigations, in my judgment, suggest.

The storyteller finishes his countless journeys as a turning point, if not *the* turning point, in history. Nietzsche himself refers to six historical events (without identifying them explicitly) that are worth all the mud and miseries of the human condition, and claims that he is the seventh. "Seven," we might note, is a number representing perfection in the Judeo-Christian tradition that he opposes. One might speculate that the six historical "events" refer to the classical Greek culture, Socrates, the Roman Empire, Christianity, the Renaissance, and the Reformation. In this list we also have three successive pairs, the first of which represents an ascent and the second its destruction.[47]

It is probably accurate to say that the storyteller does not conclude any of his journeys. For after all, the "incomplete" acts as an artistic stimulant (H; I; 199). As the seventh event, the storyteller brings forth "truths" or "certainties" that he has been hiding. Nietzsche confesses that one of the causes of his tribulations is this: "I have a subtler sense for signs of ascent and decline than any man has ever had, I am the teacher *par excellence* in this matter—I know both, I am both" (EH; "So Wise"; 1). He is both ascent and decline. And, faithful to his claim in *Twilight of the Idols* that no party to life can estimate the value of life, Nietzsche gives a numbing twist to his storytelling: he claims to possess "that freedom from party in relation to the total problem of life which perhaps distinguishes me." The "perhaps" is mysterious; it appears as a concession in a sentence that, according to him, no one else was ever in a position to utter. But if he is free from any partisan bent in dealing with "the total problem of life," then he is suggesting—whether in irony, certainty, or jest is irrelevant—that he is the only one who can evaluate life, which, of course, is what his philosophy, like any philosophy, does.

One of the clues scattered in his texts may help explain his sense of destiny. Illusions, he wrote in *Human, All Too Human*, "may be healers," and

> in the life of individuals, too, illusions that are in themselves poisons often play the role of healers; yet, in the end, in the case of every 'genius' who believes in his own divinity the poison shows itself to the same degree as his 'genius' grows old: one may recall, for example, the case of Napoleon, whose nature certainly grew into the mighty unity that sets him apart from all men of modern times precisely through his belief in himself and his star and through the contempt for men that flowed from it; until in the end, however, this same belief went over into an almost insane fatalism, robbed him of his acuteness and swiftness of perception, and became the cause of his destruction. (H; I; 164)

Is Nietzsche equating himself to Napoleon, whom he called the last great specimen of human history? One can only answer, in good Nietzschean fashion, with a resounding "perhaps." But this "perhaps" cannot blind us to the facts that Nietzsche believed in the healing power of illusions; that he proclaimed his own "divinity" and believed in himself as destiny, or fatality; that he felt contempt for the men of his times; but that, unlike Napoleon, he believed he was not robbed of "the swiftness of [his] perception." Quite the opposite: his certainty about what he had discovered, become, and represented for humankind led him, not to an inner explosion, but to that external explosion of tropicality where the individual stands "reduced to his own law-giving, to his own arts and stratagems for self-preservation, self-enhancement, self-redemtpion" (BGE; 262). Nietzsche "revealed" these volcanic eruptions in his writings, while insisting on his desire and need to be misunderstood. "[I]t is *certainty* which makes mad. . . . We all *fear* truth" (EH; "So Clever"; 4). A *"grand politics* on earth" would only begin after him (EH; "Destiny"; 1).

He is ascent, he is decline, and he is a decadent. But as we have already seen, and contrary to "real" decadents, his nature combats the decadent within him by always choosing the right means to defeat that condition. And this choosing proves that he is, essentially, a healthy specimen. In coping with the conditions that would have crushed others, he emerges victorious. Nietzsche is not claiming that the "right" means chosen by his instincts are devoid of deception and falsehood. Rather, he is saying that although the means are deceptive and false, they are the ones *required* by his nature and therefore "true." Truth is not a universal value, having the same content for all people at all times. Truth only obtains its value when it is in harmony with an individual's nature. This, of course, introduces an epistemological problem in Nietzsche's paradigm. The rhapsodist of "becoming" is also arguing that no one can change his nature. The rulers of his pyramidal society are rulers because of their nature. Strong and independent individuals are ones "prepared and predestined for command, in whom the art and reason of a ruling race is incarnated" (BGE; 61). This is another way of saying that there are human types, which are fixed by nature. Notwithstanding Nietzsche's defense of change and becoming, human types apparently belong to the sphere of being.

Nietzsche may be fatality, but in *Ecce Homo* he forgets the principle of unaccountability and, as we have seen, describes himself as the unique individual who carries the weight of all coming millennia. In *Richard Wagner in Bayreuth* (1876) he had stated that "in moments of extraordinary danger or when making important decisions about their lives," people go into an intense process of introspection that "compress[es] all their experiences" and "are able to perceive once again with uncommon sharpness the nearest and most distant things" (RWB; 1). The philosopher in Nietzsche, the one who extols danger, began to divine the future, and in 1888 he would recoil from the "most distant things." Danger was the companion of the artistic seer. He had already dreamed that "the whole primal age and past of all sentient being" continued living through him (GS; 54). This is how he believed that he had found the meaning of his fatality as a storyteller who never renounced the hybrid nature of a poetizing philosopher and a philosophizing artist (H; I; 110). He was a Homeric Greek who sought to invent his own gods; a Roman who followed the good taste and good style of the Roman nobility, as evinced in his model, Sallust; an unaccountable Olympian creature who chose to be responsible. Out of the many abysses he found in himself, he brought himself to health. He smelled the "diseased" reason of the priest and knew that it was different from his own "restored" reason. He traveled through history and restored the "old honest I" to his rightful place by ignoring the "it" into which, in Nietzsche's own words, the "I" had become.

This journeying was not a random searching. It was a selective quest, as announced in *Human, All Too Human* (1878) and in *Beyond Good and Evil* (1886). He sought to know the "heights, depths, and distances" of "the entire history of the soul *hitherto*"; he wanted to inquire into the nature of the religious men, and to survey and order their "dangerous and painful experiences" (BGE; 45).[48] The revaluation of all values was part of his intellectual pursuits since 1882, when he declared that "the weights of all things must be determined anew" (GS; 269). In 1888 he arrived at the conclusion that perhaps he, alone, could undertake the "revaluation of values" (EH; "So Wise"; 3). For in understanding his nature, that is, his instincts and physiological constitution, he had become convinced that his biography paralleled human history. "I had *discovered* the only likeness and parallels to my own innermost experience which history possesses" (EH; "Birth"; 2).

In constructing his biography as part of his storytelling, Nietzsche uses historical characters who are, he believes, spiritually bound up with his personal trajectory.[49] He describes Napoleon in a way that fits Nietzsche's own life, and similarly for Heraclitus, Schopenhauer, and Wagner. According to Nietzsche, Heraclitus "sees outside himself only error, illusion, an absence of knowledge—but no bridge leads him to his fellow man, no overpowering feeling of sympathetic stirring binds them to him. We can only with difficulty imagine the feelings of loneliness that tore through him" (PPP; 10). Such features apply equally to Nietzsche. Schopenhauer had the disadvantage of a "vain aesthete of a mother" and the advantage of a father who taught him "unbending and rugged manliness" (SE; 7). Nietzsche disowned his mother and sister, while praising the influence of his father. Wagner treats history as pliant and "malleable clay in his hands," and Nietzsche obviously does the same. Like Nietzsche, Wagner "[could] poetically infuse the individual event with the typical aspects of entire ages and thereby achieve in his representation a truth that the historian [could] never achieve" (RWB; 3). This truth was meant to be aesthetic, not objective. Like Wagner, Nietzsche views life as "the incredible manifoldness and desolateness of an apparent chaos" and sought to tie up together "what previously was irreconcilably disconnected" (RWB; 5) .

In *Ecce Homo*, the statement "nothing is dispensable" became an eloquent way to build connections and to lay a mantle of meaning over the "apparent chaos." "For [Schopenhauer] there was only one task and a hundred thousand ways of accomplishing it, one meaning and innumerable hieroglyphs with which to express it" (SE; 7). This is an apt portrayal of Nietzsche's philosophy. He, too, had one task: dissecting the past and the present to find the origins of overrated ideals and, in doing so, creating favorable conditions for the appearance of a higher species of human beings. And he had "many ways" of doing this single task: analyzing the heroic, the tragic disposition, the Dionysian, morality, decadence, nobility, modernity, Christianity, and so on. For Nietzsche, too, there was a single meaning: he was here to fulfill this task, but before doing so, he had to realize that life had no meaning. He would provide the missing meaning as a means to his own consolation, that is, as an expression of both his epic spirituality and his self-therapy. There was one meaning but many hieroglyphs, namely, the signs he read in other people's souls as well as in the past, present, and "most distant things." Wagner could not be "the prophet of the future," but he was the poetic elucidator of all past events, "the interpreter and transfigurer of the past" (RWB; 11). Nietzsche himself believed that he was one step ahead of Wagner: he was both a prophet of the future and a "transfigurer of the past."

On this interpretation, Nietzsche's assessment of Wagner's music in 1876 is equivalent to what he does in his own philosophy: "—to retranslate visible motion into soul and primal life and, on the other hand, to see the hidden fabric of the inner world as a visual phenomenon and to give it the semblance of a body" (RWB; 7). In Nietzsche's case, however, more is involved than constructing "the semblance of a body." Nietzsche constructs himself. As archaeologist, physician, and philosopher, he is the stone, the sculptor, and the tools. And he sees not only the "hidden fabric of the inner world" but also the hidden fabric of all of human history, which began as a primal, howling pack of creatures tormented by the ghosts of their past. (Hence, he suggests, we have dreams that remind us of our actions and habits in remote ages. "In outbursts of passion and in the fantasising of dreams and insanity, a man rediscovers his own and mankind's prehistory: animality, with its savage grimaces; on these occasions his memory goes sufficiently far back, while his civilised condition evolves out of a forgetting of these primal experiences" [D; 312; see also H; I; 12, 13].)

It is revealing that these descriptions of Schopenhauer and Wagner from the early 1870s turn out to be anticipatory traits, which Nietzsche later binds together in his own storytelling. And this storytelling appears, increasingly, as a philosophical reflection of an inner life discovering its place in a totality. This discovery, furthermore, opens the gate to a reconciliation with life and history. It also shuts all other avenues for Nietzsche. In one of the most beautiful sections of *Human, All Too Human,* he describes a wanderer destined to spend bad nights in the desert after finding the gates of the town, where he had expected to rest, "closed against him" (H; I; 638). The metaphor will be inverted. Nietzsche finds the gates of the town closed, but by 1888 the town had been built by himself. And far from coming from a desert populated by wild and howling beasts and attempting to get inside the town, he is already inside and trying to get out, to continue his wandering.

The reconciliation that Nietzsche cheerfully celebrates in *Ecce Homo* also adds the last brick to his epistemological prison, in which his concepts of becoming and of the body seem to collide. As quoted above, "nature . . . is horrified at the knowledge it actually needs." Is nature horrified at the knowledge of the body, a theme that takes center stage in *Ecce Homo?* For Nietzsche, the body is part of the ebb and flow of becoming, and so are the instincts. In the human body, "the whole most distant and most recent past of all organic becoming regains life and corporeality."[50] And since causes, actions, the secret war of the instincts, and reality are basically unknowable, it follows that the body, as part of reality, is also unknowable. In other words, by denying the possibility of knowing reality, Nietzsche must accept that the body, too, is unknowable to him. This epistemological conclusion should make suspect his reliance on physiology. Nietzsche, however, declines to go this far. In his view, as we have seen, the "supreme law" of nature has designed three types of human bodies, whose boundaries are fixed. He also believes in knowable connections between certain physiological defects and their moral, religious, psychological, and philosophical manifestations.

These manifestations reflect the existing configuration and arrangements of the instincts at a given moment. And since these arrangements are always in the process of change, or "becoming," it follows that the inner and unknown processes of the body express Nietzsche's concept of the Dionysian. The philosopher's body thus escapes responsibility because it is never the subject, or never the agent who wills, where the will is understood as a faculty of free deliberation and choice. Is the philosopher, then, in any position to choose and to impose one particular imprint on his inner life? Is the philosopher in any position to maintain as *permanent* a particular ranking of the instincts? Both questions presuppose that he has the power to stop "becoming"—the power to issue a formal command to his instincts. But this is not the case.

A possible, though ultimately unsatisfactory, solution to Nietzsche's dilemma may be found in the fact that Nietzsche disparages consciousness but does not deny it. He thus leaves a small space for conscious decisions that individuals may make to guide their lives. Furthermore, Nietzsche claims that certain environments spoil a philosophic nature, which suggests that the philosopher, by analyzing himself, others, and history, could make conscious choices. Nietzsche examines this idea in the *Genealogy*, where he argues that nature creates a paradox in engendering an animal—man—who first is uniform and similar, and then becomes calculable and able to make and to fulfill promises, that is, to be responsible (GM; II; 1–2). On Nietzsche's arguments, the genealogy of responsibility must be traced back to nature. At the same time, Nietzsche clearly argues that an *external* socialization could produce a particular instinct, which is the case with the instinct for personal freedom. People adhere to customs, and the suppression that is inherent in social life spawns the instinct for personal responsibility.

Nature knows no paradox, however. The unaccountability of nature, or the innocence of becoming, is the beginning and end of an epistemology that culminates in a deeply tragic knowledge. In short, Nietzsche has built, layer by layer, a series of epistemological corridors that finally become an air-tight prison. He was not crushed by the awareness of his dilemma, but he was left with no exit through his own architectural prowess.

Nietzsche's epistemological difficulties might be summarized as follows:

(1) By nature, human beings possess different quanta of power. This establishes a natural hierarchy and removes any grounds for regarding people as responsible agents.

(2) By nature, human beings are valuating animals.

(3) By nature, human beings are the only animals that need to justify life.

(4) The natural hierarchy has two major types, exemplified by the nobles and the slaves. The nobles need the slaves as a constant reminder of why they are different and superior, but in having slaves, they expose themselves to perverted forms of the will to power.[51]

(5) As valuating animals, the slaves will attempt to explain their inferior position and their suffering, which leads to sickness and the invention of morality and religion.

(6) Sickness, then, is a natural calamity, not a purposeful event.

(7) Suffering, truth, and lies are all part of nature.

(8) All of the following belong to the process of becoming: the instincts, the body, mankind, and the habits of the human mind, which are produced by our instincts; these include our ideas of time and space, logic, regularity, simplicity, causality, the need for justification, the need for "fixed forms" or concepts (without which life would not be possible), and ideas of responsibility and conscience.[52]

To summarize, all instincts are the products of becoming, even causality and logic are expressions of the instincts, and fixed forms are required by the specific nature of the human animal. All moralities and all religions are thus expressions of nature's idiosyncrasies.

Nietzsche's epistemological prison is now sealed. Any condemnation of becoming would be a condemnation of nature, and that would be a denial of the whole. Nothing is dispensable. The philosopher/archaeologist/physician finds himself in the tragic, but honest, position of acknowledging that a distinction between sick and healthy instincts and between ascending and descending life is no longer tenable. Sickness and health, ascent and decline, are all part of becoming. The stories are over. It is now time to seek refuge in the idea of eternal recurrence: the idea that this very moment, in which the last brick is placed and the last beam of light flickers out, will be repeated over and over, in the same detail, for all eternity.

"This is life. Well, once more." The wanderer whom Nietzsche had described in *Human, All Too Human* ponders over why the day is so radiant "between the tenth and twelfth stroke of the clock" (H; I; 638). In *Ecce Homo* the clock reaches the final stroke. Nietzsche's philosophy appears to be epistemologically exhausted.

Illusions as Healers

What about the innocence of becoming? It is a dead end for Nietzsche, in the sense that it is an innocence without suffering or enemies. That is, two of the fundamental requirements for training the new philosophers are absent. The new philosopher should revel in the ebbs and flows of becoming. But what becomes of the will to power in this Nirvana? The will to power should not be interpreted here as a kind of laceration that is induced by the awareness of all the past and missed opportunities of humanity, which is tantamount to suffering from the past—suffering from an "it was" that is frozen in the new philosopher's consciousness. Suffering in the present because of the past is one of the hallmarks of resentment. Since the new philosopher has redeemed himself through becoming, suffering from a permanent awareness would become predictable: it would always be suffering from the replay of the *same* past events. By being predictable, suffering becomes a lie; it becomes one of the fictions that the philosopher contrives as a way of preserving his health. In this case, he convinces himself that he is suffering from a false suffering, a suffering that is merely boredom.

I have presented the outcomes of Nietzsche's investigations. He ascertained the missed opportunities in history, the instinctual drives as the foundations of morality and religion, the "depravity" of Christianity, and so on. He adopted the stance of a savior: "What I do or do not do now is as important for everything that is yet to come as is the greatest event of the past: in this tremendous perspective of effectiveness all actions appear equally great and small" (GS; 233). He ends up like the saint, waging his own inner war with his "enemies." Granted, his demons are different from those of the usual saint, and he is not accountable to God. But is there any reason not to believe that Nietzsche's war is just as imaginary as the one that relieves the saint from boredom? An affirmative answer hinges on the reasonable contention that the guilt that, according to Nietzsche, oppresses the gullible masses is a figment of his own imagination; that his idea of the Roman Empire was a joke; that Christianity was not a secret conspiracy of the weak; and that Nietzsche's nobles perished for a variety of reasons, not necessarily because the "weak" were "cleverer." Is Nietzsche merely fighting his own boredom and passing it off as a grandiose epic? But is not this a well-known trick in the artists' arsenal when they want to produce an effect? In the realm of a type of storytelling that is bound up with the metaphysics of meaning, these questions are worth pursuing. However, they should be assessed in a different light. We should look closely at one of the features that Nietzsche attributes to the "higher human beings" and "unearth" some early fragments of his philosophy.

The "higher human being" sees and hears more than others do, but "he can never shake off a *delusion:* He fancies that he is a *spectator* and *listener* who has been placed before the great visual and acoustic spectacle that is life: he calls his own nature *contemplative* and overlooks that he himself is really the poet who keeps creating this life" (GS; 301). Of course, he is more than an spectator and listener, and he is different from the active type, that is, "the actor of this drama." In contrast to the actor, the "higher human being" has both a contemplative power and a creative power. The creative power is lacking in the actor (GS; 301). Nietzsche, I submit, acted according to his own description of the "higher human being." Certainly, he was much more than a spectator: he was the playwright and the actor of the drama. His life was the poem he invented, a poem that the "practical human being," the actor, would translate into actuality. This poem was the world that concerned him, but his storytelling and role-playing coalesced into the unity of his stories, in which Nietzsche wrote a script for something that he would represent on the stage of human history. Wagner, Nietzsche tells us, misinterpreted his own characters. It is worth asking whether Nietzsche suffered from the same malady (GS; 99).

Illusions may be healers. Good stories, as part and parcel of these illusions, are always available. In *Ecce Homo*, Nietzsche described the secret work of his instinct as follows: the "magnitude of its *higher protection* was shown in the fact I have at no time had the remotest idea what was growing within me—that all my abilities one day *leapt forth* suddenly ripe, in their final perfection" (EH; "So Clever"; 4). Illusions may be healers, but they may also play tricks, and Nietzsche has already warned us of artists who want people to believe that their works, though in fact the results of long, difficult processes, "came into being with a miraculous suddenness" and that "the complete and perfect has suddenly emerged instantaneously" (H; I; 145).

As early as summer 1872 to early 1873, Nietzsche offered an explanation of his storytelling. "We want to alter the world so drastically by means of images that it will make you shudder. And that is within our power! Plug up your ears, your eyes will see our myths. Our curses will rain down upon you!"[53] He was patient, and the curses did not rain down until 1888. But the myths he created made their debut in all his works. Nietzsche thought that he had unearthed the ascetic ideal and the theologian's instinct. He thought he had drawn back the curtain to show the "depravity" of Christianity. He had discovered the hatred of actuality underlying past characters and events. Nietzsche's storytelling was his own reordering of the past, just as an artist reorders the place that past masters have in relation to him (AOM; 147). It is my contention that he knew that his storytelling as historiobiography and as a quest for meaning through a reordering of the past could be wrong. But this did not matter to him. Why? Because the value of a good story, like the value of a good historical narrative, does not lie in its truth. It is, above all, an artistic creation. He scribbled this idea in the early 1870s, but, apparently, it stayed in his "soul" until the end of his philosophical and literary life.

In a fragment dated later in 1873, Nietzsche discussed the question of objectivity in the writing of history. The tendency to write history by interrelating events and weaving them into a totality is contrary to the notion of objectivity.

It is an artistic drive, not a drive for truth, that causes the human being to spin his web over and subdue the past. The perfected form of such historiography is simply the work of art, without even a spark of common truth. (Emphasis mine)

'The historian's objectivity' is nonsense. . . . In other words, 'objective' refers to a state of mind in the historian, artistic contemplation: however, it is a superstition to believe that the image things produce in such an aesthetically attuned person reveals the true essence of these things. Or are we to suppose that in this state of mind things simply can be photographed, are we to suppose that it is a purely *passive* state of mind? On the contrary: it is the truly creative moment of the work of art, a compositional moment of the highest sort: the will of the individual is asleep when this takes place. The picture is *artistically true,* but certainly not yet historically true; it is not the facts, but rather their interweaving and interconnection; this is a fictional invention, one that can be true by accident: but even if it is false, it is nonetheless still 'objective.'[54]

"The picture is *artistically* true," and "even if it is false, it is nonetheless still 'objective.'" Viewed in this light, Nietzsche's stories are not and were never meant to be true; they are meant to be *"artistically true."* Even if they are false, they are still "objective," where objectivity is understood as a state of mind of the historian, a state of mind characterized by "artistic contemplation." Art imparts meaning to life, and by turning man's attention away from himself, it saves the species with a spectacle of illusions and stimulants. At the same time, the artistic dimension of the theater, which Nietzsche came to see as a sign of decay, gives human beings the art of "staging and watching" themselves as heroes (GS; 78). Art becomes the supreme will to life in the intoxication of the Dionysian. The weaving of events is meant to be a fictional invention; that is to say, an artistic invention, like the stories Nietzsche crafted to give meaning to his life in the great stage of human history. "The task of painting *the* picture of life," Nietzsche wrote in *Assorted Opinions and Maxims* (1879), however often poets and philosophers may pose it, is nonetheless senseless: even under the hands of the greatest of painter-thinkers all that has ever eventuated is pictures and miniatures *out of one* life, namely their own—and nothing else is even possible. (AOM; 19)

"And nothing else is even possible." In the context of historiobiography, this describes the storyteller of meaning at his best. Let it stand as a fitting conclusion to my reflections.

Notes

Introduction

1. "Letter to Franz Overbeck, July 4, 1888," in *Selected Letters of Friedrich Nietzsche,* ed. Christopher Middleton (Chicago: University of Chicago Press, 1969).

2. "Letter to George Brandes, May 4, 1888," quoted in George Brandes, *Friedrich Nietzsche* (New York: Macmillan; London: W. Heinemann, 1909), p. 84.

3. "Moreover," Nietzsche wrote, "there is no danger that man will ever understand himself *completely,* that he will penetrate at every instant all the laws of leverage and mechanics and all the formulas of architecture and chemistry which his life requires. However, it is quite possible that the *schema* of everything might become known" (PRS; p. 18).

4. WLN; Notebook 2, Autumn 1885–Autumn 1886; section 2[106]. See also WP; 416.

5. The issue of self-creation will be addressed in more detail in chapter 1.

6. WLN; Notebook 7, End of 1886–Spring 1887; 7[2].

7. "Will one at one time say of us that we also headed West, hoped to reach an India, but that it was our fate [*dass aber unser Loos war*] to fail because of infinity [*an der Unendlichkeit zu scheitern*]?" Translation mine.

8. See "The Struggle between Science and Wisdom," in *Philosophy and Truth: Selections from Nietzsche's Notebooks of the Early 1870s,* trans. Daniel Breazeale (Atlantic Highlands, NJ: Humanities Press, 1979), p. 143. In this passage Nietzsche writes, simply, about "possibilities of life," but his philosophy as a whole is an effort to identify the best possibilities for human existence.

9. "The Struggle between Science and Wisdom," p. 143.

10. WLN; Notebook 5, Summer 1886–Autumn 1887; 5[71]; section 3.

11. "The order of rank of greatness for all past mankind has not yet been determined" (D; 548).

12. "On the Pathos of Truth (1872)," in *Philosophy and Truth,* ed. Breazeale, p. 66. At this point, Nietzsche considered art more powerful than

knowledge, in that art desires the preservation of life. He later discarded this concept.

13. Claudia Crawford provides an insightful interpretation of redemption in her essay "Nietzsche's Psychology and Rhetoric of World Redemption: Dionysus versus the Crucified," in *Nietzsche and Depth Psychology*, ed. Jacob Golomb, Weaver Santaniello, and Ronald Lehrer (Albany: State University of New York Press, 1999), pp. 271–94.

14. "Er erkennt, indem er dichtet, und dichtet, indem er erkennt."

15. The stages described in section 39 of *Human, All Too Human* will reappear, slightly modified, in section 32 of *Beyond Good and Evil* (1886).

CHAPTER ONE.   STORYTELLING AND MEANING

1. See Thomas Hobbes, *Leviathan*, ed. Edwin Curley (Indianapolis: Hackett Publishing, 1994), especially chap. 36, sections 19–20, and chap. 43.

2. See Jean-Jacques Rousseau, *A Discourse on Inequality*, trans. Maurice Cranston (New York: Penguin Books, 1984). In the preface, Rousseau states: "The most useful and the least developed of all the sciences seems to me to be that of man." He seeks to know man as "nature made him" in order to know man's "essence." He poses the question, "And how can man come to know himself as nature made him once he has undergone all the changes which the succession of time and things must have produced in his original constitution, and so distinguish that which belongs to his own essence from that which circumstances and progress have added to, or altered in, his primitive state?" (p. 67).

3. "So that sense in all cases, is nothing else but original fancy, caused (as I have said) by the pressure, that is, by the motion, of external things upon our eyes, ears, and other organs thereunto ordained" (Hobbes, *Leviathan*, chap. 1, p. 7).

4. René Descartes, *Treatise on Man*, in *The World and Other Writings*, ed. Stephen Gaukroger (Cambridge: Cambridge University Press, 1998), p. 99.

5. Julien Offray de La Mettrie, "Machine Man," in *Machine Man and Other Writings*, ed. Ann Thomson (Cambridge: Cambridge University Press, 1996), p. 31. Anticipating Nietzsche by more than a century, but still trapped within the debates of his times, La Mettrie sought to provide a materialistic and, for him, irrefutable view of the soul. "He who would learn the properties of the soul must first seek those which clearly show themselves in the

body, whose active principle the soul is. This reflection leads naturally to the thought that there are *no surer guides than the senses*. They are my philosophers" (p. 43, emphasis mine). In both *Beyond Good and Evil* and *The Anti-Christ*, Nietzsche presents the same argument. "All credibility, all good conscience, all evidence of truth comes only from the senses" (BGE; 134).

6. Contrary to Nietzsche's assertion and as previously cited, Descartes' arguments in his *Treatise on Man* make it clear that he understood the human body as a machine. In his *The Passions of the Soul* (1649), this view is also evident. See *The Passions of the Soul*, in *Selected Philosophical Writings*, trans. John Cottingham (Cambridge: Cambridge University Press, 1988), pp. 218–38. "And let us recognize," Descartes writes, "that the difference between the body of a living man and that of a dead man is just like the difference between, on the one hand, a watch or other automaton (that is, a self-moving machine) when it is wound up and contains in itself the corporeal principle of the movements for which it is designed, together with everything else required for its operation; and, on the other hand, the same watch or machine when it is broken and the principle of its movement ceases to be active" (pp. 218–20).

7. Gilles Deleuze drives a wedge between Marx and Freud, on the one hand, and Nietzsche, on the other. Deleuze argues that, in contrast to Marx and Freud, Nietzsche represents "the dawn of counterculture." While Marx and Freud intend to "cure" people through a new form of state and a new kind of family, respectively, Nietzsche places himself outside such solutions. "Marxism and psychoanalysis in a real sense," according to Deleuze, "constitute the fundamental bureaucracies—one public, the other private—whose aim is somehow or other to recodify everything that ceaselessly becomes decodified at the horizon of our culture. Nietzsche's concern, on the contrary, is not this at all. His task lies elsewhere: beyond all the codes of past, present, and future, to transmit something that does not and will not allow itself to be codified" ("Nomad Thought," in *Nietzsche: Critical Assessments*, ed. Daniel W. Conway with Peter S. Groff [London: Routledge, 1998], vol. 4, p. 78). My interpretation differs, however. Nietzsche, I argue, presents some central values as codes that allow him and his future philosophers to identify life-affirming possibilities and the concomitant culture these possibilities require. But in order to identify his codes, he must criticize the dominant moral values and show that some, if not all, have been "forgeries" of priests, philosophers, the state, and so on. Among the codes Nietzsche offers, the following stand out: the will to power; the natural order of rank; a new morality according to the rank bestowed by nature; the

relationships between physiology, psychology, philology, and philosophy that enable us to unearth the "sick" and historical basis of dominant values.

8. J. P. Stern, *A Study of Nietzsche* (Cambridge: Cambridge University Press, 1979), p. 44. Marx attempts to uncover a secret, but it is not one lodged in people's minds. Rather, it is embedded in the relations of production, that is, the way human beings produce and reproduce their material life. Along similar lines, Marx does not claim that there is a conspiracy on the part of the dominant classes. As I understand it, he holds that, regardless of people's intentions, their social position strongly influences and, in most cases, determines their material interests, as well as the political and religious ideologies they invent to preserve those interests. In Nietzsche's case, the issue of choice is more problematic than Stern's statement indicates, given the secret war of the instincts (discussed later in this volume).

9. See Arthur C. Danto, *Nietzsche as Philosopher* (New York: Macmillan, 1965); John Richardson, *Nietzsche's System* (Oxford: Oxford University Press, 1996); Richard Schacht, *Making Sense of Nietzsche: Reflections Timely and Untimely* (Chicago: University of Illinois Press, 1995); Mark Warren, *Nietzsche and Political Thought* (Cambridge, MA: MIT Press, 1988). See also Robert C. Holub, *Friedrich Nietzsche* (New York: Twayne Publishers, 1995), and Gianni Vattimo, *Dialogue with Nietzsche* (New York: Columbia University Press, 2006). Danto, in particular, is explicit and perhaps daring in his claims: the "system I offer [about Nietzsche's philosophy] must be appreciated as a reconstruction, to be understood as one must understand any theory; that is, as an instrument for unifying and explaining a domain of phenomena—in this case the domain of an individual's writings. I shall use texts as scientific theorists employ observations—to confirm my theory at this point or that. I am reasonably confident that, in at least a loose sense, this theory has a certain predictive power; that is, it allows us to know more or less what Nietzsche is going to be saying" (*Nietzsche as Philosopher*, pp. 24, 25–26).

10. Eugen Fink, "Nietzsche's New Experience of World," in *Nietzsche's New Seas: Explorations in Philosophy, Aesthetics, and Politics*, ed. Michael Allen Gillespie and Tracy B. Strong (Chicago: University of Chicago Press, 1988), p. 204.

11. I agree with Bernd Magnus's statement that "one way of reading Nietzsche is to see him telling a story about how we in the West became who we are," with the caveat that Nietzsche does not offer a single story, but rather many. Bernd Magnus, "Nietzsche and the Project of Bringing Philosophy to an End," in *Nietzsche as Affirmative Thinker*, ed. Yirmiyahu Yovel (Dordrecht: Martinus Nijhoff Publishers, 1986), p. 40.

12. Karl Marx and Friedrich Engels, *The German Ideology*, ed. C. J. Arthur (New York: International Publishers, 1988), pp. 47, 59.

13. Sigmund Freud, *Civilization and Its Discontents*, ed. James Strachey (New York: W. W. Norton, 1989), pp. 16–17, 28.

14. Sigmund Freud, *On Dreams*, ed. James Strachey (New York: W. W. Norton, 1989), p. 5.

15. In his essay "The Storyteller," Walter Benjamin invokes the decrease in "the communicability of experience" ("The Storyteller," in *Illuminations*, ed. Hannah Arendt [New York: Schocken Books, 1969], p. 86) and the emergence of information as two factors that have contributed to what he considers the vanishing art of storytelling. "The storyteller takes what he tells from experience—his own or that reported by others. And he in turn makes it the experience of those who are listening to his tale" (p. 87). But experience, in Benjamin's understanding of that term, carries with it a "practical" interest, a "counsel" that is withering away to the extent that its source, an experience that could be communicated, is disappearing. "The art of storytelling is reaching its end because the epic side of truth, wisdom, is dying out" (p. 87). If experience is in its last throes, information is in full strength. Information is a space filled with explanation and, for this very reason, is antithetical to storytelling. The story is a combination of different pieces that are left unexplained. Explanation is the reader's domain; not the storyteller's (p. 89).

Benjamin's essay carries the imprint of his epoch, which was unfolding between the First World War and Nazism. The idea of storytelling that arises from this context is not one that, I submit, could be found in Nietzsche's philosophy. This is not, of course, a critique of Benjamin or a shortcoming of Nietzsche. These two authors inhabit a different spiritual milieu, and while Nietzsche sought meaning in human history, Benjamin struggled with the meaning of history that he seemed to find in Marxism, but that was denied by the economic and cultural phenomena of his times. Yet in one respect, Benjamin's view of storytelling is entwined with Nietzsche's. The storyteller, according to Benjamin, "joins the ranks of the teachers and sages. . . . For it is granted to him to reach back to a whole lifetime (a life, incidentally, that comprises not only his own experience but no little of the experience of others; what the storyteller knows from hearsay is added to his own)" (p. 108).

16. W. D. Williams, "Nietzsche's Masks," in *Nietzsche: Imagery and Thought,* ed. Malcolm Pasley (Berkeley: University of California Press, 1978), pp. 86–87.

17. Fink, "Nietzsche's New Experience of World," p. 211.

18. Alexander Nehamas, *Nietzsche: Life as Literature* (Cambridge, MA: Harvard University Press, 1985), p. 3.

19. Ibid.

20. For Nietzsche's claim about *The Gay Science*, see "Letter to Erwin Rohde, July 15, 1882"; for his claim about *Zarathustra*, "Letter to Franz Overbeck, February 11, 1883"; see also "Letter to Carl von Gersdorff, June 28, 1883," in *Selected Letters*, ed. Middleton, pp. 187, 207, 213, respectively. Zarathustra, Nietzsche wrote Overbeck, "contains an image of myself in the sharpest focus, as I am, *once* I have thrown off my whole burden" (p. 207).

21. Nehamas, *Life as Literature*, p. 2. *The Will to Power* seems to be the driving force of Nehamas's analysis. Mazzino Montinari and Bernd Magnus have convincingly argued that this is, at least, suspect. See Montinari, *Reading Nietzsche*, trans. Greg Whitlock (Urbana: University of Illinois Press, 2003), pp. 5–22, 80–102; and Magnus's important essay, "Nietzsche's Philosophy in 1888: *The Will to Power* and the Übermensch," in *Nietzsche: Critical Assessments*, ed. Conway, vol. 2, pp. 184–203; a slightly different version of his argument is found in "The Use and Abuse of *The Will to Power*," in *Reading Nietzsche*, ed. Robert C. Solomon and Kathleen M. Higgins (Oxford: Oxford University Press, 1988), pp. 218–35. See also Wayne Klein, *Nietzsche and the Promise of Philosophy* (Albany: State University of New York Press, 1997), pp. 181–99.

22. Robert C. Solomon, "Nietzsche *ad hominem*: Perspectivism, Personality and *Ressentiment* Revisited," in *The Cambridge Companion to Nietzsche*, ed. Bernd Magnus and Kathleen M. Higgins (Cambridge: Cambridge University Press, 1996), p. 185.

CHAPTER TWO.   GENEALOGY, PHYSIOLOGY, AND NATURALISM

1. Gilles Deleuze, *Nietzsche and Philosophy*, trans. Hugh Tomlinson (New York: Columbia University Press, 1983), p. 2.

2. Michel Foucault, "Nietzsche, Genealogy, History," in *Nietzsche*, ed. John Richardson and Brian Leiter (Oxford: Oxford University Press, 1999), pp. 341, 344–45.

3. Ibid., p. 352. For a critique of Foucault's interpretation of Nietzsche's genealogy, see John Pizer, "The Use and Abuse of 'Ursprung': On Foucault's Reading of Nietzsche," *Nietzsche-Studien* 19 (1990): 462–78.

4. Raymond Geuss, "Nietzsche and Genealogy," in *Nietzsche*, ed. John Richardson and Brian Leiter (Oxford: Oxford University Press, 1999), p. 333.

5. Daniel W. Conway, "Genealogy and Critical Method," in *Nietzsche, Genealogy, Morality: Essays on Nietzsche's "On the Genealogy of Morals"*, ed. Richard Schacht (Berkeley: University of California Press, 1994), pp. 322, 323. Genealogy "shows 'only' that Christian morality originated in a slave morality; his critical interpretation of this slave heritage is delivered not by genealogy itself, but by the immanent symptomatological critique that genealogy enables" (p. 329).

6. David Couzens Hoy, "Nietzsche, Hume, and the Genealogical Method," in *Nietzsche, Genealogy, Morality*, ed. Schacht, p. 260.

7. Eric Blondel, "The Question of Genealogy," in *Nietzsche, Genealogy, Morality*, ed. Schacht, pp. 306–17.

8. Ibid., pp. 311, 313, 314.

9. Ibid., p. 312.

10. Conway claims that the prefaces written in 1886 "collectively *introduce*, via exemplification, Nietzsche's preferred strategy for reading Nietzsche: symptomatology." Conway sees this "symptomatology" as a "turn away from metaphysics." More emphatically, "Nietzsche's *Sanctus Januarius* thus marks the birth of the science of psychology, the unwitting and accidental inwardisation of science itself" ("Annunciations and Rebirth: The Prefaces of 1886," in *Nietzsche's Futures*, ed. John Lippitt [New York: St. Martin's Press, 1999], pp. 34, 38, first emphasis mine). This claim is intriguing given that the first volume of *Human, All Too Human* (1878), *Daybreak* (1881), and *The Gay Science* (1882) are replete with references to physiology and psychological explorations. In *Human, All Too Human*, Nietzsche emphasizes the importance of knowing a "chemistry of the moral, religious, and aesthetic conceptions and sensations" and tried to discern the inner states of the saints (H; I; 1, 139, 141–44). The physician is an important figure in *Daybreak*. Moreover, in *Daybreak*, Nietzsche begins to insist on the unknowable character of a person's drives. To say that the "birth" of Nietzsche's psychology occurs in 1882 and that symptomatology is introduced in the 1886 prefaces is a problematic description of the evolution of Nietzsche's thought.

11. Malcolm Pasley, "Nietzsche's Use of Medical Terms," in *Nietzsche: Imagery and Thought*, ed. Malcolm Pasley (Berkeley: University of California Press, 2000), pp. 129–30.

12. It is possible to argue that, well before Nietzsche came into contact with these authors, the contours of Nietzsche's view of the will to power were emerging in *Human, All Too Human*, *Daybreak*, and *The Gay Science*. See Gregory Moore, *Nietzsche, Biology and Metaphor* (Cambridge: Cambridge University Press, 2002), pp. 21–55.

13. Pasley, "Nietzsche's Use of Medical Terms," p. 137.

14. Thomas A. Long provides a discussion of Nietzsche's view of medicine, but his approach is to identify a Nietzschean conception of health, disease, and the patient/physician relationship. See his "Nietzsche's Philosophy of Medicine," *Nietzsche-Studien* 19 (1990): 112–28. See also Scott H. Podolsky and Alfred I. Tauber, "Nietzsche's Conception of Health: The Idealization of Struggle," in *Nietzsche, Epistemology, and Philosophy of Science: Nietzsche and the Sciences,* ed. Babette Babich and Robert S. Cohen (Hingham, MA: Kluwer Academic Publishers, 1999), vol. 2, pp. 299–311.

15. Nehamas's argument that Nietzsche seems to consider Socrates a genuine philosopher (at BGE; 212) is problematic. Nietzsche muses here about the possibility that irony was a condition for greatness of soul in the age of Socrates, but in the same passage he refers to the "malicious certitude of the old physician and plebeian," who is cutting his own flesh after opening the flesh and heart of the "noble." It is worth noticing Nietzsche's characterization of Socrates as a "plebeian," a view that he will develop in *Twilight of the Idols* (in Socrates, the rabble come to the fore). In Nietzsche's understanding, a genuine philosopher is never a plebeian. In the landscape of the soul, Nietzsche states, Socrates can say with contempt: "do not dissemble before me! Here—we are equal." Yet this notion of equality, whose roots Nietzsche traces to the notion of equality of souls, is criticized by Nietzsche in *Beyond Good and Evil,* as well as other works (for examples, see BGE; 26, 30, 43, 44, 213). For Nehamas's view, see his "Who Are 'The Philosophers of the Future'? A Reading of *Beyond Good and Evil,*" in *Reading Nietzsche,* ed. Robert C. Solomon and Kathleen M. Higgins (Oxford: Oxford University Press, 1988), p. 59.

16. See also D; 86, 368, 371, 542.

17. Solomon argues in an interesting essay that Nietzsche "saw himself and praised himself as a diagnostician, and his philosophy consists to a very large extent of speculative diagnoses, concerning the virtues and vices of those whom he read and read about, whose influence determined the temper of the times. His central strategy, accordingly, was the use of the *ad hominem* argument, a rhetorical technique often dismissed as a 'fallacy,' an attack on the motives and emotions of his antagonists rather than a refutation of their ideas as such" ("Nietzsche *ad hominem,*" p. 181). "Nietzsche is concerned not so much with the analysis and justification of philosophical concepts and doctrines but rather with an understanding of the type of people who would formulate such concepts and believe such doctrines" (p. 184). I agree with Solomon's assessment, though, in some cases, Nietzsche attacks not only the motives but also the ideas of the people he

analyzes. Thus, he criticizes the idea of sin in Christianity, the idea of causality in science, and the Socratic equation of virtue and happiness. Solomon correctly points out that an *ad hominem* approach is not always a fallacy if it "allows us to see what is *not* being said or argued, the limitations of a position as well as its possibilities" (p. 189). But he fails to mention that, in Nietzsche's case, the validity of his critiques depends, more often than not, on the accuracy and truth of his assumptions. If these assumptions are far-fetched or false, then the conclusions Nietzsche draws from his premises are suspicious. And the problem is that, very often, Nietzsche's assumptions about physiology and genealogy do not go beyond the realm of speculation. In my discussion, I prefer to call his approach archaeological rather than *ad hominem*, on the ground that Nietzsche's insistence on going down, descending, exploring the depths, and so forth, is a peculiar trait of his philosophical thinking.

18. Blondel, "The Question of Genealogy," p. 38.

19. For a discussion of Nietzsche's view of physiology and its relationship with Christianity and Buddhism, in which issues of diet and nutrition are examined, see Richard Brown, "Nihilism: 'Thus Speaks Physiology,'" in *Nietzsche and the Rhetoric of Nihilism: Essays on Interpretation, Language and Politics*, ed. Tom Darby, Béla Egyed, and Ben Jones (Ottawa: Carleton University Press, 1989), pp. 133–44.

20. See also BGE; 23, 201, 289.

21. "Letter to Franz Overbeck, Summer 1883," in *Selected Letters*, ed. Middleton, p. 214.

22. Nietzsche, assuming the role of a hermit, wonders "whether a philosopher *could* have 'final and real' opinions at all, whether behind each of his caves there does not and must not lie another deeper cave—a stranger, more comprehensive world beyond the surface, an abyss behind every ground, beneath every 'foundation'" (BGE; 289).

23. UW; Winter 1872–73; 24[9]. Goethe's use of the phrase is found in his letter to Charlotte von Stein (27 March 1784), cited in Robert J. Richards, *The Romantic Conception of Life: Science and Philosophy in the Age of Goethe* (Chicago: University of Chicago Press, 2002), p. 369.

24. "Goethe's conversation with J. D. Falk," cited in Ernst Cassirer, *Kant's Life and Thought*, trans. James Haden (New Haven: Yale University Press, 1981), p. 5. It is worth noticing that Goethe talks about being in "harmony with ourselves," a task that Nietzsche would find very difficult, if not impossible, to accomplish given his account of the secret war of a person's instincts. Yet Nietzsche's positions are not entirely incompatible with Goethe's view. The harmony that the philosopher might find is the

awareness of knowing what he is. On the other hand, though Nietzsche would accept a person's philosophy as a reflection of his individuality, he would add that, very often, a philosophy is the expression of a sick individuality. That is to say, while Goethe's statement is a celebration of the person's individuality, regardless of the nature of his philosophy, Nietzsche establishes important distinctions and regards some philosophical systems as negations of individuality. Those systems are good for the herd, not for individuals.

25. A note of caution and of interpretive methodology is in order here. According to Ken Gemes, Nietzsche's claim about the need to know ourselves and his statement that his aim is to expose the historical origins of our morality, as stated in the initial sentence of the preface to the *Genealogy*, is meant to be misleading and openly deceptive. Furthermore, "Nietzsche employs uncanny displacements and subterfuges in order to disguise his real target"—we moderns (Ken Gemes, "'We Remain of Necessity Strangers to Ourselves': The Key Message of Nietzsche's *Genealogy*," in *Nietzsche's "On the Genealogy of Morals": Critical Essays*, ed. Christa Davis Acampora [Lanham, MD: Rowman & Littlefield, 2006], p. 191). That Nietzsche deploys a rich arsenal of elliptical moves and disingenuous arguments is clear. But this should not deter us from a fundamental interpretive principle: Nietzsche believes that he is telling important truths about the past, present, and future of humankind, especially in the European context, and explicitly claims that his arguments are relevant in that they describe the way present generations have inherited the past.

26. In discussing Nietzsche's view of genealogy, Michel Haar argues, "Nietzsche's method aims at unmasking, unearthing, but in an *indefinite* way—i.e., without ever pretending to lift the last veil to reveal any originary identity, any primary foundation" ("Nietzsche and Metaphysical Language," in *The New Nietzsche: Contemporary Styles of Interpretation*, ed. David B. Allison [Cambridge, MA: MIT Press, 1985], p. 7). I think, however, that Nietzsche does intend to lift "the last veil," as attested by his analyses of the noble morality, the slave morality, the theologian, the ascetic ideal, modernity, and so forth. Haar seems to modify his position when he states the following: "The 'genealogical' critique of values consists in relating any given value to the originary direction (affirmative or negative) of volition, in unveiling the long lineage issuing from this primordial orientation, and in unraveling the remote thread of encounters that have since frozen into 'values'" (p. 12). It should be noted that, in identifying whether a value is affirmative or negative, that is, "the primordial orientation," the archaeologist/physician needs to lift the "last veil" and to dissect the type of will to power

behind those values. In a fragment dated "Spring–Fall 1887," Nietzsche explicitly states: *My purpose:* . . . to demonstrate how everything praised as moral is identical in essence with everything immoral and was made possible, as in every development of morality, with immoral means and for immoral ends" (WP; 272). The terms that Nietzsche uses here, such as "identical" and "essence," strongly suggest that his genealogical method looks for a "primary foundation."

27. A psychologist, Blondel writes, "is someone who refers a discourse to its hidden origins, while a philologist criticizes the same discourse *from the inside,* as a linguistic structure, and refers it only to another language: the language of reality, the correct language. Philology and psychology therefore designate the same taste, but the latter concentrates on the physiological origins (γένησις) while the former concentrates on the discourse (λόγος)" (*Nietzsche: The Body and Culture. Philosophy as a Philological Genealogy,* trans. Seán Hand [London: Athlone Press, 1991], p. 127). This insightful formulation expands on the issue of genealogy. Blondel's arguments assume *one* discourse that is examined and translated from two different optics: philology and psychology. But the process of referring a discourse "to its hidden origins" constructs a *new* discourse, which is then interpreted, that is, constructed again, as a physiological explanation. Blondel's reference to the "correct language" of reality is problematic in light of Nietzsche's belief that reality is unknowable (a feature that Blondel knows).

28. One important exception is Gemes's essay, "'We Remain of Necessity Strangers to Ourselves.'"

29. It goes without saying that my arguments here are informed by Hans-Georg Gadamer's conception of hermeneutics in his *Truth and Method.*

30. Christopher Janaway, "Naturalism and Genealogy," in *A Companion to Nietzsche,* ed. Keith Ansell-Pearson (Malden, MA: Blackwell Publishing, 2006), p. 347, emphasis in original.

31. Aaron Ridley, *Nietzsche's Conscience: Six Character Studies from the 'Genealogy'* (Ithaca, NY: Cornell University Press, 1998), p. 16.

32. Keith Ansell-Pearson, "A 'Dionysian Drama' on the 'Fate of the Soul,'" in *Nietzsche's "On the Genealogy of Morals": Critical Essays,* ed. Christa Davis Acampora (Lanham, MD: Rowman & Littlefield, 2006), p. 21.

33. WLN; Notebook 36, June–July 1885 36[35].

34. WLN; Notebook 7, End of 1886–Spring 1887; 7[2].

35. David Owen argues that Nietzsche turns to genealogy in order to provide a naturalistic account that could explain the taste for the unconditional. In Owen's view, this account was lacking in Nietzsche's texts prior

to the *Genealogy*. Furthermore, Owen argues, though some of Nietzsche's contemporaries were atheists, they still accepted the validity of Christian morality and thus failed to draw the right inferences from "the death of God." The genealogical method was an attempt to explain why these people were not inferring the need to reassess Christian moral values. The evolution Owen traces is compelling, but I am not convinced. Nietzsche was engaged in naturalistic accounts of morality in *Human, All Too Human, Daybreak,* and *The Gay Science.* The section Owen invokes (D; 103), in which Nietzsche accepts the validity of moral motives, is obliterated by explicit arguments in *The Gay Science* and *Twilight of the Idols*. See David Owen, "Nietzsche, Re-evaluation, and the Turn to Genealogy," in *Nietzsche's "On the Genealogy of Morals": Critical Essays,* ed. Christa Davis Acampora (Lanham, MD: Rowman & Littlefield, 2006), pp. 39–56.

36. WLN; Notebook 5, Summer 1886–Autumn 1887; 5[71]; section 1.

37. In this section, Nietzsche also claims that there is "nothing more democratic than logic," but this does not show his familiar abhorrence of democratic institutions. Here, Nietzsche asserts that logic is not a "respecter of persons" because it relies on *"compelling* agreement by force of reasons" (GS; 348).

38. WLN; Notebook 5, Summer 1886–Autumn 1887; 5[71]; section 9.

39. Few have noticed that Nietzsche wrote two genealogies: one about the nature of Greek tragedy and the other about the emergence of the slave morality. In the first, he offers no empirical evidence for his positions. In the second, he cites only a few texts to prove the hatred he identifies in the Christian church. The genealogical account in *The Anti-Christ* is an expansion of themes he had presented in the *Genealogy*.

40. Blondel, "The Question of Genealogy," p. 314.

41. Ibid., p. 316.

42. Hoy, "Nietzsche, Hume, and the Genealogical Method," p. 265.

43. Tracy B. Strong, "Genealogy, the Will to Power, and the Problem of a Past," in *Nietzsche's "On the Genealogy of Morals": Critical Essays,* ed. Christa Davis Acampora (Lanham, MD: Rowman & Littlefield, 2006), p. 100, emphasis in original.

44. WLN; Notebook 35, May–July 1885; 35[17].

45. WLN; Notebook 37, June–July 1885; 37[8]. The phrase appears in a discussion of the difficulty of breeding new masters of the earth. The idea of exploring new regions of knowledge is pervasive in Nietzsche's writings.

46. Aaron Ridley offers an excellent analysis of what he takes to be the different forms in which values can be revaluated in light of Nietzsche's philosophy. Although this is not the place to address the sublety of Ridley's

arguments, it is worth noting that Ridley attempts to solve the issue of authority, namely, the issue of identifying the grounds that would make Nietzsche's perspective authoritative and capable of furnishing reasons that adherents of other perspectives would be forced to accept. His solution is to claim that Nietzsche defends the values of self-understanding and autonomy. Self-understanding is defined as having "power over oneself." This seems to place Nietzsche in a Kantian universe that he, explicitly, rejected. (In my discussion of the secret war of the instincts I call into question the whole project of both self-understanding and autonomy.) See Aaron Ridley, "Nietzsche and the Re-evaluation of 'Values," in *Nietzsche's "On the Genealogy of Morals": Critical Essays,* ed. Christa Davis Acampora (Lanham, MD: Rowman & Littlefield, 2006), pp. 77–92, esp. pp. 88–89.

47. See also H; I; 107; and TI; "Morality"; 6.

48. Blondel seems to offer arguments similar to mine here. According to Blondel, when he speaks "as 'a physiologist,' or 'a doctor', Nietzsche does not rest at being a philologist: he is a reader of clinical signs, a decipherer of the body's text. If Nietzsche the 'philosopher doctor' consecrates himself to the affirmation of life, the philologist in him *devotes himself* to the *negative* task of genealogy: to flushing out negation, both in morality and in metaphysics" (*Nietzsche: The Body and Culture,* p. 97). My conceptualization of the genealogist/archaeologist, however, is different from Blondel's understanding of the philologist. The archaeologist reads not only "texts" or the "signs" emanating from the body or from "culture." He reads "origins" and "intentions" and scrutinizes, in broad strokes, the entire history of humankind. Furthermore, Nietzsche's view of genealogy is not the exclusive domain of the philologist. Even when genealogy takes the form of a philological examination, it is not a "negative task," since Nietzsche's aim, on my interpretation, is to create new values.

49. *Republic,* trans. C. D. C. Reeve (Indianapolis: Hackett Publishing, 2004), 408d–e.

CHAPTER THREE. *ON THE GENEALOGY OF MORALITY*

1. Ansell-Pearson, "A 'Dionysian Drama on the 'Fate of the Soul,'" p. 20.

2. Life is defined by "actual *activity,*" not by adaptation (GM; II; 12). The will to power is the organic processes in the individual, namely, the aggregate of instincts that constitutes the animal man. Life "functions *essentially* in an injurious, violent, exploitative and destructive manner, or at

least these are its fundamental processes and it cannot be thought of without these characteristics" (emphasis mine). From "the *highest biological point of view,* states of legality can never be anything but *exceptional states,* since they are partial restrictions of the true will of life, which is bent upon power, and are subordinate to its ultimate goal as a single means: namely, as a means of creating *bigger* units of power" (GM; II; 11; first emphasis mine).

3. Arthur C. Danto, "Some Remarks on *The Genealogy of Morals,*" in *Reading Nietzsche,* ed. Robert C. Solomon and Kathleen M. Higgins (Oxford: Oxford University Press, 1988), p. 18.

4. Brian Leiter, *Routledge Philosophy Guidebook to Nietzsche on Morality* (London: Routledge, 2002), p. 170. For some recent studies that enrich the discussion, see Daniel Conway, *Nietzsche's "On the Genealogy of Morals": A Reader's Guide* (London: Continuum, 2008); Lawrence J. Hatab, *Nietzsche's "On the Genealogy of Morality": An Introduction* (Cambridge: Cambridge University Press, 2008); Christopher Janaway, *Beyond Selflessness: Reading Nietzsche's "Genealogy"* (Oxford: Oxford University Press, 2007); and David Owen, *Nietzsche's "Genealogy of Morality"* (Montreal: McGill-Queen's University Press, 2007).

5. Leiter, *Routledge Philosophy Guidebook to Nietzsche on Morality,* pp. 167–68.

6. Ibid., p. 171.

7. Christopher Janaway, "Guilt, Bad Conscience, and Self-Punishment in Nietzsche's Genealogy," in *Nietzsche and Morality,* ed. Brian Leiter and Neil Sinhababu (Oxford: Oxford University Press, 2007), p. 140.

8. Janaway finds fault with Leiter's claims that Nietzsche's naturalism accepts a "methods continuity" with science, in the sense that Nietzsche's theory ought to find support in the "best sciences." Janaway counters, correctly, that "no scientific support of justification is given—or readily imaginable—for the central explanatory hypotheses that Nietzsche gives for the origins of our moral beliefs and attitudes" (Janaway, "Naturalism and Genealogy," p. 339). The absence of facts in crucial parts of Nietzsche's accounts of morality in the *Genealogy* raises doubts about any attempt to evaluate the richness of his arguments in light of scientific methodologies.

9. Ansell-Pearson's argument is well-taken: although "the bad conscience originates prior to the slave revolt in morality . . . [t]he psychical structure of pre-moral guilt created by the bad conscience . . . is certainly what makes the slave revolt in morality, and its creation of moral guilt, possible" (Keith Ansell-Pearson, "Introduction: Nietzsche's 'Overcoming' of Morality," in Friedrich Nietzsche, *On the Genealogy of Morality,* trans. Carol

Diethe, ed. Keith Ansell-Pearson [Cambridge: Cambridge University Press, 1996], p. xvii).

10. Janaway, "Guilt, Bad Conscience, and Self-Punishment," p. 144.

11. For a sustained elucidation of the idea of the animal in Nietzsche, the animal that is shaped by culture and civilization, see Vanessa Lemm, *Nietzsche's Animal Philosophy: Culture, Politics, and the Animality of the Human Body* (New York: Fordham University Press, 2009).

12. Robert Guay, "The Philosophical Function of Genealogy," in *A Companion to Nietzsche*, ed. Keith Ansell-Pearson (Malden, MA: Blackwell Publishing, 2005), p. 361.

13. Janaway, "Guilt, Bad Conscience, and Self-Punishment," p. 145.

14. Mathias Risse, "The Second Treatise in *On the Genealogy of Morality*: Nietzsche on the Origin of the Bad Conscience," *European Journal of Philosophy* 9, no. 1 (2001): 55–81, esp. p. 58.

15. Ansell-Pearson, "Introduction," p. xvi.

16. This interpretation opposes that of Leiter, who states: "Being in debt, unlike being guilty, does not involve being *morally responsible,* in the sense of being an agent who is presumed to have the capacity for autonomous or free choice" (*Guidebook to Nietzsche on Morality,* p. 230). Leiter's distinction is correct, but Nietzsche's argument is, precisely, that the sovereign individual possesses the faculty of free choice and, in this sense, he would be "morally responsible"; although Nietzsche does not reach this conclusion, I do.

17. Christa Davis Acampora, in her "On Sovereignty and Overhumanity: Why It Matters How We Read Nietzsche's *Genealogy* II: 2," in *Nietzsche's "On the Genealogy of Morals": Critical Essays,* ed. Christa Davis Acampora (Lanham, MD: Rowman & Littlefield, 2006), discusses at length the issue of the sovereign individual in Nietzsche's *Genealogy* and offers, to my knowledge, the best arguments against the view that Nietzsche envisions this individual as a higher ideal for humankind. In Acampora's interpretation, "the sovereign individual is the pinnacle of the current state of existence of *humankind*" (p. 155). If this is so, overcoming this individual, and not realizing him, is Nietzsche's goal: "Nietzsche does not call us to realize the height of our humanity in becoming sovereign individuals (a capability already characteristic of the human animal, a 'fruit' already borne), rather, he anticipates overcoming the concept of autonomy that buoys the contradictory ideal of the sovereign individual, and *that* requires the cultivation and heightening of *different* powers, which are not alien to us but which are nonetheless latent" (p. 156). Acampora's interpretation is persuasive. At the same time, I find deeply problematic her acceptance of the view that

316 Notes to Pages 82–91

the sovereign individual, to the extent that she exercises her will upon herself and thus becomes consistent, accountable, and autonomous, is the highest stage of our "current" humanity. This is implicit in Acampora's arguments and suggests that, in Nietzsche's view, the Kantian self, the autonomous self *par excellence*, is the highest stage for what we are *now*.

18. Leiter's interpretation of guilt hinges on a crucial assumption. He separates the guilt Nietzsche mentions in the second essay from the guilt that is manufactured by the ascetic ideal. "[R]eal guilt," he argues, "requires bad conscience to be put in the service of the ascetic ideal, and it is only the Third Essay that will explain why that should come to pass" (*Guidebook to Nietzsche on Morality*, p. 244; see also pp. 239, 240, 262). I am not convinced by this assumption.

19. Ibid., p. 190.

20. Contrary to Nietzsche's assumptions, there is no relation, historically, between the creation of empires and the emergence of monotheism. The Hebrews were enslaved. But for Nietzsche, the "progression to universal empires is always the progress to universal deities at the same time: despotism, with its subjugation of the independent nobility, always prepares the way for some sort of monotheism as well" (GM; II; 20).

21. Risse, "The Second Treatise in *On the Genealogy of Morality*," p. 56.

22. Aaron Ridley, "Guilt before God, or God before Guilt? The Second Essay of Nietzsche's *Genealogy*," *Journal of Nietzsche Studies* 29 (2005): 38. For Risse's reply to Ridley's arguments, see Mathias Risse, "On God and Guilt: A Reply to Aaron Ridley," *Journal of Nietzsche Studies* 29 (2005): 46–53.

23. Ridley, "Guilt before God, or God before Guilt?" p. 36.

24. My interpretation differs here from Robert Guay's. In Guay's view, once the slave revolt is over and the slaves are in power, they no longer have the nobles as an external object upon which they can discharge their hatred: "But after the slave revolt they [the weak] had no obvious enemies, so when their dissatisfaction inevitably emerged, it provoked confusion." The priests offered a convincing explanation: they alone were responsible for their suffering. "The weak needed an object to blame: striking back was their art of self-preservation. But by this time *they had assumed power*, so there was no one to turn to but themselves. They directed their hostility against the purported source of their suffering, and tormented themselves. Self-torture and self-laceration fed off the perpetual shortcomings in their humility. Their *ressentiment* turned against itself, and the 'bad conscience' was invented" (Guay, "The Philosophical Function of Genealogy," p. 360, emphasis mine). Guay's argument assumes that the story of the third essay is a

continuation of the story told in the first essay. That is to say, the herd that receives advice from the ascetic priest is constituted by the slaves who succeeded in their revolt and are already in power. This is not the case; Nietzsche does not equate the slaves with the herd. The same identification of the slaves and the herd can be found in Richard White, "The Return of the Master: An Interpretation of Nietzsche's 'Genealogy of Morals,'" *Philosophy and Phenomenological Research* 48, no. 4 (June 1988): 683–96, esp. p. 689.

25. In *Daybreak*, Nietzsche had objected to the anaesthetizing and intoxicating remedies of religions on the grounds that they worsened the real sickness (D; 52).

26. For another distinction between the ways in which Greek antiquity and Christianity understood punishment, misfortune, and guilt, see D; 78. This distinction is consistent with the argument presented in the *Genealogy*.

27. In an earlier account, Nietzsche pictured Christianity as having a special instinct for hunting people who showed a propensity toward despair, and "only a portion of mankind [was] capable" of displaying this propensity. The argument in the *Genealogy* constitutes a significant shift; here, the herd of despairing creatures is not a portion but the vast majority of human beings. See D; 64.

28. According to Leiter, "[t]he *Genealogy*, and Nietzsche's mature philosophy generally, proposes a naturalistic explanation, i.e., an explanation that is continuous with both the results and methods of the sciences." Nietzsche, as a "philosophical naturalist, aims to offer theories that explain various important human phenomena (especially the phenomenon of morality), and that do so in ways that both draw on actual scientific results, particularly in physiology . . . , but are also *modeled* on science in the sense that they seek to reveal the causal determinants of these phenomena, typically in various physiological and psychological facts about persons" (*Guidebook to Nietzsche on Morality*, pp. 8, 11). As discussed in chapter 2, I agree that Nietzsche is a naturalistic philosopher, but I am skeptical about his credentials as a physiologist, credentials that Leiter seems to accept too quickly.

29. Tracy B. Strong, *Friedrich Nietzsche and the Politics of Transfiguration*, expanded ed. (Urbana: University of Illinois Press, 2000), p. 54, second emphasis mine.

30. Strong acknowledges this point in an excellent elucidation of Nietzsche's view of causality: "The notion of causality is derived then not just from habit, let alone from a sense of causality, as Kant thought, but in fact from historical specific necessities. Men *must control* the world enough

that it appears as a series of classifiable and repeatable events; without the 'familiar to hold on to,' men are disturbed; with it, they are calmed. And . . . language is obviously *and necessarily* the main vehicle producing the 'recurring of similar cases'" (ibid., p. 67, emphasis mine). The necessity that serves as the underpinning of the notion of causality is also present in the all too human search for meaning, a search that leads to moral codes through which and in which the will to power, namely, life, asserts itself. There is no escape from this.

31. Guay, "The Philosophical Function of Genealogy," p. 364. He also claims that "the entire route that genealogy traces is, according to Nietzsche, a necessary one: there was no decisive turning point, no crucial missteps, no alternate paths." I disagree. Nietzsche's anguish about the different venues that the Roman Empire and the Renaissance represented for humanity, for example, are eloquent proofs that he envisioned other possibilities. Unfortunately, these possibilities were not realized, but this was not a matter of fate.

CHAPTER FOUR.   ARTISTS, ACTORS, AND THE AESTHETIC PROJECT

1. See also H; I; 17: "The young person values metaphysical explanations because they reveal to him something in the highest degree significant in things he found unpleasant or contemptible." Art does the same; the difference between metaphysics and art is that the former ends up denying the world by positing another world. Art, in Nietzsche's view, does not deny the world; art deceives itself about the "reality" it is describing.

2. UW; Summer–Autumn 1873; 29[223].

3. UW; Summer 1872–Early 1873; 19[173].

4. Though his principal topics are modernity and Richard Rorty's interpretations, Alexander Nehamas also offers a general discussion of Nietzsche's aestheticism in "Nietzsche, Modernity, Aestheticism," in *The Cambridge Companion to Nietzsche*, ed. Bernd Magnus and Kathleen M. Higgins (Cambridge: Cambridge University Press, 1996), pp. 223–251.

5. It is worth noticing how Nietzsche links art and religion, in the sense that both gave human beings a perspective that produced a new sensibility and allowed them to endure life. See GS; 78; and H; I; 222.

6. See also BGE; 291 and 39. Man "invented the good conscience so as to enjoy his soul for once as *simple:* and the whole of morality is a protracted audacious forgery by virtue of which alone it becomes possible to

feel pleasure at the sight of the soul. From this point of view there is perhaps much more in the concept 'art' than is generally believed" (291).

7. *"Art*—to say it in advance, for I shall some day return to this subject at greater length—art, in which precisely the *lie* is sanctified and the *will to deception* has a good conscience, is much more fundamentally opposed to the ascetic ideal than is science: this was instinctively sensed by Plato, the greatest enemy of art Europe has yet produced" (GM; III; 25).

8. "It is always as between Achilles and Homer: the one *has* the experience, the sensation, the other *describes* it. A true writer only bestows words on the emotions and experiences of others, he is an artist so as to divine much from the little he himself has felt" (H; I; 211).

9. Eberhard Lämmert has argued that the emergence of the independent writer became the "prototype" of the middle class, and he ties this to Nietzsche's view of solitude. "With control over the creative imagination as means of production, the writers unwittingly become prototypes of the middle-class individual, since the ideal of self-determination of thought and action seems to be realized in their life-style in an exemplary manner. . . . To a degree greater than ever before, Nietzsche raised the noncontemporaneity of the entrepreneurial author to a principle of thought and outward existence. With his production fired by his imagination, such an author soon was well ahead of the laborious and unmanageable emancipation of the middle-class working world, and he therefore alienated himself relentlessly from the middle class" ("Nietzsche's Apotheosis of Loneliness," in *Nietzsche: Literature and Value*, ed. Volker Dürr [Madison: University of Wisconsin Press, 1988], pp. 53, 57).

10. For a discussion of section 356 of *The Gay Science* and the question of the actor, see Paul Patton, "Nietzsche and the Problem of the Actor," in *Why Nietzsche Still? Reflections on Drama, Culture, and Politics*, ed. Alan D. Schrift (Berkeley: University of California Press, 2000), pp. 170–183.

11. The question of appearances is discussed at length in BGE; 229, 230, 232.

12. UW; Summer 1872–Early 1873; 19[162]. This is a view that Nietzsche criticizes when discussing the idea of monumental history (ULH; 2).

13. In an earlier fragment, Nietzsche wrote that "the past cannot perish in us and drives us with the disquiet of a ghost to ascend tirelessly the entire stepladder of all that human beings call great, amazing, immortal, divine" (UW; Summer–Autumn 1873; 29[98]).

14. See also AOM; 223: "[W]e require history, for the past continues to flow within us in a hundred waves; we ourselves are, indeed, nothing but that which at every moment we experience of this continued flowing."

15. In an insightful essay, Daniel Came discusses the issue of justification in Nietzsche's view of aesthetics. Came's analysis, which focuses on *The Birth of Tragedy*, offers an incisive reconstruction of how suffering can be seen as a beautiful experience, that is, as an aesthetic event that produces pleasure, without losing sight of the fact that suffering is also a constitutive element of life. Life needs the Apollonian forms, the veils that bestow beauty and, I would add, meaning to life. "If, as Nietzsche claims, unmediated experience of suffering is psychologically incompatible with life-affirmation, then perhaps that would obviate the ethical objections to adopting an aesthetic attitude towards suffering. Perhaps to attempt to see suffering as beautiful is the best that can be hoped for in the circumstances. One would therefore reject Nietzsche's proposal at the price of despair" ("The Aesthetic Justification of Existence," in *A Companion to Nietzsche*, ed. Keith Ansell-Pearson [Malden, MA: Blackwell Publishing, 2006], p. 56). Came's incisive analysis, however, is marred by the absence of a clear definition of "life-affirmation," which is, to be sure, a problem intrinsic to Nietzsche's philosophy. More important is the possibility that Nietzsche dramatically modified his views on falsification and art. In 1888 his goal appears to be the grasping of "actuality" in complete awareness that one has the strength to face life "as it is."

16. Nietzsche also argues that self-control is rooted in man's animality; that is, "self-control springs from the sense for what is real (from prudence)," a behavior that animals possess (D; 26).

17. Solomon argues that "[t]he definition of 'morality' that preoccupies Nietzsche is the definition provided by Kant—of morality as a set of universal, categorical principles of practical reason" ("A More Severe Morality: Nietzsche's Affirmative Ethics," in *Nietzsche: Critical Assessments*, ed. Conway, vol. 3, p. 324). It is true that Nietzsche criticizes the claim of universality associated with Kantian, as well as Platonic and Christian, morality. It is also true that he put forward various principles—the will to power, the order of rank, the natural law of selection—as true and universal principles that all people ought to accept. My reading is not an objection to Solomon's interpretation but, at most, a new layer. In other words, it is possible to identify a first layer in Nietzsche's view of morality in which certain principles are presented as universal. But once the first layer is affirmed, the second layer calls for particular expressions of morality according to the quanta of the will to power and the natural rank that individuals possess. It is in the second layer that Nietzsche rejects the principles of equality, universal rights, and universal morality.

18. Solomon finds a similarity between Aristotle's view of morality and Nietzsche's. Both, according to Solomon, stood for a morality of practice, not for a morality of principles. Any practice requires a context that will make room for an understanding of the virtues. "For Nietzsche as for Hegel and as for Aristotle," Solomon claims, "morality does not consist of principles but of practices. It is *doing* not willing that is of moral significance, an expression of character rather than a display of practical reason" (ibid., p. 330). Solomon also argues that Nietzsche rejects principles "without a set of practices to fall back on" (p. 330), and that for all his insistence on creating new values, Nietzsche comes up empty-handed and fails to suggest even a single new value (p. 336). Yet Solomon eschews altogether the idea that Aristotle's ethics depends on the mean, a notion too close to the idea of the average that Nietzsche rejects. Furthermore, an Aristotelian ethics is typical of rather domesticated nobles, who prefer the communitarian bonds arising from deliberations in public institutions and for the sake of a common life, not the communitarian bonds marking off warriors from the rest of people. In a word, the context for Aristotle's ethics is a herd composed of nobles. The city is thus a space in which two herds, the nobles and the plebeians, share the life of the polis. In my view, Nietzsche's philosophy (with its critique in *Beyond Good and Evil* of the Aristotelianism of morals) is not compatible with the context and content of Aristotelian virtues, which are, in turn, the foundation of Aristotle's ethics.

19. Nietzsche also discusses the relationship between "[u]nconditional honest atheism" and the ascetic ideal (GM; III; 27).

20. Nietzsche claims that the "sense for truth" is "the sense for security." It is the quest to avoid dangers, something that all animals seek (D; 26).

21. "Thucydides, and perhaps the *Principe* of Machiavelli, are related to me closely by their unconditional will not to deceive themselves and not to see reason in *reality*—not in 'reason,' still less in 'morality'" (TI; "What I Owe"; 2).

22. This is an important departure from Hobbes's arguments that treat speech as "the most noble and profitable invention of all other" and define scientific knowledge as the correct connections of consequences, but he is referring not to "the consequence of one thing to another, but of one name of a thing to another name of the same thing" (*Leviathan*, chaps. 4 and 7, pp. 16, 35).

23. See also EH; Foreword. "Do not, above all, confound me with what I am not!"

24. See also BGE; 40, 270, 289. "Every philosophy also *conceals* a philosophy; every opinion is also a hiding place, every word also a mask" (289).

25. "Men who think deeply appear as comedians when they traffic with others, because in order to be understood they always have first to simulate a surface" (AOM; 232).

26. Daniel W. Conway argues that in "[h]oping to induce the self-overcoming of Christian morality, he strove to extend his formative influence into the coming millennium, at which time he would be recognized and revered as the Antichrist" ("Odysseus Bound?" in *Why Nietzsche Still? Reflections on Drama, Culture, and Politics*, ed. Alan D. Schrift [Berkeley: University of California Press, 2000], p. 35).

27. Haar, "Nietzsche and Metaphysical Language," p. 27.

28. For a discussion of the question of solitude in Nietzsche, see Lämmert, "Nietzsche's Apotheosis of Loneliness," pp. 50–65. For Lämmert the themes of solitude, artistic creation, and the teaching of the nation characterize the German poets of the nineteenth century. "Some euphoric, some despondent, nearly all of the poets who sought fame in the period around 1800 and in the years following aspired to the inspiration of poetic genius to the point of the highest development of self and master instructor of the nation" (p. 51).

29. Though Nietzsche praises the importance of the incomplete, one should not overlook the fact that his critique of modernity entails the creation of a new social order, which is not meant to be composed of scattered fragments. I discuss Nietzsche's conception of a new social order in chapter 9. For his views on the incomplete, see H; I; 178, 199; and GS; 79.

30. Against Lämmert, it does not follow that Nietzsche's emphasis on solitude places him on a literary rather than on a philosophical tradition. Nietzsche's texts are a fusion of both. Lämmert suggests, first as a hypothesis and then as a conclusion, that Nietzsche "exemplifies the contemporary phenotype of the solitary seeker of knowledge and the visionary. He is, therefore, not to be assigned so much to a philosophical, but rather to a literary, tradition that has marked the special social status of the productive loner ever since the emergence of the independent writer in the 18th century" ("Nietzsche's Apotheosis of Loneliness," p. 51).

31. In *Twilight of the Idols*, Nietzsche writes: "My recreation, my preference, my *cure* from all Platonism has always been *Thucydides*. Thucydides, and perhaps the *Principe* of Machiavelli, are related to me closely by their unconditional will not to deceive themselves and not to see reason in *reality*—not in 'reason', still less in 'morality'" (TI; "What I Owe"; 2).

32. Nietzsche is here criticizing what he considers a mechanistic conception of the world, one that divests existence of its *"rich ambiguity"* (GS; 373).

33. "For seventeen years I have not wearied of exposing the *despiritualizing* influence of our contemporary scientific pursuits" (TI; "Germans"; 73).

34. This is Alexander Nehamas's concept of Nietzsche's aestheticism.

35. Since artists succumb to the temptation of "laying hold of actuality," Nietzsche, as already pointed out, asks: "With what success? This is easy to guess" (GM; III; 4). His discussion of Wagner in *The Case of Wagner* clarifies his "guessing."

36. Aaron Ridley, *Routledge Philosophy Guidebook to Nietzsche on Art* (London: Routledge, 2007), p. 126, quoting Julian Young, *Nietzsche's Philosophy of Art* (Cambridge: Cambridge University Press, 1992), p. 139, emphasis in the original.

37. Ridley, *Guidebook to Nietzsche on Art*, p. 127.

38. Ibid., p. 135.

39. Ibid., p. 138.

40. Ibid., p. 137, emphasis mine.

41. Ibid., p. 139.

CHAPTER FIVE. THE SECRET WAR OF THE INSTINCTS

1. Magnus, "Nietzsche and the Project," p. 40.

2. Graham Parkes is the important exception; see Parkes, *Composing the Soul: Reaches of Nietzsche's Psychology* (Chicago: University of Chicago Press, 1994), pp. 273–318. Brian Leiter comes close to examining the unconscious, but his focus is on Nietzsche's fatalism and he does not pursue the inquiry; see Brian Leiter, "The Paradox of Fatalism and Self-Creation in Nietzsche," in *Nietzsche*, ed. John Richardson and Brian Leiter (Oxford: Oxford University Press, 2001), pp. 281–321.

3. I emphasize that my discussion focuses on Nietzsche's philosophical endeavors and should not be confused with an approach that attempts to see Nietzsche's "secrets" through a reading of his life. For this second approach, see Joachim Köhler, *Zarathustra's Secret: The Interior Life of Frederick Nietzsche*, trans. Ronald Taylor (New Haven: Yale University Press, 2002).

4. "Letter to Reinhart von Seydlitz, February 12, 1888," in *Selected Letters*, ed. Middleton, p. 283. See also "Letter to Franz Overbeck, February 11, 1883," p. 207.

5. Conway finds a "turning inward" in Nietzsche's post-Zarathustra thought. "Prior to this turning," Conway writes, "he had shared Zarathustra's distaste for personal political involvement, preferring the comfortable detachment of the diagnostician to the frenzied engagement of the legislator" (*Nietzsche's Dangerous Game: Philosophy in the Twilight of the Idols* [Cambridge: Cambridge University Press, 1997], p. 10). I maintain that this inward turn is present since his early writings, expressed either in an archaeological exploration of other people's souls or in his own concern for the meaning of life. See *Schopenhauer as Educator* and *Richard Wagner in Bayreuth*. As my discussion in chapter 4 shows, Nietzsche's call for knives and vivisections, which is part of the inward turn, predates *Thus Spoke Zarathustra*.

6. See Solomon, "Nietzsche *ad hominem*."

7. In *Human, All Too Human*, Nietzsche offers another version of the good as the capacity to repay and sees evil as located in the soul of the weak (H; I; 45).

8. Wolfgang Müller-Lauter correctly asserts that Nietzsche provides several explanations for the defeat of the strong. The strong are few in number, lack the cunning of the weak, and, after vanquishing others, fight among themselves (*Nietzsche: His Philosophy of Contradictions and the Contradictions of His Philosophy*, trans. David J. Parent [Urbana: University of Illinois Press, 1999], pp. 23–40). To my knowledge, however, Nietzsche never explains why the trademark of the weak, the instinct for self-preservation, is inherited by many people. That is, he never explains why the weak are a majority in the first place. It is in this sense that, in my interpretation, he does not provide adequate reasons to account for the eventual defeat of the strong.

9. See also WP; 109: "Principle: There is an element of decay in everything that characterizes modern man: but close beside this sickness stand signs of an untested force and powerfulness of the soul. *The same reasons that produce the increasing smallness of man* drive the *stronger and rarer individuals up to greatness*." This section is dated 1885, the same year in which *Beyond Good and Evil* was written.

10. In the second, 1886, edition of *Human, All Too Human*, Nietzsche did not write a preface, which might have hinted at possible departures from the ideas he had expressed in 1879.

11. "I received absolutely no such strong impressions from the Greeks; and, not to mince words, they *cannot* be to us what the Romans are. One does not *learn* from the Greeks—their manner is too strange, it is also too fluid to produce an imperative, a 'classical' effect. Who would ever have learned to write from a Greek! Who would ever have learned it *without* the Romans!" (TI; "What I Owe"; 1, 2).

12. This is a neo-Kantian view to the extent that Nietzsche follows the Kantian argument that perception apprehends images, without ever achieving knowledge of things in themselves. But the instincts play a role in Nietzsche that will never appear in a Kantian universe, which is devoid of instincts. Furthermore, Nietzsche does not accept the notion of things in themselves, nor does he accept the Kantian argument that we possess the faculty of "apperception," which provides unity to the manifold objects that enter, through perception, into our consciousness. Appearances, Kant argues, "are not things in themselves, but rather the mere play of our representations, which in the end come down to determinations of the inner sense. . . . Now no cognitions can occur in us, no connection and unity among them, without that unity of consciousness that precedes all data of the intuitions, and in relation to which all representation of objects is alone possible. This pure, original, unchanging consciousness I will now name **transcendental apperception**" (*Critique of Pure Reason* [Cambridge: Cambridge University Press, 1998], pp. 230, 232).

13. WLN; Notebook 7, End of 1886–Spring 1887; 7[53].

14. WLN; Notebook 34, April–June 1885; 34[30].

15. Although both Hobbes and Nietzsche argue that knowledge of reality in itself is not possible, their starting points are different. Nietzsche claims that the senses perceive the objects. Hobbes argues that the objects impinge upon human senses, which he conceives of as passive organs, "[s]o that sense in all cases is nothing else but original fancy, caused . . . by the pressure, that is, by the motion, of external things upon our eyes, ears, and other organs thereunto ordained" (*Leviathan*, chap. 1, p. 7).

16. Actually, words can be hindrances to knowledge. See D; 47.

17. For the influence of these two thinkers in the formation of Nietzsche's philosophy, see George J. Stack, *Lange and Nietzsche* (Berlin: Walter de Gruyter, 1983), and Claudia Crawford, *The Beginnings of Nietzsche's Theory of Language* (Berlin: Walter de Gruyter, 1988).

18. WLN; Notebook 34, April–June 1885; 34[54].

19. WLN; Notebook 15, Spring 1888; 15[90].

20. In relation to this issue, J. P. Stern comments: "How then (Nietzsche asks), if we are incapable of positive contact with the real world, can

we sustain life? How is it that the world works? The world works on an illusion, an '*as if*' principle. We act in the world as if we were in touch with a benevolent reality, as if we were capable of comprehending its cosmic purpose, as if there were a divinity whose decrees we fulfill and who gives meaning to our individual lives—as if God were alive" ("Nietzsche and the Idea of Metaphor," in *Nietzsche: Imagery and Thought*, ed. Malcolm Pasley [Berkeley: University of California Press, 1978], p. 68).

   21. WLN; Notebook 1, Autumn 1885–Spring 1886; 1[61].

   22. WLN; Notebook 37, June–July 1885; 37[4]; Notebook 40, August–September 1885; 40[21].

   23. WLN; Notebook 15, Spring 1888; 15[90].

   24. See also WLN; Notebook 11, November 1887–March 1888; 11[120], 11[145]; Notebook 15, Spring 1888; 15[90].

   25. For an insightful discussion of Nietzsche's view of reality, see Mary Warnock, "Nietzsche's Conception of Truth," in *Nietzsche: Imagery and Thought*, ed. Malcom Pasley (Berkeley: University of California Press, 1978), pp. 33–63.

   26. Haar, "Nietzsche and Metaphysical Language," pp. 17–18.

   27. Haar, "Life and Natural Totality in Nietzsche," in *Nietzsche: Critical Assessments*, ed. Conway, vol. 2, p. 81.

   28. See, for example, ULH, especially ULH 3.

   29. Could the sick become healthy? At first sight, the answer seems to be negative, since the nobles would no longer have any opportunity to display the "pathos of distance." But on careful reflection, the answer is affirmative. However, the affirmation requires a reconciliation of philosophy and physiology similar to the one Nietzsche describes in section 57 of *The Anti-Christ*. The slaves or the lower rank ought to accept what they are, not by internalizing cruelty but by seeing their predicament as part of a natural design to preserve the higher rank of the most spiritual beings. This, presumably, relieves their pain and avoids resentment. Hence the need for a Buddhism for the masses. A detailed discussion of Nietzsche's role as physician is found in Daniel R. Ahern, *Nietzsche as Cultural Physician* (University Park: Pennsylvania State University Press, 1995).

   30. WLN; Notebook 14, Spring 1888; 14[157].

   31. WLN; Notebook 34, April–June 1885; 34[89]; Notebook 11, November 1887–March 1888; 11[115].

   32. A possible reply is that morality seeks a kind of permanence that is not present in the world for which morality attempts to legislate. I owe this to Kathleen M. Higgins. I think, however, that for Nietzsche, morality is the expression of a certain kind of life and intends the preservation of that kind

of life. This means that morality is an intrinsic part of the world in which it flourishes.

33. "The pietist, the priest of both sexes, is false *because* he is sick: his instinct *demands* that truth shall not come into its own at any point" (AC; 52).

34. See also TI; "Errors"; 3, 4, 6.

35. If, as Nietzsche tends to argue, the concepts constituting the standards of our evaluations are false, and if the paradigms of knowledge containing those evaluations are also false, what guarantee is there that when the philosopher evaluates history he is not carrying the baggage of a false conceptual framework? This is, precisely, Nietzsche's genealogy of knowledge: errors develop first and then become the standards to judge truth (GS; 110). As things stand, the philosopher goes to primeval interpretations and judges them to be false through his own epistemological paradigm, which may be false, too.

36. For a discussion of Nietzsche's "psychiatry" and his relationship with Freud, see Mitchell Ginsberg, "Nietzschean Psychiatry," in *Nietzsche: A Collection of Critical Essays,* ed. Robert C. Solomon (New York: Anchor Books, 1973), pp. 293–315.

37. As a sample of other references to the instincts in *Daybreak,* see D; 328, 346, 358.

38. For a discussion of the ego and its drives in Nietzsche's philosophy, see Graham Parkes, "Nietzsche on the Fantastic Fabric of Experience," in *Nietzsche: Critical Assessments,* ed. Conway, vol. 2, pp. 270–85. Walter Kaufmann tends to emphasize the notion of sublimation in his discussion of the drives; see his *Nietzsche: Philosopher, Psychologist, Anti-Christ* (New York: Meridian Books, 1956), pp. 182–222.

39. Nietzsche repeats this argument in D; 129.

40. My account differs from that of Ruth Abbey in her *Nietzsche's Middle Period* (Oxford: Oxford University Press, 2000), pp. 17–33. She claims that in the works that belong to Nietzsche's "middle period," namely, *Human, All Too Human, Daybreak,* and *The Gay Science,* the issue of free will is surrounded by many tensions. At times, she argues, Nietzsche defends the doctrine of free will, and at other times he explicitly leaves room for the free will, especially in the case of the free spirits. In replying to Abbey's interpretation, I offer two arguments. First, the tensions embedded in Nietzsche's critique of free will continue to be present in *Beyond Good and Evil,* when he debunks the "old I" and then defends the idea of self-responsibility for the philosophers (BGE; 17, 212). These tensions are also present in the *Genealogy* (the ascetic priest is sick, but he is described as the

agent responsible for the propagation of the weak); in *Twilight of the Idols* (no one is responsible for what he is, but modernity knows what it is doing); and in *The Anti-Christ* (theologians lie, and they *know* that they are lying, an act that presupposes an element of choice). Second, and more important, Abbey's analysis misses the passages I mention from *Daybreak* (sections 109, 119) and the fact that Nietzsche's view of the instincts continues in *The Gay Science, Beyond Good and Evil,* and *Twilight of the Idols.* Without denying the evident tensions in Nietzsche's critique of free will, I argue that there is a rather consistent trail that ascribes obdurate influences to the instincts.

41. See BGE; 158: "To our strongest drive, the tyrant in us, not only our reason but also our conscience submits."

42. My "finally" assumes that chronology is not important here. The first four books of *The Gay Science* were published in 1881, before *Beyond Good and Evil* (1886).

43. "[M]ost of a philosopher's conscious thinking is secretly directed and compelled into definite channels by his instincts" (BGE; 3).

44. In chapter 7, I examine in more detail the complex relationship between instincts, thought, and language in Nietzsche's philosophy.

45. WLN; Notebook 11, November 1887–March 1888; 11[113].

46. For a discussion of Nietzsche's opposition to Descartes' view of consciousness, see Kathleen Marie Higgins, *Comic Relief: Nietzsche's "Gay Science"* (Oxford: Oxford University Press, 2000), pp. 127–50.

47. Haar, "Nietzsche and Metaphysical Language," p. 9.

48. Gemes, "'We Remain of Necessity Strangers to Ourselves,'" p. 199. Gemes's arguments are an excellent exposition of Nietzsche's assertion in the *Genealogy* that we are strangers to ourselves.

49. Thomas Heilke argues that "[t]he knowledge of self—not of God or nature—becomes for Nietzsche the beginning of all wisdom" (*Nietzsche's Tragic Regime: Culture, Aesthetics, and Political Education* [DeKalb: Northern Illinois University Press, 1998], p. 152). This is the view that Nietzsche proposes in *Schopenhauer as Educator,* but his insistence on the unknowable nature of instincts and even actions indicates a different perspective. In *The Gay Science* he advocates a vision of individuality, which seeks what is authentic in the individual (this presupposes knowledge of authenticity), and in *Beyond Good and Evil* and subsequent works, he stresses the centrality of nature in defining one's real identity (which presupposes knowledge of a person's "real" nature). Nietzsche's philosophical program seems to be caught up between the Socratic imperative ("know yourself") and the awareness of its impossibility.

50. Along similar lines, "[o]ur character is determined even more by the lack of certain experiences than by that which we experience" (AOM; 36).

51. Thomas L. Pangle argues: "Even the warrior who can lay claim to having won the most complete and generous sort of victory, reflecting the victory within himself of the most expressive and fruitful concatenation of passions, will sooner or later discover (or be forced in battle to admit) that a flaw has surfaced in his temporarily structured and *partly subconscious* psychic constitution. Some new concatenation of passions, hitherto regarded as 'low,' 'devilish,' 'shameful,' or *'evil,'* will assert itself as the source of a neglected possibility, a new way of life with unheard-of-demands" ("The 'Warrior Spirit' as an Inlet to the Political Philosophy of Nietzsche's Zarathustra," in *Nietzsche: Critical Assessments*, ed. Conway, vol. 4, p. 243, first emphasis mine). I agree, with minor qualifications. First, it is not entirely clear whether the warrior will discover something new in his inner domain; and second, the warrior's psychic constitution is not "partly subconscious." Rather, it is part of hidden and unknown struggles that will bring liberation or exhaustion to the individual, though he will not be able to identify the causes of his mental states.

52. WLN; Notebook 34, April–June 1885; 34[46].

53. WLN; Notebook 11, November 1887–March 1888; 11[145].

54. Is there any room for truth and knowledge in Nietzsche's philosophy? Maudemarie Clark's study, *Nietzsche on Truth and Philosophy*, is, in my view, one of the standards to assess Nietzsche's conception of truth. Though a thorough treatment exceeds the boundaries of the present project, the preeminence of inner processes concealed from us and, accordingly, unknowable, requires some clarifications about the issue of whether Clark's interpretations are powerful enough to settle the issue of a factual reality, which is knowable and asserted as "true." Though Clark does not examine the role that the instincts play in Nietzsche's philosophy, she traces his idea of truth and concludes, "In the six books that follow BG, there is no evidence of Nietzsche's earlier denial of truth: no claim that the human world is a falsification, no claim that science, logic, or mathematics falsify reality" (*Nietzsche on Truth and Philosophy* [Cambridge: Cambridge University Press, 1900], p. 103). Contrary to Clark's categorical statement, Nietzsche insists that, while scientific knowledge has been possible to the extent that it has accepted the evidence of the senses, there are still realms impervious to this evidence. He proceeds to list metaphysics, psychology, and epistemology, and adds: "*Or* science of formulae, sign-systems: such as *logic* and that applied logic, mathematics. In these *reality does not appear at all,* not even as a problem; just as little as does the question what value a

system of conventional signs such as constitutes logic can possibly possess" (TI; "Reason"; 3, second and third emphases mine).

In this passage, logic, a system that seeks to describe reality, is treated by Nietzsche as one that does not even touch reality ("reality does not appear at all"), which I take to mean that logical descriptions *falsify* their objects. But he expands upon something, perhaps, of far-reaching consequences. In *Twilight of the Idols,* Nietzsche discusses how a sensation is brought to the surface by a particular instinct ("the cause-creating drive") as "meaning," namely, as part of a causal connection. This "meaning" requires a "motivation." The outcome is that the motivation comes *late,* but is presented as the *cause* of the sensation. "The ideas *engendered* by a certain condition have been misunderstood as the cause of that condition." The fact of a sensation comes to our consciousness "only *when* we have furnished it with a motivation of some kind." Our memory, "which in such a case becomes active without our being aware of it," recalls earlier states and "the causal interpretations which have grown out of them—*not* their causality" (TI; "Errors"; 4).

This suggests a chasm between the real and true causality and the "causal interpretations" that some occurrences have registered in our memory, an activity that takes place "*without our being aware of it.*" This "great error" means that "true" causality is separated from causal interpretations that have become dominant, which in turn means that causality is upside down. We take, according to Nietzsche, causes for their effects and vice versa. This causality is, precisely, the logic that has *prevailed.* And if this is so, Clark's argument that Nietzsche does not assert that logic falsifies reality in his last six published books is not tenable.

55. Leslie Paul Thiele, *Friedrich Nietzsche and the Politics of the Soul: A Study of Heroic Individualism* (Princeton: Princeton University Press, 1990), pp. 68–69.

56. Ibid., p. 66.

57. Ibid., pp. 66–95.

58. "Morality is merely sign-language, merely symptomatology: one must already know *what* it is about to derive profit from it" (TI; "Improvers"; 1).

59. WLN; Notebook 34, April–June 1885; 34[46].

60. These statements by Nietzsche are probably gymnastic mental moves, but in a web of stories this is no longer a serious objection. His quest for meaning stands. And he is well aware that the quest for meaning is meaningless, but he keeps trying. No wonder, then, why he called himself the first tragedian as well as the first nihilist.

61. WLN; Notebook 11, November 1887–March 1888; 11[99].

CHAPTER SIX. THE METAPHYSICS OF MEANING

1. The epigraph is quoted in Stephen Crites, *Dialectic and Gospel in the Development of Hegel's Thinking* (University Park: Pennsylvania State University Press, 1998), p. 47.

2. WLN; Notebook 2, Autumn 1885–Autumn 1886; 2[191].

3. In the *Genealogy of Morality* (1887), Nietzsche did not emphasize severity and cunning as prerequisites of the strong. The strong (the nobles) enjoy the pleasures of the body. The ones who practice cunning are the slaves, and it is the ascetic priest who now transforms severity into its goal and purpose in life.

4. See also WLN; Notebook 7, End of 1886–Spring 1887; 7[39]. In this passage Nietzsche refers to the powerful soul as one that can emerge even stronger from its painful experiences.

5. My interpretation differs from that of Deleuze, for whom the root of the problem of existence is suffering. On his argument, if existence is blameworthy, this blame entails suffering, which, in turn, entails atonement. "Existence seems to be given so much by being made a crime, an excess. It gains a double nature—an immense injustice and a justifying atonement. It is Titanised by crime, it is made divine by the expiation of crime" (*Nietzsche and Philosophy*, p. 20). This view, he claims, is present in both the Greek and the Christian religious and moral horizons, although Christianity invented the notion of original sin that brought forth the bad conscience. In my interpretation, Nietzsche conceives of suffering as part of his spiritual training and does not divinize it. The metaphysics of meaning I find in Nietzsche's philosophy is not suffering from life, where life is an abstract category. Suffering is not an experience that is equally applicable to all individuals. The nobles' suffering is completely different from that of the slaves. The metaphysics of meaning appears as Nietzsche's own despair after the realization that *his* life has no meaning, but he cannot avoid valuating it. This realization leads him into the heroic dimension, in which he suffers from his life but is willing to endure it.

6. This was the argument presented in *Human, All Too Human* (1878). "Everything is necessity—thus says the new knowledge; and this knowledge itself is necessity. Everything is innocence: and knowledge is the path to insight into this innocence" (H; 107). Nietzsche returns to the idea of necessity in *The Anti-Christ*.

7. For an examination of the question of the philosophers of the future, see Nehamas, "Who Are the 'Philosophers of the Future'?"

8. See TI; "Morality"; 6; "Errors"; 8.

9. It is important to notice that Nietzsche establishes a direct relationship between the will to power and the Greek word "pathos," whose dominant meaning is one of suffering and passion.

10. "Perspectivism is only a complex form of specificity. My idea is that every specific body strives to become master over all space and to extend its force (—its will to power:) and to thrust back all that resists its extension. But it continually encounters similar efforts on the part of other bodies and ends by coming to an arrangement ('union') with those of them that are sufficiently related to it: thus they conspire together for power. And the process goes on" (WP; 636).

11. As Kathleen Higgins comments, "The human race, Nietzsche contends, has a periodic need for belief that life has a purpose. And so, although the comic view will always triumph, the tragic view will recurrently arise and satisfy this human need" ("Nietzsche and Postmodern Subjectivity," in *Nietzsche as Postmodernist: Essays Pro and Contra*, ed. Clayton Koelb [Albany: State University of New York Press, 1990], p. 203). I am not sure that Nietzsche's arguments justify Higgins's conclusion that the comic view, whatever this term means, "will always triumph."

12. In contrast to the tragic understanding of suffering, wandering, and identity, it is hard to find persuasive examples in the Judeo-Christian tradition in which life is equated with suffering or in which suffering is viewed as a precondition of wisdom. In the Old Testament, wisdom is a good to be sought, and in the New Testament, wisdom is a divine gift incarnated in Christ. In the Judeo-Christian tradition, there is punishment for one's deeds, but punishment ought to lead to repentance, *not* wandering. The generation that spent forty years in the desert were not wanderers in the Greek sense. They were not seeking redemption, nor were they doing penance; they were simply prevented from entering the Promised Land.

13. Karl Löwith, "Nietzsche's Revival of the Doctrine of Eternal Recurrence," in *Nietzsche: Critical Assessments*, ed. Conway, vol. 2, p. 175. I agree with Löwith, although for different reasons. For other valuable examinations of the doctrine of eternal recurrence, see Bernd Magnus, *Nietzsche's Existential Imperative* (Bloomington: Indiana University Press, 1978); Joan Stambaugh, *Nietzsche's Thought of Eternal Return* (Baltimore: Johns Hopkins University Press, 1972); and Stambaugh, *The Problem of Time in Nietzsche* (London: Associated University Presses, 1987). As an aside, the Aztecs and the Mayas also suscribed to a cyclical conception of time. See Tzvetan Todorov, *The Conquest of America: The Question of the Other* (New York: HarperPerennial, 1985), pp. 63–123.

14. Pierre Klossowski, "Nietzsche's Experience of the Eternal Return," in *The New Nietzsche*, ed. David B. Allison (Cambridge, MA: MIT Press, 1985), p. 108.

15. Ivan Soll, "Reflections on Recurrence: A Re-examination of Nietzsche's Doctrine, *Die Ewige Wiederkehr des Gleichen*," in *Nietzsche: Critical Assessments*, ed. Conway, vol. 2, p. 378.

16. Ibid., p. 379. Klossowski presents a similar argument ("Nietzsche's Experience of the Eternal Return," p. 113). For an attempt to offer a scientific explanation of the eternal return, see Pierre Klossowski, *Nietzsche and the Vicious Circle*, trans. Daniel W. Smith (Chicago: University of Chicago Press, 1997), pp. 93–120. For another view of the eternal recurrence, see Thomas J. J. Altizer, "Eternal Recurrence and Kingdom of God," in *The New Nietzsche*, ed. David B. Allison (Cambridge, MA: MIT Press, 1985), pp. 232–46.

17. Haar, "Life and Natural Totality in Nietzsche," p. 84. In this regard, Klossowski's expression is not felicitous: eternal recurrence is not "the necessary circular movement to which I yield myself, to which I deliver myself," since the circular movement will occur regardless of my will. See Klossowski, "Nietzsche's Experience of the Eternal Return," p. 109.

18. Klossowski also emphasizes the importance of forgetting and revelation. "In fact," he writes, at the moment when I am struck by the sudden revelation of the Eternal Return, *I no longer am*. In order for this revelation to have any meaning, it is necessary that I lose consciousness of myself, and that the circular movement of the return be merged with my unconsciousness until such time as it leads me back to the point where the necessity of living through the entire series of my possibilities is revealed to me." I do not think that revelation is necessary to Nietzsche. A culture infused with a belief in the eternal recurrence suffices. But Klossowski's emphasis on forgetting is well-placed. For example, if I receive the "revelation" of eternal recurrence at the age of thirty, it does not follow that I will immediately know all the thoughts I will hold and all the actions I will carry out. Eternal recurrence is the *awareness* that a life was lived before and will be relived in the future. It does not entail knowledge of any detail pertaining to that life. Otherwise, the individual will be in a position to derail the recurrence of *the same*. See Klossowski, "Nietzsche's Experience of the Eternal Return," p. 109.

19. Soll correctly points out that "[t]he supra-historical character of recurrence, by leaving open the possibility of any kind of meaning within the cycle of history, is, contrary to Nietzsche's conclusion, not 'the most extreme form of nihilism: the nothing (the "meaninglessness") eternally'

(WP, 55). It also allows the 'meaningful' to be repeated eternally" ("Reflections on Recurrence," p. 383).

20. Nietzsche's theory of total unaccountability and his sense of moral obligation are difficult to reconcile. On the one hand, nature and life are not moral, and the quest for moral principles in the world is futile. Morality is depicted as an inner phantom that we project on the external world. On the other hand, Nietzsche insists on the duty to act honestly. But honesty, as a moral value, alters the idea of total unaccountability as expressed in *Human, All Too Human* and *Twilight of the Idols*. This predicament gives credence to the centrality of the tragic in his philosophy.

21. WLN; Notebook 36, June–July 1885; 36[27].

22. On my interpretation, Haar errs when posing the following dichotomy: "*Either there is a whole*," and one needs to justify it rationally; namely, "to reintroduce God as 'the consciousness of the totality in becoming'"; or "*there is no totality*" and, accordingly, no room for a "joyful fatalism . . . and becoming loses itself in indefiniteness" ("Life and Natural Totality in Nietzsche," p. 87). In my view, the whole does not entail the need for a suprahistorical and rational justification, which Haar sees as the "reintroduction" of God. The whole is the form in which becoming shows its intricacy

23. Higgins, *Comic Relief*, pp. 148–49.

24. "[W]o ich nich fand, was ich *brauchte*, es mir künstlich erzwingen, zurechtfälschen, zurechtdichten mußte (—und was haben Dichter je Anderes getan?)" (*Menschliches Allzumenschliches und Andere Schriften*, Werke1, p. 246).

CHAPTER SEVEN. TRUTH AND REASON

1. Jonathan Raban, "My Holy War: What Do a Vicar's Son and a Suicide Bomber Have in Common?" *The New Yorker*, February 4, 2002, p. 29.

2. See also WS; 17. "He who explains a passage in an author's 'more deeply' than the passage was meant has not explained the author but *obscured* him."

3. For some of Nietzsche's views on interpretation in *Human, All Too Human*, vol. 1, see sections 126, 127, 134, 135, 270, 271.

4. Further, "He [Nietzsche] has good reasons for his demand. Yet he doesn't manage to do it. Indeed, when it comes down to it, he does not want to do it. In *Ecce Homo* he repeats Zarathustra's words: 'No longer-*willing*, no longer-*valuing*, no longer-*creating*—oh may this great fatigue remain far from me!' (Volker Gerhardt, "Self-Grounding: Nietzsche's Mo-

rality of Individuality," in *The Fate of the New Nietzsche*, ed. Keith Ansell-Pearson and Howard Caygill [Aldershot: Avebury Ashgate Publishing, 1993], p. 286).

5. This sentence is presented in the form of a question, but there is no doubt about Nietzsche's answer. The preeminence of "hithertos" in his discussion of psychology shows his conviction that it is a flawed enterprise.

6. Nietzsche praises "the indomitably strong and tough masculinity of the great German philologists and critical historians" who, in his view, contributed to a *"new* conception of the German spirit" (BGE; 209).

7. Blondel, *Nietzsche: The Body and Culture*, p. 93.

8. Gerhardt argues that "in everything essential to him," Nietzsche "retained" a moral interpretation of phenomena. Gerhardt lists "the aristocratic identification of value" and the elements of Epicurean and Stoic ethics as proofs of this moral interpretation of phenomena ("Self-Grounding," p. 289).

9. See Laurence Bergreen's excellent book, *Over the Edge of the World: Magellan's Terrifying Circumnavigation of the Globe* (New York: Perennial, 2004), p. 219.

10. WLN; Notebook 11, November 1887–March 1888; 11[99].

11. Ibid.

12. WLN; Notebook 5, Summer 1886–Autumn 1887 5[71]; section 11.

13. WLN; Notebook 5, Summer 1886–Autumn 1887 5[71]; section 9.

14. WLN; Notebook 5, Summer 1886–Autumn 1887 5[71]; section 14.

15. WLN; Notebook 2, Autumn 1885–Autumn 1886; 2[127].

16. WLN; Notebook 5, Summer 1886–Autumn 1887; 5[71]; sections 4–5.

17. WLN; Notebook 9, Autumn 1887; 9[35].

18. WLN; Notebook 9, Autumn 1887; 9[41].

19. WLN; Notebook 5, Summer 1886–Autumn 1887; 5[59].

20. WLN; Notebook 11, November 1887–March 1888; 11[104].

21. WLN; Notebook 5, Summer 1886–Autumn 1887; 5[71]; section 6.

22. In his description of nihilism as a cleansing process, Nietzsche sees an opportunity to determine and to specify the attributes of the strongest. WLN; Notebook 5, Summer 1886–Autumn 1887; 5[71]; section 14.

23. WLN; Notebook 11, November 1887–March 1888; 11[99]; section 1.

24. WLN; Notebook 5, Summer 1886–Autumn 1887; 5[71]; section 12.

25. These are two different conditions. To flow *with* entails consciousness of difference; the agent, as a different entity, flows along with the innocence of nature. To flow *in* is to lose oneself in the fluidity of nature; the pathos of distance between the individual and nature is lost. He is now Dionysus.

26. In 1886, Nietzsche identified the Greek poets as the origin of a concept of actuality. The poets possess a "joy in the actual" as a compensation for their lack of sagacity. Nietzsche understood the Greek state and its religion as determined by a conscious regard for "*all human actuality*" (AOM; 220).

27. I leave aside the issue of whether nothingness can be treated as a value.

28. Though his point of departure is different from mine, Maurice Blanchot's reflections on nihilism are apposite: "Nihilism is tied to being. Nihilism is the impossibility of coming to an end and finding an outcome in this end. It tells of the impotence of nothingness, the false renown of its victories; it tells us that when we think nothingness, we are still thinking being" ("The Limits of Experience: Nihilism," in *The New Nietzsche: Contemporary Styles of Interpretation,* ed. David B. Allison [Cambridge, MA: MIT Press, 1985], p. 126).

29. Michael Allen Gillespie presents an interesting trajectory of the figure of Dionysus in Nietzsche's texts following *The Gay Science.* He argues that while Nietzsche describes himself as an atheist and free spirit in his middle period and identifies himself with "Zarathustra the godless," his self-portrayal changes significantly in *Beyond Good and Evil.* "At the end of *Beyond Good and Evil, Twilight,* and *Ecce Homo* Nietzsche thus describes himself as the last disciple of the philosopher Dionysus. In the end, he portrays himself as the vessel of Dionysus who aims at the transfiguration not merely of German culture but of Europe as a whole" (*Nihilism before Nietzsche* [Chicago: University of Chicago Press, 1995], p. 217). This account has some textual evidence on its side, but it also moves away from substantial aspects of Nietzsche's own revisions. True, Dionysus's appearance at the end of *Beyond Good and Evil* distills the energy of new theoretical projects, although Nietzsche, with his insistence on hidden places and secret paths, is not forthcoming about what his status as a disciple of Dionysus might represent for the future. It scarcely helps that he is aware that he is the *last* disciple. Though Nietzsche talks about the appearance of new free spirits (*Human, All Too Human, Gay Science*) and new philosophers of the future (*Beyond Good and Evil*), he never claims to see new followers, let alone new disciples, of Dionysus. This is a status that Nietzsche reserves for himself.

My arguments suggest that in *Beyond Good and Evil* and the texts written in 1887 and 1888, Dionysus is a mask that has worn out. There is little creative energy in *Ecce Homo.* There is a call to reconciliation, the same call that Nietzsche makes in *Twilight of the Idols.* The eternal recurrence is a test for meaning, the meaning of a strong and affirming life. It is not a Dionysian predicament and does not contain destruction or a new creation. Chaos is absent, since chaos that repeats itself is no longer chaos but a predictable succession of moments. Becoming, too, is absent, by definition. Eternal recurrence is the repetition of the same life with its intrinsic sameness, a life that, as a sign of its strength, can simply proclaim "Once more" and interpret this utterance as the confirmation of a self-inflicted meaning.

30. Nietzsche's depiction of Schopenhauer cannot be separated from his own philosophy; that is, he finds in Schopenhauer's thought the problems he considers important from the standpoint of his own philosophy. For Nietzsche, Schopenhauer's greatness "lies in the fact that he dealt with the picture of life as a whole in order to interpret it as a whole." Nietzsche follows the same approach in his own philosophical explorations. Furthermore, Schopenhauer's philosophy must be interpreted "by the individual for himself alone, in order to gain insight into his own misery and need, into his own limitations, in order to become acquainted with antidotes and consolations" (SE; 3).

31. See Z; Prologue; 5. The "last man" depicted by Zarathustra represents the deepest disintegration of man. This "last man" is unable to "give birth to a star" and "makes everything small."

32. Nietzsche might reasonably argue that he is also suffering for being the heir of so many erroneous interpretations, which have truncated the better possibilities for his life. Still, those better possibilities are only "better" in light of an interpretation, which depends on "thinking" and on a person's needs (WP; 481).

CHAPTER EIGHT. MODERNITY, PLATO, AND THE PERSIAN TURN

1. See, for example, D; 184.

2. See Rousseau, *A Discourse on the Origin of Inequality.*

3. Though this point is abundantly clear, it is worth repeating: Nietzsche's conception of nobility was not anchored on economic power. Nobility meant manners, gestures, the blood of one's ancestors, the pathos of distance, the will to command, and the awareness of a person's power as what nature intended him to have.

4. Rousseau, *The Social Contract,* Book 2, chapter 11. Equality implied that "no citizen shall ever be wealthy enough to buy another, and none poor enough to be forced to sell himself" (*The Social Contract and Discourses* [London: Everyman, 1993], p. 225).

5. David Samuels, "The Confidence Men," *The New Yorker,* April 26–May 3, 1999, p. 153. This essay discusses the relationship between a con artist and one of the Gilded Age barons, Jay Gould.

6. "Schopenhauer never wants to create appearances, for he writes for himself, and no one likes to be deceived, least of all a philosopher who has made this his law: Never deceive anyone, not even yourself!" (SE; 2).

7. The lack of authenticity as a problem for Nietzsche's view of individuality is an issue that is overlooked in Ruth Abbey's *Nietzsche's Middle Period.*

8. Philippa Foot mentions Nietzsche's mistrust of the motives guiding human actions, but this is not a central issue in her arguments, since her main goal is to criticize the grounds of Nietzsche's attack on morality ("Nietzsche's Immoralism," in *Nietzsche: Critical Assessments,* ed. Conway, vol. 3, esp. pp. 57–59).

9. Along similar lines, the "openhearted . . . probably always acts in accordance with secret reasons, for he always has communicable reasons on his lips and practically in his open hand" (GS; 194).

10. "It is the *most sensual* men who *have* to flee from women and torment their body" (D; 294).

11. A good example is provided in D; 303.

12. See GS; 14; AOM; 263, 269, 277.

13. In *Daybreak,* Nietzsche claims that "Napoleon belongs to the mankind of antiquity" (D; 245).

14. According to Rockefeller, Napoleon "was a human being and virile because he came direct from the ranks of the people. There was none of the stagnant blood of nobility or royalty in his veins." Cited in Ron Chernow, *Titan: The Life of John D. Rockefeller, Sr.* (New York: Vintage Books, 1998), p. 529. For Emerson, see "Napoleon; or, the Man of the World," in *Ralph Waldo Emerson: Essays and Lectures* (New York: Library of America, 1983), p. 742.

15. "For one must admit how completely the whole species of a Heraclitus, a Plato, an Empedocles, and whatever else these royal and splendid hermits of the spirit were called, is lacking in our modern world" (BGE; 204; see also 253).

16. Tracy B. Strong, "Nietzsche's Political Aesthetics," in *Nietzsche's New Seas: Explorations in Philosophy, Aesthetics, and Politics,* ed. Michael Allen Gillespie and Tracy B. Strong (Chicago: University of Chicago Press, 1988), p. 170.

17. See, in this regard, Patton, "Nietzsche and the Problem of the Actor."

18. In his discussion of Nietzsche's aesthetics, Matthew Rampley argues that Nietzsche is deeply concerned with the disappearance of the present in modernity. This claim is problematic to the extent that Rampley uses, as his main evidence, Nietzsche's essay on history in the *Untimely Meditations*. In Nietzsche's later work, especially *The Gay Science* and *On the Genealogy of Morality*, he argues that the present is too close and the philosopher must keep it at bay. Equally important, he shows his disgust toward his own times and calls for an overcoming of that present in which he lives. Rampley also emphasizes the importance of the incomplete and the fragmentary in Nietzsche's aesthetics. This is correct, as long as one includes Nietzsche's critique of modernity as an environment in which the fragments are so small that they disable any attempt to build something great, not to mention something lasting. See Matthew Rampley, *Nietzsche, Aesthetics and Modernity* (Cambridge: Cambridge University Press, 2000), pp. 135–65.

19. See *Republic* 382a–d; 414b–c.

20. Cited in Barbara Goldsmith, *Other Powers: The Age of Suffrage, Spiritualism, and the Scandalous Victoria Woodhull* (New York: Alfred A. Knopf, 1998), p. 340.

21. Christopher Haigh, *The Plain Man's Pathways to Heaven: Kinds of Christianity in Post-Reformation England, 1570–1640* (Oxford: Oxford University Press, 2007), pp. 165, 167, 170.

22. Ibid., pp. 173–74.

23. Ibid., p. 180, emphasis mine.

24. Two insightful studies of Nietzsche and his relationship with Christianity are Jörg Salaquarda's "Nietzsche and the Judaeo-Christian Tradition," in *The Cambridge Companion to Nietzsche*, ed. Bernd Magnus and Kathleen M. Higgins (Cambridge: Cambridge University Press, 1996), pp. 90–118, and his "Dionysus versus the Crucified One: Nietzsche's Understanding of the Apostle Paul," in *Nietzsche: Critical Assessments*, ed. Conway, vol. 3, pp. 266–91.

25. For a discussion of Arius's teachings, see Richard E. Rubenstein, *When Jesus Became God: The Epic Fight over Christ's Divinity in the Last Days of Rome* (New York: Harcourt Brace & Co., 1999). See also Timothy D. Barnes, *Athanasius and Constantius: Theology and Politics in the Constantinian Empire* (Cambridge, MA: Harvard University Press, 1993).

26. See UW; Summer–Autumn 1873; 29 [96].

27. "The perils in the way of the evolution of the philosopher are in truth so manifold today one may well doubt whether this fruit can still ripen at all" (BGE; 205).

28. The issue of war is examined in more detail in Book 5.

29. Deleuze argues that Nietzsche ridicules institutions ("Nomad Thought," pp. 79–80), but in fact Nietzsche's thought reveals a consistent defense of institutional devices, ranging from education to the state, which are necessary to lay the groundwork for a more spiritual culture.

30. According to Pangle, in *Thus Spoke Zarathustra* Nietzsche looks for a synthesis of priests and warriors. "In the Zarathustrian dispensation, each rank-ordering, because it is perspectival, is never free from controversy: each rank-ordering, one may say, *exists* as controversial, has its mode of being in controversy" ("The 'Warrior Spirit' as an Inlet to the Political Philosophy of Nietzsche's Zarathustra," p. 244). This is not the view that Nietzsche delineates in *The Anti-Christ*.

31. Nietzsche's insistence on a natural hierarchy conflicts with Thiele's argument that "[t]o realize his potential, man must struggle such that his higher self may rule" (*The Politics of the Soul*, p. 67). For Nietzsche, it is not man, understood as a universal category, who has to struggle, but the few and particular individuals who are destined for independence. "Man may choose," Thiele asserts, "to his advantage or disadvantage, which of his inherited traits to follow" (p. 74). But Nietzsche denies both free will and the ego, which are prerequisites for the choice Thiele describes.

Chapter Nine.   The Trapped Dionysus

1. The epigraph is from Carnap's essay in *Heidegger and Modern Philosophy*, ed. Michael Murray (New Haven: Yale University Press, 1978), p. 34.

2. "How does one compromise oneself today? By being consistent. By going in a straight line. By being less than ambiguous. By being genuine" (TI; "Expeditions"; 18).

3. The problem is not one of believing that the gods belong to another realm, but of believing in another world that is conceived as the "true" one, to the extent that it denies our world. Nietzsche does not complain about the Greek gods, for example, because the world they inhabited was not a denial of the Greek world. He holds the same opinion about the God of the ancient Israelites, and the root of his argument is his belief that there can be different types of gods.

4. WLN; Notebook 34, April–June 1885; 34[135].

5. Along similar lines, health shows its mettle in its relation to sickness, in "how much of the sickly it can take and overcome—how much it can make healthy" (WP; 1013).

6. Solomon, "A More Severe Morality," p. 323.

7. Robert C. Solomon, "Nietzsche, Nihilism, and Morality," in *Nietzsche: A Collection of Critical Essays,* ed. Robert C. Solomon (New York: Anchor Books, 1973), p. 217.

8. Ibid., p. 223.

9. I have in mind Nehamas, *Life as Literature,* and Solomon, "A More Severe Morality."

10. My argument relies on the following distinctions. A perspectivist might accept and even *know* that some interpretations are better than others. A relativist argues that all interpretations are equally valid, and this position could be presented as a knowledge claim. The skeptic can partake of both the perspectival and the relativistic predicament. Skepticism is distinguished from both perspectivism and relativism by its claim that it is not sure, that is, it does not know whether some interpretations are preferable to others. But in these three cases, there is a core agreement that independent and neutral grounds, which could serve as the foundations to determine why some interpretations are better than others, are absent. Both perspectivism and relativism seem to pose this absence as something they *know,* as the *certainty* behind their claims about ambiguity and a plurality of equally valid views. If perspectivism claims that it knows that some interpretations are better, this "knowledge" is confined within specific boundaries: it does not stem from independent grounds but from the belief that the chosen interpretations make more sense than other interpretations, in the light of the assumptions or the goals that perspectivism seeks. Or, put another way, the chosen interpretations make more sense in the light of the stories the perspectivist thinker narrates. When one accounts for the absence of independent grounds to establish an epistemologically privileged standpoint, perspectivism and relativism are not substantially different. The irony is that a perspectivist "knowledge" is given by stories (the assumptions and goals the perspectivist thinker strives for), and both the perspectivist's and the relativist's uncertainty is based on an undisputed "certainty," namely, the absence of neutral grounds or the inability to find or to construct them.

11. My view differs from that of Ken Gemes, who argues that Nietzsche always sees truth as valid only within particular contexts. "Nietzsche is always a local rather than a global thinker. He will not simply condemn for

instance, the will to truth, but rather will condemn it within a given context. The point is what ends it serves in a given context" ("'We Remain of Necessity Strangers to Ouselves,'" p. 197).

12. Although neither emphasize the concepts I list, Steven D. Hales and Rex Welshon argue that Nietzsche defends an ontology that they term "a perspectivist ontology of power" (see Steven D. Hales and Rex Welshon, *Nietzsche's Perspectivism* [Urbana: University of Illinois Press, 2000], pp. 57–84).

13. Other references to Napoleon are found in H; I; 362; GS; 362; TI; "Germans"; 4; TI; "Expeditions"; 44, 48, 49; and GM; I; 16.

14. Niccolò Machiavelli, *The Prince,* ed. Quentin Skinner and Russell Price (Cambridge: Cambridge University Press, 1988), chap. 20, p. 74.

15. This last citation refers to Nietzsche's discussion of the "historical sense" but is equally applicable to new philosophers.

16. WLN; Notebook 2, Autumn 1885–Autumn 1886; 2[97].

17. WLN; Notebook 10, Autumn 1887; 10[87].

18. WLN; Notebook 5, Summer 1886–Autumn 1887; 5[71]; section 5.

19. See WLN; Notebook 40, August–September 1885; 40[46].

20. WLN; Notebook 10, Autumn 1887; 10[3].

21. The passage continues: "For the present we know of no other means by which that rude energy that characterizes the camp, that profound impersonal hatred, that murderous coldbloodedness with a good conscience, that common fire in the destruction of the enemy, that proud indifference to great losses, to one's own existence and that of one's friends, that inarticulate, earthquake-like shuddering of the soul, could be communicated more surely or strongly than every great war communicates them: the streams and currents that here break forth, though they carry with them rocks and rubbish of every kind and ruin the pastures of tenderer cultures, will later under favourable circumstances turn the wheels in the workshops of the spirit with newfound energy. Culture can in no way do without passions, vices and acts of wickedness" (H; I; 477).

22. "The normal condition is the state of *war:* we make *peace* only for limited periods of time" (UW; Summer 1872–Early 1873; 19[69]).

23. *The Prince,* chaps. 14 and 21. According to Machiavelli, "It was necessary that Cyrus should have found the Persians discontented under the rule of the Medes, and that the Medes should have been *soft and weak because of the long peace*" (chap. 6, p. 20, emphasis mine).

24. "[H]ow deeply human beings can suffer almost determines their order of rank—the harrowing certainty, with which he is wholly permeated

and coloured, that by virtue of his suffering he *knows more* than even the cleverest and wisest can know, that he is familiar with, and was once 'at home' in, many distant, terrible worlds of which '*you* know nothing!'" (BGE; 270).

25. A similar view is presented in *Daybreak:* "Of all the means of producing exaltation, it has been human sacrifice which has at all times most exalted and elevated man" (D; 45).

26. In *The Gay Science* Nietzsche avers that only great pain "compels us philosophers to descend into our ultimate depths" (GS; P; 3).

27. "Letter to Peter Gast, Genoa, April 6, 1883," in *Selected Letters*, ed. Middleton, p. 211.

28. WLN; Notebook 7, End of 1886–Spring 1887; 7[39].

29. "The men of the world of antiquity knew better how to *rejoice:* we how *to suffer less*" (AOM; 187).

30. WLN; Notebook 37, June–July 1885; 37[8].

31. Conway's argument that, for a nihilist like Nietzsche, the quest for self-knowledge lacks justification, is problematic. Conway argues that self-knowledge for Nietzsche is not attainable, and that "the real justification of the pursuit of self-knowledge lies . . . in a vague anticipation of the type of person one might become in the process" ("Odysseus Bound?" p. 32). Furthermore, even if the quest reveals a "tragic insight," this achievement "could never be considered an adequate justification for the pain and hardship endured." I leave aside Conway's characterization of Nietzsche as a nihilist, an issue that I explored in chapter 8. My argument here is that this runs counter to Nietzsche's craving for suffering and hardship, which are of a noble character. Conway also argues that Nietzsche "remains forever unknown to himself." As shown in chapter 5, the secret war of the instincts makes self-knowledge impossible. Yet, Nietzsche does claim to possess some knowledge about what he is, as I argue in this volume.

32. "But it is music which reveals to us most clearly what masters we are in the rapid and subtle divination of feelings and in empathising: for, though music is an imitation of an imitation of feelings, it nonetheless and in spite of this degree of distance and indefiniteness often enough makes us participants in these feelings, so that, like perfect fools, we grow sad without there being the slightest occasion for sorrow merely because we hear sounds and rhythms which somehow remind us of the tone-of-voice and movements of mourners, or even of no more than their customary usages" (D; 142).

33. "To *overthrow idols* (my word for 'ideals')—that rather is my business" (EH; Foreword).

34. This comment, written in the Spring–Fall of 1887, should be compared to his view in the *Genealogy*: "The sick represent the greatest danger for the healthy; it is *not* the strongest but the weakest who spell disaster for the strong. Is this known?" (GM; III; 14).

35. Other references to solitude are found in D; 323, 325, 491.

36. Conway claims that decadent philosophers, like Nietzsche, are doing nothing more than "clutching a single, nihilist thread" and that this thread is that they "know nothing" about the epochs under their scrutiny ("Odysseus Bound?" p. 32). This is difficult to accept in Nietzsche's case. Nietzsche claims to know how to distinguish life-ascending possibilities from life-denying ones, and, as we have seen, he says a lot about the achievements of the Greeks and the Roman Empire. Conway's description of Nietzsche as a "decadent" philosopher should be compared to Nietzsche's self-evaluation in *Ecce Homo*, where he argues that he is decadent but is also the opposite, since he always chooses the right means to overcome his conditions and thus proves that he is *"fundamentally healthy"* (EH; "So Wise"; 2).

37. Here I agree with Nehamas's view of Nietzsche as a philosopher of the future who already exists in the present. In this sense, Nehamas argues, *Beyond Good and Evil* can be read self-referentially, as a text in which the narrator describes the philosopher of the future he considers himself to be. However, I take issue with Nehamas's argument that "[o]ne is a genuine philosopher only to the extent that one produces a coherent and livable picture of life—coherent and livable at least for oneself. . . . What is also necessary is to embody these thoughts and values [of a coherent picture] into a coherent self, a coherent character, and, in our case, a coherent narrator" ("Who Are the Philosophers of the Future?" p. 65; see also p. 60). Although Nietzsche's scripts and vignettes about history contain many coherent elements, his philosophy in general tends to shun coherence and proudly announces this as his personal disposition. In *The Gay Science*, he describes genuine individuals as ones who are willing to float and to avoid the consistency of being a "castle" (GS; 46; 305). In *Twilight of the Idols*, he criticizes both systems and systematizers, two entities that praise and require "coherence" (TI; "Maxims"; 26). For Nietzsche, systems and systematizers are the opposite of a philosophy of becoming, and "convictions," which are symptoms of "coherence," are prisons (H; I; 483; AC; 54).

38. UW; Summer 1872–Early 1873; 19[73].

39. WLN; Notebook 36, June–July 1885; 36[27].

40. *"Everything* human deserves to be viewed ironically so far as its *origin* is concerned: that is why irony is so *superfluous* in the world" (H; I; 252). See also D; 44.

41. "Letter to Franz Overbeck, May 21, 1884," in *Selected Letters*, ed. Middleton, p. 225.

42. Nietzsche claims that "the evil and suspicious, the animal and backward, . . . the barbarian, the pre-Greek and Asiatic . . . still lived on in the foundations of the Hellenic nature" (AOM; 220).

43. "Letter to Franz Overbeck, May 21, 1884," in *Selected Letters*, ed. Middleton, p. 225.

44. "Letter to Franz Overbeck, February 11, 1883," in *Selected Letters*, ed. Middleton, p. 206.

45. "Letter to Jacob Burckhardt, January 6, 1889," in *The Portable Nietzsche*, ed. Walter Kaufmann (New York: Viking Press, 1954), p. 686.

46. For a discussion of *Ecce Homo* as a text of self-therapy and self-parody in which Nietzsche "documents his failure to overcome resentment," see Daniel W. Conway, "Nietzsche's Döppelganger: Affirmation and Resentment in *Ecce Homo*," in *The Fate of the New Nietzsche*, ed. Keith Ansell-Pearson and Howard Caygill (Avebury: Ashgate Publishing, 1993), pp. 55–78.

47. If the list of six events should refer only to individuals, another possibility is: Heraclitus, Aeschylus, Socrates, Julius Caesar, Sallust, and Napoleon.

48. For Nietzsche's interest in surveying all "kinds of human passions" and even in studying "the moral effects of different foods," see GS; 7.

49. For an examination of the relationship between Nietzsche's personal tribulations and his ideas in *Thus Spoke Zarathustra*, see David B. Allison, *Reading the New Nietzsche* (Lanham, MD: Rowman & Littlefield, 2001), pp. 111–79.

50. WLN, Notebook 36, June–July 1885; 36[35].

51. Nietzsche's wish that the slaves accept and even be glad of their function as fertilizer for the nourishment of a stronger species is bound to clash with the valuating nature of human beings.

52. WLN; Notebook 34, April–June 1885; 34[46], 34[49], 34[81], 34[89]; WLN, Notebook 37, June–July 1885; 37[4].

53. UW; Summer 1872–Early 1873; 19[69].

54. UW; Summer–Autumn 1873; 29[96].

Bibliography

Abbey, Ruth. *Nietzsche's Middle Period.* Oxford: Oxford University Press, 2000.

Acampora, Christa Davis, ed. *Nietzsche's "On the Genealogy of Morals": Critical Essays.* Lanham, MD: Rowman & Littlefield, 2006.

————. "On Sovereignty and Overhumanity: Why It Matters How We Read Nietzsche's *Genealogy* II: 2." In *Nietzsche's "On the Genealogy of Morals": Critical Essays,* edited by Christa Davis Acampora, 147–61. Lanham, MD: Rowman & Littlefield, 2006.

Ahern, Daniel R. *Nietzsche as Cultural Physician.* University Park: Pennsylvania State University Press, 1995.

Allison, David B. *Reading the New Nietzsche.* Lanham, MD: Rowman & Littlefield, 2001.

Altizer, Thomas J. J." "Eternal Recurrence and Kingdom of God." In *The New Nietzsche: Contemporary Styles of Interpretation,* edited by David B. Allison, 232–46. Cambridge, MA: MIT Press, 1985.

Ansell-Pearson, Keith. "Introduction: Nietzsche's 'Overcoming' of Morality." In *On the Genealogy of Morality,* translated by Carol Diethe, edited by Keith Ansell-Pearson. Cambridge: Cambridge University Press, 1996.

————. "The 'Meaning' of the Transhuman Condition." In *Nietzsche's Futures,* edited by John Lippit, 189–206. New York: St. Martin's Press, 1999.

————. "A Dionysian Drama on the 'Fate of the Soul.'" In *Nietzsche's "On the Genealogy of Morals": Critical Essays,* edited by Christa Davis Acampora, 19–38. Lanham, MD: Rowman & Littlefield, 2006.

Barnes, Timothy D. *Athanasius and Constantius: Theology and Politics in the Constantinian Empire.* Cambridge, MA: Harvard University Press, 1993.

Benjamin, Walter. "The Storyteller." In *Illuminations,* edited by Hannah Arendt, 83–109. New York: Schocken Books, 1969.

Bergreen, Laurence. *Over the Edge of the World: Magellan's Terrifying Circumnavigation of the Globe.* New York: Perennial, 2004.

The Bible: Authorized King James Version with Apocrypha. Edited by Robert Carroll and Stephen Prickett. New York: Oxford University Press, 1997.

Blanchot, Maurice. "The Limits of Experience: Nihilism." In *The New Nietz-sche: Contemporary Styles of Interpretation*, edited by David B. Allison, 121–28. Cambridge, MA: MIT Press, 1985.

Blondel, Eric. *Nietzsche: The Body and Culture. Philosophy as a Philological Genealogy.* Translated by Sean Hand. London: Athlone Press, 1991.

———. "The Question of Genealogy." In *Nietzsche, Genealogy, Morality: Essays on Nietzsche's "On the Genealogy of Morals,"* edited by Richard Schacht, 306–17. Berkeley: University of California Press, 1994.

Brown, Richard. "Nihilism: 'Thus Speaks Physiology.'" In *Nietzsche and the Rhetoric of Nihilism: Essays on Interpretation, Language and Politics*, edited by Tom Darby, Béla Egyed, and Ben Jones, 133–44. Ottawa: Carleton University Press, 1989.

Came, Daniel. "The Aesthetic Justification of Existence." In *A Companion to Nietzsche*, edited by Keith Ansell-Pearson, 41–57. Malden, MA: Blackwell Publishing, 2006.

Carnap, Rudolf. "The Overcoming of Metaphysics through Logical Analysis of Language." In *Heidegger and Modern Philosophy*, edited by Michael Murray, 23–34. New Haven: Yale University Press, 1978.

Cassirer, Ernst. *Kant's Life and Thought.* Translated by James Haden. New Haven: Yale University Press, 1981.

Chernow, Ron. *Titan: The Life of John D. Rockefeller, Sr.* New York: Vintage Books, 1998.

Clark, Maudemarie. *Nietzsche on Truth and Philosophy.* Cambridge: Cambridge University Press, 1990.

Comte-Sponville, Andre. "The Brute, the Sophist, and the Aesthete: 'Art in the Service of Illusion.'" In *Why We Are Not Nietzscheans*, edited by Luc Ferry and Alain Renaut, 21–69. Chicago: University of Chicago Press, 1997.

Conway, Daniel W. "Nietzsche's Döppelganger: Affirmation and Resentment in *Ecce Homo*." In *The Fate of the New Nietzsche*, edited by Keith Ansell-Pearson and Howard Caygill, 55–78. Avebury: Ashgate Publishing, 1993.

———. "Genealogy and Critical Method." In *Nietzsche, Genealogy, Morality: Essays on Nietzsche's "On the Genealogy of Morals,"* edited by Richard Schacht, 318–33. Berkeley: University of California Press, 1994.

———. *Nietzsche's Dangerous Game: Philosophy in the Twilight of the Idols.* Cambridge: Cambridge University Press, 1997.

———. "Annunciations and Rebirth: The Prefaces of 1886." In *Nietzsche's Futures*, edited by John Lippitt, 30–47. New York: St. Martin's Press, 1999.

————. "Odysseus Bound?" In *Why Nietzsche Still? Reflections on Drama, Culture, and Politics,* edited by Alan D. Schrift, 28–44. Berkeley: University of California Press, 2000.

————. *Nietzsche's "On the Genealogy of Morals": A Reader's Guide.* London: Continuum, 2008.

Crawford, Claudia. *The Beginnings of Nietzsche's Theory of Language.* Berlin: Walter de Gruyter, 1988.

————. "Nietzsche's Psychology and Rhetoric of World Redemption: Dionysus versus the Crucified." In *Nietzsche and Depth Psychology,* ed. Jacob Golomb, Weaver Santaniello, and Ronald Lehrer, 271–94. Albany: State University of New York Press, 1999.

Crites, Stephen. *Dialectic and Gospel in the Development of Hegel's Thinking.* University Park: Pennsylvania State University Press, 1998.

Danto, Arthur C. *Nietzsche as Philosopher.* New York: Macmillan, 1965.

————. "Some Remarks on *The Genealogy of Morals.*" In *Reading Nietzsche,* edited by Robert C. Solomon and Kathleen M. Higgins, 13–28. Oxford: Oxford University Press, 1988.

Deleuze, Gilles. *Nietzsche and Philosophy.* Translated by Hugh Tomlinson. New York: Columbia University Press, 1983.

————. "Nomad Thought." In *Nietzsche: Critical Assessments,* edited by Daniel W. Conway with Peter S. Groff, vol. 4, 78–85. London: Routledge, 1998.

Descartes, René. *The Passions of the Soul.* In *Selected Philosophical Writings,* edited by John Cottingham, 218–38. Cambridge: Cambridge University Press, 1988.

————. *Treatise on Man.* In *The World and Other Writings,* edited by Stephen Gaukroger, 99–169. Cambridge: Cambridge University Press, 1998.

Emerson, Ralph Waldo. "Napolean; or, the Man of the World." In *Ralph Waldo Emerson: Essays and Lectures.* New York: Library of America, 1983.

Fink, Eugen. "Nietzsche's New Experience of World." In *Nietzsche's New Seas: Explorations in Philosophy, Aesthetics, and Politics,* edited by Michael Allen Gillespie and Tracy B. Strong, 203–19. Chicago: University of Chicago Press, 1988.

Foot, Philippa. "Nietzsche's Immoralism." In *Nietzsche: Critical Assessments,* edited by Daniel W. Conway with Peter S. Groff, vol. 3, 49–60. London: Routledge, 1998.

Foucault, Michel. "Nietzsche, Genealogy, History." In *Nietzsche,* edited by John Richardson and Brian Leiter, 341–59. Oxford: Oxford University Press, 1999.

Freud, Sigmund. *Civilization and Its Discontents.* Edited by James Strachey. New York: W. W. Norton, 1989.

———. *On Dreams.* Edited by James Strachey. New York: W. W. Norton, 1989.

Gadamer, Hans-Georg. *Truth and Method.* Translated by Joel Weinsheimer and Donald G. Marshall. 2nd rev. ed. New York: Continuum, 1989.

Gemes, Ken. "'We Remain of Necessity Strangers to Ourselves': The Key Message of Nietzsche's *Genealogy.*" In *Nietzsche's "On the Genealogy of Morals": Critical Essays,* edited by Christa Davis Acampora, 191–208. Lanham, MD: Rowman & Littlefield, 2006.

Gerhardt, Volker. "Self-Grounding: Nietzsche's Morality of Individuality." In *The Fate of the New Nietzsche,* edited by Keith Ansell-Pearson and Howard Caygill, 283–301. Aldershot: Avebury Ashgate Publishing, 1993.

Geuss, Raymond. "Nietzsche and Genealogy." In *Nietzsche,* edited by John Richardson and Brian Leiter, 322–40. Oxford: Oxford University Press, 1999.

Gillespie, Michael Allen, *Nihilism before Nietzsche.* Chicago: University of Chicago Press, 1995.

Ginsberg, Mitchell. "Nietzschean Psychiatry." In *Nietzsche: A Collection of Critical Essays,* edited by Robert C. Solomon, 293–315. New York: Anchor Books, 1973.

Goldsmith, Barbara. *Other Powers: The Age of Suffrage, Spiritualism, and the Scandalous Victoria Woodhull.* New York: Alfred A. Knopf, 1998.

Guay, Robert. "The Philosophical Function of Genealogy." In *A Companion to Nietzsche,* edited by Keith Ansell-Pearson, 353–70. Malden, MA: Blackwell Publishing, 2005.

Haar, Michel. "Nietzsche and Metaphysical Language." In *The New Nietzsche: Contemporary Styles of Interpretation,* edited by David B. Allison, 5–36. Cambridge, MA: MIT Press, 1985.

———. "Life and Natural Totality in Nietzsche." In *Nietzsche: Critical Assessments,* edited by Daniel W. Conway with Peter S. Groff, vol. 2, 74–90. London: Routledge, 1998.

Haigh, Christopher. *The Plain Man's Pathways to Heaven: Kinds of Christianity in Post-Reformation England, 1570–1640.* Oxford: Oxford University Press, 2007.

Hales, Steven D., and Rex Welshon. *Nietzsche's Perspectivism*. Urbana: University of Illinois Press, 2000.

Hatab, Lawrence J. *Nietzsche's "On the Genealogy of Morality": An Introduction*. Cambridge: Cambridge University Press, 2008.

Heilke, Thomas. *Nietzsche's Tragic Regime: Culture, Aesthetics, and Political Education*. DeKalb: Northern Illinois University Press, 1998.

Higgins, Kathleen M. "Nietzsche and Postmodern Subjectivity." In *Nietzsche as Postmodernist: Essays Pro and Contra*, edited by Clayton Koelb, 189–215. Albany: State University of New York Press, 1990.

———. *Comic Relief: Nietzsche's "Gay Science"*. New York: Oxford University Press, 2000.

Hobbes, Thomas. *Leviathan*. Edited by Edwin Curley. Indianapolis: Hackett Publishing, 1994.

Holub, Robert C. *Friedrich Nietzsche*. New York: Twayne Publishers, 1995.

Hoy, David Couzens. "Nietzsche, Hume, and the Genealogical Method." In *Nietzsche, Genealogy, Morality: Essays on Nietzsche's "On the Genealogy of Morals,"* edited by Richard Schacht, 251–68. Berkeley: University of California Press, 1994.

Janaway, Christopher. "Naturalism and Genealogy." In *A Companion to Nietzsche*, edited by Keith Ansell-Pearson, 337–52. Malden, MA: Blackwell Publishing, 2006.

———. "Guilt, Bad Conscience, and Self-Punishment in Nietzsche's Genealogy." In *Nietzsche and Morality*, edited by Brian Leiter and Neil Sinhababu, 138–54. Oxford: Oxford University Press, 2007.

———. *Beyond Selflessness: Reading Nietzsche's "Genealogy."* Oxford: Oxford University Press, 2007.

Kant, Immanuel. *Critique of Pure Reason*. Translated by Paul Guyer and Allen W. Wood. Cambridge: Cambridge University Press, 1998.

Kaufmann, Walter. *Nietzsche: Philosopher, Psychologist, Anti-Christ*. New York: Meridian Books, 1956.

Klein, Wayne. *Nietzsche and the Promise of Philosophy*. Albany: State University of New York Press, 1997.

Klossowski, Pierre. "Nietzsche's Experience of the Eternal Return." In *The New Nietzsche: Contemporary Styles of Interpretation*, edited by David B. Allison, 107–20. Cambridge, MA: MIT Press, 1985.

———. *Nietzsche and the Vicious Circle*. Translated by Daniel W. Smith. Chicago: University of Chicago Press, 1997.

Köhler, Joachim. *Zarathustra's Secret: The Interior Life of Frederick Nietzsche*. Translated by Ronald Taylor. New Haven: Yale University Press, 2002.

La Mettrie, Julien Offray de. "Machine Man." In *Machine Man and Other Writings*, edited by Ann Thomson, 1–40. Cambridge: Cambridge University Press, 1996.

Lämmert, Eberhard. "Nietzsche's Apotheosis of Loneliness." In *Nietzsche: Literature and Value*, edited by Volker Dürr, 50–65. Madison: University of Wisconsin Press, 1988.

Leiter, Brian. "The Paradox of Fatalism and Self-Creation in Nietzsche." In *Nietzsche*, edited by John Richardson and Brian Leiter, 281–321. Oxford: Oxford University Press, 2001.

———. *Routledge Philosophy Guidebook to Nietzsche on Morality*. New York: Routledge, 2002.

Lemm, Vanessa. *Nietzsche's Animal Philosophy: Culture, Politics, and the Animality of the Human Body*. New York: Fordham University Press, 2009.

Long, Thomas A. "Nietzsche's Philosophy of Medicine." *Nietzsche-Studien* 19 (1990): 112–28.

Löwith, Karl. "Nietzsche's Revival of the Doctrine of Eternal Recurrence." In *Nietzsche: Critical Assessments*, edited by Daniel W. Conway with Peter S. Groff, vol. 2, 175–83. London: Routledge, 1998.

Machiavelli, Niccolò. *The Prince*. Edited by Quentin Skinner and Russell Price. Cambridge: Cambridge University Press, 1988.

Magnus, Bernd. *Nietzsche's Existential Imperative*. Bloomington: Indiana University Press, 1978.

———. "Nietzsche and the Project of Bringing Philosophy to an End." In *Nietzsche as Affirmative Thinker*, edited by Yirmiyahu Yovel. Dordrecht: Martinus Nijhoff Publishers, 1986.

———. "The Deification of the Commonplace: *Twilight of the Idols*." In *Reading Nietzsche*, edited by Robert C. Solomon and Kathleen M. Higgins, 152–81. Oxford: Oxford University Press, 1988.

———. "The Use and Abuse of *The Will to Power*." In *Reading Nietzsche*, edited by Robert C. Solomon and Kathleen M. Higgins, 218–36. Oxford: Oxford University Press, 1988.

———. "Nietzsche's Philosophy in 1888: *The Will to Power* and the Übermensch." In *Nietzsche: Critical Assessments*, edited by Daniel W. Conway with Peter S. Groff, vol. 2, 184–203. London: Routledge, 1998.

Marx, Karl, and Friedrich Engels. *The German Ideology*. Edited by C. J. Arthur. New York: International Publishers, 1988.

Montinari, Mazzino. *Reading Nietzsche*. Translated by Greg Whitlock. Urbana: University of Illinois Press, 2003.

Moore, Gregory. *Nietzsche, Biology and Metaphor.* Cambridge: Cambridge University Press, 2002.

Müller-Lauter, Wolfgang. *Nietzsche: His Philosophy of Contradictions and the Contradictions of His Philosophy.* Translated by David J. Parent. Urbana: University of Illinois Press, 1999.

Nehamas, Alexander. *Nietzsche: Life as Literature.* Cambridge, MA: Harvard University Press, 1985.

———. "Who Are 'the Philosophers of the Future'?: A Reading of *Beyond Good and Evil.*" In *Reading Nietzsche,* edited by Robert C. Solomon and Kathleen M. Higgins, 46–67. Oxford: Oxford University Press, 1988.

———. "Nietzsche, Modernity, Aestheticism." In *The Cambridge Companion to Nietzsche,* edited by Bernd Magnus and Kathleen M. Higgins, 223–51. Cambridge: Cambridge University Press, 1996.

Owen, David. "Nietzsche, Re-Evaluation and the Turn to Genealogy." In *Nietzsche's "On the Genealogy of Morals": Critical Essays,* edited by Christa Davis Acampora, 39–56. Lanham, MD: Rowman & Littlefield, 2006.

———. *Nietzsche's "Genealogy of Morality."* Montreal: McGill-Queen's University Press, 2007.

Owen, David, and Aaron Ridley. "Dramatis Personae: Nietzsche, Culture, and Human Types." In *Why Nietzsche Still? Reflections on Drama, Culture, and Politics,* edited by Alan D. Schrift, 136–53. Berkeley: University of California Press, 2000.

Pangle, Thomas L. "The 'Warrior Spirit' as an Inlet to the Political Philosophy of Nietzsche's Zarathustra." In *Nietzsche: Critical Assessments,* edited by Daniel W. Conway with Peter S. Groff, vol. 4, 229–65. London: Routledge, 1998.

Parkes, Graham. *Composing the Soul: Reaches of Nietzsche's Psychology.* Chicago: University of Chicago Press, 1994.

———. "Nietzsche on the Fantastic Fabric of Experience." In *Nietzsche: Critical Assessments,* edited by Daniel W. Conway with Peter S. Groff, vol. 2, 270–85. London: Routledge, 1998.

Pasley, Malcolm. "Nietzsche's Use of Medical Terms." In *Nietzsche: Imagery and Thought,* edited by Malcolm Pasley, 123–58. Berkeley: University of California Press, 1978.

Patton, Paul. "Nietzsche and the Problem of the Actor." In *Why Nietzsche Still? Reflections on Drama, Culture, and Politics,* edited by Alan D. Schrift, 170–83. Berkeley: University of California Press, 2000.

Pizer, John. "The Use and Abuse of 'Ursprung': On Foucault's Reading of Nietzsche." *Nietzsche-Studien* 19 (1990): 462–78.

Plato. *Republic*. Edited by Lewis Campbell and Benjamin Jowett. Vol. 1. New York: Garland Publishing, 1987.

———. *Republic*. Translated by C. D. C. Reeve. Indianapolis: Hackett Publishing, 2004.

Podolsky, Scott H., and Alfred I. Tauber. "Nietzsche's Conception of Health: The Idealization of Struggle." In *Nietzsche, Epistemology, and Philosophy of Science: Nietzsche and the Sciences*, edited by Babette Babich and Robert S. Cohen, vol. 2, 299–311. Hingham, MA: Kluwer Academic Publishers, 1999.

Raban, Jonathan. "My Holy War: What Do a Vicar's Son and a Suicide Bomber Have in Common?" *The New Yorker*, February 4, 2002, 28–37.

Rampley, Matthew. *Nietzsche, Aesthetics and Modernity*. Cambridge: Cambridge University Press, 2000.

Richards, Robert J. *The Romantic Conception of Life: Science and Philosophy in the Age of Goethe*. Chicago: University of Chicago Press, 2002.

Richardson, John. *Nietzsche's System*. Oxford: Oxford University Press, 1996.

Ridley, Aaron. *Nietzsche's Conscience: Six Character Studies from the "Genealogy."* Ithaca, NY: Cornell University Press, 1998.

———. "Guilt before God, or God before Guilt? The Second Essay of Nietzsche's *Genealogy*." *Journal of Nietzsche Studies* 29 (2005): 35–45.

———. "Nietzsche and the Re-evaluation of Values." In *Nietzsche's "On the Genealogy of Morals": Critical Essays*, edited by Christa Davis Acampora, 77–92. Lanham, MD: Rowman & Littlefield, 2006.

———. *Routledge Philosophy Guidebook to Nietzsche on Art*. London: Routledge, 2007.

Risse, Mathias. "The Second Treatise in *On the Genealogy of Morality*: Nietzsche on the Origin of the Bad Conscience." *European Journal of Philosophy* 9, no. 1 (2001): 55–81.

———. "On God and Guilt: A Reply to Aaron Ridley." *Journal of Nietzsche Studies* 29 (2005): 46–53.

Rorty, Richard. *Contingency, Irony, and Solidarity*. Cambridge: Cambridge University Press, 1989.

Rousseau, Jean-Jacques. *A Discourse on Inequality*. Translated by Maurice Cranston. New York: Penguin Books, 1984.

———. *The Social Contract and Discourses*. Translated by G. D. H. Cole. London: Everyman Publishing, 1993.

Rubenstein, Richard E. *When Jesus Became God: The Epic Fight over Christ's Divinity in the Last Days of Rome*. New York: Harcourt, Brace & Co., 1999.

Salaquarda, Jörg. "Nietzsche and the Judaeo-Christian Tradition." In *The Cambridge Companion to Nietzsche,* edited by Bernd Magnus and Kathleen M. Higgins, 90–118. Cambridge: Cambridge University Press, 1996.

———. "Dionysus Versus the Crucified One: Nietzsche's Understanding of the Apostle Paul." In *Nietzsche: Critical Assessments,* edited by Daniel W. Conway with Peter S. Groff, vol. 4, 266–91. London: Routledge, 1998.

Samuels, David. "The Confidence Men." *The New Yorker,* May 3, 1999, 150–61.

Schacht, Richard. *Making Sense of Nietzsche: Reflections Timely and Untimely.* Chicago: University of Illinois Press, 1995.

Soll, Ivan. "Reflections on Recurrence: A Re-examination of Nietzsche's Doctrine, *Die Ewige Wiederkehr des Gleichen.*" In *Nietzsche: Critical Assessments,* edited by Daniel W. Conway with Peter S. Groff, vol. 2, 370–87. London: Routledge, 1998.

Solomon, Robert C. "Nietzsche, Nihilism, and Morality." In *Nietzsche: A Collection of Critical Essays,* edited by Robert C. Solomon, 202–25. New York: Anchor Books, 1973.

———. "Nietzsche *ad hominem:* Perspectivism, Personality and *Ressentiment* Revisited." In *The Cambridge Companion to Nietzsche,* edited by Bernd Magnus and Kathleen M. Higgins, 180–222. Cambridge: Cambridge University Press, 1996.

———. "A More Severe Morality: Nietzsche's Affirmative Ethics." In *Nietzsche: Critical Assessments,* edited by Daniel W. Conway with Peter S. Groff, vol. 3, 321–29. London: Routledge, 1998.

Stack, George J. *Lange and Nietzsche.* Berlin: Walter de Gruyter, 1983.

Stambaugh, Joan. *Nietzsche's Thought of Eternal Return.* Baltimore: Johns Hopkins University Press, 1972.

———. *The Problem of Time in Nietzsche.* London: Associated University Presses, 1987.

———. "Thoughts on the Innocence of Becoming." In *Nietzsche: Critical Assessments,* edited by Daniel Conway with Peter S. Groff, vol. 2, 388–401. London: Routledge, 1998.

Stern, J. P. "Nietzsche and the Idea of Metaphor." In *Nietzsche: Imagery and Thought,* edited by Malcolm Pasley, 64–82. Berkeley: University of California Press, 1978.

———. *A Study of Nietzsche.* Cambridge: Cambridge University Press, 1979.

Strong, Tracy B. "Nietzsche's Political Aesthetics." In *Nietzsche's New Seas: Explorations in Philosophy, Aesthetics, and Politics,* edited by Michael Allen Gillespie and Tracy B. Strong, 153–74. Chicago: University of Chicago Press, 1988.

———. *Friedrich Nietzsche and the Politics of Transfiguration.* Expanded ed. Urbana: University of Illinois Press, 2000.

———. "Genealogy, the Will to Power, and the Problem of a Past." In *Nietzsche's "On the Genealogy of Morals": Critical Essays,* edited by Christa Davis Acampora, 93–106. Lanham, MD: Rowman & Littlefield, 2006.

Thiele, Leslie Paul. *Friedrich Nietzsche and the Politics of the Soul: A Study of Heroic Individualism.* Princeton: Princeton University Press, 1990.

Todorov, Tzvetan. *The Conquest of America: The Question of the Other.* New York: HarperPerennial, 1985.

Vattimo, Gianni. *Dialogue with Nietzsche.* New York: Columbia University Press, 2006.

Warnock, Mary. "Nietzsche's Conception of Truth." In *Nietzsche: Imagery and Thought,* edited by Malcolm Pasley, 33–63. Berkeley: University of California Press, 1978.

Warren, Mark. *Nietzsche and Political Thought.* Cambridge, MA: MIT Press, 1988.

White, Richard. "The Return of the Master: An Interpretation of Nietzsche's 'Genealogy of Morals.'" *Philosophy and Phenomenological Research* 48, no. 4 (1988): 683–96.

Williams, W. D. "Nietzsche's Masks." In *Nietzsche: Imagery and Thought,* edited by Malcolm Pasley, 83–103. Berkeley: University of California Press, 1978.

Young, Julian. *Nietzsche's Philosophy of Art.* New York: Cambridge University Press, 1992.

Index

and reason, 18–22
relationship to genealogy, 20–22,
25, 32, 43, 66, 69, 281–82

Raban, Jonathan, 194
Rampley, Matthew: *Nietzsche,
Aesthetics and Modernity*, 339n18
reality, 255–64, 275, 320n16, 321n21,
322n31, 325nn12, 15, 20, 326n25,
329n54
fact vs. interpretation, 30–31, 120,
135, 149–50, 151, 153, 158, 159, 165,
166–67, 198–200, 209–10, 216,
229, 232, 251–52, 256, 258–64,
285, 341n10
hatred of, 204, 240, 242, 298
relationship to art, 114, 213, 254–55,
318n1, 319n8, 320n15, 323n35
relationship to language, 26,
119–20, 121, 150–52, 153, 159, 171,
209–10, 311n27
See also becoming; knowledge;
truth
reason, 26, 66, 260
Hegel on, 168
Kant on, 4, 18
Nietzsche on, 3–4, 163, 167, 193,
200, 201, 290, 295, 312n37,
321n21, 322n31, 329n54
Plato on, 15, 238
and quest for transparency, 18–22
Reformation, the, 17, 287
Luther, 98, 208, 265
relativism, 262–63, 341n10
religion
Greek gods, 5, 14, 15, 16–17, 97,
108, 125, 232, 233, 234, 290,
340n3
invention of gods, 98, 125, 233,
290
monotheism and empires, 316n20

and politics, 17–18
sin, 53, 72, 84, 86, 89, 90, 91, 92,
93, 94, 95–97, 98, 99, 102, 132,
216, 229, 248, 261, 308n17
and storytelling, 13–14
See also asceticism; Buddhism;
Christianity; Hindu caste
system; Jews and Judaism
Renaissance, the, 16–17, 22, 23, 265,
287, 318n31
resentment/*ressentiment*, 64, 93, 155,
250, 264, 287, 296, 345n46
and asceticism, 59–60, 64, 94,
100–101, 231, 316n24
and Christianity, 21, 55–56
and democracy, 21, 265
and French Revolution, 21
in modernity, 59–60, 132, 241–42,
245, 265
among slaves, 53, 79–80, 90, 91,
96, 144–45, 157, 223, 247, 265,
281, 326n29
Richardson, John, 20, 304n9
Ridley, Aaron
on aesthetic justification of life,
131, 132–33
on *amor fati*, 134
on bad conscience and guilt, 88
on Christianity and guilt, 86, 87
on *Ecce Homo*, 134–36
on genealogy, 47
on Nietzsche and the Dionysian,
131–32
on Nietzsche's honesty, 134–35
on revaluation of values, 312n46
Risse, Matthias
on Christianity and guilt, 86
on genealogy of guilt, 79
Rockefeller, John D.: on Napoleon,
225, 338n14
Rolph, William, 38

of truth, 172, 192, 193–94, 195–202,
196, 251–54, 261–62, 289, 298
the whole as source of, 202–3
See also morality
Vattimo, Gianni, 304n9
Voltaire, 39

Wagner, Richard, 1, 172, 248, 259,
286, 291, 292, 297, 323n35
as decadent, 226–27
as deceiver, 129
instincts of, 41, 42, 129, 162
as sick, 40, 212, 228, 278
Warnock, Mary, 326n25
Warren, Mark, 20, 304n9
weakness/the weak, 34, 43, 51, 54, 55,
56–57, 59, 74, 85, 87, 128, 143,
146, 148, 157, 189, 203–4, 260,
262, 275, 324n7, 327n40
conspiracy of the weak, 242, 243,
247, 249, 297
sickness of the weak, 58, 60, 61,
154, 344n34
slaves as weak, 56–57, 100, 107,
154, 242, 263, 274
standard of weakness, 11, 179,
324n8
Welshon, Rex, 342n12
White, Richard, 316n24
Williams, W. D., 26–27
will to power, 30, 33, 38, 77, 123, 125,
133, 182, 187, 189, 203, 303n7,
307n12, 317n30, 332n10

of ascetic priest, 41, 45–46, 50–51,
96, 100–101, 154, 248
as essence of life, 25, 56, 65, 70,
108, 119, 143, 154–55, 158,
173–74, 178, 253, 254, 263, 278,
313n2
and eternal recurrence, 184–85,
187–88
as fact, 30, 261, 320n17
as healthy, 60–61, 285
and interpretation, 59, 251–52,
284–85
and metaphysics of meaning,
173–74, 178
of nobles, 28, 51, 154, 260
as pathos, 173–74, 332n9
relationship to cruelty, 51, 74,
101–2
relationship to instincts, 70, 251,
285
relationship to suffering, 269,
296, 332n9
relationship to value, 173–74, 178,
210–11, 262, 310n26, 320n17
vs. self-preservation, 28, 101, 143,
158, 259, 260
and self-responsibility, 278–79
as sick, 46, 60–61, 62, 64, 101–2,
103–4, 106, 155, 210–11, 248,
285, 295
of slaves, 28, 105, 107, 154–55,
295
Young, Julian, 131

Roberto Alejandro

is professor of political science

at University of Massachusetts at Amherst.